12

The Britten Companion

Benjamin Britten, sketch by Kenneth Green, 1944

The
BRITTEN
Companion

edited by
CHRISTOPHER
PALMER

ff

faber and faber
LONDON·BOSTON

First published in 1984
by Faber and Faber Limited
3 Queen Square London WC1N 3AU
Typeset by Wyvern Typesetting Ltd, Bristol
Printed in Great Britain by
Redwood Burn Ltd, Trowbridge, Wiltshire
All rights reserved

This collection © Faber and Faber Ltd 1984

British Library Cataloguing in Publication Data

The Britten Companion
1. Britten, Benjamin
I. Palmer, Christopher
780'.92'4   ML410.B853

ISBN 0-571-13147-6
ISBN 0-571-13168-9 Pbk

Contents

Contents

Contents

Contents

Illustrations

Benjamin Britten, sketch by Kenneth Green, 1944 *frontispiece*

between pages 224 and 225

Illustrations

Editorial Preface

We cannot claim that our *Britten Companion* is altogether without precedent. In fact, during his lifetime and after his death in 1976, there has been more than one symposium, most of them, however, taking an individual work as their topic, e.g. the 1948 collection of essays on *Lucretia* and more recently Philip Brett's handbook on *Peter Grimes* (1983).

But there is one principal exception, *Benjamin Britten: a Commentary on his works from a group of specialists* (1952), edited by Donald Mitchell and Hans Keller, which was put together when the composer was alive and in full creative spate. This new *Companion*, inevitably, departs from that model. For one thing, alas, the composer is dead, which means that an element of retrospection cannot be avoided, though it may strike readers that a high proportion of the contributors anticipate or imply a pretty bright future for Britten's music. Another difference is a proportional one. The 1952 *Commentary* included only a relatively small amount of already published work, whereas this 1983 *Companion* has consciously gone about retrieving what the editor considers to be some of the best writing on Britten and his music that has yet appeared, much of it no longer easily accessible. He has searched diligently and not overlooked the composer as author, rare though Britten's ventures were into print or the broadcast word.

But the main body of the book, like the *Commentary* of just over thirty years ago, is entirely new and fresh, and divulges as many opinions of and approaches to Britten as there are contributors. The *Companion* is new too in a way that the *Commentary* was not and could not be. Britten's death has meant that in the years since 1976 an immense amount of information, both musical and biographical, has become available through the establishment at Aldeburgh, Suffolk—within the precincts of Britten's own home—of the Britten–Pears Library and Archive of his manuscripts. The existence of the latter,

Editorial Preface

and the generous collaboration of the Archivist and trustees, has illumined and influenced the *Companion* in more ways than it is possible to enumerate here. The extent of this influence, however, clearly emerges from the new light that is shed on Britten, his musical personality and works, and by our contributors' use of the documentary and manuscript sources of the Archive, which must represent one of the most comprehensive collections anywhere of the manuscripts and sketches of a leading twentieth-century composer.

Without access to the riches of the Archive, this *Companion* would be much the poorer in information and insight. The editor and his collaborators, while gratefully acknowledging their debt to the Archive, also recognize the achievement of the composer's trustees in establishing an Archive that not only includes the manuscripts retained by the composer's Estate but also, on permanent loan to the Britten–Pears Library, those manuscripts that are owned by the British Library on behalf of the nation. It was the epic determination and tireless negotiating skills of Isador Caplan (one of the trustees) that led to the successful creation of the Archive, an institution that will benefit generations of scholars and researchers still to come; and not only them, but lovers, admirers and performers of Britten's music, for all of whom our *Companion* was designed and by whom, we trust, it will be greatly enjoyed. Britten himself, we may be certain, would have been able to raise only two Forsterian cheers for the idea of an Archive. The only 'archive' that mattered to him, quite simply, was music: his own, his contemporaries' and that of his great predecessors. It is the diverse wealth of *his* contribution to that living archive that the contributors to this *Companion* diversely, brilliantly and fascinatingly explore.

Acknowledgements

Grateful acknowledgements are due to Boosey & Hawkes Music Publishers Ltd for music examples from the following works by Benjamin Britten: *Billy Budd*, Op.50, *Canticle II: Abraham and Isaac*, Op.51, *Diversions*, Op.21, *Gloriana*, Op.53, *Les Illuminations*, Op.18, *The Little Sweep*, Op.45, *A Midsummer Night's Dream*, Op.64, *Night Piece*, *Nocturne*, Op.60, *Noye's Fludde*, Op.59, *On this Island*, Op.11, *Our Hunting Fathers*, Op.8, *Peter Grimes*, Op.33, Piano Concerto, Op.13, *The Prince of the Pagodas*, Op.57, *The Rape of Lucretia*, Op.37, *Saint Nicolas*, Op.42, *Scottish Ballad*, Op.26, *Serenade*, Op.31, *Seven Sonnets of Michelangelo*, Op.22, *Sinfonia da Requiem*, Op.20, *Six Metamorphoses after Ovid*, Op.49, String Quartet No.1 in D, Op.25, Suite, Op.6, Symphony for Cello and Orchestra, Op.68, *War Requiem*, Op.66; and for Britten's realizations of works by John Gay (*The Beggar's Opera*, Op.43) and Henry Purcell (*The Blessed Virgin's Expostulation*, *Dido and Aeneas* (with Imogen Holst) and 'I attempt from Love's sickness to fly'); to Faber Music Ltd for the music examples from the following works by Britten: *Death in Venice*, Op.88, *Owen Wingrave*, Op.85, *Paul Bunyan*, Op.17, *Quatre Chansons Françaises*, Second Suite for Cello, Op.80, *Songs and Proverbs of William Blake*, Op.74, String Quartet No.3, Op.94, *Welcome Ode*, Op.95 and *Young Apollo*, Op.16; and to the Britten Estate for music examples from the incidental music to *King Arthur* and Britten's sketches for *The Prince of the Pagodas*.

The illustration from Britten's autograph manuscript score of *Billy Budd*, his article 'The Composer's *Dream*', his interview with Donald Mitchell, and excerpts from his sketches, letters and diaries are © The Britten Estate and not to be reproduced without written permission. The page from W. H. Auden's draft for *Paul Bunyan* is © 1984 by the Estate of W. H. Auden; reprinted by permission.

Thanks are due to the editors of the *Gramophone* for permission to

Acknowledgements

reprint John Culshaw's '"Ben"—A Tribute to Benjamin Britten', and the *Observer* in which 'The Composer's *Dream*' was first published.

Acknowledgement is made to the publishers and editors of the following books and magazines in which articles reprinted here first appeared: Donald Mitchell and Hans Keller (eds.), *Benjamin Britten: a Commentary on his works from a group of specialists*; Wilfrid Mellers, *Caliban Reborn: Renewal in Twentieth-Century Music*; David Drew (ed.), *The Decca Book of Ballet*; Benson & Hedges Music Festival Programme Book (1977); *Musical Times*; *Opera*; *San Francisco Opera Magazine* and *Tempo*; to the BBC and CBC for articles derived from broadcast talks and the Decca Record Company Ltd for articles derived from sleeve-notes and booklets accompanying the boxed sets of recordings of works by Benjamin Britten. Chapter 20 first appeared in *Tempo*, No.146, September 1983.

The editor and publishers are particularly grateful for the encouragement and support of the Executors of the Britten Estate and of the staff of the Britten–Pears Library, Aldeburgh. Special thanks are also owed to Jill Burrows, Patrick Carnegy, Paul Courtenay (who drew the music examples), John Evans, Sally Lane (who designed the book), Philip Reed, and Ruth Smith.

Key to Principal References

BA *Britten and Auden in the Thirties: The Year 1936* Donald Mitchell

BMM *Britten* (Master Musicians Series) Michael Kennedy

BR *Britten* (Great Composers Series) Imogen Holst

BS *Benjamin Britten: A Commentary on his works from a group of specialists* (The Britten Symposium) Donald Mitchell and Hans Keller (eds.)

BT *The Music of Britten and Tippett* Arnold Whittall

MBB *The Music of Benjamin Britten* Peter Evans

OBB *The Operas of Benjamin Britten* David Herbert (ed.)

PG *Benjamin Britten: Peter Grimes* (Cambridge Opera Handbook) Philip Brett (ed.)

PL *Benjamin Britten 1913–1976: Pictures from a Life* Donald Mitchell and John Evans

SW *Benjamin Britten: Peter Grimes* (Sadler's Wells Opera Book) Eric Crozier (ed.)

TBB *Tribute to Benjamin Britten on his Fiftieth Birthday* Anthony Gishford (ed.)

WB *Working with Britten* Ronald Duncan

For details of these and other principal publications, see the Select Bibliography on pp.455–6.

All books cited in the text and bibliography are published in London unless otherwise indicated.

PERSPECTIVES

1
What do we know about Britten now?

DONALD MITCHELL

From Benjamin Britten's personal diary:

> It is the composer's heritage to take what he wants from
> whom he wants—and to write music.
>
> (18 March 1936)

> Listen to Webern conducting Mahler's 4th Symphony
> from London Regional. This work seems a mix-up of
> everything that one has ever heard, but it is definitely
> Mahler.
>
> (23 April 1936)

Before setting out to attempt this introduction to *The Britten
Companion*, I read again (as I had not done for some ten years)[1] the
introductory piece—'The Musical Atmosphere'—that I wrote for the
Britten Symposium that I edited with Hans Keller.

What struck me most forcibly was how the intervening three
decades have modified the perspective. It seems to me still that the
points of view I expressed in 1952 made quite tolerable sense and
perhaps even here and there touched on what have since proved to be
genuine and enduring aspects of Britten's personality and his art. But
1952 was 1952, and not only did he look very different then—and
also in contrast to the editors' judgement look very different to a
significant part of our musical establishment: hence the 'need' for our

---

[1] It was for a reprint of the Britten Symposium in 1972, which was able to accommodate
some modest revisions and corrections, that I last reread the opening chapter. The
Symposium—cumbersomely (and also wrongly) subtitled *A Commentary on his
works from a group of specialists* (some were not)—was first published in 1952.

Donald Mitchell

Symposium—he was, too, a very different composer from the one who died in 1976: in 1952 there was twenty-four years' music yet to come. Moreover, it was not only the unknown future that would necessarily modify the perspective, but also the unknown past. One knew little, in 1952, of Britten's musical origins, of early influences and enthusiasms, of his training and earliest attempts at composition, or, for that matter, of a whole range of early published works which—for reasons I shall return to—were rarely performed and lay curiously mute and unexplored in the composer's catalogue.

It is not just that Britten has since died and become a perfectly proper subject of research and investigation; that the living composer, who was always busy with the *next* piece, has suddenly become an archive whose main business is to arrest the past, analyse and memorialize it. The perspective of 1952—our understanding of Britten at that time—was defined by what then seemed to us important, by what music was accessible and frequently performed, and above all by the complex relationship between the composer, his public and his critics (both his proponents and his adversaries). It was a relationship that was, and continued to be, in a state of continuous flux. Our Symposium of 1952 represented a set of attitudes, froze them, and preserved them in print: a snapshot of how a figure looked in a particular landscape of opinions and responses at a particular moment in time. A decade later, the image would have altered: some features would still be recognizable—indeed might be more clearly perceived—but some would have disappeared and others been added. Two decades on, and the modifications would have been even more marked. However, the analogy will entirely mislead if one factor is overlooked. The subject of the snapshot varies, but so too does the stance of the photographer, who is not only himself a *part* of the changing landscape but in a state of continuous evolution as his experience and the flow of information available to him subtly influence his angle of approach.

While it is not my intention to check off in any methodical way one set of observations (from 1952) against another (their 1984 equivalents), there are a few cases, I think, where 1952 can usefully be brought into relation, or compared, with 1984. The exercise may tell us a little about what we ought to know about Britten seven years or so after his death in December 1976.

One observation I made in 1952 particularly intrigued me when I reread it: the suggestion that there was a whole category of Britten's

What do we know about Britten now?

tunes which, although not really like folksong, none the less had about them a quality that transcended time, place and occasion (perhaps even the composer's persona), and mysteriously convinced one that they were tunes that must have existed for ever and were made known through, rather than by, the composer.[2]

One might argue that this was no more than a knack for writing a good tune; and I should certainly not want to deny that. But Britten in fact wrote very many different kinds of tunes, which include the most elaborately constructed and unpredictable melodies as well as this particular category of the immediately memorable tune, instant communication made manifest, which somehow corresponds—to what? To a stock of basic melodic and rhythmic patterns that we are born with and carry round inside us, awaiting release?

We have to regret that the little *Welcome Ode*, Op.95, for young people's chorus and orchestra, completed in August 1976, proved to be the last composition that he was able to bring to an end.[3] But there is a curious rightness that this minor, but wholly characteristic work, which sustains the long tradition of music for children and young people that Britten founded, should also include a telling example of one of those extraordinary tunes to which I have been referring— 'Round about, round about, in a fine ring a:', the tune of the Roundel (Ex.1). The old knack was as evident, and as strong, at the end of Britten's life as it was in early days—in fact, in very early days.

[2] The tunes I specifically mentioned in 1952 were the third audience song from *The Little Sweep* (but why not all four of them?), the children's ball game from *Albert Herring* (Act I scene 2), the wordless waltz from the Finale of the *Spring Symphony*, and Billy's F major ballad from *Billy Budd* (Act IV scene 1). I am not too enthusiastic now about the rhetoric of thirty years ago but I think a genuine observation just manages to shine through the fog: 'It may be countered that these examples are not more than evidence of a capacity for writing "a good tune", a judgement which is partly relevant. But it was the critic who observed that the audience songs from *The Little Sweep* had almost established themselves as national folksongs who approached the heart of the matter. Not, I believe, *factually*—since all the instances [I quote] seem to me to be fundamentally far removed from folk art—but *intuitively*: this critic was aware of the special nature of the attraction of these audience songs for the audience participant. Somehow it was sensed that Britten was making an assault on the deepest strata of our musical consciousness (as perhaps the best folk art does), tapping a creative source in himself and finding a creative response in his audience, which may have both been dormant for centuries, or perhaps never before utilized by a creative artist in this manner. In these [songs] Britten seems to have effected a real union (probably unconscious on all sides) between the artist, the public and the common heritage of our musical culture, however harassed or suppressed that culture may have become.'
[3] At the time of his death he was working on a setting of Edith Sitwell's poem; 'Praise We Great Men', for solo quartet, chorus and orchestra.

23

Ex.1

Indeed, I think that one of the most fascinating aspects likely to be revealed by a methodical scrutiny of his juvenilia will be the early manifestation of a pronounced melodic gift. It was certainly something he recognized in himself, and very occasionally remarked upon as a possible merit of his music. He took obvious pleasure in singing the tune of the Roundel to me on my return from a journey overseas. There was life, I was to understand, in the old dog yet.

One looks at the Roundel and one thinks: predictable. Yet the phrase-lengths and the distribution of the accents are rather characteristically unpredictable; and as for the little tune itself, its predictability strikes one only after one has heard it, and then in the sense that I have tried to describe above, i.e. as one of those tunes that must have existed for ever but is only given life by Britten: unpredictable until he lent it predictability.

The truth is, I submit, that Britten's powerful and prodigal melodic invention—with respect not only to the limited class of tunes which I have been discussing but to his melody as a whole—is one of his strongest characterizing features. It was also one of the features which marked him off, quite sharply, from many of his contemporaries— and conspicuously so from much Modernist aesthetic, which paid little attention to melody or was actively contemptuous of it. It is interesting to find that it is precisely this feature of Britten's music which has impressed composers from wholly different traditions, Lutoslawski and Messiaen among them.

The mention of Messiaen may surprise some readers. But in fact his most recent experience of *Peter Grimes* at the Paris Opéra (in 1981)—he had heard the opera only once before, in Hungary, when he had not understood it so well—suggested to him that the work was a 'masterpiece'. He was struck in particular, it seems, by its dramatic power, superb orchestration and the strength, memorability and basic simplicity of its melodic lines. One of Messiaen's perceptions of the work seems to me to be strikingly original and illuminating: that the music of *Grimes* was not neo-classical but all diatonic—'something very brave in its own way for its time'. Of particular scenes and interludes he liked especially the 'Dawn' (first) sea interlude and the 'fog'—i.e. 'mad'—scene, which he thought magnificent theatre. He cared less, apparently, for the dance music (Act III), though finding it appropriate to its context: 'in a large work one must be able to express everything from the sublime to the vulgar: as in Shakespeare'. (I am much indebted to a pupil of Messiaen's, George Benjamin, for this fascinating account of a conversation, of which I report only part, with his eminent teacher.)

I shall mention the topic of Britten's melodic invention again, but let me turn for a moment to the question of his contemporaries. On the whole, this was not an area about which we had much to say in 1952: the scrutiny was concentrated, rather, on influences, on 'European' influences in particular. Two senior contemporaries, Schoenberg and Stravinsky, were mentioned from time to time in a general way, and substantially by Hans Keller in his chapter 'The Musical Character' (pp.334–51), but in neither case was there much specific or detailed commentary. For our supposed 'neglect' of, or 'indifference' to, Stravinsky we were chastised by William Glock. I confess that my own relative ignorance of Stravinsky at that time may well have contributed to the impression of narrow vision. But I continue to wonder, even though we now have both Stravinsky's and Britten's *oeuvres* before us, more or less in their totality, and allowing for what ought to have been said in 1952 that was not said, whether the mounting of a major study of Stravinsky's influence on Britten would in fact get us very far beyond the observation of absolutely obvious and inescapable technical debts the younger composer owed his senior. On the other hand it would surely make emphatically clear the contrast in musical characters.

As for Schoenberg, in 1952 it seemed that the contrast in musical character and technique could scarcely be deeper: Schoenberg appeared to be the very antithesis of Britten. The only direct comment on any work of Britten's showing a Schoenberg influence was made by Erwin Stein, in his chapter 'The Symphonies', about Britten's Opus 1: 'The *Sinfonietta*, I believe, is the only work of Britten's in which Schoenberg's influence is directly apparent' (p.247). That looked right in 1952 and perhaps was right for 1952. Now I find it looks very odd indeed, especially in the light of the works composed after 1952 which reveal Britten's use of serial principles: not serial technique in the classical sense but undeniably serial thinking and serial practice. I have in mind *The Turn of the Screw*, the *Cantata Academica*, *A Midsummer Night's Dream*, *Songs and Proverbs of William Blake*, *Death in Venice* and, above all, *Owen Wingrave* (1970). It is true that in none of these works—perhaps 'excepting the *Screw* and the genial cantata—would it be appropriate to describe Schoenberg's influence as 'direct'. But then direct influence is very often the most superficial form of influence, as well as the most obvious. What counts, and what habitually counted with Britten, is the modification or development of his compositional techniques brought about by his encounter with another and possibly very different mode of compositional practice. It is in this significant sense that I believe Schoenberg came, however unexpectedly, to be influential in Britten's music: in no way a question of style but altogether a way of thinking.[4] Britten would not have thought that way if it had not been for Schoenberg's example. And one knows in

[4] There is a fascinating passage in the early *Quatres Chansons Françaises*—the orchestral song-cycle (settings of Verlaine and Hugo) Britten composed in the summer of 1928, at the age of 14½—which almost unfolds all twelve notes of the chromatic scale within a narrow space. But this in fact is not the most interesting aspect of it. How Britten chooses to organize his resources is strikingly prophetic of his later practice of mobilizing and exploiting all twelve notes. Admittedly the passage I quote here (voice part omitted), from the first and most 'advanced' of the songs, 'Nuits de Juin', is used for colour rather than as a constructive principle—part of the cycle's 'Impressionism'—but none the less it is remarkable evidence of the very young Britten's open and omnivorous ear, open, distinctly, to air from another planet:

1983, as one did not know thirty years ago, the extent of the youthful Britten's knowledge of Schoenberg's music and his enthusiastic response to some (not all) of the works he heard. Schoenberg's position in Britten's landscape has radically altered since 1952: his shadow has grown distinctly longer.

But it was not only his more or less immediate contemporaries who influenced Britten. There was also the past, perhaps especially the recent European past which, in the case of certain composers, was also—at least for English musicians—an unfamiliar past.

The most prominent example was that of Mahler; and he was conspicuously placed in my 1952 introduction as one of the major formative influences on Britten. The conspicuousness was heightened by two considerations: first, Britten's own declared admiration—though in 1952 it was not clear, as it is now, how early Britten's admiration for and experience of Mahler had begun—and second, that to us in the 1950s, the battle to establish (serious) criteria by which Britten should be judged was part of the same battle to win Mahler a hearing and (serious) critical attention. In introducing Mahler into the argument one was saying something serious not only about Britten but about Mahler too.

The general proposition seems to me to be as true as ever, though now in a rather different way. For example, I would not now strenuously argue that Mahler's influence showed in Britten's *Seven Sonnets of Michelangelo* and in particular in Sonnet XXX (cf. BS, pp.41–5); I should want to point in this same song to the clear technical evidence of the formation of a highly personal melodic style—a style, moreover, which was to remain immediately identi-

---

Perhaps something of Berg's stimulated this particular idea. Colin Matthews suggests that it may have been owing to the radical influence of Frank Bridge himself or one of his radical works; or perhaps the boy had come across some ear-opening scores in his teacher's possession. Among the works that Britten heard and studied immediately before and during the period he was composing the *Quatre Chansons* were the following (all entered in his 1928 diary): Bridge, *Three Idylls* (for string quartet) and *An Irish Melody*; Debussy, *L'Après-midi*; Ravel, *Introduction and Allegro*, *Sonatine*, and *Miroirs*, No.1. On 27 June he played the triangle in a performance of Samuel Coleridge-Taylor's cantata *A Tale of Old Japan* (his mother was in the chorus): 'We had a practice with Soloists in the Afternoon, and then in the evening we had the actual thing. It might have been a great deal worse.' See also an important study of the songs by Christopher Mark, 'Britten's Quatre Chansons Françaises', in *Soundings*, no.10, summer 1983, pp.23–35. Mr Mark spends some time on the possible influence of Berg on the first song, a point I raised in the first of three BBC Radio 3 documentaries on Britten and his early years, broadcast on 4 April 1980.

fiable and yet capable of embracing opposed poles of feeling. And whereas in 1952 *Paul Bunyan*[5] was still an entirely unknown quantity, we are now able to juxtapose the exalted love song from the *Michelangelo Sonnets* (probably composed between spring and October 1940)[6] with Tiny's 'sentimental' song from *Paul Bunyan* (almost certainly composed shortly before the work's première in New York in May 1941)[7] and perceive precisely the same techniques—which is to say, the same composer—at work. And it is the total working method that is involved, not just the common feature of the Lydian fourth, characteristic though that is, and the common key (see Exx.2a–d). I find it fascinating that the song, which is quite deliberately modelled on the lyric 'number' from the Broadway musical—a genre Britten had undoubtedly made it his business to get to know: hence the harmonization of the melody at the song's opening (cf. Ex.2c), which, rightly in the context of *Bunyan*, eschews the austerity of Sonnet XXX (cf. Ex.2a)—should move, so artlessly and yet so artfully, into a melodic shape whose only model was the composer's

Ex.2a Sonnet XXX

[5] The operetta Britten wrote with W. H. Auden in the United States in 1940–1, withdrawn after its first performance. It resurfaced at the end of Britten's life and had its first British radio and stage performances in 1976.

[6] Sonnet XXX is undated but the cycle as a whole is inscribed 'Oct. 30th 1940' and the earliest dated song, the second, is inscribed 'March 15th 1940'.

[7] Act I, No.15a. According to Helen Marshall, the original Tiny of 1941, 'I had been singing in a madrigal group with Peter Pears and when he found out that Dr [Milton] Smith had cast me in the show he evidently said something to Ben about the fact that I could sing a little bit; and so, the first time I met Ben, he said, "Please, Helen, what is your range?" So I told him what my vocal range was and the next night he had the Mother aria written for me. It was not in the original score. . . .' She commented on the speed with which the piece was composed—'Just overnight . . . no problem at all.' Milton Smith recollected that 'In the original version, although it called for a soprano lead singer, [Tiny] had nothing to sing but chorus, and . . . there was a main tenor who had nothing to sing except in the choruses, and I insisted that each of them had to have something to sing, so the boys [Britten and Auden] obliged.'

Ex.2b Sonnet XXX

Ex.2c Tiny's Song

Ex.2d Tiny's Song

Donald Mitchell

own prototype (cf. Exx.2b and 2d). Thus a composer's personality, i.e. his technique, unifies, the seemingly diametric opposition of lyric number and art song. (The Romance from the *Diversions*, Op.21, for piano (left hand) and orchestra (also composed in 1940) shows the same melodic type and much the same textural layout, though here chains of fourths replace scales and arpeggios.) That qualifying digression does nothing to alter the fact of Mahler's importance for Britten. Indeed, when Britten reheard *Paul Bunyan* after thirty-five years, he drew my attention to a passage in it that showed 'how well I knew my Mahler in 1941'. Ex.3 gives the beginning of the orchestral bars in question (from Act I, No.8b, Exit of Lumberjacks):

Ex.3

It seems odd that Britten thought, in 1976, that there was something specifically Mahler-inflected about Ex.3 and its continuation. It is Mahlerian surely only in the most general sense, i.e. we respond to a few highly expressive bars, whose intensive chromaticism makes manifest the expressiveness—a kind of lyric rhetoric of which Mahler was indeed a master. But I think that what may in fact have prompted Britten's remark was not an identity of style but rather a show of overt expressiveness which he associated with Mahler—which is different from the replication of another composer's voice.

But there are passages and works where Britten's comment might have seemed altogether more meaningful; for example, the Adagio for orchestra with which *Death in Venice* comes to an end, or the last song of the *Nocturne* (the Shakespeare sonnet). There we do feel, and were probably meant to feel, Mahler's presence.[8] And there are plenty of other examples, either direct, such as the dramatic timpani strokes at the very beginning of the *Sinfonia da Requiem* or numerous vivid details of the writing for wind in the Cello Symphony, or indirect, for instance the very concepts of the 'dramatic' symphony or 'symphonic' song-cycle. To take only one example from the last category, *Our Hunting Fathers*, the orchestral song-cycle of 1936: the shape of that extraordinary work and, above all, its ambitiousness—I refer to the brilliant development for orchestra alone which forms the climax of the 'Dance of Death'—are clearly rooted in Mahler, in particular in *Das Lied von der Erde*.

The influence, the impact, is there all right; but the striking thing is how much *Our Hunting Fathers* owes in compositional *principle* to *Das Lied von der Erde* and how little in terms of personal *style*, apart from an odd touch here or there (for example the muted brass fanfares one bar before Figure 22). The virtuoso orchestral development in the 'Dance of Death' not only makes the point about principle—the passage could scarcely have existed without its Mahlerian precedent—but is also an example of the emphatic contrasts in personality (i.e. style): both are funereal set pieces but one is a very fast scherzo, all unrestrained bite and ferocity, while the other is a very slow march, all elegiac melody and contained dissonance.

Thus if I were writing now about the Britten–Mahler relationship, I should concentrate on shared technical principles rather than on observation of common features of style. It is an approach, I believe, that aids us to come to a conclusion about Britten's assimilation of his 'influences', and throws general light on his musical character. While it remains true that he was indeed an eclectic composer, and avowedly so, his eclecticism, far from manifesting itself as an array of diverse and identifiable styles, in fact resides in a process that is the very opposite. His 'style', his 'profile', is singularly and immediately recognizable and 'individual', but the techniques that service the style often represent the summation of astonishingly heterodox compositional principles drawn from a variety of distant and recent pasts and presents. It is precisely in the nature of his resources and equipment

---

[8] Especially so in *Death in Venice*, I think, not because Britten was confusing Aschenbach with Mahler (as Luchino Visconti did in his film), but because an elegiac Mahlerian Adagio was a wholly appropriate musical salutation to the type of artist of which Aschenbach, the writer, was a representative. See also the prelude to Act II of the opera (cf. Ex.5, below).

that Britten's authentic eclecticism reveals itself; and our understanding of this clarifies the paradox with which we have previously been saddled: how was it that so eclectic a composer should always sound so conspicuously like no one but himself? I am convinced, moreover, that it is just this synthesizing aspect of Britten's technical thinking that will prove particularly influential on and appealing to succeeding generations of composers.[9] For it is clear now that he did not unswervingly pursue some compromised road of orthodoxy but on the contrary ruthlessly and comprehensively ransacked past and present, orthodox and unorthodox, fashionable and unfashionable, traditional and innovative, and took whatever was useful to him; and that was a lot. It could well be that Britten's 'eclecticism', newly defined and understood, will offer composers and music a way forward.

I have suggested that one of the differences that distinguishes writing about Britten in 1983 from writing about him in 1952 is an awareness of the difference between direct influence on style and influential technical principle. All the odder, then, that in 1952 one of the composers whom I now think should be acknowledged as a direct influence, and perhaps more than that, received no mention at all: not Berg or Bartók—though neither was very adequately commented on—but Shostakovich (b. 1906). Perhaps in the light of that curious omission, the absence of Prokofiev, who likewise finds no place in the index, strikes one as less surprising.

So the Symposium presented a somewhat constricted view of what in 1952 seemed to be the principal European sources of influence on Britten—a good deal about Stravinsky and Mahler, and Berg and Bartók somewhere in the picture, though scarcely in the foreground

---

[9] Any such reassessment of the character of Britten's technical achievement will be substantially aided by Peter Evans's masterly analytical account, *The Music of Benjamin Britten.* I have seen some adverse comment implying that Professor Evans's approach is too dauntingly analytic—as if Britten's music and vigorous analytic method were somehow mutually exclusive. In fact Professor Evans's study shows just the opposite: that Britten's music can support, or is susceptible to, analysis as complex as any that one may find applied to other contemporary composers, whether to his predecessors or to composers of his own generation, not to speak of a later one. Professor Evans would be the first to agree that analysis cannot be the final instrument of judgement. But in this particular case it can, and does, tell us a great deal about the complex organization of Britten's major music and about the rich and diverse techniques that serve it, knowledge of which must certainly precede the making of any serious critical evaluation, adverse or enthusiastic. This point would scarcely be worth making were it not for the oddity of some of the composer's admirers *and* opponents sharing the same illusion.

or very sharp in definition; but of the Russians not so much as even a ritual acknowledgement. Once again, it is the view that has changed. What we know now of Britten's works up to 1939, when he left for North America, opens up a very different perspective. It is not only that our knowledge of the music, including some hitherto unknown works, has increased, but that we know much more than we did about the youthful Britten's musical environment: about his tastes, his prejudices, his preoccupations, the music he heard, and the music he played. It was an environment coloured, and for Britten very darkly coloured, by the political events of the decade and above all by the rise of Fascism in Europe.

I am not going to cover ground that I have already mapped out elsewhere (*BA*, especially pp.71–3), but a minimal amount of historical information is necessary if we are to understand the particular interest Britten would have had in Shostakovich in the 1930s. The appeal of Shostakovich—seven years older than Britten and like him prodigiously gifted as a young composer—was bound up not only with the fact of his talent but also with his nationality. That he was a *Russian* (Soviet) composer added an extra dimension to the appeal because it was the Russians, at this particular time, who seemed to be the spearhead of the resistance to Fascism; they were certainly so viewed by many of the groups of artists with whom Britten was directly associated.[10]

Thus there was an extra-musical, *political* reason why Shostakovich would have made a particular impact on Britten in the mid-1930s. We know that Shostakovich's music formed a vivid part of his experience at this time: he got to know some of it at the piano (e.g. the Piano Concerto No.1 for piano, trumpet and strings, Op.35) and in the concert hall: he heard a concert performance of *Lady Macbeth of the Mtsensk District* on 18 March 1936 and wrote about it both in his diary[11] and in the opening issue of *World Film News*. The music of the

[10] A great deal of heat has been generated by those with conflicting opinions about the political convictions of the groups and personalities involved. I make no judgement of the politics but simply observe how some of the participants themselves saw the situation.

[11] See 'Britten on *Oedipus Rex* and *Lady Macbeth*', *Tempo*, No.120 (March 1977), pp.10–12. The entry he made in his diary after the performance reveals his views of *Lady Macbeth* in more detail than the published review: 'Of course, it is idle to pretend that this is great music throughout—it is stage music and as such must be considered. There is some terrific music in the entr'actes. But I will defend it through thick & thin against these charges of "lack of style". People will not differentiate between style & manner. It is the composer's heritage to take what he

immensely gifted and then conspicuously iconoclastic, 'outrageous' young Soviet composer was an established feature of the contemporary musical scene. It would have been surprising if Britten had not in some way reacted positively to the model of the slightly senior Shostakovich, not only for the reason I have already adduced, but also because the two composers interestingly shared some common characteristics which have their roots at perhaps a deeper level than those of manner and gesture. Indeed, the only surprising aspect of the whole matter is that the relationship has gone virtually unnoticed and its potentialities unexplored. Yet if we take Shostakovich into account, and place him not so much in our present landscape but in Britten's, in the mid-1930s, some works come into sharp focus. I am thinking not of recently rediscovered pieces like *Russian Funeral*, whose topic would in any case have required the making of an audible and recognizable fraternal gesture,[12] but of such works as the 1938 Piano Concerto, Op.13, its finale especially, and the discarded Recitative and Aria (the original slow movement, abandoned in 1945), in which there was a conspicuous element of parody and burlesque.[13] We may understand the character of the latter work, or at

---

wants from whom he wants—& to write music. There is a consistency of style & method throughout. The satire is biting & brilliant. It is never boring for a second—even in this form. Some of the vocal writing is extravagant. But he may have special singers in view. . . . The "eminent English Renaissance" composers sniggering in the stalls was typical. There is more music in a page of Macbeth than in the whole of their "elegant" output!'

[12] *Russian Funeral*—to which Britten referred as his 'War and Death'—for brass and percussion, was composed and first performed in 1936 (see *BA*, pp.70–8). The quick middle section, 'War', is distinctly Shostakovich-like in conception; and by a strange coincidence the authentic Russian melody Britten used in 1936 for his march was used in 1957 by Shostakovich in his Eleventh Symphony. The slow funeral march, 'Death', which frames 'War', is emphatically Mahlerian. Thus *Russian Funeral*, in juxtaposing two models of particular importance for Britten, also neatly places Shostakovich alongside one of *his* principal models, Mahler, who proves to be one of the more important links between Shostakovich and Britten. For evidence of how well Shostakovich knew Mahler in *his* youth (cf. Britten's statement, referred to above, n.11), one need look no further than *Lady Macbeth*, particularly Act II scene 5, Fig.315f. The melody for strings here is a marvellous re-creation of a Mahlerian melody. One will search in vain for anything comparable in Britten's work; and his own example, from *Paul Bunyan* (see p.30), pales into insignificance by the side of Shostakovich's.

[13] In the first part of the movement, called Recitative, which is a kind of cadenza for the piano in dialogue with solo woodwind. The oboe, clarinet, bassoon, flute and finally two horns all contribute to a mosaic in which the solo piano runs through a provoking sequence of popular idioms, e.g. *quasi polka*, *quasi 'blues'*, *tempo di valse*, before the movement settles down into an extended tutti, *lento molto*. If the recitative is all Satire, then the Aria is all Sentiment. While there is no case for restoring the original

least one of its principal sources, more fully if we bear Shostakovich in mind as a probable model or point of departure, and also bear in mind that for Shostakovich, *his* model was probably Prokofiev, an *enfant terrible* and specialist in satire and grotesquerie of an earlier vintage.[14]

It is, perhaps, the common use of parody which constitutes the really significant relationship between Britten and Shostakovich, an emphatic feature of both composers' styles but also something more deeply rooted: an important feature of their creative personalities as youthful artists. If we look for direct influence, for manifestations of identical style, then we shall come up, as always, with a relatively trivial haul. For example, it is highly interesting to compare Britten's orchestral song-cycle, *Our Hunting Fathers* (composed between May and July 1936), of which satire and parody are prominent components, if not *raisons d'être*, with Shostakovich's satirical opera, *Lady Macbeth*, of which, as I have already mentioned (above, and n.11), Britten heard the original (1932) version for the first time in March 1936, just a few weeks before beginning to work seriously on his own song-cycle. The comparison certainly reveals how receptive was Britten's ear. The glacial xylophone ostinato that takes over in the song-cycle's Funeral March, for example: Britten surely owed that to Shostakovich's example.[15] And in general it is fascinating to hear how two composers in whom the satirical vein was strong often chose to exploit the orchestra through identical means. For example, Shostakovich's bold use of instrumental contrasts projected at the extreme range of the instruments involved, of unconventional and often radically lean instrumental accompaniments, and of unconventionally selected solo instruments (in an orchestral context) is

---

movement—clearly, Britten thought it belonged exclusively to the *manners* rather than the *spirit* of the time—an occasional performance of the 1938 version of the Concerto is to be welcomed in so far as it throws specific light on an important aspect of the composer's style in the late 1930s. (Incidentally, a series of miniature cadenzas for brass and woodwind, and finally piano, is a feature of the Burlesque from *Diversions*, composed in 1940.)

[14] It has always struck me that Prokofiev was a major voice in the March in the later *Diversions*, though now I hear the variation as Prokofiev filtered through Shostakovich. However, it is unlikely that this was the result of any influence by the left-hand Concerto Prokofiev wrote in 1931 for the same patron, Paul Wittgenstein. Wittgenstein never played that work, though the score remained in his possession, and it was not performed until 1956. It is just possible that he showed Britten the score—perhaps as an example of what to avoid! Britten's own collaboration with Wittgenstein was not without difficulties.

[15] And, of course, Mahler's: i.e. the formal idea of the march is Mahlerian, the predominant instrumental sonority Shostakovichian.

broadly matched by technical features that show up not only in *Our Hunting Fathers*, but, albeit much modified, throughout Britten's works.[16]

However, once that has been said, the differences that remain are a good deal more substantial than the practices that unite the two composers. For example, to return to the first topic I touched on in this chapter, how relatively lacking in rich melodic invention is Shostakovich's *Lady Macbeth*. There are of course some marvellous melodic inspirátions, but one does not leave the work with an impression of a boundingly fertile melodic gift, as one does, I suggest, *Our Hunting Fathers*. Furthermore, while Shostakovich's vocal writing certainly reflects the characteristic exaggeration of the drama (huge leaps, for example), it shows nothing of the innovatory quality that Britten in 1936 brought to the voice part of his song-cycle, which may—probably intentionally—have had an element of exaggeration about it but, at the same time, represented a dazzling extension of the potentialities of the voice. The boundaries of what technically could be done, given the right singer, were significantly enlarged; and many composers since, knowingly or unknowingly, have benefited from Britten's pioneering.

Shostakovich's pioneering is to be found rather in his brilliant orchestral imagination which, as I have already suggested, must have had a particular appeal for the youthful Britten in the 1930s; and yet even here, and despite the admiration he expressed for the orchestral interludes in *Lady Macbeth*,[17] how sharply contrasted are the two composers' sound-worlds. If in particular we react to, and conceivably against, the piercing character of Shostakovich's sound or, no

[16] For instance, the remarkable use of extreme contrast in range and colours towards the end of *Death in Venice* (Act II scene 17, Fig.320): the combination of solo flute and two solo double-basses which precisely—and in part because of the complete absence of any orchestral middle—embodies the emptiness of the beach and the total draining of Aschenbach's moral centre. This example is particularly interesting because it shows a basic historical principle at work. A good claim could be made that instrumental writing at the extreme of the instruments was prompted in the first place by the need for a style to accommodate, to embody, extreme feelings; and parody, satire, burlesque are (in the main) a sub-category of extreme feelings—after all, parody feeds on *exaggeration*. The new technique becomes part of the established grammar, of the total resources of the language, and eventually can be used in situations far removed from those which originally prompted the technique into life. The process must be peculiar to the individual composer, but in Britten's case, I suggest, some of the boldness of his late expressive style had its roots in (probably long forgotten) techniques he had developed in the service of parody and satire.

[17] The notorious *Entr'actes*, Britten's memory of which (along with the interludes from *Wozzeck*) may well havce influenced the way he put *Peter Grimes* together.

less, its bludgeoning character (when the drama calls for it), it is because the extremist style of the orchestration is often pressed into the service of a massive, grinding dissonance: the aural assault is conducted as it were on two fronts simultaneously.

If I say that we find nothing like that in Britten—and we don't (I believe he would have been almost physically incapable of generating quantities of 'ugly' sound)—I run the risk of confirming suspicions that this Shostakovich–Britten juxtaposition is no more than an exercise in the sterile game of playing off one composer against another, and in this round Shostakovich comes off second best. But the comparison, in particular the last point I have made, will enable us to come to conclusions which may transcend the triviality of competitive ratings. Our observation that the piled-up dissonances of Shostakovich's *Lady Macbeth* never formed part of Britten's compositional practice is a way of making an important aesthetic discrimination. Britten was virtually untouched by the Modernism which the young Shostakovich so provocatively affirmed and of which *Lady Macbeth* was a particularly exuberant example. That Britten eschewed Modernism reminds us that whereas Shostakovich's shock-tactics (a feature of Modernist doctrine) were conspicuously part of the landscape of the 1920s, with the onset of the 1930s—Britten's, the younger man's, formative period—Modernism had passed its peak, both as a fashion and as a stimulating influence, and was in decline. Thus the juxtaposition of two distinctive decades, when spelled out in the personalities and creative practice of the two composers, permits us to see what Britten took from the twenties, and what he rejected. In my account of Britten and Auden (*BA*) I tried to show Britten in relation to, and in part as a maker of, the thirties. His relationship to the twenties, however, has hardly been looked at; and I suggest that through the use of Shostakovich as a landmark we can begin to map out a hitherto unexplored area of Britten studies.

A final point, possibly the most significant. The strength of Shostakovich's appeal to Britten rested, it is clear, on a diversity of attractions. As I have already mentioned, there was the political dimension; there was also perhaps the example of Shostakovich's own working life, which during the twenties and thirties was so often linked with the Soviet theatre and film studio. In this respect, indeed, Britten's working life in the thirties provides a kind of English paraphrase of the Soviet composer's. But these connections are marginal to my main argument: that it is the shared vein of parody and satire which provides the common ground. This was one of Shostakovich's principal techniques during the twenties and thirties, one which made him famous inside and outside Russia and represented for him a particularly powerful mode of expression. It would be absurd, of course, to suggest that for the youthful Britten parody was the only way forward. His list of works shows that not to be true; but parody was certainly *one* of the principal ways forward for him. If one takes into account the vast mass of incidental (and largely unknown) music that he wrote in the thirties, some of the most striking of which relied on parody and satire, and also the published works,[18] some of the best and most successful of which— *Variations on a Theme of Frank Bridge*, for example—likewise depend substantially on parody as a compositional principle, the total investment in parody is surprisingly extensive. Without exaggeration, it was one of the principal modes of composition that Britten practised, to the end of the thirties and just beyond. His basic model in this field, I believe, was Shostakovich; and the sympathetic response of the younger English composer to Shostakovich's own special brand of parody and satire seems to me the most interesting feature of the relationship, much more interesting than the unveiling of a direct influence. It was not so much that Britten was stirred to imitate: his exercises in parody, indeed, have little of the sheer belligerence of Shostakovich's—a difference we may wish to attribute to the evolution of the twenties into the thirties, but perhaps is better explained in terms of the development of Britten's own creative personality. In his hands, parody became more complex and sophisticated, more affectionate (from time to time) and, if it is sound alone that we are considering—dare I say it?—*more musical*. In short, he remarkably extended the range of parody, the scope of its forms, its content. So it was not admiring mimicry; rather, Shostakovich stirred into life a singular gift that was to characterize large stretches of the music Britten composed between 1933 and 1941. Perhaps these thoughts may stimulate investigation of a debt that as yet has hardly been recognized.[19]

---

[18] We are also able, in 1984, to take into account some early works that were performed but not published and which make substantial use of parody, e.g. the *Three Divertimenti* for string quartet (1936) and the *Temporal Variations* for oboe and piano (1936), the March from which powerfully evokes Prokofiev.

[19] The parallel was drawn relatively early by a distinguished composer in the United States. The New York première of Britten's Violin Concerto, in 1940, was attended by Elliott Carter, who heard the work as 'an English counterpart of recent Prokofiev

What do we know about Britten now?

The impact on Britten of his travels to the Far East in 1955–6 has often been remarked upon. It was audible, first in the full-length ballet, *The Prince of the Pagodas*, composed on his return from the Orient, and then, substantially later, in the first of the church parables, *Curlew River*, composed in 1964 and based on one of the most famous Japanese Noh plays, *Sumidagawa* (a performance of which had greatly impressed Britten when he was in Tokyo).[20] Crudely speaking, one might say that the *Pagodas* was bound up with the visit to Bali, *Curlew River* with the visit to Tokyo.

One might well imagine, then, that these journeys east in 1955–6 were responsible for the very radical development in Britten's compositional techniques in the 1960s and after; and substantially that would be a perfectly correct view. The score of the *Pagodas* showed the direct influence of Balinese music in the shape of a brilliant evocation of a gamelan orchestra, and some seven years later it became clear that what in the *Pagodas* might have been no more than an immediate but isolated response to the narrative and geography of the ballet's scenario was in fact a clear precursor of a much more significant and far-reaching reaction to the exotic musical experiences of 1955–6. But while we must recognize that the history of Britten's creative encounter with the Orient *effectively* begins in the mid-1950s, that history itself has a fascinating prehistory. If we are to locate the very beginnings of the techniques derived from oriental music which became so important an aspect of the last thirteen years of Britten's life, we have to look back as far as 1939, to the years Britten spent in New York on Long Island, first as a guest and then as a member of the Mayer family.[21] There Britten met Colin McPhee

---

and Shostakovitch music' (quoted by Arnold Whittall, *BT*, p.47). Carter's mention of Shostakovich was made in a positive context: ' . . . nobody could fail to be impressed by the remarkable gifts of the composer, the size and ambition of his talent'. A decade later another American composer, Virgil Thomson, was referring to Britten in connection with cultures that exploit 'the vein of public-pleasing serious music. That is Russia's specialty and a little bit England's, with Benjamin Britten a local Shostakovich.' (*A Virgil Thomson Reader* (Boston: Houghton Mifflin Co., 1981), pp.332–3.)

[20] Britten and Pears were accompanied on this part of their trip by the Prince and Princess of Hesse and the Rhine, and from the diary of Prince Ludwig (partly published in *TBB*, pp.56–65), we learn the date of the performance, 11 February 1956, besides other details of this historic encounter with *Sumidagawa*. But it seems from Britten's correspondence with William Plomer that in fact there were discussions about a project based on a Noh play *before* the composer had actually visited Japan and seen and heard the Noh theatre for himself.

[21] For information about the Mayers see *PL*, plates 112–76.

(1901–1964),[22] a friend of the Mayers who was both a gifted composer and at the time the leading authority on Balinese music: he lived on Bali during the thirties and indeed could only recently have left the island when he first met Britten in New York in 1939.

Among McPhee's many published studies of Balinese music was a set of transcriptions for two pianos, four hands, *Balinese Ceremonial Music*, published by Schirmer in 1940; and not only was the music published: it was also issued in the same year as a set of gramophone records (78 rpm, shellac discs), volume 17 of the same publisher's *Library of Recorded Music*. The discs contained the two-piano transcriptions and also three pieces for flute (the flautist was Georges Barrère, the French virtuoso) and piano; the two-piano transcriptions were recorded by Colin McPhee and Benjamin Britten.

Thus Britten's first exposure of any substance to 'exotic' music[23] was a result of his meeting, on the other side of the Atlantic, with McPhee. We may safely assume that the two composers would have discussed what, compositionally, might be transferred from east to west or prove fertile in a fresh context. McPhee would, undoubtedly, have been enthusiastic about such transfers: some of his own compositions attempt a synthesis, a marriage of two cultures. But interestingly enough, Britten seems not to have been persuaded, even though he was McPhee's partner in performing and recording the two-piano transcriptions. McPhee's inscription on the copy of the *Balinese Ceremonial Music* he gave Britten in April 1940 reads 'To Ben—hoping he'll find something in the music, after all':[24] scarcely an inscription to a convert! Yet whatever Britten's reluctance or (more probably) ambivalence, he *did* find something in McPhee's transcriptions and used it in the 1940s. (Many years later he found much more, but by then his experience was not of a transcribed Bali but of the magic island itself.)

[22] See *PL*, plate 125. McPhee was of American nationality but Canadian origin. See further below, n.21 pp.206–7.

[23] There is no mention in his diaries of music from any of the countries of South East Asia, but he was very much taken by a concert of Indian music and dancing which he attended on 6 May 1933 and about which he wrote: 'I go to Amb. Th. [Ambassadors Theatre] at 8.45—ticket paid for by Miss Fass—to see Uday Shan-kar & his Hindu dancers (inc. Simkie & Robindra—quite young) & musicians (inc. Vishnu Dan—marvellous drummer & Timir Bawan). I haven't seen anything for ages which has thrilled me more. Marvellously intellectual & perfectly wrought dancing. Finest I have yet seen. Music, full of variety, rhythmically & tonally. One perfect creation of Shan-kar—an ecstatic dance. Tandawa Nrittya was a longer ballet with a very exciting fight.'

[24] See *PL*, plate 176.

What do we know about Britten now?

I have mentioned that our approach to Britten in 1983 must be conditioned by our acquisition of knowledge of works that have hitherto been unfamiliar or inaccessible, or even unsuspected. *Paul Bunyan*, withdrawn in 1941 and not rescued until 1976, is one of those early, unknown works that prove to have been seminal; and in the Prologue to Act I of the operetta, in the brief, chiefly orchestral passage that heralds the unusual phenomenon of the moon turning blue (Figures 11–12), we discover that—'after all', I am tempted to say—Britten's ear and imagination had seized on something in the McPhee transcriptions and put it to bold, if brief, use. The passage represents, albeit in very simple though effective form, the pure heterophonic principle with which Britten had become familiar through his acquaintance with McPhee and with McPhee's pioneering work as transcriber. Ex.4 gives the complete passage. The importation of an exotic technique into *Paul Bunyan* (which otherwise had more to do with Broadway than Bali) would be inexplicable were it not for the model that *Balinese Ceremonial Music* provided. It is true, of course, that something alien and unexpected was musically required in order to match the exceptional dramatic moment (a blue moon) and Britten was stimulated to seek out a kind of music that was equally outside everyday expectation. However, that it took the shape it did was entirely due to the meeting in New York with McPhee—one of those fateful encounters which lastingly influences a creative life, though its significance may pass unnoticed at the time. I am sure that Britten, when composing his bit of heterophony, was not conscious of anything other than putting to use an idea, a technique, which was particularly appropriate to the particularly dramatic event. Least of all would he have been conscious of what retrospectively has proved to be (to my knowledge) his first heterophonic exercise.

And yet something undoubtedly went on resonating in Britten's mind and ears. In March 1944, after his return from New York, he gave a two-piano recital in London with Clifford Curzon at the Wigmore Hall which included McPhee's transcriptions—their first English performance.[25] So he had not altogether lost touch with the transcriptions; and some fresh research by David Matthews on *Peter Grimes*, which was then very much at the forefront of Britten's composing activity, suggests that the *Balinese Ceremonial Music*

[25] See *PL*, plate 174.

41

Ex.4

surfaced not only in his first opera but again in his second (*PG*, pp.122–4).

While major research on Britten's use of heterophony must address itself to *The Prince of the Pagodas* and the works after 1963, it is clear that the prehistory, which I have only outlined, also merits attention. And paradoxically, what seems to have been Britten's initial reluctance to respond, to get involved, makes his later, profound involvement the more telling. Something was touched off in him, of which he was obliged to take notice, perhaps even against his will, and to which eventually he was irresistibly drawn. It is a remarkable story enabling us to discern a line, straighter and certainly longer than one had supposed, linking Britten's first opera, *Paul Bunyan*, of 1941, with his last, *Death in Venice*, of 1973. Perhaps it is fanciful to suggest that in Britten's Venetian bells—for example in the Overture, between Figures 43 and 45—we hear an echo of the syncopated ceremonial Balinese bells, whose characteristic sound McPhee tried to make his keyboards yield.[26] But there is nothing fanciful at all in pointing to a passage like Ex.5, from *Death in Venice*, Act II, which is

Ex.5

[26] Cf. for example some bars from the first of the transcriptions, *Pemoengkah*:

worlds (and decades) apart from the 'blue moon' music of *Paul Bunyan* and yet is served by the same heterophonic technique.

Yes: Britten's landscape looks very different in 1984. Now we have

There is a similarly striking passage in the second of the five two-piano numbers, the *Rébong*, which Britten and McPhee recorded in 1940, an item which is not included in the published set of three pieces.

The opening of the second published transcription, the *Gambangan*, offers a characteristic example of one of the freely improvised solo flourishes that are so prominent in Balinese music:

Gambangan

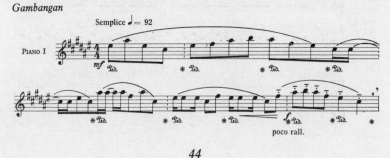

to take both east and west into simultaneous view, something that was certainly no part of our horizon in 1952; and yet, as we have seen, it all started in the late 1930s and early 1940s. There could hardly be a more powerful illustration of the composer taking what was to hand, choosing what was technically useful to him, and making it his own. He continued to use these particular techniques to the end of his life; though by then, one might seriously claim, they had in part taken *him* over. So the hope that Colin McPhee expressed in his inscription of *Balinese Ceremonial Music* came 'after all' to be fulfilled.

The gesture must have stayed with Britten all his life—his memory of it doubtless powerfully reinforced by his visit to the island in 1956—so that he was able to revive it, as to the manner born, in *Death in Venice*. See, for instance, Act II, Figure 214 (and also 1 bar before Figure 26); Britten's glockenspiel=Bali's metallophone:

Death in Venice

2

Working for Benjamin Britten (I)[1]

IMOGEN HOLST

When the editor of the *Musical Times* asked me to set down some of my 'impressions and memories' of Benjamin Britten, I decided that the most practical contribution I could make would be to mention a few of the things I learnt while working for him.

It is difficult to describe his energy, which always left the rest of us far behind. He could go straight from a rehearsal to a committee meeting and then to a discussion with a librettist, putting the whole of his mind from one thing to another without any hesitation. People have often remarked on the speed with which he wrote his music; but he nearly always thought about each work for a long time before beginning to write it. The *Missa Brevis in D*, for example, was written in only a few days, but he had been thinking about it for more than six months. Whenever he was actually writing, his concentration was impregnable: I remember one pouring wet day when he got soaked through while sitting indoors at his desk because he hadn't noticed that the rain was coming in on him.

I first met him in 1943, and during the next few years did various odd jobs for him. Then, in 1952, when I was already training the Aldeburgh Festival Choir, he asked me to orchestrate *Rejoice in the Lamb* for that year's Aldeburgh Festival as he hadn't time to do it himself. It was a formidable request. Luckily he approved of my instrumentation, and soon afterwards he suggested that I should come and live in Aldeburgh, to work as his amanuensis and to help in the running of the Festival.

That was in September 1952, and he had just begun writing *Gloriana*, which had been commissioned to celebrate the Coronation

[1] From the *Musical Times*, 118 (March 1977), pp.202–6.

in June 1953. The Royal Opera House, Covent Garden, wanted the vocal score by the middle of February, so he planned a timetable for getting each act finished. Every morning he wrote from about 8.30 to 12.30; then he took the manuscript to the piano and played through what he had written. He usually went back to work at 4, and kept at it until 7.30 or 8. His pencil sketches were remarkably clear to read. My job was to write out the vocal score so that it could be reproduced for the singers. He gave me helpful advice about my piano reductions, telling me to add a *tremolando* in brackets for a gradual *crescendo* on slow sustained brass chords, and to indicate in small notes above the stave any rapid 'out-of-reach' woodwind passages. He never allowed a convenient pianistic division between the two hands on the keyboard to disguise the clear outlines of the music.

He began the full score of *Gloriana* in February 1953 and we then had to work for at least ten hours a day in order to get through it in a month. I prepared the 34-stave pages for him, spacing the bar-lines, writing the clefs and signatures, copying out the vocal lines, and eventually filling in any instruments that were to be doubled. We sat side by side at separate tables, and I was dismayed to see how quickly he wrote—he could get through twenty-eight pages in a day. I thought I should never catch up with him. On one occasion he had reckoned to get to the end of a scene by four o'clock, but he finished it just after midday, and, as usual, he turned round while he put in the last note, saying: 'Now in the *next* scene . . .'. He seldom had to stop and think. There were a few momentary queries: could trombones *glissando* a fourth fairly low down? Could the bass clarinet flutter-tongue? What were the shakes that the bassoon couldn't manage? My first chance to keep pace with him was when he reached the *tutti* contrapuntal entries at 'Green leaves are we, / Red rose our golden Queen'. Here, to my great relief, he stopped and thought for nearly three-quarters of an hour, matching the details of the woodwind tonguing or the string bowing with the subtle sound of each final consonant in the words.

He was always patient about my many mistakes. It is true that he could be very angry; but he was fundamentally a calm person. He was often depressed, especially after a bad performance. In a letter he wrote to me in 1948 he said: 'How *essential* good performances are! I have recently heard several performances of my own pieces and I felt so depressed that I considered chucking it all up! Wrong tempi, stupid phrasing and poor technique—in fact non-sense.'

He was frequently weary. I remember once, when he was halfway through a full score, he asked: 'Did your father *always* enjoy working?' And when the vast score of *The Prince of the Pagodas* was at last finished he wrote to me, saying: 'Thank God it is over and done with (all except those . . . metronome-marks).' It was the strain of having to live the double life of composer-performer that was the chief cause of his weariness. Foreign orchestral concert tours were particularly exhausting. In a letter he wrote to me from Aldeburgh in 1968 he said: 'Just off to Germany—what a life!—how I wish one could sit quietly and just get on with work; but it won't last for ever, and one day I'll be able to relax a bit, and try and become a good composer.'

Proof-reading often had to be dealt with while he was travelling from one country to the next. When we were writing a book together, called *The Story of Music*, I used to get pages of his criticism sent from abroad:

That old vexed question of nature v. art!! I suggest that the paragraph should end—'An artist needs to have courage and imagination, as well as energy and skill, for he has to create something that will have a life of its own, with the vitality of Nature's own creations.' That gets rid of what I don't like, the suggestion of *rivalry* with Nature.

During the years when I was his amanuensis there was always plenty of variety in the unexpected jobs that had to be done. While he was writing *Gloriana* he had been unable to begin Act II scene 3 because he didn't know the steps and figures of a pavane, galliard, volta or coranto. So I took the day off and went and had lessons on how to dance them, in order to teach him what he needed to know before he wrote the appropriate tunes. (He said that I was to swear to tell him directly the music began to 'turn into a pastiche'.) During rehearsals of *The Turn of the Screw* one of my jobs was to teach the 13-year-old David Hemmings to pretend to be playing Miles's piano solo on the bare surface of a table while the actual sound came from the orchestral pianist in the pit: each gesture had to look sufficiently convincing to deceive the audience in the Venice opera house. In *Noye's Fludde*, Britten had had the idea of hitting teacups with teaspoons to represent the sound of the first raindrops falling on the ark, but he came round to me one afternoon saying that he'd tried it out at tea-time and it wouldn't work. By great good fortune I had once had to teach Women's Institute percussion groups during a wartime 'social half-hour', so I was able to take him into my kitchen and show him how a row of china mugs hanging on a length of string could be hit with a large wooden spoon. Other unexpected jobs included rehearsing the 'tongs and bones' in *A Midsummer Night's Dream*, and conducting the offstage trumpets in the recording of *The Prince of the Pagodas*. He used to find recording sessions more exhausting than anything else and dreaded the days when he had to stop writing a new opera in order to record the one before last.

Many other things threatened to interrupt his regular hours of work. There were innumerable letters to be written to all the young musicians who asked for his advice. There were the many friends in distress who had to be helped if possible: 'One can't pick up *every* pebble on the beach, because one's hands aren't large enough to hold them.' There were the amateur members of the Aldeburgh Music Club, turning up in a state of terrified ecstasy when he offered to play the viola with them in the Schubert C major Quintet. And there was his own conscience, nagging him because of his dislike of the music of certain established composers: every now and then he used to read an unloved score as a bedside book from 11 p.m. onwards, taking another look to be quite sure he hadn't been mistaken: 'Anyway, I've done Brahms now and needn't get him out again for another three years or so.'

The Aldeburgh Festival, which he cared about so passionately, took up a great deal of his time and energy. In our frequent three-hour discussions about programmes he was quicker and clearer than anyone else. And he was always aware of the difficulties of organizing a festival. Long before Snape Maltings became available, he knew that we should have to have our own theatre. But there were many problems. In a letter to me from Hong Kong in 1956 he wrote: 'I was a little alarmed by the reticence of [a few of the committee's] approval of the *whole* Theatre project (much doubt being expressed as to whether it's a good idea) and without that can one *really* go ahead and raise money for the site? That's a kind of responsibility that I can't face alone.' The Festival may often have seemed a burden to him, but it was an essential part of his working life. Among its many blessings it helped to teach him how to conduct. Readers who first knew him as a great conductor during the 1960s may not realize that he was trying to get his technique better and better throughout the 1940s and 1950s. At the 1953 Aldeburgh Festival, when he was having trouble with his arm as a result of writing too many pages every day, he said: 'I'll have to learn a different way of conducting if I'm to get through this weekend: I suppose it's because I'm too tense nearly all the time.' Six months later he was saying that he would have to learn to conduct with very small movements, and that it would be a lesson in control, which was what he felt he needed more and more.

In 1964 I had to give up working as his amanuensis because of the increasing demands for performances and recordings of my father's music. I went on working for the Aldeburgh Festival, and there were occasional writing jobs for Britten, such as helping him to edit a concert version of Purcell's *The Fairy Queen*. This was an enthralling task which I enjoyed as much as any of the things he had ever asked me to do for him. I have often wished that I had written down what he said about the technical problems we were trying to solve.

When I first began working for him in 1952 I kept a diary, but soon had to give it up because there was never time to spare. On rereading it, I have been reminded of several of his characteristic remarks. For instance, on the day when *Benjamin Britten: A Commentary on his works from a group of specialists* was published he said: 'I've come to the conclusion that I must have a very clever subconscious.' Then once, after a depressing committee meeting, he said that he wanted in future to be able to 'think more and more about less and less'. And on my first evening in Aldeburgh the entry in my diary says: 'We were talking about old age and he said that he had a very strong feeling that people died at the right moment, and that the greatness of a person included the time when he was born and the time he endured, but that this was difficult to understand.'

One day in 1953 he said: 'What you and Peter and I have got to remember is that we're going to have a music school here one day.' The 'school' came to birth in 1973 with a Snape Maltings weekend for singers directed by Peter Pears, and it has gone on growing ever since. The very last concert that Britten heard in the Maltings, a few weeks before his death, was a programme of madrigals and motets given by groups of students, with the whole audience singing rounds.

The recent appeal for funds to convert an additional wing of The Maltings for our music school is now linked to the need for a practical memorial to him, to 'ensure the continuity' of his sort of music-making.[2] It is good to know that working for Benjamin Britten is something that will go on for a long time to come.

[2] The Britten–Pears School for Advanced Musical Studies was opened by H.M. Queen Elizabeth The Queen Mother on 28 April 1979. [C.P.]

3

Working for Benjamin Britten (II)

ROSAMUND STRODE

'How did you come here, and what exactly do you *do*?' people would say. It was almost impossible to give a satisfactory answer; it usually ended with my muttering one or two inadequate remarks, smiling, and changing the subject as soon as possible. Perhaps it wasn't easy, for one thing, to admit that my career as a singer hadn't taken off as it should—or to voice my own constant amazement at finding myself working for Benjamin Britten at all. Certainly the main difficulty was in trying to define the job so that other people could begin to see what kind of support Britten needed from his music assistant. He was, after all, busy as a performing musician and the mainspring of the Festival in addition to his primary occupation as a composer.

Imogen Holst has already described her work with him from 1952 and when I became her official successor in 1964 I naturally continued along similar lines. But her skills and experience far exceeded mine so that, in order to survive at all, I had to strike one or two bargains with the composer from the start. 'No piano reductions' was the main thing; I am a shamefully bad pianist and also lacked the necessary compositional expertise to produce good keyboard work. That agreed, other things fell into place and I found Britten consistently courteous, kind, patient and helpful to work for. He was also demanding (of himself, as well as of his staff), and a perfectionist with the ruthlessness that genius seems to need if it is to realize the goals it sets for itself.

I had, in fact, already done a good deal of work for Britten by the time I joined his staff in 1963. I had met him from time to time when he came with Peter Pears to Dartington Hall, particularly in December 1948 when he conducted one of the earliest performances of *Saint Nicolas*. That had been during my first term in the music department there as a postgraduate student of Imogen Holst's—I had recently left the Royal College of Music, where I had studied singing and viola—and it was to prove the crucial step towards Aldeburgh. From Dartington, in 1950, I went to London to study singing and for several years earned a precarious living doing chorus work and taking solo engagements whenever they turned up. There was also a variety of *ad hoc* musical jobs—some, like string-class teaching, far removed from solo singing. In the autumn of 1952 Imogen Holst, by then in Aldeburgh, wrote to say that, at the suggestion of Peter Pears, she was about to form a small, partly professional group of singers to be available to perform at the Festival and elsewhere, and would I like to join? Of course the answer was 'yes', and what was later to become the Purcell Singers came into being, starting with five voices rehearsing in a London mews office. The next summer the group (by then a little larger) came to Aldeburgh for a week's rehearsal, and from the seventh Aldeburgh Festival in 1954 the Purcell Singers appeared annually for many years—most memorably, perhaps, in the series of late-night concerts in the Parish Church given under Imogen Holst's direction from 1958 to 1968.

Preparing the music for concerts, when rehearsal time is limited for financial and other reasons, is absolutely fundamental, and it was characteristic of both Imogen Holst and Benjamin Britten to ensure that the basic material should be ready in every detail before the performers met. Only then could the 'one per cent inspiration' of Edison's definition of genius be allowed to flower, the way cleared for it by the ninety-nine per cent of perspiration that had gone before. From occasionally helping Imogen with the Purcell Singers' music it was natural for me to graduate to other Festival work (including materials needed by Britten) and so to become an extra copyist for his own large-scale full scores. The first of these was *The Prince of the Pagodas*, due to be performed in September 1956. I had a desperate telephone call from Imogen in mid-July: things were behind schedule, and could I spare a few days to come to Aldeburgh and help? I ruled bar-lines and put in clefs for three days (which saw to Act II) but Britten became ill and the mammoth score could not be completed in time; the première actually took place on New Year's Day 1957.

This failure of his to meet a committed date was quite exceptional for Britten, who understood all too well how many people's

livelihoods depended upon his finishing a work on time. Early in
1966, when an unexpected abdominal operation forced him to break
off the composition of *The Burning Fiery Furnace* for a few weeks, he
told me that one night he had counted up the number of jobs
dependent on him that summer—having reached around sixty he'd
stopped counting out of fright. (Luckily that time all went well and
the work was achieved.)

My status as a kind of extra-mural assistant to Britten became
regularized in 1961 when he began paying me a small quarterly
retainer for odd jobs done in London, and felt he could now ask me to
come to Aldeburgh occasionally if the need arose. I helped to organize
and teach a boys' choir (the London Boy Singers) which met in
Finchley every Saturday; this was to fulfil Britten's wish to have
available a boys' choir trained in the continental method as taught by
George Malcolm to the boys of Westminster Cathedral Choir. This
released and exploited the natural robust energy and timbre of a boy's
voice, in contrast to the traditional English cathedral style, which
Britten found insipid and inadequate.

The full score of the *War Requiem* meant some work for me at home
over Christmas 1961, and in the early summer of 1963 Britten asked
whether I would consider coming permanently to Aldeburgh to work
for him. The job would include working for the Festival and dealing
with background musical matters throughout the year. (The Festival
Office permanent staff at that time consisted only of Stephen Reiss,
the Secretary and Manager, with part-time secretarial assistance.) I
should need to be in Aldeburgh for three or four days a week, and if all
went well was to take over as Britten's music assistant from Imogen
Holst when, in due course, she retired. These arrangements fitted in
well with my own plans, leaving me one free day in London and
allowing me to continue with the boys' choir on Saturdays. As it
turned out Imogen Holst relinquished her work for Britten in 1964
(sooner than she had thought) to concentrate on the music of Gustav
Holst, and as my job in Aldeburgh became full-time I gave up my
London commitments.

Britten's fiftieth birthday year in 1963 brought a good deal of
concert activity for him. As a result, some of the more ordinary (but
important) tasks were getting left behind, and I was quickly involved
with, among other things, the routine matter of preparing scores for
publication. The list of works then awaiting attention was formidable;
being constantly in demand and continually working on new

compositions, it was simply not possible for Britten and his publishers to keep up with the number of older pieces still remaining unpublished in full score. This time-consuming matter tended to be done in the autumn and we settled into a more or less regular annual routine, with the June Festival as its peak. Britten liked to keep December to February free for composing, resisting requests to give concerts then, though there were concert tours with Peter Pears from time to time, and some memorable Christmastide concerts of Bach at St Andrew's, Holborn, in the late 1960s. If he were engaged on a large piece to be performed at the Festival, its final preparation and rehearsals naturally took up most of the remaining months before June. There were also the smaller new compositions to be fitted in, and performances of works by other composers which Britten was to conduct at the Festival. Some of these (such as Mozart's *Idomeneo* and Schumann's *Scenes from Goethe's 'Faust'*) needed an enormous amount of 'house' editing to make the music available to the performers at all.

The Festival entailed much other detailed work for Britten. He wrote programme notes for his own pieces, and often for other composers' works he was to perform. The rehearsal schedule and orchestra calls had to be worked out minutely so that no precious time would be wasted; this could be done as far ahead as January if necessary. He had to mark his conducting scores with dynamics for the whole orchestra, bowings for the strings, and maybe a few editorial 'fixings'—perhaps to make orchestral economies possible— in time for his assistant to put them into each individual player's part. Programme Book proofs were always read and commented upon by both Benjamin Britten and Peter Pears; that often led to last-minute changes causing some editorial despair, but always produced more interesting final results. And this does not take into account the higher reaches of Festival planning which continued all the year: working out artists' availabilities, dates and programmes, filling out thin places—and those terrible last-minute crises arising because of sickness (such as Mstislav Rostropovich's enforced absence in 1963) or disaster (the Maltings fire in 1969), all of which bore heavily on Britten.

One could not always relax much after the Festival, though some kind of breather was absolutely necessary by then. As he conducted more, increasing demands were made on Britten to perform outside Aldeburgh. There were concerts at the City of London, King's Lynn

Working for Benjamin Britten (II)

and Edinburgh Festivals, the Henry Wood Promenade Concerts, the Aldeburgh Festival's own weekends of Bach at Long Melford early in September from 1962 to 1967, late summer concerts at Snape Maltings in the early 1970s and, for these and other audiences, always the chance of hearing a recital by 'the old firm'—that incomparable partnership of Peter Pears, tenor, accompanied by Benjamin Britten, piano.

As for my own work, the autumn turned out to be the best time to cope with the publication backlog. One had first to edit the master copy of the existing full score (a dyeline reproduction, usually of a copyist's copy but sometimes of Britten's own manuscript), which entailed making a painfully slow note-by-note comparison of it against all available materials. There were Britten's own conducting copies and the published piano reductions with corrections (and sometimes minor amendments or revisions) to be incorporated, and of course the master score had to be checked against the manuscripts whenever possible. A number of discrepancies would be found which meant keeping long lists of queries to present to Britten at the next opportunity. 'Ben, your composition sketch and the full score disagree with each other and with the published vocal score at this point; which is right?' 'There is no dynamic to the solo line here; what should it be?' (Sometimes the surprising answer to that one was 'Leave it as it is without anything; I want them to *think* about it.') 'Are the horns still muted here? They were, last time they played.' 'Should this chord have double-bass pizzicato notes in it, as before?' 'This phrase comes at a page-turn and seems to finish in mid-air; how should it end off?' And (worst of all) 'The first time this passage appeared you used staccato dots, the next time dashes, and now it has neither. Which do you want, and should they be the same each time?'

Britten found this last kind of detail particularly irritating and tedious to sort out, though he agreed that the matter had to be settled. We would normally have tea-time sessions on such queries, with lists and odd pages spread out on the drawing-room sofa. The age of the composition I was wrestling with never seemed to matter, for even in the throes of writing a new piece he was apparently able to put himself back twenty or thirty years quite easily; he never wanted to make changes for change's sake, though just occasionally he altered something slightly to fit in with his current publishing style. Or he might have conducted a performance of the work concerned, and seen

55

then that the look of the music on the page did not exactly convey what he wanted.

The visual aspect of his music mattered very much to Britten, who had a cultivated and perceptive eye for everything about him. He also had a constantly inventive and sure approach to working out notational puzzles, such as the barring in *Curlew River*, which itself gave birth to the 'curlew' sign, invented specially for this opera and used by Britten frequently thereafter.[1]

So the edited score went to the publisher, and one got on with other jobs. Months later that edited score returned, this time with the first proofs. The checking began all over again, and there would be new lists of queries for the composer; humiliating to find how many things had been overlooked before, though the new layout always produced unforeseen problems of its own. Second proofs—and, for tricky pages, sometimes third—followed, and then another silence. The finished scores suddenly appeared when one least expected them, looking better than one had dared to hope—but Britten invariably (and unnervingly, even to himself) found a flaw on the first page he looked at. It would become the first on a list of corrections that was to accumulate until that particular score was up for reprinting and could be set to rights.

Music processing has undergone enormous changes in recent years, somehow epitomized by Britten's own composing career. As a young man he had had to work on traditional lines, making his own full scores or fair copies in ink from the original pencil composition sketch. These would go to the publishers for engraving, and the whole job had to be done as quickly as possible because upon that stage depended the availability of material to performers and the public. Sometimes if time were very short the full score could not be recopied before the work's première (a set of instrumental parts had, of course, first to be made from it), so the composer's manuscript then became the conductor's full score. Conductors tend to use coloured crayons, often very freely, to find their way through unfamiliar new scores, and the effect of two or three different hands on an original manuscript can well be imagined.

Developments in the use of photography, among other things,

---

[1] Britten defined it thus: The sign ⌒ ('curlew' sign) over a note or rest shows that the performer(s) concerned must listen and wait until the other performers have reached the next bar-line or meeting-point—i.e. the note or rest may be longer or shorter than its written value.

have changed all that. An original pencil manuscript may now be reproduced by the dyelining method—a photochemical process, giving sharp black results—which, although the copies exude ammonia fumes at first and turn yellowish in strong sunlight, at least makes it possible for a work to be reproduced immediately without the laborious and expensive business of engraving. The copies will be only temporary, but serve well for initial performances—and leave the original manuscript unscathed.

These technical advances suited Britten well, partly because they came in just as he began to need more freedom in committing his ideas to paper. Latterly none of his works was available in print before it had received its first performance and he had had time to make revisions to it, if he wished. He did not like to send anything but a final version out into the world, and, apart from the expense involved (an important consideration to publishers these days) he knew only too well how difficult it is to circulate revisions once an early version has taken root. The only exceptions to this rule were opera librettos: those of the three church parables, and *Owen Wingrave* and *Death in Venice* were all brought out in small first editions (giving the audience something to follow and cherish at the time of the premières) and second editions were soon put in hand to keep pace with the changes that had evolved since the original text went to press.

There were, of course, musical revisions. Sometimes they would be substantial alterations, crucially affecting the balance of an entire work, and at others more of a final burnishing to an already completed whole. One realized that when something wouldn't go quite right with a composition it took endless and agonizingly hard work on Britten's part to get it as he knew it had to be; 'almost' wasn't good enough for him. *Curlew River* had an intractable place at the climax towards the end, where the Spirit of the Boy appears to the Madwoman. At first this passage was designed using all seven instruments, and was a sizeable piece of agitated music, with the monks' evening hymn tune, 'Custodes hominum', appearing in the bass. The first edition of the libretto described the action at this point: 'The Spirit comes out of the tomb. Repeatedly she tries in vain to embrace him; he returns to the tomb. She falls, weeping.' The final version, very spare in instrumentation and much shorter, consists of a disembodied piccolo tune over a shimmering, almost static accompaniment of one held organ note and small repetitive phrases on the harp lightly reinforced by double-bass, viola and horn; it was reached after at least six other clearly distinguishable intermediate attempts to get the mood, the stage action and the music just right. The libretto now reads: 'The Spirit circles slowly round the Madwoman, who appears transformed. He returns to the tomb.' What a difference—and who now could imagine *Curlew River* with anything but tranquillity at this point! Yet it only came about by persistent effort, mostly at a very late stage when the work was already in rehearsal.

For me there was usually plenty of copying to be done—every one of those *Curlew River* instrumental parts, for instance, with continuous cue-lines for each player; and the revisions just mentioned had to be incorporated overnight, ready for the next morning's rehearsal. From 1963 Britten used a high-quality 16-stave folio manuscript paper specially ruled and printed for him by Boosey & Hawkes. It withstood the attacks of his pencil erasers well and the rather narrow staves, spaced further apart than usual, exactly fitted his neat, fluent hand. I particularly enjoyed making ink fair copies straight from the composition sketches of the smaller-scale pieces, though after *Who are these children?* had been particularly troublesome to its creator, demanding constant revisions and adjustments over several months, Britten insisted that I, too, should work in pencil. This was, again, because he wanted to feel absolutely free to make changes; all the same, it was he who minded the extra labour involved in my correcting an ink copy and not I, who much preferred the predictable clean lines of a square-cut nib and black ink.

To his assistant, Britten's own performances sorted themselves out into two main kinds: those in which he was the conductor, and the others when he played the piano, as an accompanist or as a member of a chamber group. When he was conducting I was not, of course, usually occupied during the performance itself, although (particularly during recording sessions) there might be some fringe job, such as page-turning for a keyboard player or keeping a note of metronome marks. My main work—dealing with the instrumental parts—was already done, though unforeseen crises, small and large, often meant a flurry of activity. I learnt to take a copying-kit about with me: scissors and paste, needle and thread, an assortment of pieces of manuscript paper in varied rulings—and a few finger-dressings. Britten liked to use a particularly lightweight baton, about 12 inches long including the cork handle: he found that what really suited him best was to snap off the last couple of inches from a 14-inch baton. It gave a nice balance, but left a sharp, jagged end, which more than once he managed to drive into his left hand, which resulted in blood all over the score as he turned the pages.

Page-turning for other people is a notoriously fraught activity, though it was something I enjoyed doing for Britten when he played the piano, despite the latent perils. In the first performance of *Songs and Proverbs of William Blake*, for instance, the piano copy, weakened by much handling, suddenly bent backwards over the top of the music desk so that the upper half became invisible. As this happened in the middle of the ferocious 'Tyger, Tyger', there wasn't much time for reflection: I had to stand up and hold the top centre taut for a few pages till the danger was past. (After that nasty experience, everything went into card covers.) But the oddest duty was once to have to place a pair of spectacles on a pianist's nose while he was playing, already several bars into a piece. This happened during a concert at Snape in 1968, when four distinguished singers with Claudio Arrau and Britten (playing at his preferred bass end of the keyboard) gave an encore of one of the Brahms *Liebeslieder* waltzes. Britten had taken off his glasses at the end of the complete performance and forgotten to replace them for the encore. Fortunately his desperate, muttered 'Put my glasses on!' was just loud enough to hear; the spectacles were in his top pocket, and the first lunge with them landed them safely on target. What a relief!

Though Britten certainly did have darker moods, he enjoyed things and people, and there were many moments of fun and hilarity. I remember surprise expeditions—being plucked from work to go on a picnic, accompany him to a school music competition, join in a privileged (and most memorable) look at the Sutton Hoo ship burial site during re-excavation. There were slow drives in the open-topped Alvis along narrow lanes to woods where chiff-chaffs and nightingales sang (he was a keen bird watcher and loved all birdsong, except the dreary cries of those suavely handsome collared doves) or to small churches with some special feature that he wanted to look at. He would always give good, practical topographical advice: 'If you are going there, use *this* road—it's shorter and much nicer—and then you can call in on that village church where there's a stunning Norman door.' I learnt much of Suffolk and East Anglia from him.

From the late summer of 1972 Britten's health, never very robust, began to show serious signs of strain. He had to cancel all performing activities to concentrate only on finishing *Death in Venice*, which was scheduled for performance the following June. The composition sketches of the opera were completed in December; then began the massive task of coping with the orchestral score. I went ahead of Britten, ruling up the pages (in pencil, of course!) and putting in all the voices. Colin Matthews, who had made the vocal score, helped by writing in many of the more routine orchestral passages, which all saved Britten a considerable amount of physical effort. The score was finished by the end of March, and Britten (who was in fact far more ill than he had realized) had to undergo medical tests in London at the beginning of April. His precarious state of health was quite evident to me, and the importance of trying to get the *Death in Venice* notes as correct as possible from the very start seemed all the greater. There were long lists of small details to be distributed to singers, repetiteurs and the conductor, Steuart Bedford, who had the tremendous responsibility of conducting this première without the help of the composer's eye and ear. (Steuart was also conducting the first stage performance of *Owen Wingrave*, at the Royal Opera House, Covent Garden, that May.) Britten's operation, to replace a valve in the heart, took place on 7 May, and he spent the rest of that summer convalescing.

There had to be many adjustments after the operation, which, although it improved the heart condition, did not turn out to be the miracle-cure we had all hoped for. Indeed there was now a serious new drawback, for a slight stroke he had suffered during the operation had left Britten with impaired movement on his right side. It made walking none too easy, and writing was difficult and often painful. He did a little revising (mostly subtle reinforcement of the scoring) to *Death in Venice* after its première, and early in 1974 he revised the 1931 String Quartet in D. Next, after gentle hints from various close friends, he finally took *Paul Bunyan* off the metaphorical shelf where it had rested since he and W. H. Auden had discussed revisions just after its first not altogether successful presentation in 1941, and prepared some of the numbers for performance at the 1974 Aldeburgh Festival.

Then in July he finished the first new piece for eighteen months, *Canticle V: The Death of Saint Narcissus*, written for the new performing partnership of Peter Pears with Osian Ellis. Everyone (including Britten himself) was delighted that he was composing again, and although he could now work for only short periods each day, he really was 'in business'. He preferred to write sitting in an armchair, with a board across his knee, and we had to exercise some ingenuity over the problem caused by that limited arm movement, eventually finding that the best thing was simply to cut down the height of the manuscript paper. Britten felt that his writing was now unclear and difficult to read; true, it did not look quite so precise and even as before, but there was very rarely any doubt as to what a particular note might be. Even the manuscript condensed score of the String Quartet No.3, parts of which looked at first glance to be too cramped to be readable, turned out to be totally clear and legible; all the same it was perhaps the most difficult copying job I ever had to do for him.

Undoubtedly the greatest deprivation of all to Britten in these last years was that he could no longer play the piano. Apart from personal pleasure thus lost, this seriously affected some aspects of his work, for although he never composed 'at the piano', he always played things through once they were written, exercising his critical faculties aurally. Colin Matthews again helped here, providing just the right sort of competent (but not too dazzling!) piano playing, allied to a composer's understanding, which Britten so badly needed. They worked in this way on *Phaedra*, the String Quartet No.3 and his last (finished) composition of all, *Welcome Ode*, which Colin also scored under Britten's direction.

I am still asked what exactly do I do, and it is just as difficult as it ever was to give a straight answer. There is still a good deal to be done on the publishing side; some 'new' works have been brought out, from the quantity of unpublished material, both early and late, left shelved and unreviewed by the composer; and those constant corrections to be maintained. I have not worked for the Festival since Britten became ill in 1972, but other administrative office jobs have increased, and to sort out the biographical and archival material seems a never-ending task. All this is part of the general business of the Britten Estate, which is run by his Executors. But the main development has been that of the Britten–Pears Library at the Red House. It has already taken its place as the foremost centre for Britten research and is visited by scholars from all over the world. The composer's original manuscripts have been microfilmed (they include many in private hands, lent to the Library for that purpose) and relevant materials gathered together—especially those ephemeral concert programmes, on so many of which, over a period of thirty years, the names of the Library's founders appear as performers. So 'Working for Benjamin Britten' continues; and it is still an extraordinary privilege.

4

'Ben'—A Tribute to Benjamin Britten[1]

JOHN CULSHAW

This piece is included not only for its relevance to the present context but also as a tribute to the author, whose death in 1980 at the age of 55 was even more premature than Britten's. John Culshaw was devoted to Britten and his music, and it was largely due to him that we have an invaluable documentation of the composer conducting a substantial part of his oeuvre—a legacy comparable to CBS's Stravinsky records. For further details of Culshaw's working relationship with Britten in the studio, particularly during the recording of the War Requiem, *readers are referred to his autobiography* Putting the Record Straight *(Secker & Warburg, 1981). After leaving Decca Culshaw joined BBC Television as Head of Music Programmes, in which capacity he supervised the television recordings of* Peter Grimes *and* Owen Wingrave. *[C.P.]*

'Our job', he once said, 'is to be useful, and to the living.' And he was. He was a consciously practical composer in that, so far as I can recall, he never wrote a note unless it was going to be useful to someone. He liked to write with specific people in mind, not just because of their professional skills but because of their qualities as human beings: Peter Pears, Kathleen Ferrier, Joan Cross, Owen Brannigan, Janet Baker, Dietrich Fischer-Dieskau, Mstislav Rostropovich and a host of others. *Owen Wingrave* was cast before it was written, because he wanted to think about human beings rather than dramatic abstractions. I am writing this in Adelaide, South Australia, on 7 December 1976, the day of his funeral in Aldeburgh, and it is hard to collate

[1] Edited from *Gramophone*, February 1977, pp.1251–2.

memories of the twenty-five years or so that we worked together in recording or television, partly because there are so many and partly because it is too soon to accept that, at 63, he is dead. The happiest hours I have spent in any studio were with Ben, for the basic reason that it did not seem that we were trying to make records or video tapes; we were just trying to make music.

He was a complex character, and superficially full of contradictions. He was world famous but he did not care for the trappings of fame. He was a marvellous pianist and conductor, yet he did not enjoy performing and the prospect of a concert sometimes made him literally sick. As he grew older, he seemed to harbour increasing doubts about his own works—doubts which were not shared by his colleagues or by the public: witness the triumph of *Death in Venice* at the Metropolitan, New York, in the autumn of 1975. He could be very stern with an undisciplined orchestra or chorus. Professional musicians of the toughest order revered him all the same, and after a difficult session would retire to the nearest pub, and drown their misbehaviour in pint after pint while speaking in awe of his professionalism. He was a gentle person, and loved gentle pictures like those painted by his neighbour Mary Potter. But then he also loved fast cars, and before his illness he would drive brilliantly through Suffolk lanes narrow and twisty enough to frighten a cyclist, let alone his passengers, although there was no need for fear because he knew every tree and every curve and every place where a stray cow might be lurking; and he knew his stopping distance. When he found out that I held a private pilot's licence he hired a Cessna for a Sunday morning joyride up and down the Suffolk coast, a prospect which didn't seem to frighten him or Peter Pears one little bit.

There are several ways of driving from Aldeburgh to London, but whenever I drove him to the city we took a scenic route which he had worked out in order to pass through some of the most exquisite parts of Suffolk and Essex, and hit the sprawl of north London as late and as deviously as possible. If we left the Red House shortly after nine in the morning we would arrive at the last genuinely country pub in time for a Bloody Mary around noon and still reach his London home for lunch. He did not like London; I don't think he liked any modern cities. He was really at peace only in Aldeburgh (and, perhaps, some years ago in Bali). To be a weekend guest at the Red House was to relax completely; although, before his illness, Ben's own ideas about relaxation might not totally coincide with those of a city-dweller. Of course nothing was obligatory, and I enjoyed the long country walks, not least because he was an expert ornithologist, whereas I cannot tell a curlew from a duck; but I confess that more often than not I dodged the early morning swim before breakfast because I had been awakened hours earlier by the dawn chorus of birds which those who live in the country never seem to hear. By the time the birds had shut up I would be fast asleep again, and Ben and Peter would be in the pool or walking the dogs in the garden or at breakfast. One of the cruellest ironies of Ben's early death is that he had kept himself so fit. He was no health fanatic, but until the final illness he enjoyed the outdoor life: he walked regularly, he swam, he played tennis. He did not smoke, but he enjoyed a drink if there was conversation to go with it. He loved good food, and the best food of all was at the Red House because it was fresh, like fish straight out of the sea with vegetables from the garden. The last time we had a meal together there we had grilled sprats which, he remarked, 'really are worth the awful smell they make in the kitchen'. Maybe it seems trivial to mention such things, but I don't think so, because they show the other side of a shy public figure. However well read, however sensitive, however concerned about the state of music and indeed the state of man, he was at heart, like Elgar with whose music he eventually came to terms, a countryman. A deceptive simplicity, an earthiness, lies behind all his music, just as it lies behind the music of his beloved Schubert.

He was a reluctant performer both in public and in the studio, and yet he never lost command of his forces. In concert performances of the *War Requiem* he chose to conduct the chamber ensemble and thus relinquish overall control to another conductor; but in the recording he conducted everything, and I have still to hear a better performance. It was made in January 1963 in Kingsway Hall and because of the importance of the occasion, and without Ben's knowledge, my colleagues at Decca 'wired' the hall and the control room in such a way that we were able to record every word of the rehearsals and the comments during playback in the control room. Had we told Britten what we were up to he would, at worst, have refused to proceed or, at best, have been inhibited by the cunningly hidden additional microphones. But there was a friendly purpose in this exercise, for over the coming months the hours and hours of rehearsal tapes were reduced to just under one hour; a major security clamp was placed on both the extracted and the residual material; and eventually one record was produced bearing a properly printed Decca label with the serial number BB50. It was then packed in an embossed leather sleeve and presented to Britten for his fiftieth birthday—22 November 1963—by Sir Edward Lewis. When he left the office Ben said to me, with a mischievous grin, 'I shan't forgive you quickly for this!' But he did.

Apart from anything else, the *War Requiem* rehearsals revealed all over again his amazing ability to control and communicate with children. He loved writing for children, and he loved working with them. He always wanted them to understand just what they were doing, and just what the music was meant to convey. When it came to boys' voices, he preferred a rougher quality than the 'pure' sound of the cathedral choirs, which in his view put the emphasis in the wrong place. It was a view that he applied generally. 'Frankly', he once said to me when we were discussing a casting problem, 'I'm not very interested in beautiful voices as such. I'm interested in the person behind the voice.' In other words, a beautiful voice controlled by a mind was a blessing indeed, whereas a mindless beautiful voice was of no interest to him. The same, of course, went for instrumentalists and, not unexpectedly, other composers, although in the last fifteen years or so of his life his tastes broadened, and sometimes in unexpected directions.

I don't think he ever came round to Wagner, though many years ago when he was going to India he told me he was taking a score to study (I think it was *Götterdämmerung*). He was invited to conduct at Bayreuth, but declined (if he was going to conduct Wagner anywhere for the first time, Bayreuth would be the last place). His love for Purcell, Bach, Mozart and Schubert was evident whenever he conducted or played a note of their music. He didn't care for the florid school of Italian opera, which he wickedly lampooned in *A Midsummer Night's Dream*, but he was passionate about mature Verdi. He was, I think, unsure about Tchaikovsky as a symphonist, but he loved the ballet music. Then there were the personal enthusiasms: the music of Frank Bridge, and not just because Bridge had been Britten's teacher, and of Percy Grainger, because Grainger's music had a simplicity which spoke to him directly. Elgar did not appeal to him until late in life, and it would have been unimaginable in the 1950s to suggest that one day he would record *The Dream of Gerontius* and the *Introduction and Allegro*.

In the summer of 1965 Ben and Peter invited me to go and explore an old building at Snape which might, by a considerable stretch of the imagination and a lot of money, be converted into the kind of multi-purpose hall that was so urgently needed by the Aldeburgh Festival. We walked round the Maltings and then clambered inside. It was all but impossible to imagine what it would be like when gutted, because it consisted of floor upon floor with no through sight-line. We kept on descending until we reached the ovens in the basement. And yet . . . there was a feeling about the place, about its setting by the river with the view of Iken Church through the reeds and across the marshes, that made it right. If Ben was to have a concert hall on his doorstep, this was it; and in 1967, thanks to a superb conversion job by Ove Arup and Partners, who joined in close acoustical collaboration with Decca and the BBC, the Maltings at Snape was opened by the Queen. Two years later it burned down to a cinder, yet in 1970 it was open again and, if anything, better than ever.

The Maltings is Ben's monument, although I am not sure he would have liked me to put it that way. It is not a monument in the sense of Bayreuth, because it was not built to serve the music of one composer: it was built to serve all music. It has proved to be a marvellous concert and recital hall; it can accommodate opera without strain; the many Decca recordings made there prove its quality as a recording location; and on at least three occasions—for *Peter Grimes*, *Winterreise* and *Owen Wingrave*—the BBC turned it literally into a television studio. But, most important of all, its existence encouraged Britten to make many recordings which might otherwise never have been made, since they would have involved him in prolonged trips to London. At the Maltings he could work in peace, and in the environment that inspired so much of his work; the warmth and welcome of the building were, and will remain, a reflection of the man.

The first music of his that I ever heard was the *Serenade* for tenor, horn and strings. I was a serviceman at the time; it was towards the end of the war; and it was the original Decca recording. No other piece of contemporary music had spoken so directly to me or meant so much. I had no reason to suppose that within five or six years I would be working with Ben and Peter in Decca's No.1 studio in West Hampstead, at the start of a long relationship which was to involve a lot of hard work, but also some fun. There was one evening when, after two *Lieder* sessions, they tried to remember a couple of cabaret numbers Ben had written years earlier to words by W. H. Auden,[2] until both the words and the music ran out. Then there was the

[2] Now published as *Four Cabaret Songs* (Faber Music, 1980).

seemingly impossible problem of making David Hemmings in *The Little Sweep* sound as if he were up a chimney; the solution was to get him to sing into a globe rather like a goldfish bowl, of which there was only one, and which he promptly dropped.

I believe Ben's doubts about recording have been exaggerated or at least misinterpreted on the basis of the speech he made at Aspen, Colorado, in the 1960s.[3] Nobody who actually disapproved of recording could have made as many records, and with such enthusiasm, as he did; but he sounded a warning with which few, I imagine, would disagree. Nothing in musical performance is ultimately definitive, and to that extent a recording is only representative of the artist's approach at the time of recording. His approach to *Peter Grimes* when he conducted it for the BBC television production in 1969 was quite different from the one he brought to the Decca recording ten years earlier. His playing of *Winterreise* darkened and deepened over the years, magnificent though it was from the start. He could never be stale or complacent.

I saw him for the last time during the 1976 Aldeburgh Festival. He was very frail, but he made a massive and perhaps damaging attempt to attend as many events as possible. It was the right thing for him to do, whatever the risk, because it was not in him to admit defeat. I am glad that he was present in the Maltings to witness the triumph of his cantata, *Phaedra*. The audience may have marvelled at how, under such adversity, he could have written such a piece, and it was an emotional moment when he rose to acknowledge the applause; but finally it was the music that was being applauded, because it had communicated, and for Ben, communication was what music was all about.

[3] *On Receiving the First Aspen Award.*

5

The Ceremony of Innocence

CHRISTOPHER PALMER

There was a time when meadow, grove, and stream,
The earth, and every common sight,
To me did seem
Apparell'd in celestial light,
The glory and the freshness of a dream.
It is not now as it hath been of yore;—
Turn whereso'er I may,
By night or day,
The things which I have seen I now can see no more.

Wordsworth,
Ode: Intimations of Immortality from
Recollections of Early Childhood

When Britten's enchanted childhood yielded to adolescence and maturity there 'pass'd away a glory from the earth' which he sought in vain to recapture throughout his adult life. But in dim and weary twilight hours, who can recall the splendour of the dawn? It is a fact of life that the childhood vision, once clouded over, can never be recaptured in its pristine purity; a fact of life that Britten was never able to come to terms with. None perceived more plainly or more painfully than he that children, before they are corrupted by systematized education, possess the artistic emotion or sensibility in its quintessence; they resemble primitive man before he was subjected to the so-called 'refining' influence of civilization. As Wordsworth knew, the ecstasy of the artist is but a remnant of the childish vision; and the child looks at the world through 'magic casements' (Keats). The man is nothing more than the child primed with all manner of advantages in the realms of intellect and technique, but much deprived of imaginative vision and intuitive perception. A few composers have preserved almost intact the 'vision splendid' of those early years, and have supplemented it by the acquired attributes of experience, age and instruction. Ravel was one; Britten was not. His tragedy was that, much as he admired the basic childlike quality—unselfconsciousness—in other artists, he was never able to achieve it himself, because the fall from grace had irremediably taken place within himself, and he knew it. He was at odds with the universe because it had burdened him with self-consciousness; he was, in fact, self-conscious about his own self-consciousness. He gave memorable expression to his feeling for innocence beleaguered, 'blackly, malignantly invested under the heavy sky' (Geoffrey Grigson) in 'Before Life and After', the last poem in the Hardy cycle *Winter Words*, set to music eloquent of cosmic despair:

> *A time there was—as one may guess*
> *And as, indeed, earth's testimonies tell—*
> *Before the birth of consciousness,*
> *When all went well. . . .*
> *But the disease of feeling germed,*
> *And primal rightness took the tinct of wrong;*
> *Ere nescience shall be reaffirmed*
> *How long, how long?*

This is a recurrent burden of every major work from *Peter Grimes* onward. In the texts chosen for, say, *Songs and Proverbs of William Blake*, we find 'The tygers of wrath are wiser than the horses of instruction. If the fool would persist in his folly he would become wise.' Blake was a lifelong literary love of Britten's, and it was to be expected that sooner or later a complete Blake song-cycle should take shape; for Blake's *Songs of Innocence and of Experience* (published as a single volume in 1794, illuminated with his own designs) were intended to show 'the Two Contrary States of the Human Soul'. The innocent joys and happiness which are the subject of the first collection are turned by 'experience', in the second, into woe, misery and wrath. Experience and wordly wisdom are for Blake synonymous with man's fall from grace. Britten, like Blake and Wordsworth, saw himself as a victim of this in one sense natural, yet in another profoundly *un*natural, train of events. In our infancy Heaven lies about us; shades of the prison-house begin to close upon us in childhood; in youth, though leaving that supernal brightness ever farther behind us, we are still 'Nature's priests', still attended by the 'vision splendid'; then, inevitably, 'At length the Man perceives it die away, / And fade into the light of common day.'

Not until we are turned out of Paradise do we realize that we were there. Most of us accept the fact and try to make the best of such fragments of divine intuition as remain to us; but Britten never could accept it. The man Britten felt himself doubly isolated: as a child in an adult's world and as a homosexual in a heterosexually orientated society. According to Ronald Duncan and Hans Keller, who knew him well, his sexual ethics were too conventional to permit him to come fully to terms with his 'deviation' or 'inversion'; and if it aroused strong guilt feelings in him, this would have served only to increase his feeling of alienation. Surely we need look no further for an explanation of one of Britten's most dominant traits, his personal and professional insecurity. Neither was justified, but no one as deeply troubled as Britten by lack of self-confidence can ever be convinced that they have nothing to worry about. Peter Pears notes that an inferiority complex began to assert itself in the early days of contact with W. H. Auden; in his and his associates' company Britten felt keenly the 'provincialism' of his background, and the fact that he had never attended a university caused him in later life to look sceptically at academic institutions. In this respect we may note a parallel with Elgar. Both were superbly equipped professional musicians, yet neither could ever feel totally assured of the soundness of his standing. They believed the world was prejudiced against them, and naturally they retaliated. In Britten's case this meant primarily a withdrawal from the centralized hurly-burly of professional musical life in London into a world of his own making at Aldeburgh. For Britten the parable of the prodigal son, which he later retold in his own musical terms, had a deeply personal significance. Auden appears in the role of the Tempter: it was he who urged upon the young Britten that life was passing him by, that the world was calling him, that the fruits of experience were waiting to be tasted. Britten tasted them, and enjoyed their sweetness and their bitterness; but during his stay in North America he began to reap what he had sown. 'Your pleasures must be paid for: pay what is due!' cries the Tempter; but Britten had already paid in depriving himself of the soil he needed for his genius to flourish, and now he hurried home. Aldeburgh, situated in Suffolk and by the North Sea which had been familiar to him from earliest childhood, became a buffer between him and the world.

People of Britten's strength of character and steadfastness of purpose can always create circumstances conducive to bringing out the best in themselves, can exert an almost magnetic attraction over those whose participation is essential to accomplishing the Great Work. His founding of the Aldeburgh Festival, his conversion of the Snape Maltings into a concert hall and his contract with Faber Music (formed in 1966 to publish his music) were all aspects of the composer's concern to form an environment sympathetic to himself, in which he could realize his potential to the full and minimize the encroachments of alien forces. This need was recognized by Auden in a letter to him written early in 1942, shortly before he returned with Pears to England from the United States:

> Wherever you go you are and probably always will be surrounded by people who adore you, nurse you, and praise everything you do. . . . Up to a certain point this is fine for you, but beware. You see, Bengy dear, you are always tempted to make things too easy for yourself in this way, ie to build yourself a warm nest of love . . . by playing the lovable talented little boy (*BA*, pp.161–2).

Auden's habitual and frequently irresistible attempts to create all his friends in his own image caused him to lose sight of the fact that artists of Britten's calibre have their own built-in survival kit: they know instinctively what is best for them, they are determined to succeed and they show undeviating single-mindedness, bordering occasionally on ruthlessness, in succeeding. And while we need to be aware of those 'abnormal sensitivities' (Donald Mitchell's phrase) with which Britten had to contend all his life, we should not underestimate that streak of toughness which enabled the composer both to realize an astonishing number of major projects and to overcome the antagonism his work, his success, his political stance and his sexuality often aroused in the early part of his career.

Britten's childlike vulnerability was nowhere more striking than in his lifelong hypersensitivity to unfavourable criticism. From his friends and colleagues he demanded unblemished loyalty, and woe betide anyone discovered to have been making 'critical' remarks behind the composer's back. Many have been puzzled to discern this allergy in an artist of Britten's range and brilliance of accomplishment. Paranoia is characteristic of charlatans, ill-prepared men ever fearful lest their lack of proper technical equipment for the task in hand be discovered by the world which is paying them homage; but Britten was the very antithesis of a charlatan. Again the insecurity is that of the primitive, the innocent, who finds himself cut adrift in a world of sophisticates and highly evolved intellects. Because he *is* a primitive his instinctive reaction is one of fear, and fear results in fight and flight. Compare Elgar's lack of academic training, Mahler's 'threefold' homelessness, Britten's 'provincialism'—the pattern recurs and in all cases results in some form of paranoia or persecution mania.

Much could be written about Britten's affinities with the above-mentioned composers, but another deserves special mention in this context, one whose mind as reflected in his music throws much light on Britten's: Percy Grainger. The central fire within both Grainger and Britten was the purity of the primitive, the innocent, the child. Both were faced with the problem of reconciling the ideal of primitivism with the highly complex and sophisticated phase of development that the technology of music had reached when they encountered it. Grainger was a colonial, born in Melbourne and introduced at an early age to the vast and untamed Australian country scene. As a real child of nature, he yearned for a complete return of all humanity and culture to nature. For him, nature and culture were complementary, nature and civilization diametrically opposed. He wanted to make music free to express the state of primordial innocence to which he himself aspired. In later years he devoted much of his time to his 'free-music' machines: machines that would give voice to a music totally unfettered by the conventional limitations of rhythm, scales or intervals. Like Britten, Grainger was one of those artists who, owing to a combination of factors in their temperament and upbringing, never really outgrow the myth of childhood. Almost every aspect of his creative life was in some way related to this urge to perpetuate childhood. In a quest for identity, roots and security resembling Britten's, he ransacked the world for folksong, which has the quality of *belonging* that he prized. Folksong and its singers gave him a sense of stability. Folksong of course is a kind of 'free music'—the music of the people, of the earth, of nature—and it deals in those qualities which Grainger admired above all others because of their freedom from the contaminating influence of civilization. Small wonder, then, that Britten took Grainger's folksong settings as models for his own;[1] even *The Ballad of Little Musgrave and Lady Barnard*, not based on any actual folk material, bears a Graingerian stamp and may well have been modelled on Grainger's masterly setting of Swinburne's *The Bride's Tragedy*. Britten's and Grainger's harmonic and textural idioms have little in common, but their basic approach was similar. Grainger wasn't interested just in preserving or fixing a tune, like a fly in amber; he wanted to take full account of the emotional or dramatic implications of the text to which the song was sung, and if appropriate turn it into a self-contained musico-dramatic entity. A case in point is the *tour de force* 'Hard Hearted Barb'ra (H)Ellen', a kind of extended scena embodying a musical realization of all the tragedy's successive phases as recounted in the text. One wonders if Britten was familiar with it, since merely to read Grainger's performance instructions is to broach the technical world of the church parables and *Death in Venice*—e.g. a sequence of piano chords 'does not have to dovetail exactly' with the voice; 'singer takes rhythmic initiative; pays no attention to chords in piano'; 'play this passage again and again at same speed (faster than singer's speed)'; 'pianist fits in the chords just when he pleases'. What a pity that Britten and Pears never recorded this masterpiece. Pears tells us of Britten's concern to recreate folk melodies, to take the tune as if he had written it himself and 'think himself back as to how he might turn it into a song' (sleeve note for Decca SXL 6793). Graham Johnson has suggested (below, chapter 27) that Britten the folksong setter was much influenced by Britten the opera composer, and certainly his theatrical, exhibitionistic streak (also a childlike trait) finds a ready parallel in Grainger's. Although, unlike Grainger, Britten was never galvanized to creativity by folksong, he was greatly affected by popular music in the widest sense—music of the people, music with roots. Roots for Britten were a *sine qua non*. Much of his music was inspired by the North Sea and by the peculiar climatic and atmospheric qualities of East Anglia. By an odd coincidence Grainger himself once described a 'North Sea mood' in music: 'There seems to be some climatic influence at work here—some Rembrandtian fog of the sea, the soil, and the soul—that . . . which produces a soaring

---

[1] Britten expressed unbounded enthusiasm for Grainger's folksong settings when he first encountered them in the early 1930s; see his diary entry for 3 March 1933, after listening to the radio: '. . . two brilliant folk-song arrangements of Percy Grainger—17 come Sunday, & Father & Son, knocking all the V. Williams and R. O. Morris arrangements into a cocked-hat.' (Quoted in *PL*, plate 353.)

ecstasy of yearning wistfulness that is quite distinct from, let us say, the occasional melancholy of Russian music and the sombreness of Spanish music.'[2] This captures the essence of *Peter Grimes*, and it could also serve to sum up the character of the one work in which Britten pays conscious tribute to Grainger, the *Suite on English Folk Tunes*, 'lovingly and reverently dedicated to the memory of Percy Grainger' (Britten follows the wording of Grainger's dedication of his *British Folk Music Settings* to Grieg). A folk tune is quoted in full only in the last movement, 'Lord Melbourne', which Grainger himself collected and set in what is generally thought to be his masterpiece for wind band, the *Lincolnshire Posy*. Britten's quite different treatment is perhaps the bleakest and most desolate of his many East Anglian marsh- and fen-scapes: the tune's last distant echo on the flute is actually extinguished before it can reach the last note, and the scene settles into complete silence. The *Suite* is prefaced by the lines from Hardy Britten had set as the finale to *Winter Words* (quoted above, p.69). Of all his laments for lost innocence this is one of the most poignant, and it is significant that it should have been inspired by a composer for whom, in a sense, the ceremony of innocence never was drowned.

Britten confessed to having been attracted above all by Grainger's 'earthiness'—a synonym for naturalness or innocence. Innocence implies a belief in the freedom to act in accordance with the dictates of one's own nature, not in conformity with an illiberal man-made morality. Grainger, in writing to one of his friends about his setting of *The Bride's Tragedy*, described it as

> . . . my personal protest against the sex-negation that our capitalistic world . . . offered to young talents like me. A man cannot be a full artist unless he is manly, & a man cannot be manly unless his sex-life is selfish, brutal, wilful, unbridled. But the main stream of tho[ugh]t in our age sets its face against such manliness as has always seemed right and proper to me.[3]

Frustration, anger and bitterness are implicit in *Albert Herring* and *Peter Grimes*, though no doubt many even today are unaware of the personal anguish that motivated those operas. *Herring* may be in theory and in practice a comic opera, but inasmuch as it is the story of

---

[2] 'Grieg—Nationalist and Cosmopolitan' (the second part of a four-part essay), *The Etude* (Philadelphia), July 1943, pp.428 and 472.
[3] Quoted in Bird, *Grainger*, p.136.

a man lauded and fêted by an insensitive, hypocritical society for failing to realize his manliness, it is deeply serious. Elsewhere Grainger wrote that '. . . on the whole I think the entire musical world is oblivious of the whole world of bitterness, resentment, iconoclasm and denunciation that lies behind my music'. We could possibly give more thought to the presence of these emotive forces in Britten's music. Its strong vein of aggressiveness has often been commented upon, and Hans Keller pointed out long ago that a defiantly expressed pacifism can often conceal a strongly repressed sadism. Grainger could discuss his sado-masochistic impulses quite objectively, and the supercharged masculinity of much of his work reflects what his doctor called the 'sizzling time-bomb within him', which he defused in sado-masochistic practices. Yet he wrote *The Power of Rome and the Christian Heart* as a protest against the useless sending of countless thousands of young men to their deaths in the First World War, while Britten's *War Requiem* is perhaps the most powerful anti-war tract of modern times. As in children, their energy is often synonymous with belligerence. Grainger wrote:

> . . . one reason why things of mine like 'Molly [on the Shore]' & 'Shepherd's Hey' are good is that there is so little gaiety & fun in them. Where other composers would have been jolly in setting such dance tunes I have been sad or furious. My dance settings are energetic rather than gay.[4]

So too with Britten's many dance movements, e.g. the Burlesque in the *Three Divertimenti*, the 'Dance of Death' in *Our Hunting Fathers*, the Tarantella in the *Diversions*, the tournament music in *Gloriana*, 'Hankin Booby' and 'Hunt the Squirrel' in the *Suite on English Folk Tunes*, the Jig in the *Welcome Ode*. None of these has any real jollity or fun, whatever the superficial impression; the keynote in all cases seems rather to be anguish or aggression.

Other child-like characteristics of Grainger's reflected in his creative work are his love of percussion instruments of all kinds, and his urge to break away from conventional instrumental combinations. One of his reasons for urging composers and conductors to take the kitchen department more seriously was that it offers wonderful opportunities for *children* to participate enjoyably in orchestral performance. He advocated percussion instruments like the marimba

[4] Quoted in Bird, *Grainger*, p.62.

and vibraphone which were common in jazz and theatre bands but had yet to find a place in the symphony orchestra. In his ballet score *The Warriors* he exploits this new range of sonorities to great effect, clearly influenced by the sound of the Balinese gamelan (percussion orchestra) which had fascinated Debussy (whose *Pagodes* Grainger transcribed for the very medium that had inspired it) and which Britten was to evoke so skilfully in *The Prince of the Pagodas*. This point of contact between Grainger and Britten seems crucial when we remember that Britten also was constantly concerned to involve children and amateurs in music-making and frequently discarded conventional notions of vocal and instrumental orchestration to do so. Percussion was always very important in his scores, and like Grainger he gave much time and thought to concocting novel percussion effects. Grainger in his *Tribute to Foster* makes his chorus rub their fingers around the rim of glasses filled with water to produce a high pedal effect. In *Noye's Fludde* Britten writes for 'slung mugs' (see above, p.48), and at the end of the work (from the climactic entry of all the voices singing 'The Spacious Firmament on High' in eight-part canon) they are used in conjunction with Grainger's favourite handbells and pianos, again to produce a curiously gamelan-like effect. Pentatonic formations predominate here, as they do in Britten's work as a whole; not unexpectedly, since the five-note scale is a basic form of innocent or unselfconscious musical utterance—hence its ubiquity in most folk music cultures. (Britten's oft-noted fondness for the major second as a harmonic entity almost certainly sprang, like Debussy's, from its pentatonic connotations. Nor is it surprising that Britten stocked so large a part of his melodic and harmonic vocabulary with the staple formula of the triad, the common chord. To quote just one relevant instance: in the *Dies irae* of the *War Requiem* the brass thrill with the sound of triads warring in bitonal close combat. So do the brass in Grainger's *'The Duke of Marlborough' Fanfare*, intended according to the composer to evoke both distant memories of war and war in the present: presumably a coincidence, but the affinity of mind is striking.)

In the 1960s Britten collaborated with the percussionist James Blades to produce a variety of unusual instruments for the three church parables, for instance a multiple whip and a set of tuned wood blocks for *The Burning Fiery Furnace*. Finally in *Death in Venice* a gamelan-like percussion ensemble plays a crucial dramatic role, representing the remoteness of the world of Tadzio and his companions and its utter inaccessibility to the ageing Aschenbach (just as the boys' voices in the *War Requiem* represent an extreme of non-communication with the world of fighting men). Percussively the most elaborate of Britten's scores is that of *Children's Crusade*, which calls for six solo percussion and tutti percussion divided into three groups, tuned, rhythmic and clashed. Add to this a combination of piano duet and electronic organ—the latter a surrogate for Grainger's long-suffering harmonium—and the result is a proto-Graingerian orchestration.

Both Grainger and Britten were driven by an urge to democratize their music—to make it available on a practical level, not only to children, but to as wide a range of numbers and talents as possible. Grainger developed a principle which he called 'elastic scoring' that enabled his works to be played by a variety of numbers and combinations of instruments. It is worth noting that both composers were intensely professional practical musicians and exceptionally fine orchestrators. Both instruct each performer in the most painstaking detail how to play his part, so that even if the performer isn't particularly musical his performance will be. The master orchestrator exacts a high level of virtuosity from his performers without causing them practical discomfort, the result being the peculiar sense of exhilaration which we experience in listening both to Grainger and to Britten. In such works as *The Little Sweep*, *Saint Nicolas* and *Noye's Fludde* Britten's policy was to include parts tailored to the limited techniques of amateur singers and instrumentalists. In all of them prominent use is made of the piano. Grainger was a pioneer in the orchestral use of the piano and Britten was one of his most assiduous disciples. (Walter Piston's classic treatise, *Orchestration*, cites the opening bars of Britten's *Sinfonia da Requiem* as one of the most striking instances of the use of piano sonority in modern orchestral literature.) Grainger's purpose in this respect was partly educational:

> Above all, let us press into orchestral playing as many young music-lovers as possible. Whether they are to become laymen or professionals, they need some experience of musical team-work before they can become *practical* musicians, *real* musicians sensing the inner soul of their art. . . . Let us use in our orchestras the vast mass of keyboard players . . . that preponderate everywhere in our musical life. Pianists . . . are more in need of some kind of musical

team-work (to offset their all too soloistic study activities) than almost any other class of musicians.[5]

Britten shared this passion for making music more of a communal practical experience and its expression has many ramifications in his scores. Audience participation, for example, as in *The Little Sweep, Saint Nicolas* and *Noye's Fludde*; putting performance directions in English rather than Italian (with more moderation than Grainger, who carried the principle to an extreme); and integrating 'solo' instruments within the orchestra. Grainger never wrote a concerto because he thought the form 'undemocratic'. Britten's works in concerted form were, with one notable exception, all written in the early part of his career. Later everyone in the orchestra is a soloist at one time or another. This applies not only to small orchestral groupings as in the chamber operas or the *Nocturne*, but also to the big scores of symphonic dimensions like *Billy Budd* or the *Spring Symphony*. Significantly the piece for cello and orchestra written for Rostropovich is called a cello *symphony*, not a concerto; and it is remarkable how the solo instrument sounds like a natural extension of the speaking voice of the orchestra, and vice versa. At the beginning of the fourth movement, for example, the trumpet is just as much a solo instrument as the cello.

The more we cherish a memory, the more we naturally seek to recreate the context in which that memory flourished. For anyone brought up, as Britten was, in an English middle-class environment in the early twentieth century, the church was bound to be one of the most palpable realities of childhood, and it is therefore no surprise to find it playing a very large role in Britten's creative life. Not that he was especially prodigal of music for liturgical use; *Rejoice in the Lamb, A Ceremony of Carols* and the church parables were composed for performance *in a church building*, which is a different matter. But specific qualities associated with churches and church music that may be reckoned part of his childhood heritage return to colour his music again and again. A very large proportion of his choral music is texturally conceived in terms of a reverberant church or cathedral acoustic, and loses immeasurably if performed in a concert hall or studio.[6] The 1957 recording of *A Boy Was Born*, made in a Decca studio, proves the point: the problem is not that the part-writing is

[5] Quoted in Bird, *Grainger*, pp.286–7.
[6] See also below, pp.217–18.

congested but that the individual parts have no room to breathe, hence the generally turgid impression. One of the most moving moments in *Saint Nicolas* fails completely if it is not performed in a church: the canonic entries of the six distinct semichoruses of trebles at 'Let the legends that we tell praise him, with our prayers as well', the climax of 'His piety and marvellous works' (Ex.1). A dead acoustic kills the effect of gigantic ripples spreading and expanding on a water-surface. *A Ceremony of Carols* is particularly interesting in

Ex.1

(cont.)

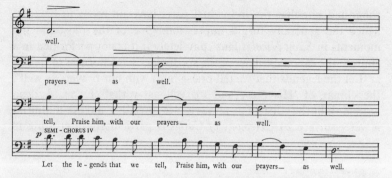

this respect. Whoever heard of accompanying a carol sequence for church performance with a *harp*? But Britten knew not only that the instrument would create a new style of accompanimental texture, but also that a church or cathedral acoustic would automatically enhance its naturally reverberant properties. The canonic writing in 'This little Babe' has an increased urgency and a depth and intimidating bigness of sonority because the acoustic amplifies and multiplies each part *ad infinitum* as in a series of endlessly (and nightmarishly) reflecting mirrors; the impression is of ever-increasing numbers joining in a frenzied pursuit, a perfect example of the dramatic element in Britten's art asserting itself in the unlikeliest of contexts. Much the same applies to the weird and shadowy 'In freezing winter night', in which the first treble voice carries the melody, the second follows it canonically like a *Doppelgänger* and the third relates closely to the icy fingerings of the harp. (Here, in fact, for one of the first times in Britten's music, is the technique of heterophony, in which plain and elaborated versions of the same melodic line are heard simultaneously.) Moreover, in its framing use of plainsong (the Christmas 'Hodie Christus natus est') as processional and recessional, *A Ceremony of Carols* can be seen as the progenitor of the church parables. In these much later works, which develop the process of germination and growth from plainsong to an unprecedented degree, a reverberant acoustic is central to the textural complexity: both to the oriental or medieval technique of heterophony and to the cloudy chord-clusters built up and sustained by the organ. *Voices for Today* is also conceived specifically for such an acoustic: the boy's chorus is to be placed apart from the main chorus (if possible in a gallery) and the *ad libitum* organ part 'should be used primarily when the resonance of the building is inadequate'. The character of the writing is related directly to this desired 'resonance'. The same of course applies, on a much larger scale, to the *War Requiem*, in which Britten continues with Mahler's experiments in spatial differentiation for dramatic effect. For Britten, massed voices—especially when unaccompanied —remained throughout his life associated with the context in which he first encountered them as a boy.

Britten's lifelong attachment to hymnody may perhaps be similarly accounted for. The *Scottish Ballad* is based primarily on the hymn tune 'Dundee' ('The people that in darkness sat'); the *Suite for Harp* incorporates 'St Denio', and the overture *The Building of the House* the tune best known as 'Vater Unser' ('O quickly come dread judge of all'); and 'The Choirmaster's Burial' from *Winter Words* makes telling use of 'Mount Ephraim'. Act II of *Peter Grimes* brilliantly en-compasses an entire church service as ironic counterpoint to the increasingly turbulent scene between Peter and Ellen taking place on the beach: introductory hymn, 'Now that the daylight fills the sky'; Confession; *Benedicite*; Creed. A similar Sunday morning scene occurs in *The Turn of the Screw*, in which the sound of church bells in the preceding variation (incorporating the fourths of the 'screw' theme) leads into the children's *Benedicite*, a song this time not of the bounties of the earth and the heavenly hosts but of all the hierarchy of evil: again Britten diverts (or rather perverts) a keen childhood enthusiasm to superb dramatic effect.[7] In *Albert Herring* the children's 'Glory to our new May King' is clearly an intentionally comic hymn-tune parody (perhaps partly derived from Wesley's 'Hark how all the welkin rings' and W. H. Monk's tune 'Würtemberg'). Both more and less conventional is the use of actual hymns in *Saint Nicolas* and *Noye's Fludde*, the intention being to involve the audience as participants in the rite. John Culshaw has testified to the power of these hymns (specifically in *Noye's Fludde*) to shake normally impervious men to their foundations. The hymns touch something

[7] Bells too—real or imitation—re-echo throughout Britten's *oeuvre*: in the finales of *A Boy was Born*, *Noye's Fludde* and the *Temporal Variations* for oboe and piano, in Act II of *The Prince of the Pagodas*, in Act II of *Albert Herring*, in the *Missa Brevis in D* (altar bells), in the introduction and coda of the *Cantata Academica*, in the *War Requiem*, in *The Building of the House*, in the magnificently Turneresque Venice music in *Death in Venice*, and in the bass ostinato of the Finale of String Quartet No. 3. In *A Ceremony of Carols* they clash in rhythmic exultation in 'Wolcum Yule' and 'Deo Gracias', and boom and hum as if heard from the inmost depths of a cathedral in the transparently beautiful 'There is no rose': As early as 1934 the *Te Deum in C* has a unifying bell-like figure, first heard in the organ pedals in the opening bars and rarely absent until at the climax ('Vouchsafe, O Lord') it develops into a long pealing proclamation.

deep down in our subconscious, something older than the present organization of our nature, something innocent of the fall from grace.[8] Much the same applies to plainsong, which assumes increasing importance as Britten's career progresses—it is a framing device in *A Ceremony of Carols*,[9] generates the invocatory opening and closing sections of *A Hymn to St Peter* and finally takes pride of place as the *fons et origo* of the church parables.

Once we accept that Britten's child-like-ness was the mainspring of his creativity, we are not surprised by the proliferation of compositions in which children themselves participate. In *Let's Make an Opera*, *Canticle II*, *Saint Nicolas*, *The Turn of the Screw*, *Noye's Fludde*, *The Golden Vanity* and *Children's Crusade* they are both dramatis personae and performers. Other works exploit, with a consistency and appositeness peculiar to Britten, the distinctive timbre of boys' voices, notably *Rejoice in the Lamb*, *A Ceremony of Carols*, *Voices for Today*, *A Boy was Born*, the *War Requiem*, the *Spring Symphony*, the three church parables and *A Midsummer Night's Dream*. Mahler's use of the *Chor seliger Knaben*, 'chorus of blessed boys', in the Eighth Symphony and, more particularly, in the fifth movement of the Third, in which boys' voices and bells are compounded in a vision of joy and the morning—a work with which we know Britten was familiar as he made a version of the second movement for reduced instrumentation—may well have been a

[8] In *Canticle II: Abraham and Isaac* (whose text, like that of *Noye's Fludde*, was derived from the Chester Miracle Cycle) the development or expansion of the main theme to which the final 'For ever and ever, Amen' is set is virtually identical with the last line of 'All people that on earth do dwell', perhaps still fresh in Britten's mind from *Saint Nicolas*:

Abraham and Isaac

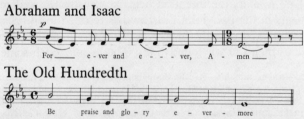

The Old Hundredth

[9] Michael Dawney ('Some Notes on Britten's Church Music', *Tempo*, No.82 (Autumn 1967), pp.13–21) has traced part of this plainsong to the antiphon of the Vespers on Christmas Day, and identifies the death of Nicolas in *Saint Nicolas* as being marked 'by the first psalm-tone with termination D_2, as classified in the *Liber Usualis*'. The music of the finding of the Heavenly Babe in *Canticle IV: Journey of the Magi* is based on 'Magi videntes stellam', the antiphon before the *Magnificat* at First Vespers for the Feast of the Epiphany.

stimulus, but Britten far exceeds Mahler in the range and diversity of the demands he makes on his youthful collaborators. He treats children, in fact, as fully fledged professionals and writes children's adult music for them, not adults' children's music. His attitude to children is neither condescending nor sentimental, nor is there any element of self-conscious simplification in the music itself. George Peele's driving boy who whistles in Part I of the *Spring Symphony* is a real boy, not an escapist idealization of one; and the great apotheosis of the Finale ('Sumer is i-cumen in'), in which the boys' choir is required to ride in triumph over the full orchestra and (adult) chorus, demands real flesh-and-blood vitality.[10]

But of course Britten's children are real, since he himself was a child. He would never have wanted them to forswear their natural 'animal' instincts or fancy themselves as the incarnation of human perfectibility fondly imagined by some adults. These are falsities perpetrated by 'the disease of feeling'. Britten was fascinated not only with the sound *per se* of children's voices; for him they represented a world of untarnished purity and never-ending springtime, an ever-present Garden of Eden. At the climax of the *Spring Symphony* they crown the height of summer with 'Sumer is i-cumen in'; yet in the *War Requiem* they connote a zenith of disembodied coldness, the marmoreal non-humanity of religious ritual tradition—as if Britten were placing his well-loved associations of choirboys' voices and the Anglican Church in an ironic perspective. It is touching and significant that his last completed utterance should have been not the weightily introspective *Death in Venice* nor its parergon String Quartet No.3, but the freshly, joyously unpretentious *Welcome Ode* written for the Suffolk Schools' Choir and Orchestra, its finale a hymn to the everlasting summer (literal and metaphorical) of childhood. It was in every way a fitting envoi.

[10] In his 'Music: some Aspects of the Contemporary Problem', *Horizon*, 10, No.55 (July 1944), Edward Sackville-West defined as one of the 'youthful influences' on Britten 'what I can only describe as the Fun Fair—that glorious conglomeration of popular music, balladry, coconut shies and merry-go-rounds, and all the caps-back-to-front paraphernalia of the English *festa*, with its echoing overtones from childhood, schooldays, nonsense jokes, family cosiness, and the entrancements of the Christmas tree' (p.71). Miss Hudson, Britten's housekeeper, recalled that Britten loved a traditional Christmas, with turkey, a large ham, plum pudding, cakes with icing and mince pies. The Christmas tree is clearly visible in the photograph showing a 1946 meeting of the English Opera Group at Oxford Square (plate 27) and one can imagine with what relish Britten accepted a BBC commission in 1947 to write variations on 'God rest ye merry, gentlemen' for the Christmas Day Broadcast *Men of Goodwill*.

STAGE WORKS

6
Mapreading

BENJAMIN BRITTEN
in conversation with
DONALD MITCHELL

Britten was never enthusiastic about giving interviews. He agreed, however, to discuss with me the project of writing an opera for television. This was Owen Wingrave, commissioned by the BBC and first transmitted on 16 May 1971. As emerges very clearly, the new undertaking was much influenced by his experience of working on the BBC Television production of Peter Grimes, transmitted on 2 November 1969. Our conversation began with Wingrave as the principal topic, but as it proceeded and Britten grew more relaxed, I was able to introduce other subjects. Some of his replies touch on areas which he referred to rarely if at all in public (and not much in private), and in the end a quite surprising amount of ground was covered.

In transcribing the interview for this, its first publication in any form, I have precisely followed Britten's spoken words. If he had lived and had an opportunity to scrutinize the text, he would have corrected the many imperfections, inconsistencies and inelegancies I have preserved. I have made virtually a verbatim transcript because I found that when I tried to edit Britten's speech, a great deal of character was lost without any great gain in clarity of meaning. Moreover, I was reluctant to put words in his mouth which he had not spoken. I have not been quite so purist about my questions. The tape of the interview is available for consultation in the Archive at the Britten–Pears Library; in a few instances the rhythm of Britten's speech reinforces his meaning. The interview took place at the Red House, Aldeburgh, in February 1969, and was first broadcast by the BBC on 10 May 1971. The recording was originally made for use by the Canadian Broadcasting Corporation.

[D.M.]

Benjamin Britten

DONALD MITCHELL: Earlier this year you were heavily engaged in the television production of *Peter Grimes*. I know it was a great physical strain for you, because it must have been an enormous undertaking. But I think you were impressed and intrigued— were you not?—by all the possibilities of putting one of your major operas on television?

BENJAMIN BRITTEN: It was a very great experience. It was, as you say, also rather alarming and tiring, simply because the handling of this enormous force of performers, and also of course fitting in with the wishes of the cameramen and the producers and directors, was something that I had never tried before. It was a much bigger enterprise than I had imagined I could ever try. But actually the people I was working with were so musical and understood the musical side of the work so well that my task was made much easier.

DM: Do you think, Ben, as a result of this experience with television—which took place, almost literally, on your own doorstep—that television opera has got a great future? That the possibilities for opera on television are really very considerable?

BB: I think the answer is a definite 'yes' for that, but I think there are one or two lessons that one must learn before really committing opera to television; and if I can be slightly technical for a moment I would like to say what they are, these lessons. One is that I am sure the opera must have a musical intensity on television: it must not get broken up into a vehicle for the cameras only. I have seen quite a few television versions of operas, and I think the danger can easily come that they are made, if I may say so, too reasonable, too realistic. And then one asks—I am sure the audience, the non-operatic audience, asks itself—why in the blazes people are singing and not speaking. You have got to keep this knife-edged balance between the photograph, the picture, which of course in a television medium must be rather realistic, it has that realistic impact on one, and also the musical excitement. And I think what I have learnt from the television [production] of *Peter Grimes* is that the drive forward of the music, the singing of the tunes, the elaboration of the ensembles, must never be forgotten. If you do, you get a kind of misfire, which is neither straight drama nor good opera. And that is the sort of thing that I've learnt and I'm trying to put into practice in this opera I'm now writing for television.

DM: I wanted to ask you a question about that, whether in fact your experience with *Grimes* will be taken into account in this television opera that you are now just about to start writing?

BB: Yes. . . . Well, I've learnt—I mean, I'm deeply thankful that I did have that experience with *Grimes* before I actually put pen to paper in this new opera.

DM: Could you tell us briefly what the new television opera is to be? It's a short story by Henry James, isn't it?

BB: Yes. It's a very remarkable short story called 'Owen Wingrave'. It's like all Henry James's work: very reasoned, very intelligent, and full of very strong atmosphere. I've learnt, of course, a lot from doing *The Turn of the Screw*, and I'm also using the same librettist, Myfanwy Piper, for *Owen Wingrave* as I had for *The Turn of the Screw*. I won't tell you the story because people can always find the story in volume 9 of *The Collected Short Stories*. It's a very provocative story and a very strange one, but I think it's a very powerful one, and I hope it is a good choice for one's first television opera. It's not got a big chorus, in fact it's got scarcely a chorus at all. It's got a small number of characters, all of which I think is a good thing for the television medium. Although I think with careful handling large forces can be made to be successful.

DM: So this will be virtually a chamber opera?

BB: Yes. I shall use a slightly bigger orchestra than I used for *The Turn of the Screw*, because I need rather other effects, but it will not be a big orchestra. It will be an orchestra I think of slightly Mozart size, although not necessarily Mozart style.

DM: This will be a work, then, specifically designed for the television medium?

BB: Entirely designed.

DM: Have you got some special ideas in this respect?

BB: Oh yes. We're using the camera consciously throughout. I mean, it's quite an effort for me, but I'm being very careful to think throughout of the television medium and not of the stage. I've no doubt that one will, at a later date, be able to adapt it for the stage, but it will take a considerable amount of rewriting. But what is perhaps more interesting than my just talking about a work in the future is that one has learnt from this *Peter Grimes* experience so much that I've changed the libretto which was sketched before we started the television [production] of *Peter*

Grimes. I've changed a great deal of it because of the lessons that I learnt in that. And it's all gone back to the operatic form of opera and away from the realistic form of opera. In fact I've been in the last days with Myfanwy Piper—we've been adding arias galore. Because I am convinced—and this comes from my recent television experience—that the audience needs the tunes, it needs the lyricism of the aria and the ensemble, rather than the realistic side of perpetual recitative. Which would prompt, as I suggested, the question 'Why in the blazes is he singing and not speaking?'

DM: Yes, so in a way what you're saying, Ben, is that the successful television opera is more likely to succeed in so far as specifically musical forms in a sense predominate, and the drift away from realism is pronounced?

BB: Yes, that's exactly what I feel about it. And I'm glad to say that John Culshaw, who is the producer of this opera, is in entire sympathy with my feelings about that.

DM: I think this really is an extraordinarily interesting discovery or conclusion to have come to as a result of the *Grimes* filming.

BB: It's a very surprising one, quite honestly.

DM: It's a surprising one—I wouldn't have expected that. I'm sure that this is right in fact.

BB: Well, it's certainly right for *me*, and I'm sure that what one apologist for television opera said to me, I think entirely mistakenly, that the greatest praise that a television opera can have was that the viewer forgot it was opera—I'm sure that is the greatest mistake. One should enjoy it *because* it's opera.

DM: Ben, how far have you a clear picture, compositionally speaking, of the work in your mind? I put this as a general question because it would very much interest me to know how this happens when you're approaching a new piece. Whether you come with your ideas already pretty fully formulated, or whether a lot happens once you get down to your desk.

BB: I never start a work without having a very clear conception of what that work is going to be. When I say conception, I don't mean necessarily tunes or specific rhythms or harmonies—or old-fashioned things like that!—but I mean the actual shape of the music—the kind of music it's going to be rather than the actual notes, they come very much later. But notes at this stage, which is about two or three weeks away from the first note to be put on paper—the notes are beginning to come already. Not necessarily the beginning, but little schemes throughout the work. I am beginning to plan it all from a textural point of view throughout. But there is always this element of chance, of improvisation, which happens once the work gets under way. I think E. M. Forster describes that very well in *Aspects of the Novel*, when he says that one must always be prepared as a creative artist to let the characters take charge. And I can quite often go to the paper perfectly clear that what I'm going to do, and to find that it doesn't work out quite like that. And I think one has got to have faith in one's subconscious, that it's going to direct one rightly. Quite often, you see, when you put a thing down on paper it lacks a certain quality which it may have in your imagination, which is not quite so precise as the actual instructions for the performers. Then you have to be prepared to adjust, and that particularly in opera when, as E. M. Forster says, the characters take over, where the characters do exist in a very big way. It's very difficult to remember precisely something which one wrote such a long time ago, but I know that the first drafts for *The Turn of the Screw* were in what one called then the normal three-act form, and even I think the libretto was written in that shape. And I realized there was something wrong. It was partly what was wrong I think because we had omitted some of James's own episodes, and put others together, and he planned that story, as one slowly found out, so very carefully that if you miss one rung in the ladder you miss your footstep, and something goes wrong. I then discovered that what we were really planning was something in a certain number of scenes which must follow very closely. And I was then looking for an idea which could be varied through these scenes which then would turn out to be a series of variations. Because really the story could be rather fancifully described as a theme with variations. Incidentally there are many close similarities between the two stories, 'Owen Wingrave' and 'The Turn of the Screw'.

DM: So in some ways the new piece will be a companion piece?

BB: Yes, I think it will be. In the number of characters it's comparable, in the intensity of it, and in the short scenes and the interludes, although I don't think I shall do it in the same variation form.

DM: Ben, I know dreams, sleep, night have clearly meant a great deal

Benjamin Britten

to you as a creator. 'Night and Silence, these are two of the things I cherish most': that's a phrase of yours I've always remembered.

BB: Silence of course, these days, becomes a rarer and rarer presence, particularly in this house where we're sitting now, where the aeroplanes land with unfailing regularity close to the house. But night and dreams—I have had a strange fascination by that world since a very early age. In fact I can remember, rather precociously, when I was at my private school, saying to myself, the last thing before I went to sleep, or naming to myself, an algebraic problem which I had to solve the next day. Someone told me—I don't remember whom—that if you do that it gives a chance for your subconscious to work when your conscious mind is happily asleep. Whether that was a successful method I don't remember well enough, except I was fairly successful in mathematics when I was young. But I do treasure that moment and that's why I think I get so disturbed and distressed if I don't sleep, I find that I wake up in the morning unprepared for my next day's work.

DM: Of course, in a work like *A Midsummer Night's Dream*, for example, one does there—poetically—experience the healing power of sleep, because after the dream-world of the wood, and the imposed sleep of the spells, everything does come right in the end; and this is an image perhaps of what you've just been saying about the therapeutic effect of a good night's sleep. At the same time it is true—isn't it?—that night does also have a more disturbing aspect for you?

BB: Yes. It can release many things which one thinks had better not be released; and one can have dreams which one cannot remember even, I find, in the morning, which do colour your next day very darkly. And it's always very puzzling to me that I can't remember something which has had such a big emotional effect on the next day, on the next days even. Similarly, of course, it can have a very blessed effect on your next day. My recent dream about meeting Schubert in Vienna blessed the following days in a way that I seldom remember in my life before.

DM: I think you must in fact be the only composer known to me who has written a whole work virtually devoted to sleep and dreams—the *Nocturne*, the orchestral song-cycle.

BB: Yes. Well, the *Serenade* gets near to it.

DM: Yes, the *Serenade* leads into the later song-cycle—doesn't

92

it?—with Keats's 'Sleep' sonnet. This foreshadows really the world to which the *Nocturne* is devoted in its entirety. Although that piece—I think it is true, isn't it?—does deal too with the disturbing aspects of sleep . . .

BB: Very much so, yes.

DM: . . . nightmare, for instance. It's not by any means all happy dreams.

BB: No. The Wordsworth I think is a very nightmarish poem—the dream about the French Revolution. And of course the *Nocturnal* which I wrote for Julian Bream also has some very, to me, disturbing images in it, linked, of course, inspired by this— the Dowland song, which of course itself has very strange undertones in it. Dowland was a person who perhaps even consciously realized the importance of dreams.

DM: Ben, you've often said to me that you've never had any desire or ambition to teach. Do you still feel that way, even though we might possibly live in a time when some teaching from you might be thought to be extremely valuable?

BB: Yes, I don't exactly know why I'm so shy about teaching. I know that when young people come to me with their works it gives me great pleasure to go through them—these works—with the young composers. I think I'm frightened of imposing my own solutions on their problems. Although I do believe strongly that even the personality of the teacher can be absorbed without much detriment to the scholar. Because if the personality of the scholar is strong enough it can absorb it easily, and perhaps get richer from it. But I have seen so many cases in my life where the tricks, the mannerisms of the teacher have been picked up by the scholar. And sometimes when the teacher has not been a professional composer they have been really unhealthy influences, I feel. They've been a secondhand version of the tricks of other composers and it produces so often a stilted quality in the music of these young chaps that has sometimes been almost impossible to eradicate. I think that the great composer, the great writer, painter, will survive almost any kind of treatment. But the great composers can look after themselves. It's the minor composers, the people who can make our lives so much richer in small ways, that I want to preserve and to help. Also, I do think that at this moment of acute change in music that I perhaps am *not* the right person to guide young composers. My methods, which are entirely personal to me, are founded on a time when the language was not so broken as it is now. I think this is a moment of lack of confidence which I shall outgrow, but at the moment I feel that the young composer would not be interested in my criticisms. Because virtually really all a teacher can do to help a student is to say 'Is this what you mean? And if not, let's try and find out what it is.' In other words, to shine a brighter light on the music than the scholar really has . . . is yet in possession of; and to make him see his work more clearly in order to get it, the real re-creation of what is in his mind. My methods, I feel, of doing that would be a little unacceptable to some of the young composers; and that I think is why at the moment—apart of course from the major one of lack of time—but I think that's one of the major reasons why I haven't taught.

DM: You do feel, do you, that this is a time of acute change in music? I think you're quite right to feel that, but . . .

BB: Yes, I do. And I don't always follow the new directions, and nor do I always approve of them, but that is only purely personal to me. I mean, that there should be new directions is obvious. Any new thought, in whatever language it's couched, has got to have this new element. But I sometimes feel that the seeking after a new language has become more important than saying what you mean. I mean, I always believe that language is a means and not an end.

DM: Of course language is a means of communicating; and I would have thought that you would regard yourself, as an artist, as a communicator.

BB: Entirely. I mean, why bother to write your music down, if you don't want to communicate it?

DM: Exactly. But I would have thought that the acute change to which you refer was bound up with the total abolition of the idea of comprehensible language on the one hand and of the idea of communicating on the other.

BB: Yes.

DM: This does seem in fact really to represent the immense gulf that has opened up in the arts in our time.

BB: I think one mustn't exaggerate that. I think it's only the very vocal few who make these extreme remarks . . .

DM: . . . or who take up extreme positions?

BB: Yes, because in my experience, and I do see really a great deal of young composers' work, this only belongs to the very, very few.

Mapreading

And I can name many young composers—I mean, of those already reaching maturity and those who have not yet reached maturity—who are passionately interested in telling us what they want to say. I think that one of the bores of the enormous newspaper coverage, and radio and television coverage, of opinions, is that the very vocal ones become very well known. And I think quite often they are not the best. But I do find in a young composer like John Tavener, for instance, who is writing very hard and very interestingly in this country at the moment, he is profoundly interested in telling us what he means. And I think he and many of his generation are swinging far, far away now from what I call the academic avant-garde, who have rejected the past. He and many others like him *adore* the past and *build* on the past. After all, language is a matter of experience. When we're talking together now, we're using symbols which have been used by the past. If we rejected the past we should be just making funny noises.

DM: Ben, you were talking about some composers—some, only—young composers, who reject the past. Well, of course, certainly this has never happened in your case. To a composer standing at the point of his life where you do today, you have a great inheritance, not only in your own music but also with regard to the past. I would like to ask you how it feels standing in that situation? And are you conscious of this wonderfully exciting but also great *burden* of tradition behind you?

BB: [*A long pause.*] I'm *supported* by it, Donald. I couldn't be alone. I couldn't work alone. I can only work really because of the tradition that I am conscious of behind me. And not only the painting, and architecture, and countryside around me, people around me. [*Pause.*] This may be giving myself away—if so, I can't help it. I feel as close to Dowland, let's say—because we mentioned him earlier in our talk, a few hundred yards back—I feel as close to him as I do to my youngest contemporary. I was reading a play of Euripides in bed this morning—*Ion*—which I had read before, but I hadn't reread for some time. And really, the first chorus of that—written, what, nearly three thousand years ago?—seemed to me as if it was being written about a crowd visiting the Maltings, looking around and making comments: 'What's this?'; 'Where do we go here?' I feel that there's no difference except the difference of environment, between

Euripides and ourselves today. And we all have that feeling reading the Bible, reading any old sagas from Iceland or India. I cannot understand why one should *want* to reject the past. After all, we sit in this room surrounded by pictures and an amphora from Armenia, a very beautiful thing, which is five thousand years old. I'm given *strength* by that tradition. I know it changes—of course traditions change. But the human being remains curiously the same.

DM: It would be true then that you feel this sense of tradition as an aid and as an assistance in your own work. Could we just turn for one minute to one particular example: I was thinking we might choose possibly the *War Requiem*. Did you feel there when approaching this after all very big creative task, great precedents and examples of the Mass—for example, the settings of the Mass for the Dead—behind you in that work?

BB: I'd like to answer that question, Donald, in a rather roundabout way, by an example. Not long ago there was a young composer who had a first performance of an opera not far from here. And at the same time there were other operas being performed in the neighbourhood. I know it was probably because of the tightness of time, and the absorption in his own job, but it seemed to me very strange that he didn't want to go and see how Mozart solved *his* problems. If he were setting out, from here to Newmarket, to drive, naturally he would use maps to find out how to get there. Why, if he used maps to get to Newmarket, didn't he use maps which show how to write an opera? I know he was trying to say something different, just as we are probably driving a different car to Newmarket from the mapmaker's, but after all, there are many similarities between all works presenting dramatic ideas to audiences, and I would think, even though he may have rejected it—just as one can find a new way of going to Newmarket—that it's useful to know how someone else has gone there. And actually, as far as we can know, achieved getting there. And I think that I would be a fool if I didn't take notice of how Mozart, Verdi, Dvořák—whoever you like to name—had written their Masses. I mean, many people have pointed out the similarities between the Verdi *Requiem* and bits of my own *War Requiem*, and they may be there. If I have not absorbed that, that's too bad. But that's because I'm not a good enough composer, it's not because I'm wrong.

7

Paul Bunyan:
The American Eden

WILFRID MELLERS

Opera is a musical-poetic form that deals in theatrical projection with the myths people live by. Since Wagner, almost all operas that carry conviction have been concerned with personal stresses that can also acquire archetypal qualities; Britten's operatic myths are rooted deep in his personal psychology, yet at the same time speak of and to us all. We are obsessed with innocence because we have lost it, and for the same reason we persecute those who have not. In dealing with innocence and persecution Britten knew what he knew, both from his obsession with the presumptive Eden of his childhood and from the alienation caused by his homosexuality. The grandest, most tragic statement of this motif is in *Peter Grimes*, the opera that made him famous; its most painfully concentrated statement, *The Turn of the Screw*, stands at the centre of his creative life; while its most explicitly poignant revelation occurs in *Death in Venice*, in several senses his consummatory work.

Britten cannot have been consciously aware that this was to be the central theme of his work at the time when, in his mid-twenties, he left this country, a few months after W. H. Auden, possibly to settle in the United States. This suggests that genius knows where it is going long before it knows that it knows; for Britten's migration to America was not so much a rejection of moribund Europe as a discovery of a New World that, in being new, was a potential Eden. At a basic geographical level Britten was exploring his essential theme, out of which he produced his first musical-theatrical piece which, even after he realized that he was destined to be an opera composer, he for many years wanted to forget. Interestingly enough, the New York

97

commission offered to Auden and Britten in 1940 was for a
music-theatre piece for young people. Choosing as his theme the
American folk legend of Paul Bunyan, Auden made a book that was
not so much an opera libretto as a play for music, using techniques
derived from English ballad-opera, from music-hall and musical
comedy, from Gilbert and Sullivan and, more sophisticatedly, from
Brecht and Weill. Britten responded appropriately, incorporating a
considerable number of vocal parts, all of them negotiable by
untrained singers, and scoring for the orchestra habitual to the larger
American schools and colleges, plus a few exotica such as extra
percussion, saxophone and bass clarinet. Idiomatically he exploited
the eclecticism for which he was already famous or notorious, in that
the music's manners range unselfconsciously from English and
American folk ballad through Gilbert and Sullivan and parodies of
Italian opera to the blues and the blander kinds of jazz. Far from
denying personal identity, this eclecticism is endemic to the theme:
America's raw newness is patched together from the ragbags of
Europe. *Paul Bunyan* may be an unpretentious piece, but is far from
trivial in its implications; its rather grand theme is the relationship
between Nature and Nurture.

We open with a Prologue in the American wilderness. Old Trees
sing of Nature's seamless-seeming eternity before the advent of man,
and Britten invents for this state a musical image as inspired as it is
rudimentary: a C major scale that sways slowly up and down, with a
semiquaver flutter on the third of the four beats, and with Lydian
sharp fourths in the harmony. The pace doubles as Young Trees
argue with the venerable ancients. The young, being bored with their
vegetative state, want to grow towards consciousness; they are
snappily dismissed by the Old Trees as being 'sick', 'silly', 'crazy',
dangerously subversive 'Reds' who will soon grow out of it, since 'it's
only a phase'. Wild Geese fly over in a still faster metre, with
wing-flickering semiquavers and a tune arching through major and
minor thirds—one of the earliest intimations of this Britten
fingerprint. Being a stage further towards consciousness, they
annunciate man's transformatory arrival. As they chant in chorus
with the trees their arpeggio-founded melody—

A man is a form of life
That dreams in order to act
And acts in order to dream

Paul Bunyan: *The American Eden*

—flowers from their initial chains of thirds. When they announce that this mythic man will be born at the next Blue Moon, the Old Trees scoffingly laugh off such an implausibility: which immediately occurs. So they have no choice but to accept it, in a gravely homophonic chorus centred on E major but with persistent flat sevenths, and with vacillations back to their preconscious C major.

The Young Trees respond very differently to the Geese's incantation. Their 6/8 tune frisks fatuously up and down the scale, yearning to proceed from their 'natural' state to 'civilized' transmutation into houses, ships, chairs, even a dado! Their prophecies are rounded off with a repetition of the Blue Moon chorus, sung with modified implications by the Young Trees in consort with the Wild Geese. After this Paul Bunyan's birth is recounted by the Narrator in the First Ballad Interlude—an American-style country number in symmetrical duple rhythm and unsullied diatonicism, veering between D major and F major. Paul grows to gigantic dimensions because he is more than an individual; he is to represent mankind who enters 'a forest full of innocent beasts', where 'there are none who blush at the memory of an ancient folly, none who hide beneath dyed fabrics a malicious heart'. Not surprisingly this evocation of the American Eden provokes the first essentially Britten-like sounds in the score: morning noises on woodwind, over sustained and elided tonic, dominant and subdominant chords on strings. Being a legendary giant, Bunyan himself neither sings nor appears on stage (his supposed height would preclude that). He is confined to oracular speech, and the first ostensibly human song comes from the lumberjacks whom he summons to subdue with their axes the vast American forests.

They come from Sweden, a forest-pervaded country, and although they are to effect the transition from Nature to Nurture, they are not so far from savagery themselves. They yell a metrically pounding, perfunctorily primitive tune with leaping octaves agitated by chromatics, over a lurching oompah bass. Individual lumberjacks tell of their variously European origins; all join in the refrains to celebrate how, with saw and axe, they are 'melting the forests away'. In the succeeding quartet these embryonic men predictably quarrel as to who shall be their leader. A Western Union Boy, harbinger of electric technology, arrives on a bicycle, trundling in boogie rhythm through a perky E flat march, bearing a telegram from the King of Sweden. This message from the Old World establishes some crudely

99

hierarchical order, and a few cannier types assume necessary roles as foreman (Hel Helson), bookkeeper (Johnny Inkslinger), and cooks (Sam Sharkey and Ben Benny). Over a conventionally arpeggiated accompaniment, with a tonic pedal reiterated on the tuba, the two cooks vocally entwine in a Donizetti-style paean to the virtues of soup and beans, the measure of their culinary accomplishment.

At this point Auden introduces domestic animals, a dog and two cats, to bridge the gulf between Nature and emergent man. Again unsurprisingly, these beasts sing characteristic Britten music, the dog bouncing in linearly staccato thirds in semiquavers, the cats mewling in harmonically parallel thirds. They can effect, they tell us, a transition between man's destructive instincts as hunter and his more benignly human motivations: 'He needs the deep emotions I can give,' the dog remarks, while the pussies perceive in man 'a common passion for the lonely hour'. Bunyan bids everyone goodnight in five diaphanously modal bars in a calm 3/2: the first passage specifically to remind us of an American composer (Aaron Copland), as distinct from the sundry echoes of American demotic musics relevant to the scene and story. After the lumberjacks have gone to bed, four male voices sing a blues in a modal C sharp minor, brooding, in the silence of the night, over the perils as well as the hopes inherent in the creation of civilization from chaos. The music is sombre, more disturbing than anything so far encountered: grave in its arpeggiated phrases and thudding beat, with a boogie rhythm more suggestive of a funeral march than of jazz exuberance, though there are intermittently blue false relations. The middle section modulates restlessly, before the C sharp minor darkness envelops all.

With morning come, the Narrator sings the Second Ballad Interlude, in the same American country style as the first, this time in the Aeolian mode. He tells the story of Bunyan's marriage, which is part of the folk legend, though it hasn't much relevance to the main theme and was probably a late accretion. Paul needs a wife; he finds it difficult to discover one of appropriate size, but eventually succeeds and sires a daughter on his Carrie. The marriage proves unhappy; Carrie returns to her native land, sickens and dies. Bunyan rushes too late to her death-bed and returns to the camp with his daughter who, since she is called Tiny and proves disturbing to the lumberjacks, is presumably of normal dimensions. While waiting for Paul's return the lumberjacks yawp a facetious chorus in Gilbert and Sullivan style protesting about the eternal soup and beans. Inkslinger, being literate

Paul Bunyan: *The American Eden*

and more 'conscious' than the rest, effects civilized compromises, introducing Slim, a good cook as contrasted with soup-and-bean-purveying Sam and Ben. Slim brings too a deeper dimension to the music, singing a country-style song concerned with something more than material survival.

> In fair days and in foul
> Round the world and back,
> I must hunt my shadow
> And the self I lack

he sings, floating his wide-spanned 3/2 lyrical melody over a 6/4 oompah on pizzicato strings and piano. Civilization is not merely a conflict between man's will and brute creation, but also a search for self-knowledge: a theme developed after Bunyan has returned and Inkslinger has sung a touching song about the precarious equilibrium between Nature's simplicities and Culture's sophistications. He'd love to 'paint St Sebastian the Martyr' or 'compose a D major sonata', but has to admit that 'a guy gotta eat', and that he has no right to feel superior to the lumbering lumbermen, let alone to Slim. Intellectual sophistication is manifest in the song's shifty modulations and jazzily chromatic chords, but the bluesy false relations are wistfully vulnerable.

There is a dramatic complement to this duality between Nature and Nurture, for Tiny's arrival at the camp wreaks havoc. The lumberjacks all fall for her and vie with one another in comic attempts to ingratiate themselves. Tiny deflates them by singing a lovely elegy for her mother, arching in waves in a subtly syncopated 6/4, and in a G major piquantly pricked with Lydian fourths. As she reflects on the lot of a motherless girl confronted with the wild wastes of a new world, the lumberjacks join her song, morosely commenting on their own mortality, in a rhythm of four minims crossed with her swinging 6/4. Inkslinger affectingly muses, over woodwind scales in contrary motion, on the difficulty of human communication—the number again dissipating on a false relation. The act ends as Bunyan speaks another goodnight over Nature's C major triad with flat seventh, punctuated by the chitters of nocturnal creatures, suggesting that the hero who has returned 'to the humble womb . . . may be pacified and refreshed'.

Act II opens with more morning noises, over which Bunyan recounts the march of civilization, probably through many years.

'Loneliness has worn lines of communication. Irrational destruction has made possible the establishment of a civilized order.' Forest-destroying axe-men are being replaced by barley-producing farmers, who sing a number sturdy in rhythm, Mixolydian in tonality, its bucolic affirmation compromised, however, by major–minor oscillations in the harmony. For the advance of civilization brings its own problems. Loutish Helson, the original foreman, can't recognize that 'He will never, never, never be great' and resents being superseded by the farmers, who in turn cannot stomach his arrogance. They taunt him cruelly, and he seeks consolation from the domestic beasts. The sentimental dog relishes this but the cats, 'Aristotelian and proud', reject both Hel and hound in a fast modal waltz with dismissive cross-rhythms. The action blows up in a furious fight, musically very primitive, as is appropriate, in which Bunyan puts down the subversive Helson, presumably because he is inimical to Progress. But this human confrontation is juxtaposed with a positive human collaboration in the form of a love duet between Slim and Tiny. He is a country boy who has learnt to dream, she is the daughter of the American life-force that is forging an industrial future; their gently flowering melody—related to their earlier solo numbers—proves more durable than the disruptive music of the fight. A mock funeral march, chorically sung over the prostrate Helson, comically echoes the gravity of the first act's closing Quartet of the Defeated and is consummated in a hymn of mutual forgiveness, incorporating the love song into a Stravinskian ostinato pattern, both rhythmic and harmonic. The 'great day of discovery' tells us that any new world worth the having must be based on personal acts of love: 'lost is the world I knew / And I am lost, dear heart, in you'. The music attains a grandeur that remains simple, if no longer innocent.

The Third Ballad Interlude describes, in the familiar country idiom, the reconciliation of Hel and Bunyan, of the Savage Man and Progress. The last scene ties up ends in a Christmas party which marries off the lovers and brings back the Western Union Boy with another telegram, promising Inkslinger fame and fortune in Hollywood, making movies (and perhaps ballad-operas?) about the Wild West. Inkslinger calls on Bunyan, in a lilting tune affectionately exploiting drooping fifths, to pronounce a general benediction: which he does, praising man's taming of the wilderness but reminding us that the harder task is ours, since 'all but heroes are unnerved / When love and life must be deserved'. In the final Litany men and women and domestic animals appeal for salvation. Helson wildly wonders what will become of inarticulate him and of America when Paul leaves; but Bunyan restates the opera's burden: 'America is what you do . . . America is what you choose to make it.' The message of Auden's cleverly articulate text and of the young Britten's resourcefully simple music still rings clear, in any country, through the forty years since the opera was created.

8

On Playing Peter Grimes[1]

PETER PEARS

What sort of a man is Peter Grimes? Is he what the bus conductor used to call him when the No. 19 bus stopped outside Sadler's Wells: 'This way for Peter Grimes, the sadistic fisherman'? Grimes reacts most irritably and unreasonably to criticism and can be clumsily violent, but I don't think he is a sadist at all. All of us are capable of anger, many of us of striking in anger, and the helpless and incompetent can very easily arouse irritation, fury even, in quite decent people. Grimes would have been treated as a criminal two hundred years ago, but today he would be considered a case for specially interested care.

I do not believe Grimes killed his apprentices. Indeed we know he didn't kill the second one, and the first was drowned in a rough sea. But his treatment of them led to their destruction, just as his own behaviour led to his self-destruction. I see him as an oversensitive being: too unstable, too strong in his reactions, too unsure of himself—but not a rough brute nor a hysterical maniac. To me the clue to Grimes's character is the beautiful and haunting phrase in Act I scene 2: 'Who can turn skies back and begin again?' I find him not unsympathetic.

When Ben and I were first planning the outline of the opera,[2] we thought that some scene from Grimes's background and earlier life at home would be needed to suggest why he had developed as he did. In Crabbe's poem, Grimes was from childhood stubborn and rebellious, as an adult drunken and violent to his father, a poacher and a pilferer,

---

[1] Edited from a talk in the series *Characters from Opera*, first broadcast by BBC Radio 3 on 7 August 1974.
[2] For a full analysis by Philip Brett of the genesis of the libretto see *PG*, chapter 3 [C.P.].

who felt the world was against him: 'And as these wrongs to greater numbers rose / The more he looked on all men as his foes.' Crabbe describes his madness superbly, with such shrewd insight and sensitivity that one stops thinking of Grimes as a villain and sees him much more sympathetically and objectively. Can a man be *so* black and yet recount his experiences, real or imagined, so touchingly? So the character of the operatic Peter Grimes moved away from unrelieved villainy to a more interesting and complicated character— a frustrated person with imagination enough to aspire to a better condition.

In Crabbe, Ellen Orford does not appear in the same poem as Grimes, although one feels there is no reason why she should not have known him, so lifelike and convincing are Crabbe's stories of the Borough. A heart-breaking series of misfortunes—a drunken father, seduction by a nobleman, a husband who 'turned Methody' and hanged himself, an idiot daughter and a lively and charming son who ended on the gallows—all these Crabbe gave Ellen Orford as though her life was a more or less normal one in his time. At last she becomes the Borough schoolmistress, respected and loved, and that is where the opera finds her.

The principal roles of the opera are, on the one hand, Peter Grimes himself and, on the other, a composite picture of a community, the Borough, consisting of the coroner (Swallow), the Rector, the landlady of the Boar (Auntie) and the Apothecary (Ned Keene), and widows, children, fishermen and others who form the highly important chorus. Peter may be acquitted of the manslaughter of his young apprentice—'accidental circumstances' is the verdict—but the Borough simply calls it murder and is dead set against him, regardless of his daring and skill as a fisherman.

There are one or two who are prepared to go along with him, as long as it profits them. There is one experienced student of mankind, Balstrode, a retired skipper, who is intrigued by him and tries to help him. Balstrode can sympathize with Grimes: the aria of longing and frustration in Act I scene 1 when Peter gives his version of the apprentice's death—the genuine utterance of a sensitive character, even if it is offset by a sort of bitter ambition—appeals to him. And there is the schoolmistress, Ellen Orford, who loves him. She would do anything for him and tries to keep him on the rails. He cannot then be wholly brutal and insensitive. To some extent he is lovable, but he won't accept pity, any more than he will take criticism: he longs to accept Ellen's love but refuses—not till he is in a proper position to do so, till he has established himself.

The great storm in Act I scene 2 does not worry Grimes. On the contrary, his nature is a stormy one, violently emotional, and the wild manifestations of nature appeal to him deeply. The storm releases tension in him and makes him creative, a poet. He is exalted, taken out of himself, and further than ever isolated from the humdrum gossipy Borough, as personified by the crowd sheltering in the Boar. When Peter finally walks in out of the storm and feels compelled to utter his great question 'Who can turn skies back and begin again?', the Borough is uncomprehending and totally unsympathetic. He must be either mad or drunk. He is neither mad nor drunk, but inspired by nature's great upheavals to an imaginative fancy quite out of the range of the down-to-earth townsmen. The others start singing a song at the instigation of Balstrode, who is trying to patch up a deteriorating and quarrelsome situation. The song is a sort of cross between a jingle and a shanty, lively and fun, but light years away from Grimes and his 'Great Bear and Pleiades'.

The new apprentice arrives; work goes on from day to day and the boy seems to be settling down. Ellen keeps a kindly eye on him, hoping secretly that her care for the boy will bring her nearer to Peter and that perhaps one day they will all three share a home. Then one Sunday morning, by the beach near the church, in the bright sunshine, she chats with the boy and finds a bruise on his neck—evidence of rough treatment. She tries to reassure him, but at that very moment Grimes appears, in high excitement, having caught sight of a phenomenally large shoal, and he and his apprentice must put to sea at once. When Ellen tries to keep him back, to persuade Peter to let the boy stay with her—after all, it is Sunday, his day of rest—Peter will not listen. And when she finally reproaches him with the word 'failure'—'We've failed!'—in exasperation he actually strikes her.

It is a savage and brutal act. Men are frequently brutal when infuriated, and Grimes *is* infuriated. He has been touched on a very sore spot. His pride, his ambition, his whole overwrought frustration, his inability to admit failure as possible, his feelings of betrayal, are all concentrated into a savage attack on his one true loving friend. Off he storms to his hut with the boy to collect the nets and be off fishing the shoal that will make their fortune.

The whole scene has been observed by inquisitive watching eyes and for the first time the Borough decides to take action. The men of the town, led by the village constable beating the drum, march off in an orderly fashion to Grimes's hut. In the meantime, Grimes has reached his hut and is madly irritated by the child's weakness and slowness. In the frantic efforts to get down from the hut on the cliffs to the shore the apprentice slips and falls to his death.

The audience knows that there has been a bad accident and we could witness that Grimes was not—directly—responsible for it. Again: accidental circumstances. The men of the Borough know nothing, although Balstrode senses that something is wrong and will later seek out Ellen Orford and hope to be of practical use. For the Borough it is a disappointment, an anticlimax and, as often at an anticlimax, some other distraction is necessary: in this case, the Act III dance at the Boar. A lot of drink is consumed and the ladies of the town (Auntie and her two nieces) entertain any gentleman who cares to drop in. Meanwhile, Mrs Sedley, the self-appointed crime investigator, by eavesdropping on Ellen Orford and Balstrode, discovers a clue which suggests that the apprentice and Grimes have disappeared. (Ellen has found the boy's jersey on the beach.) Mrs Sedley presumes, accurately, that the boy is dead and that Grimes is on the run.

The orderly investigation of Grimes and his hut which took place in Act II is now replaced by a full-scale manhunt, a dance of death. The cries of 'Peter Grimes!' echo round the town and countryside as the pursuers stampede through the marshes and into the woods with any weapons they can find. It is a lynching scene: the Borough is out for Peter's blood. There is only one road out of the town and they will have blocked that. Grimes knows that he is trapped and that no one will believe the boy's death was an accident. There is no hope for him. The hysterical man runs wildly through the woods and marshes in the foggy night until he is exhausted and demented. All we hear is the foghorn, Grimes's pursuers and Grimes himself. Even the night birds are silent. His frustrations, his guilt, his longings, his inadequacy, his resentment—all now find expression. He even has an imaginary quarrel with Ellen. There is no one to answer him, to give in to him or to stand up to him. Ellen comes in with Balstrode, who persuades him that the only way is to go out to sea and go down with his boat. The Borough has beaten him.

9

Chaos and Cosmos[1] in *Peter Grimes*

CHRISTOPHER PALMER

It is paradoxical that when Britten came back from the United States to settle in England he chose precisely the kind of small, staid community in which he, as an 'outsider' (both as conscientious objector and as homosexual) might expect to feel most uncomfortable and self-conscious; such people normally seek the anonymity of big cities. Yet for Britten the urge to return to base—to the type of small-time, small-town community he was born and grew up in—overrode all other considerations. The result was that in Suffolk his art found local occasion and expression; yet both *Peter Grimes* and *Albert Herring* bear signs that his attitude to the type of circumscribed milieu to which he had voluntarily shackled himself was, at least initially, somewhat ambivalent, compounded of fear and hate as well as love and understanding. For instance, in *Grimes*, it is the Borough's own music—the Moot Hall dance band in Act III—that provides the wherewithal for the most vicious climax of all: the great chorus of hate and hysteria upon which the Borough disperses to hunt Grimes is based on the vacuously merry little clarinet tune first heard earlier when Mrs Sedley is impressing upon Ned Keene that 'everything points to Peter Grimes. He is the murderer.' Why, if Britten was aware of the dangers of this narrowness of life-style, did he choose it?

To begin at the beginning, he was born in Lowestoft, Suffolk, where 'his parents' house faced the North Sea, and the winter days and nights were filled with the buffeting of the cold north-east wind

---

[1] The title of a tone-poem Britten composed as a prep-school boy, 'though I fear I was not sure what those terms really meant' (*The Composer and the Listener*, BBC radio broadcast talk, 7 November 1946).

and the sound of the huge waves breaking on the pebbles and the distant squawking and screeches of the herring-gulls swooping and circling above the fishing-boats'.[2] Britten himself recalled that 'my life as a child was coloured by the fierce storms that sometimes drove ships on to our coast and ate away whole stretches of the neighbouring cliffs'.[3] The Britten children spent their summer holidays at a farmhouse near Butley, about 30 miles south of Lowestoft, where there were walks across the marshes

> . . . with the wind blowing from the sea. As they went on their way, the tall reeds and rushes moved with them, leaning over with a swishing sound, while high overhead the curlews and redshanks called to each other. Beyond the marshes, the farthest walks led to Shingle Street, a small row of cottages on a pebbly beach, where there was nothing in sight except a vast expanse of sea and sky . . . on a still day, the light can have the delicate outlines of a Japanese picture. On a stormy day, even in summer, the grey sea batters itself against the shelf [of pebbles], dragging the shingle down with a scrunching, grating, slithering sound. To anyone born on the Suffolk coast, this sound has always meant home.[4]

One can easily imagine Britten's reaction when, in self-imposed exile in faraway California during the early years of the war, he encountered E. M. Forster's *Listener* article about Crabbe and

> . . . Aldeborough, on the coast of Suffolk. It is a bleak little place: not beautiful. It huddles round a flint-towered church and sprawls down to the North Sea—and what a wallop the sea makes as it pounds at the shingle! Nearby is a quay, at the side of an estuary, and here the scenery becomes melancholy and flat; expanses of mud, saltish commons, the marsh-birds crying. Crabbe heard that sound and saw that melancholy, and they got into his verse.[5]

They were to get into Britten's music too; no wonder that when he read this passage it brought on 'a feeling of nostalgia for Suffolk, where I had always lived', and a longing 'for the realities of that grim and exciting seacoast around Aldeburgh'.[6] Forster could be writing of Britten as much as of Crabbe when he maintains that 'Even when he

[2] *BR*, p.13.
[3] 'Introduction', *SW*, p.8.
[4] *BR*, pp.13–15.
[5] *Listener*, 29 May 1941.
[6] *SW*, p.7.

Christopher Palmer

[Crabbe] is writing of other things, there steals again and again into his verse the sea, the estuary, the flat Suffolk coast, and local meannesses, and an odour of brine and dirt—tempered occasionally with the scent of flowers.' As Eric Crozier (the producer of the first performance of *Grimes*) has said, 'He evoked the place, the people, the landscape, the movement of wind and clouds and waves and birds and grasses, with a knowledge as detailed as that of Crabbe himself.'[7] Most of *Grimes* was composed during 1944 in the Old Mill at Snape, then Britten's home, where the all-embracingness of East Suffolk sky and marsh made a round-the-clock impression on him.

The importance of the sea in Britten's life and work[8] calls for some discussion here. In a highly original theory of the creative unconscious, based on an analysis of poetic images of earth, air, fire and water, of space and of the world of dreams, the French philosopher Gaston Bachelard distinguished between two funda-mental types of creative imagination, the formal and the material.[9] The material imagination, he argues, does not seek out form in picturesque or changeable external objects but penetrates to the core of things where form is enveloped in substance; it dramatizes the world in depth, discovering in the innermost heart of substances symbols of the innermost secrets of life. Britten's imagination as revealed in *Grimes* was surely of this 'material' kind, which is further elucidated by a composer with whom he had much in common, Percy Grainger.[10] The latter, in describing his *English Dance* for large orchestra and organ as an 'impersonal presentation of cosmic energy', points out that in the scoring

> . . . the somewhat grey and certainly monotonous scheme of Bach's colouring (as instanced in the first chorus of the *Matthew Passion* and in the Brandenburg Concertos, etc.) has been preferred to the more heterogeneous, shorter-breathed, broken-up brush-work of modern orchestration habits. By putting the minimum of emphasis on tonal 'colour', by adopting an instrumentation of mainly 'neutral' tints, I feel it is possible to concentrate the whole appeal

[7] *OBB*, pp.25–6.
[8] See also below, p.255.
[9] *L'Eau et les rêves* (Paris, 1942) and other studies published at intervals during the 1940s. While Bachelard was concerned primarily with literature, his theories are applicable to other expressions of the imagination. See also E. Lockspeiser, *Debussy: His Life and Mind* (Cassell, 1965), vol.2, pp.278–81, and Robert Henderson, 'In Britannia's Kingdom', *Daily Telegraph*, 13 September 1980.
[10] See above, pp.72–8.

upon what appears to me to be the strongest of all musical elements—purely *intervallic* expression. In nature at its sublimest (the desert, the ocean, and the like) a certain monotony is generally present; the smaller elements of contrast do not intrude upon the all-pervading oneness of the larger impression.[11]

'Grey . . . monotonous . . . purely *intervallic* expression . . . nature at its sublimest'—this strongly suggests Britten, *Grimes* and the core of things where form is enveloped in substance.

But in this essential, indeed elemental, aspect, *Grimes* had a predecessor in Britten's output, a work intimately related not only to *Grimes* but also, more obviously, to that final consummatory celebration of life, death and the sea, *Death in Venice. Young Apollo*, for piano and string orchestra, a work whose brevity belies its significance, was composed in 1939 (but published only in 1982) and is based on the last lines of Keats's unfinished 'Hyperion': '—and lo! from all his limbs / Celestial . . .'. Apollo, called to be the new god of beauty by Mnemosyne, the goddess of memory, foresees his destiny, and in one final convulsion throws off his mortal form. He stands before us, the new sun god; and the music was actually inspired, according to Britten, by 'such sunshine as I've never seen before'.[12] The sea is nowhere explicitly referred to, but everywhere implied, first of all in Keats. As the older order of the gods comes to realize its end is nigh, Saturn appeals for counsel to the God of the Sea, Oceanus, who speaks of his successor, Apollo:

> *Have ye beheld the young God of the Seas,*
> *My dispossessor? Have ye seen his face?*
> *Have ye beheld his chariot, foam'd along*
> *By noble winged creatures he hath made?*
> *I saw him on the calmed waters scud,*
> *With such a glow of beauty in his eyes,*
> *That it enforc'd me to bid sad farewell*
> *To all my empire. . . .*

We find here a familiar mythological paradox in the association of fire (=sunlight) with water, two incompatibles; yet part and parcel of the solar myth is the idea of death and rebirth through the perilous night journey under the sea. The elemental-ness of water and the sea is

[11] Preface to the full score of *English Dances* (New York: G. Schirmer, 1924).
[12] Letter to Enid Slater, 29 July 1939, quoted in sleeve-notes to ASD 4177.

familiar as a recurrent theme in Wagner. Senta plunges into the sea at the end of *Der fliegende Holländer*; Tristan and Isolde drown (figuratively) in the waves of love and the sea in *Tristan und Isolde*; Brünnhilde goes through fire and water at the end of *Götterdämmerung* and we see the world end. The water is the River Rhine, symbol of the chaos before creation,[13] and the first self-generated gods are depicted as emerging from it in search of some foothold of solid matter. The E flat arpeggios of the opening of *Das Rheingold* are primordial murk. Wagner thought of this music as 'the beginning of the world', and science suggests that life came from the waters. Then *lux facta est*, light brought form to the void and gave birth to consciousness (the very 'consciousness' which Britten and Hardy so deplored). *Young Apollo* begins with a notably similar symbol of cosmic void: an empty and (because deprived of its third) indeterminate chord of A, prolonged through a total of thirty-two bars, static yet kept tense—a world in travail—through a heterophony of rhythmic figuration: in other words (as in *Das Rheingold*) the chord remains constant as a sonority but is continually changing shape before our ears. This is the elemental backdrop, the 'state of nature'. Then the thunderbolt, the irruption of primordial light: sparkling rills burst from the piano, rippling wave-like major scales, first at intervals then in rapid succession. The intermingled musical images of water and light are unmistakable, and evoke

> . . . the sight of this living figure, virginally pure and austere, with dripping locks, beautiful as a tender young god, emerging from the depths of sea and sky, outrunning the element—it conjured up mythologies, it was like a primeval legend, handed down from the beginning of time, of the birth of form, of the origin of the gods.

But this is from Mann's *Death in Venice*, set to music by Britten over thirty years after *Young Apollo*. Musically the link between them is no less strong—the 'Apollonian' key of A major, with the Lydian sharpened fourth, the key in Britten not merely of light but of *light-on-water*.[14] So it is no surprise to discover that A major, Lydian fourth and all, is the key of the sea music that begins and ends *Grimes* and of both what is perhaps the most poignant, painful and passionate

---

[13] See Robert Donington, *Wagner's 'Ring' and its Symbols* (Faber and Faber, 1963).

[14] It is perhaps significant that in Britten's only underwater sea-picture, Tennyson's 'Kraken' in the *Nocturne*, the basic tonality, B flat minor, is constantly under attack, as it were, from the resonant, ringing A naturals of the pizzicato strings—like rays of light trying to penetrate the murk and being refracted into nothingness.

moment in the opera—Peter's aria 'What harbour shelters peace'—
and its later corollary, 'And she will soon forget her schoolhouse
ways', Peter's vision of heaven. The choice of key tells all: Peter's
home, his harbour, his nemesis, is 'calm in deep water'. A curious
chronology. It is as if the sun god, Apollo, revealed himself to Britten
at the start of his career, then went into hiding for some thirty years
and finally emerged incarnate as Tadzio in *Death in Venice*. But the
journey back to the sun and the sea of the south had to be made via the
sea of the north—the North Sea of *Grimes*.[15]

The sea is arguably the major protagonist in *Grimes*. The first we
hear of it is in the 'Dawn' Interlude leading into the first scene; the
entry of the violins is like a breath of fresh sea-air after the dry,
clipped, claustrophobic sonority (chiefly woodwind and brass) of the
courtroom Prologue. The very first notes show us Britten's orchestral
imagination working simultaneously on two complementary levels,
the functional and the poetic: the flutes supply both necessary support
to the high violins and the veiled, grey colour of the sky over the
North Sea. Eric Walter White hears the wind in this first motif; since
it later moves into a kind of ostinato pattern which remains suspended
(as it were poised in mid-air) over the rest of the orchestra for long
periods, I would regard it also as a representation of sky with sea-birds
wheeling (see Ex. 1). In the violas, harp and clarinets the water laps in

---

[15] Towards the end of his life Britten gave a great deal of thought to the idea of a *Sea
Symphony* for chorus and orchestra, a kind of companion-piece to the *Spring
Symphony* (see Alan Blyth, ed., *Remembering Britten*, p.135).

'natural' thirds. For Britten the triad seems to symbolize a state of nature (as it did for Wagner: many of the *Ur*-motifs in the *Ring*—those of the Rhine, the Gold and the Sword—are rooted in it). At the same time the chordal brass motif—the scrunch of the shingle—acidly pits A major against the now firmly established A minor, thereby fixing the key and the colour of the working chorus with which Act I opens.[16] The hymn-like character of this chorus has often been remarked. It looks both forward to *Noye's Fludde* ('Eternal Father, strong to save' is sung at the height of the storm at sea) and, less obviously, back to the main theme of *Young Apollo*, which undergoes a chorale-like transformation (Ex.2).

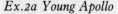

Ex.2a Young Apollo

Ex.2b Peter Grimes

A word at this point on the genealogy of Britten's sea music. A debt to *La Mer* is self-evident: the acciaccatura F dropping on to the E in Ex.1, and the heavy chordal motif in the brass, are probably both derived from the 'Dialogue du vent et de la mer'. Yet as far as we can establish the sea revealed herself in music to the young Britten in the form not of *La Mer* but of Bridge's *The Sea*, of which he arranged the slow movement, 'Moonlight', for piano and organ(!) for a recital he gave in St John's Church, Lowestoft, in July 1934. Bridge's *The Sea* belongs to 1910 and his relatively conservative early period, and is a

---

[16] Both the spacing and the scoring of these brass chords (especially when they underlie the chorus) are important *agents évocateurs*. The doubling of thirds in the lower octave always produces an opaque sonority; the trumpets, sparingly used, are confined to their lowest plain-chocolate-brown or black-grey register. This obtains even at the climactic recapitulatory moment of this music in the last act ('Then back to sea with strong majestic sweep') from which clarinets and oboes—instruments of brightness and light in their upper registers—are also excluded.

relatively conservative example of romantic Impressionism. Yet certain features might well have pulled the young Britten up short, particularly the unusually exposed, almost chamber-like, character of some of the instrumentation in the first two movements, 'Seascape' and 'Sea-foam': for example, in the former, the opening solo for tutti violas and, just before the coda, an extraordinary passage for solo woodwind, elusive of definition but very much an authentic proto-*Grimes* sea-sound (perhaps an altercation amid a passing flock of gulls?). But whereas Bridge's 'Moonlight' is a stylized romantic genre picture, lyrical, melodious and lusciously scored, Britten's is more essentially Impressionistic, more realistic: night and the sea-swell are mirrored in the gently heaving chords for low strings and woodwind, interspersed with flickers of moonlight (downward-glancing flute and harp triplets). In the big chordal surge forward to the climax and then back again (as in 'Dawn') the presence of the sea is evoked almost as a living creature, sensed but not seen. And while in his 'Storm' Bridge is content merely to paint tempestuous gestures, Britten in *his* 'Storm' Interlude actually re-enacts the elemental process. The link with Wagner is also apparent here: the turbulent, turbid, appoggiatura-laden chromaticism of a motif such as Ex.3 recalls the sea music of *Tristan*, and both works make the boiling sea symbolic of inner storm and stress—paranoia in the one work, love-passion in the other.

Ex.3

Britten achieves a sense of sea-pervasiveness by landing in the Interludes a catch of textures, tonalities and motifs which he then distributes selectively throughout each ensuing scene. An intriguing example, in Act I, is the Borough's outraged reaction when Ellen volunteers to look after the new apprentice on his way home from the workhouse: 'What? And be Grimes' messenger?'—but the sound of the chorus, as it intones the line to the major seventh chord of the 'Dawn' sea music, is curiously angelic, almost implying that Ellen as Grimes's 'Messenger' is heaven-sent, sea-delivered, joined with Grimes in elemental unity. This may of course be reading much more into the music than is actually present, but the composer's own recording gives this passage a haunting, poetic quality absent from the Colin Davis / Jon Vickers version. Less equivocal is the 'Sunday Morning' Interlude (with its 'natural' overlapping thirds in the horns suggesting the hum and jangle of bells in the air), which firmly implants a baleful deep-tolling B flat bell and chord in the midst of its glittering sunlit D major—an omen of 'Grimes is at his exercise'. Occasionally too Britten reverses the process: e.g. Peter's 'What harbour shelters peace' occurs in the scene immediately *preceding* the 'Storm' Interlude, in which it forms an enclave of (albeit beleagured) stillness. Less obvious is the prevalence of what we might interpret as sea rhythms, shapes and colours, for instance the churning *andante pesante* rhythm of the 'capstan' ensemble ('I'll give a hand'); the sweeping wave-like melodic rise and fall of Ellen's 'Let her among you without fault cast the first stone'; the slow, measured, bell-like woodwind ostinato slapping like water against the side of a boat all through her 'Child, you're not too young to know / Where roots of sorrow are', which culminates prophetically in 'After the storm will come a sleep / Like oceans deep'; the gentle sea-swell-like rhythm which underpins the trio for Auntie and the Nieces, and the close-knit quality of its vocal texture which suggests the sea bright-gleaming in the distance; Grimes's 'the whole sea's boiling', evoked with stunning simplicity by *tremolando ponticello* strings on a D major chord with added C sharp, and then as it were expanded colouristically as well as harmonically by flutes, clarinets and harp, *ppp leggiero*, in 'They listen to money'.

In a sense, however, the most eloquently oceanic music of all is that of the Passacaglia, in which no explicit reference is made to the mighty monster. Here form is of the essence. In attempting to measure in music the immeasurable (Nature) a composer ideally needs a structural discipline that allows a maximum of internal freedom within a framework which, like the earth itself, is fixed, unchanging, ever-recurring. The passacaglia form has precisely such a rock-steady regularity and inexorability. The link with *Noye's Fludde* here is strong: in the words of Wilfrid Mellers, 'although the Flood is in one sense a destructive force, it is in another sense (as it was in the biblical myth) *a necessary return to the unconscious waters* . . . though it generates the storm's excitement, the passacaglia theme [of the Flood episode] is also *God's law which is beyond change* . . .' (my italics).[17] We are reminded of Grainger's conviction that, in nature music, the 'smaller elements of contrast' should not intrude upon the 'all-pervading oneness of the larger impression'. The fugue is another structure which contains a basic element of predictability, of sameness, but which at the same time can take off in an infinity of different directions, attract an infinity of new musical entities; it has too a feeling of unimpedable growth, inevitability, cumulative intensity—hence Britten's use of it, magnificently and thrillingly, in the 'storm-cone' chorus (Act I scene I), in which he wanted to portray the inexorable on-coming, in-driving of a storm at sea. Fugal too is the texture of Peter's 'Great Bear and Pleiades' aria: and was the inscrutability, the steady slow-movingness, the immanence of the universe ever better portrayed in music?

In the sixth and final Interlude the thick, all-enveloping blanket of fog which rises up from the sea to befuddle and enshroud not only the Borough but Grimes's mind is well is contained in a dominant seventh chord sustained by muted horns *pianissimo* throughout; and through and around this impassively spectral sound weird contortions of earlier themes stumble in, dally and fidget, and disappear inconclusively. The sea in *Grimes* is basically a sinister power, always lying in wait for man and ready to devour him the moment he relaxes his vigilance. Peter, however, is not so much man as part of the elements. He belongs to the sea. Peter Garvie has searchingly examined this aspect of *Grimes*:

> Peter is natural man, responsive to both the metamorphoses and the unalterable in nature. The tide is his symbol and makes his epitaph; never the same, but in its larger rhythm never to be altered. . . .[18] [His personality defines itself] only in relation to

17 See below, pp.154 and 158–9.
18 Adam Woolfitt's photograph (plate 38) perfectly expresses this oneness of Grimes with the elements.

nature. . . . There is something of the child in him too, especially in his easy drift between fantasy and reality. . . . He is as alone with his unconscious as he is with the sea.[19]

The 'deep water' *is* his own unconscious and cannot be avoided. The first time we see Peter in the main body of the opera he comes out of the sea ('Hi! Give us a hand!') and at the end the sea takes him as one of her own. Like Tennyson's King Arthur 'From the great deep to the great deep he goes'. So the horn chord of the last Interlude sounds like a siren song calling Peter back literally into his element. Of the Rhinemaidens' destructive crying and calling in *Das Rheingold* Donington remarks:

> It is the old enchantment, the familiar pull backwards into irresponsible bliss, the *perennial unconscious fantasy of return to the mother's embrace*. . . . All the joy and all the poetry in our adult lives are flooded through with emotions the undertow of which derives from what we felt as infants when mother was herself the source of life. . . . What we stand to gain by going repeatedly back to this source is immeasurable, but only if we have sufficiently internalized and confronted it to bathe in it without drowning[20] (my italics).

The dangers, according to Donington, are that one may (a) project the mother-image on to other people and (b) abandon oneself to nostalgia for infanthood past recall. 'But the spontaneity of the infant and the unrivalled force and directness of its emotions are assets the more of which we can carry forward into adult life the more richly we shall live—provided it really is adult life.' This says as much about Britten as about Grimes, perhaps more: about his need to return to Aldeburgh (= the sea = Mother), about his preoccupation with childhood, and about the strengths and weaknesses of the style he evolved to reproduce 'the spontaneity of the infant and the unrivalled force and directness of its emotions'. It also reveals a dimension of affinity between Grimes and Britten of which the latter was almost certainly unaware, since it lies so deep beneath the surface. Grimes, at the start of Britten's operatic career, comes from the sea and returns to it; Tadzio, at its end, emerges Apollo-like from the waves and is perceived at the last by the dying Aschenbach to be walking out to the sea, to nothingness, to Plato's 'vast sea of beauty'; Britten himself

[19] 'Plausible Darkness: *Peter Grimes* after a Quarter of a Century', *Tempo*, No.100 (1972), p.13.
[20] *Wagner's Ring and its Symbols*, pp.246–7.

was born by the sea and died by it. So calling the muted horn chord a 'siren song' is not simply a poetic flight of fancy, especially since the chord involved is a dominant chord (a seventh as opposed to the Rhinemaidens' ninth); and dominant chords in these contexts always possess a beguiling, insidious sweetness simply because they lead somewhere (they *must* resolve), point forward, beckon (like sirens), and sound euphonious (which is why the Impressionists in music—Wagner, Debussy, Britten—were so fond of them). The distant voices of the Borough in pursuit eventually lose all identity; Peter (and the audience) hear them as nature voices merging with and enveloping the foghorn's semitones (another siren song of the elements), lulling him to sleep with a gentle but inexorable sea rhythm, *diminuendo al niente*. Then Balstrode dispatches him in his boat to all eternity, and the reprise of the Act I sea-work song, in a great *fortissimo* descending tidal-wave-like surge, follows him down, down, down to death and dissolution ('Then back to sea with strong majestic sweep / It rolls yet terrible and deep'). But being submerged and swept away by a torrent of water is an image also of rebirth; if Peter is to be redeemed he has to return, like Noah and his family, and ultimately like Aschenbach, to the unconscious waters, whence— well, who knows? Man is nothing, nature alone endures; perhaps, in the last analysis, the truest lesson *Grimes* has to teach us is that of the vanity of all human endeavour. *Grimes* is a quintessentially Hardyesque work. As Peter Garvie puts it, 'The passing bell is tugged by human hands to signify the end of human time for each of us; but the bell-buoy sounds for ever to the movement of the tides.'[21]

21 'Plausible Darkness', p.9.

10

The Rape of Lucretia

CHRISTOPHER HEADINGTON

It is not my task here to debate whether or not *The Rape of Lucretia* is a 'great' opera, whatever the meaning of that well-worn adjective; but that it is not a 'grand' opera is beyond dispute. It neither has nor needs the spectacle, sweeping crowd scenes and symphonic utterance of *Peter Grimes*. (It is twenty minutes shorter too, but that is less important.) Of course, to ascribe smallness to *Lucretia* is provocative; if I do so it is to call attention to the opera's stature and originality.

It would be disingenuous to ignore Peter Pears's remark to me in 1979 that 'Whether we would have moved away from big-scale opera had Joan [Cross] stayed at Sadler's Wells is a question possibly worth debating.' Yet practical and artistic reasons often intertwine, and fruitfully: would Handel have written *Messiah* had the public not been tiring of his operas, or Stravinsky composed *The Soldier's Tale* if the First World War had not made lavish ballet productions economically difficult? That Britten and Pears left Sadler's Wells because of its change of policy and were then left without a theatre (as it were) of operations is significant, but not the whole story. The composer himself once exclaimed rather irritably that 'some people seem to want another *Grimes*. . . . I have different challenges before me and I respond to them.' After finishing *Grimes* he had thought of writing a comedy in collaboration with Ronald Duncan, who had helped him to assemble the final text of the mad scene in the Crabbe opera; but, according to Duncan, he was also hankering after the greater musical clarity of 'a Mozartian ensemble . . . and looked forward to tackling the problems of obtaining a full musical effect with fewer instruments'.[1] The whole scenario of *The Rape of Lucretia*

---

[1] For this and other relevant information about *Lucretia*, I am indebted to Duncan's *Working with Britten*.

was sketched out together with its musical architecture, and the score of Act I actually written, before John Christie offered to produce the opera at Glyndebourne. In other words, *Lucretia* was not born of necessity; indeed Duncan assures us that Britten was attracted to the idea of chamber opera even before the production of *Peter Grimes*.

But in any case it is not only the deliberately restricted vocal and instrumental forces that give *Lucretia* its 'chamber' quality: the work has an enclosed feeling. I am not forgetting Tarquinius' ride to Rome or the bright morning of Act II scene 2, but in neither are we altogether free of oppression—in the one we are driven on with the Prince and his 'blood furious . . . desire impetuous', while in the other we are warned by Bianca of a day that is to be 'unbearably hot . . . by evening it will thunder'. Another adjective that one might apply to *The Rape of Lucretia* is 'intimate'. (In view of its subject-matter that may seem too like the language of the popular Sunday newspapers, yet Britten himself was not above occasional light-heartedness concerning this highly serious work, quoting Lucretia's motif in *Albert Herring* when Superintendent Budd mentions 'rape'.) This inward-turned quality in *Lucretia* might make us, as helpless spectators of the human tragedy, feel a certain claustrophobia, did we not have the Male and Female Chorus to 'stand between' us and the drama with their Christian commentary.

And, quite naturally, this quality belongs to the music as well as to the story and its treatment as a libretto. Over thirty years ago, in the Britten Symposium, Donald Mitchell and Hans Keller identified the 'parent cell' of the opera, the harp figure contained within a minor third that evokes the sound of crickets in Act I scene 1. That minor-third interval seems to tighten the atmosphere, perhaps because of what Deryck Cooke called the 'tonal tensions' of the diatonic system.[2] According to Cooke, western composers since the time of the *Dies irae* have 'expressed the "wrongness" of grief by means of the minor third', and among other examples he offers a Britten passage, from *Peter Grimes*, with the protagonist singing a phrase that closely foreshadows the so-called 'Lucretia' motif in the later opera (Ex.1). But these interlocking minor thirds are in any case characteristic of Britten: compare the cry of 'Silly fellow!' in *Rejoice in the Lamb* and Miles's '*Malo, Malo*' in *The Turn of the Screw*. (And at the opening of *Death in Venice*, Aschenbach's interlocking *major*

[2] *The Language of Music* (Oxford University Press, 1959), p.57.

Ex.1a *Peter Grimes*

Un-til the Bor-ough hate ——— pois-ons your mind.

Ex.1b *The Rape of Lucretia*

Lu - cre - - tia!

seconds seem to represent a further tightening, almost to paralysis, of the inner tension so integral to Britten's art.)

The minor-third interval is heard throughout *The Rape of Lucretia*, at such key points as the first mention of the Tarquins, the 'noise of crickets' harp figure, the phrase with which the Male Chorus introduces the generals in their camp and the opening of the ride to Rome. Reference to these passages reveals the considerable emotional range the composer draws from the interval. Even in the wholly different ambience of Lucretia's quiet, ordered home it has its place: consider the opening harp solo of Act I scene 2, and the beautiful alto flute melody of the lullaby that revolves around the note E within the interval D–F in a C major context. Thus when Tarquinius reaches the bedside and contemplates the sleeping Lucretia, how natural it *is* that he should use it to caress the thought of the candlelight that knows her nakedness (Ex.2). As we approach the rape itself, the minor third becomes obsessive, hypnotic.[3] The Prince sings 'To wake Lucretia with a kiss' to Ex.2, and as he takes her in his arms the Female Chorus, *pianissimo*, tells us in the same music that, dreaming of her husband Collatinus, she 'desiring him draws down Tarquinius'. Her awakening brings all the expected shock, a crack of the orchestral whip and a change to *fortissimo* and *allegro agitato*. Yet how strangely right it is that Britten stays exactly with this same minor third, C sharp–E, for their first exchanges.

Ex.2

How luck-y is this lit-tle light,

The shock is thus not wholly a surprise. In this, libretto and music are at one. In André Obey's play, the immediate source, Lucretia is

---

[3] Can the dramatic resemblance to Act IV of *Otello* be coincidental? There too, we have the minor third of Desdemona's 'salce, salce'.

The Rape of Lucretia

given a clear motive for her comparatively easy surrender, in that Tarquinius threatens to kill her and one of her slaves and testify that he caught them in the act of intercourse (Obey here followed his classical sources). Duncan and Britten removed this element of the story. Just as in the earlier opera Crabbe's villainous Grimes had been made more complex and sympathetic (at Britten's instance), so Lucretia is no mere symbol of cool chastity but every inch a woman. We learn that she has been attracted to Tarquinius: 'In the forest of my dreams / You have always been the Tiger.' Morally she is wholly unwilling to yield, but we cannot tell whether he is mistaken when he declares that

> *The linnet in your eyes*
> *Lifts with desire,*
> *And the cherries of your lips*
> *Are wet with wanting.*

At any rate, it is because of her 'shame' that Lucretia ordains her own death, calling herself a 'Roman harlot'. Collatinus spells out his own love and understanding—'If spirit's not given, there is no need of shame'—but Lucretia seems to admit the stain of sin in her

> *Even great love's too frail*
> *To bear the weight of shadows. . . .*
> *See, how my wanton blood*
> *Washes my shame away!*

So much for the libretto's evidence of Lucretia's involvement—the word 'corruptibility' suggests itself, and though this is probably too strong, it links the characterization of Lucretia to one of the major themes in Britten's creative world. What of the music? Tarquinius and Lucretia share the minor third, but so do other characters and atmospheres of the opera; what seems more significant is that *interlocking* minor thirds bring the two into a curiously close relationship. Compare Lucretia's motif (Ex.1b) with Tarquinius' characteristic falling figure, the four notes with which he identifies himself (Ex.3). This is the figure which dominates the orchestral accompaniment to the 'goodnight' sequence in Lucretia's house at the

I am the Prince of Rome!_

end of Act I, and it is also to this music that she makes her desperate plea to Tarquinius' better nature before he rapes her, 'Is this the Prince of Rome?'

Other characters also are given identity by the intervals they use. Lucretia's husband is a less interesting (if more virtuous) person than Tarquinius—or even perhaps than Junius, whose Iago-like role is of considerable dramatic strength: without him Tarquinius would not have undertaken his escapade. If we examine Collatinus' music we find innocence and directness, symbolized intervallically by the perfect fourths that characterize his gentle reproach to Junius in Act I and his crucial though vain acceptance of his wife near the end. How strange, and at the same time how natural, that his music is a 'perfected' upward version of Tarquinius' Ex.3, encapsulated with complete simplicity in Lucretia's first utterance of his name (Ex.4).

Ex.4

But in terms of motive structure the minor thirds and perfect fourths are only part of the story. We also have, memorably, the yearning upward leaps of sevenths and ninths in the spinning scene as Lucretia thinks of her absent husband, Bianca of her lost youth and young Lucia of love and lovers. And then there are the sixths that emerge so naturally as inversions of the predominant third. Consider the lyrical moment for Tarquinius as he stands at the head of Lucretia's bed before awakening her, 'Within this frail crucible of light'; and there are two other important examples, themselves related in contour, in what has been called the framing hymn for Male and Female Chorus and the theme of the passacaglia 'finale of epitaphs' after Lucretia's death. I have reserved, too, until this stage any mention of the important recurring theme which appears twice in each act and which Norman Del Mar goes so far as to call the 'motto melody' of *The Rape of Lucretia*. Now, however, it will be clear how this too is a natural flowering from the parent cell of the minor third (Ex.5). It is Lucretia who gives us the final statement of this theme ('Oh, my love, our love was too rare'); then she stabs herself and dies in a series of seven falling thirds and one final 'purified' fourth. In the nearest thing to a big chorus that chamber opera permits, the passacaglia epitaph by the remaining characters comments bitterly on

The Rape of Lucretia

Ex.5

the brevity of beauty, with a falling-third motif, finally E–C sharp, to the words 'It is all! It is all!' But the Male and Female Chorus now frame the work from their Christian point of view and reaffirm mankind's hope.[4] The framing hymn ('Whilst we as two observers stand') now appears with what seems the inevitability of mastery. Nevertheless the thirds remain inexorably in the *ppp* woodwind exchanges and string tremolandi until the *quasi niente* ending of the opera.

In opera there are other tensions besides tonal and melodic ones that the composer quite naturally employs as part of his expressive language:[5] those of key, rhythm and vocal-instrumental texture. Of course all these interrelate: in the opening of the opera, for example, not only the harsh tutti scoring but also the *crescendo*—from *fortissimo*; the apparent *accelerando*; the repetition of a single chord, itself a strange dissonance of C, D flat and E flat (that minor third *ab initio*!); and finally perhaps the un-Brittenish C minor, suggesting Beethoven's 'Roman' mood in the *Coriolan* overture; all these together and indissolubly create the oppressed, explosive mood of a Rome governed 'by force and . . . sheer terror'. Donald Mitchell has commented to me on the 'bleached' sound of *The Rape of Lucretia*. The word suggests a pallor as of exposed bones, and certainly the large stretches of piano-accompanied recitative give something of that quality to the music, not only in the substantial sections at the beginning of each act, but also for example in the rapid and increasingly quarrelsome exchanges between the generals in their tent

---

[4] Duncan's account of the shaping and incorporation of the Christian element in the libretto (*WB*, pp.74–7) is of interest.

[5] 'Naturally', simply because that is the way a composer thinks. I am not sure whether Norman Del Mar is right to talk of 'exceedingly skilful . . . elaborate motivic integration' in this work. An artistic masterpiece does not arise from cleverness: as Britten himself said (of Schubert), the mystery remains (*On Receiving the First Aspen Award*, p.18). (See also Britten's disarming comment on the publication of the Britten Symposium quoted above, p.50 [C.P.].)

125

in Act I. Though Britten was to use recitative in later operas, it is not until *Death in Venice* that we again meet such a secco style, so rich in its austerity. (These two operas also have an Italian setting in common, and something more: in both the protagonist may only dream—literally—of a forbidden love.)

Britten's characteristic skill in instantly establishing a sound-world is evident too in the quiet commentary of the Male Chorus setting the heavy evening scene outside the generals' tent. And how effective is the instrumental clothing for the joyless drinking scene itself: horn (*naturale* or *cuivré*) and bass drum (ordinary or hard stick) with swirling unison woodwind are all Britten needs for the first two of the three stanzas. Felicities of this kind abound in the opera. But in one quite substantial passage even Britten's acute judgement seem to have failed him: the final exchange between Junius and Tarquinius beginning at Figure 34 of Act I with the words 'What makes the Nubian / Disturb his heavy mountain?' For Duncan's dense imagery the composer chose an *allegro agitato* tempo with off-beat continuous quavers for a string quartet accompaniment; the language is chromatic too, while the two singers have phrases of up to thirteen bars with no space to draw breath and in the final (third) stanza have to sing in canon. The effect is fussy and problems of ensemble hard to surmount—witness even the composer's own recording. But the passage is worth examining: both technically and artistically, Britten's comparative failures remain of interest. A more fruitful point is adumbrated by the mention of stanzaic form. At the time of *Peter Grimes* the composer had written of his interest in 'the general architectural and formal problems of opera' and his preference for 'the classical practice of separate numbers' rather than a Wagnerian continuous flow.[6] Ronald Duncan has described how, having made a synopsis of each *Lucretia* scene, Britten and he 'proceeded to break this up into its appropriate musical forms: recitative, accompanied recitative, arias, and ensembles'. Strong architecture seems to me to be one of the finest features of the opera. In a way Britten, like his admired late Verdi, had the best of the two post-Wagnerian operatic worlds. *Lucretia* is doubly buttressed: the separate-numbers technique gives it articulation, while the use of motivic methods unifies all. The young but very experienced Britten of 1946 succeeded admirably in his aim (in *Lucretia*'s last words) 'to harness song to human tragedy'.

[6] 'Introduction', *SW*, p.8. (Britten adhered to this preference even when preparing the structure of his television opera, *Owen Wingrave*: see above, pp.89–90 [C.P.].)

11
Albert Herring [1]

ERWIN STEIN

This piece, on an aspect of Albert Herring *which has received little critical attention, is wholly representative of the music-critical style of a man who from the first was one of the composer's staunchest supporters. Erwin Stein was a distinguished Schoenberg pupil who became an authority on his master's music. His profound knowledge of composers and composing lends what he writes a very special touch of distinction.*

[C.P.]

Britten's success as an opera composer comes primarily from the excitement of his dramatic expression, but this would not come off effectively unless the form were arranged for every detail to stand out with its right emphasis. I can see a distinct development in the composer's handling of formal problems from *Peter Grimes* to *The Rape of Lucretia* and *Albert Herring*; in particular, transitions and recitatives have become more integrated, though naturally the structure of the comic opera remains light and loose. There are fewer opportunities for slow movements and lyrical expansion than in musical drama. To find sufficient contrast and variety within the narrower scope needs much creative imagination; and to shape loosely built parts as components of an integrated whole, still more resourcefulness. I really wonder why people in judging an opera speak so much about the libretto—which anyhow cannot be separated from the music—and so little about the musical form. To me, here is the point which marks the distinction of a composer. He would be none who had no imagination, yet musical creation is not inventing a nice tune, but shaping a piece of music. A good tune, after all, must be well

---

[1] Edited from *Tempo*, No.5 (Autumn 1947), pp.4–8.

shaped; on the other hand, much of the best music has been built out of what one would have thought was poor material.

Britten does not write his opera acts as large quasi-symphonic forms, as many composers since Wagner have done; he returns firmly to the old distinction between recitative and set piece and integrates into a unity clear-cut sections, however contrasting in form and character. Recitatives play a prominent part in *Albert Herring*. By re-establishing the secco on the lowest level of dramatic expression, Britten has a wide scope for shaping the comedy. The loose form easily follows the vivid action and is adaptable to any nicety of the dialogue. The pace of the parlando may quicken or slow down, it may turn gradually or suddenly into song; the accompaniment may consist of supporting chords only, may gain more definite shape, or may cease altogether. By alteration with set pieces the form remains clear cut.

There are also instances where both forms penetrate each other or are combined. A happy example of this kind occurs in the first scene when candidates for a May Queen are suggested. Britten inscribes the music 'recitative (*alla ballata*)', but it grows into a definite if loosely knit form. Between varied repetitions of the ballad verse, with the traditional accompaniment in the piano, there are contrasting phrases of voice and orchestra as each of the suggestions is rejected in turn. The music develops while the proposals become shorter, the refusals longer, and when the piece concludes with the ballad, sung as a quartet in the minor key, something like a rondo has taken shape. The setting of the quartet is peculiar: the voices sing in canon but out of time, while the piano continues the steady ballad accompaniment. Recitative ensembles of another kind occur in Act II when the guests at the banquet all sing together, each his own phrase and everyone again out of time. An exhilarating musical description of a talking dinner party is the result. Indeed, the ancient tree of recitative yields uncommon fruits to Benjamin Britten.

The first scene falls under three headings: The Assembly, The Defeat of the Proposed Candidates and Albert's Election. Each of the three parts is in three sections, the first comprising the housekeeper's bustling introduction and frustrated aria, the recitative of the Committee of Four, and Lady Billows's entry. The recitative stands between two set pieces; it is formally a secco recitative—though the expression 'dry' can hardly be applied to dear Miss Wordsworth's florid passages. The pace becomes gradually more dramatic until the four characters begin talking simultaneously. Her Ladyship's entry and reception are kept very formal by the stiff rhythms of three musical shapes: a stilted melody, chordal sequences and finally a developed fugato.

When the committee sits down to work, there are two arias from Lady Billows, one before and one after the above-mentioned recitative-rondo. The first aria, in which the election of a May Queen is proposed, has a fairly loose form and the voice is largely kept declaiming, while the following recitative, in which none of the girls is found sufficiently virtuous, develops into a set piece of almost lyric character. Here, and in other places, the distinctive features of aria and recitative have partly been assimilated or reversed for the sake of dramatic expression; where necessary there may be reciting in an aria, or singing in a recitative. Yet when Lady Billows expresses her fury about the failure of the meeting, she does it in a formal aria, a typical set piece. It ends on a low note and there is general depression.

The police superintendent reopens the discussion by proposing the election of Albert as May King in an emphatic recitative with subsequent song, while the others continue in the secco way. A cello solo introduces Lady Billows's desperate 'I am a very disappointed woman'. At this dramatic moment her one phrase has almost the weight of an entire aria, but formally it is only a transition to the Vicar's cavatina on virtue. The following brilliant ensemble finale concludes the scene in the initial key of C.

An orchestral interlude, 'The Village Children', anticipates the music of the next scene and when the curtain rises on Albert's shop the children are singing and playing outside. This scene is very loosely constructed, but consistency is reflected on it by the music of the preceding interlude. Once the children stop singing, even recitative is too articulate for their exclamations, and the orchestra must carry the burden of expressing their sensations, a burden which becomes fairly heavy when Sid catches the boy pinching apples. The scene is the counterpart to that which has introduced the notables in the previous scene; here the simple folk are brought in, the children, Sid and Nancy, and of course Albert. Starting with Albert's entry the music develops gradually from secco recitative to Sid's merry aria, describing the joys of life unknown to his friend. When Nancy comes into the shop her recitative with Sid is on a 'sentimental' level, sung rather than recited, and the little love duet which follows, and in which Albert timidly joins, forms a lyric climax.

Albert, left alone, feels frustrated and wants to escape. His solo scene is shaped as an aria of three varied verses and concludes with a broad melody of great intensity; we learn here that he is not the simpleton he appears to be. Actually the aria is once interrupted by a customer, but that is the sort of thing that happens to Albert.

A finale starts when Florence enters to herald the May Day committee. It is in three sections, the first a loosely shaped trio of Mum, Florence and Albert; the second a formal ensemble set piece when the committee arrives and Lady Billows pompously addresses Albert (her hymnic stanzas alternate with hurried conversation in semiquaver rhythm—another kind of recitative); and finally we have the duet of Mum and Albert in which he resents his coronation as May King—it is a stretto and at the climax the children join in with their song.

The May Day fanfare opens the short prelude to Act II. There are three set pieces, linked by secco recitatives, before the feast begins: Flo's song chiding the tardy Sid; Sid's aria describing the church celebrations; and Miss Wordsworth's delightful rondo with the children, as they rehearse their Festive Song. Another secco recitative, while Sid pours rum in Albert's lemonade, precedes the elaborate finale, which is built from a great variety of set pieces and recitatives. The entry of the festive party is in the form of a loosely shaped introduction: each person brings with him a few bars of his own music, linked by the May Day fanfare of the bells. The Festive Song of the children is the first set piece of any length; then the form becomes loose again when they sing their ditties between the short recitative ensembles of the guests.

Now the finale begins in earnest, with speeches by Lady Billows, the Mayor, Miss Wordsworth and the Superintendent; they are set pieces bound together into a larger form by the Vicar's recitatives, which recur like variations of a ritornello. Actually the speeches are, as the word implies, recitatives elevated to arias. It well reflects Lady Billows's pomposity that anything she says has the emphasis of an aria, and the more commonplace her utterances, the more florid her singing becomes. Sandwiched between the stilted Mayor and the effusive Superintendent, Miss Wordsworth is the poet; everyone has music appropriate to his banalities, including the smooth Vicar. Amazing how their platitudes are vested in a musical form which is exhilarating as well as accomplished! When it is Albert's turn to speak we realize from the expressiveness of the short orchestral phrases how embarrassed he feels before he can utter his brief 'Thank you very much'. In this society his aria can hardly be longer. A short ensemble leads to the last set piece of the finale, the Vicar's hymn, repeated by the guests and culminating in three cheers for Her Ladyship. Albert drinks the rum. The recitative ensemble during Albert's hiccups is a transition to the fugue of the interlude. Its theme derives from the Vicar's hymn, which in turn elaborates the May Day fanfare; apparently the high spirits of the fugue picture the banquet. The interlude gradually slows down and changes to a nocturnal duo of bass flute and bass clarinet, and this continues when the curtain rises on the empty shop.

It is the evening after the feast. Albert enters gaily and recapitulates the events of the day. A large scena follows in which his mind and feelings are fully revealed. During this musical monologue recitatives, arioso passages and developed arias, loose forms and set pieces alternate as his thoughts wander or concentrate, and an impressive aria arises when he comes to ponder on Nancy, on Sid's daring, and on his own shyness. In the middle of the scena a secco recitative and spirited love duet of Sid and Nancy occurs. Albert observes them through the window, he hears his name mentioned and listens to their sympathy and pity. His temper is roused and now his mind is fixed in one direction: to escape from his shameful position. There is one great aria ending with his final decision and departure. The music of the notturno begins again as Mum enters wearily and goes to bed, thinking Albert fast asleep.

Unusual formal devices are employed in the last act. An ostinato side-drum rhythm, symbolizing the restless search for the vanished Albert, goes through the music until at his *fortissimo* climax the Mayor, the Superintendent and Sid solemnly carry in Albert's coronation wreath, making everyone believe that Albert is dead. The rhythm is elaborated in the *prestissimo* prelude (in ternary form), when it gains melodic shape and passes in canons and figurations through all the instruments. When the curtain rises Nancy is alone in the shop and an expressive clarinet solo reflects her self-reproach: the rum they gave Albert caused all the trouble. With frequent interruptions by the ostinato Nancy sings three lovely verses in duet with the clarinet. Sid enters and they have a quarrel duet. The Superintendent joins them with an accompanied recitative in which the side-drum rhythm is again prominent. Mum's aria of lament leads to a beautiful quartet. But now Lady Billows appears raging with fury (recitative), and her duet with Florence takes up the music of the manhunt and leads to its

Erwin Stein

climax. All these set pieces are linked and often rudely interrupted by the ostinato rhythm, and during the recitatives it often remains as background.

The following threnody is the centre-piece of the act. One verse is repeated by the chorus of the ensemble while each singer emerges in turn to sing his own stanza: at first everyone is accompanied by the chorus, but later all sing their individual verses in ensemble. At the climax they join in unison lament.

But the bell rings and Albert appears, prompting the most striking anticlimax which Britten has ever written. Dumbfounded only for a moment, all round on him to the music of the manhunt, and an insistent questioning follows in secco recitative. Albert's narration of his nocturnal experiences is a large aria in which he mocks at the hypocrites and settles his account with his mother, but the music changes to a pleasant string melody, descriptive perhaps of Albert's newly gained self-assertion. The finale is short and loose, the children come in and the friends join in a cheerful final song, sending the unwanted May Day laurel wreath skimming over the heads of the audience.

I have given in this present survey a few examples of how stage action and musical form in *Albert Herring* are interlocked. Music in opera, and particularly in comic opera, does not exist entirely in its own right. The interest of a comedy rests primarily in the action, but the music enhances the enjoyment by re-creating the events of the stage in a new medium. The musical form shapes the scene, directs the tempo of the action and sets any detail into new relief. It is one of the merits of the libretto of *Albert Herring* that its variety and gaiety challenged the composer to write music of very light and loose structure, but highly organized form.

12

Salvation at Sea:
Billy Budd[1]

PHILIP BRETT

The association of Benjamin Britten and E. M. Forster is one of the more interesting in the annals of opera. Less startling than the contemporaneous collaboration of Stravinsky and W. H. Auden (over *The Rake's Progress*, also completed in 1951), which by comparison was like two stars from different galaxies passing in unusual orbit, it seems to have been an almost predictable match between a literary-minded composer and a musical novelist who shared country, class and, to a large extent, beliefs. It also contained, for Britten at least, an element of the fateful. The two had met in 1936 under the auspices of Auden (then a major influence on Britten) and Christopher Isherwood (a close friend of Forster) during the staging of a play of theirs for which Britten had written the incidental music. Forster, then nearing 60, was the 'anti-heroic hero' (to use Isherwood's phrase) of this group of young liberal artists. He had given up writing novels after *A Passage to India* had appeared in 1924, but his creative energy was undiminished, and the tough words on personal liberty and humanitarian principle that issued in disconcerting ways from his superficially mild, understated demeanour shone as a guiding light to many in those days of gathering darkness. 'I hate the idea of causes, and if I had to choose between betraying my country and betraying my friend, I hope I should have the guts to betray my country':[2] this is the most famous sentence from Forster's essay on his personal philosophy which, whatever its limitations, successfully maintained the primacy of personal relationships at a

---

[1] Revised version of an article first published in *San Francisco Opera Magazine*, 1978.
[2] 'What I Believe', *Two Cheers for Democracy* (Edward Arnold, 1951), p.78.

time when most intellectuals were succumbing to the siren songs of one ideology or another.

The independence Forster so cleverly maintained sprang not only from his Victorian liberal heritage but also from a profound distrust of authority that is common among members of a minority, but rarely in so articulate a form. Forster's acceptance of his homosexual nature, although on the one hand it caused him to stop writing fiction, had on the other strengthened his resolve and ability to be true to himself and his feelings. When Auden and Isherwood emigrated to the United States in 1939, they discovered similarly (as Isherwood reports)[3] that their support for the various left-wing causes they had espoused simply could not take precedence over their personal destinies as men and writers. Britten and Pears soon followed Auden and Isherwood to the United States, probably with similar ideas in their heads. But Britten could not settle down, and Forster played an important part in the next stage of his life. By chance the composer came across an article by the novelist on the minor Suffolk poet George Crabbe beginning with the words 'To talk about Crabbe is to talk about England'.[4] And this clinched Britten's decision not only to return to England, but to take up residence in his native county in Crabbe's own town, Aldeburgh. The article also sent him to Crabbe's major poem, *The Borough*, where in the character of Peter Grimes he found the subject of his first and still most widely known opera.

The association then proceeded with overtures and pleasantries. Britten's third opera, *Albert Herring*, was dedicated to Forster—quite appropriately, for it contains whiffs of Forsterian social comedy and a good dose of the message of the early novels. The famous novelist was also invited to the First Aldeburgh Festival in 1948 to lecture on Crabbe, and in so doing he remarked, 'It amuses me to think what an opera on Peter Grimes would have been like if I had written it.'[5] The hint was pondered, and when in the same year Britten was commissioned to write an opera for the projected Festival of Britain he suggested they should collaborate. Forster was excited but hesitant because he lacked stage experience. Eric Crozier, the librettist of *Albert Herring*, was called in to help, and at this point Forster accepted. A subject had still to be found, however, and it is reported that the composer and novelist almost simultaneously hit upon

---

[3] *Christopher and his Kind* (New York: Farrar, Straus & Giroux, Inc., 1976), pp.317ff.
[4] In the *Listener*, 29 May 1941.
[5] 'George Crabbe and Peter Grimes', *Two Cheers for Democracy*, p.190.

Salvation at Sea: Billy Budd

Herman Melville's *Billy Budd* as the perfect choice.[6] It was certainly an unusual one, but when Crozier raised objections—for instance to the idea of an all-male opera—they are said to have been too impatient to listen; and it is safe to conclude that the subject answered a need for both of them.

Forster had written sympathetically about Melville (and perceptively about *Billy Budd* in particular) in his *Aspects of the Novel*. But the story offered him more than purely critical delight. He often gave sex as his reason for retiring from fiction: 'weariness of the only subject that I both can and may treat—the love of men for women & vice versa', he wrote in his diary as early as 1911.[7] But in *Billy Budd* there was the opportunity to write about profound relationships between men: symbolically to evoke the power of homosexual love without being in any way sexually explicit. His first task, as he wrote to William Plomer, was to 'rescue Vere from Melville', that is to say to correct Melville's excessive respect for authority, education and aristocracy as embodied in the Captain. This explains why Vere refuses in the opera to launch into the tirade that Melville causes him to deliver to his junior officers at the drumhead court. 'How odiously Vere comes out in the trial scene!' Forster exclaimed in a little-known explanatory document.[8] The resulting vacuum, both in the plot and in Vere's character, is filled by the most daring of all the Forsterian

[6] This and much other information is taken from P. N. Furbank's excellent biography of the novelist: *E. M. Forster: A Life* (Secker & Warburg, 1977, 1978), to which I am deeply indebted. See vol.2, pp.283–6, for the account of his work on the opera. Britten's own account, possibly a little idealized, appears in 'Some Notes on Forster and Music', *Aspects of E. M. Forster*, ed. Oliver Stallybrass (Edward Arnold, 1969), pp.85–6.

[7] Furbank, *Forster*, vol.1, p.199.

[8] A 'Letter to America', written in September 1951 for the *Griffin*, the still-extant monthly organ of the Reader's Subscription Service in the United States. This letter, kindly brought to my attention by Mr Furbank after my essay was written, appears in certain ways to contradict what comes through in the opera. Perhaps, with his lack of operatic experience, Forster did not clearly perceive how firmly Britten was steering the ship, and in what direction. Forster thought the librettists' main problem was 'how to make Billy, rather than Vere, the hero'. For him, 'Melville got muddled', 'his respect for authority and discipline deflected him', and 'every now and then he doused Billy's light and felt that Vere, being well-educated and just, must shine like a star'. That the opera ultimately came out almost the opposite of what Forster intended, at least for one perceptive observer, appears from Andrew Porter's article in *Music & Letters*, 33 (1952), p.112: 'The librettists have made this secondary relationship [between Billy and Vere] the principal theme of their opera, and Vere its chief figure. The roles of Billy, the natural hero, and Claggart are reduced to those of actors who bring about Vere's tragedy and, indeed, the action is conceived as "having been called up by Vere".'

salvations: for just as the crippled Rickie (in *The Longest Journey*) is saved by the boisterous Stephen Wonham, just as Maurice is saved by the love of that other gamekeeper of English fiction, Alec Scudder, so the intellectual Captain Vere is saved by the love of his handsome sailor Billy—with less reason, perhaps, and certainly more poignancy, for Vere still orders his destruction.

If Vere is vocal in Melville, Claggart is not. And in an effort to breathe life into the depraved Master-at-arms, Forster engineered a great aria towards the end of Act I about which he subsequently wrote to Britten, 'It is my most important piece of writing and I did not, at my first hearing, feel it sufficiently important musically . . . I want *passion*—love constricted, perverted, poisoned, but never the less *flowing* down its agonizing channel; a sexual discharge gone evil. Not soggy depression or growling remorse.'[9] Clearly for Forster the apprehension of Billy's beauty and goodness by both Claggart and Vere includes sexual passion among other feelings. Forster himself was wont to project his feelings this way, as we learn from a most honest and revealing personal memorandum: 'I want to love a strong young man of the lower classes and be loved by him and even hurt by him. That is my ticket, and then I have wanted to write respectable novels.'[10] Billy was for him the centre of the story, and perhaps in his creation of the young sailor there was an element of the wish-fulfilment that is evident in *Maurice* and some of the posthumously printed stories.

For Britten, *Billy Budd* must have seemed a logical and necessary further exploration of themes he had already broached—most notably in *Peter Grimes* and *Albert Herring*. The heroes of these two earlier operas are both outsiders, odd-men-out in ordered and repressive societies. Grimes is destroyed by that society, but not before destroying himself by internalizing the oppression he suffers. *Herring*, as Andrew Porter rightly claims,[11] is the happy counterpart of *Grimes*, in which Albert, the repressed youth tied to his mother's apron-strings, breaks out after being unexpectedly 'saved'. I have argued at length[12] that *Grimes* is fundamentally an allegory of homosexual oppression, and that in writing it Britten was somehow coming to terms with—by artistically experiencing the dark side of his

[9] Quoted in Furbank, *Forster*, vol.2, pp.285–6.
[10] Quoted as a personal memorandum of 1935 by Oliver Stallybrass in his introduction to *The Life to Come and Other Stories* (Edward Arnold, 1972), p.xiv.
[11] *New Yorker*, 3 July 1978.
[12] *Musical Times*, 118 (December 1977), pp.995–1000, and reprinted in *PG*.

feelings towards—the embattled society to which he was returning when he left the United States. While it is dangerous to connect an artist's personal life with his work too closely, it might even be suggested that there is some connection between the happiness and warmth of *Albert Herring* and the success of that particular decision in terms of the acceptance Britten found among English society. This 'acceptance' grew over the years, and as Britten became more established so his mistrust of—even his connection to—society seems to have diminished, and his own private and deeply spiritual preoccupations came closer and closer to the surface: the corruption of innocence, the poignancy of age and decay, the theme of human reconciliation, compassion for the weak, lonely and helpless, and the Christian notion of salvation.

In *Billy Budd* the setting is still a hostile, uncomfortable environment dominated by oppressive forces. The hero, like Grimes, is destroyed by these forces, but in this instance he is pure, he is not alone against the crowd, and he is untouched by self-hatred. Instead, as innocent as Parsifal if more obviously flawed, he conquers the real evil and then 'saves' the morally ambiguous figure who orders his destruction. Compared with *Grimes*, then, tragedy here is purified and made transcendental. And by framing the action between reminiscences of the ageing Vere (whom Melville kills off shortly after the hanging), the opera is given a further push in the direction of a parable of redemption.

First and foremost among the difficulties in setting the libretto was the sheer technical problem of making an opera work without female voices. The composer thrived on such challenges and, as in this case, made them work to his advantage. The musical language of *Budd* as a whole is less demonstrative and colourful, more subtle than that of *Grimes*. It suggests most convincingly a certain grey monotony of life at sea, as well as the inner greyness of a character like Claggart in whom dwells, as Melville puts it, 'the mania of an evil nature, not engendered by vicious training or corrupting books or licentious living, but born within him and innate'.[13] The scoring forgoes the

13 The standard edition of *Billy Budd*, ed. Milton R. Stern (Indianapolis: Bobbs-Merrill, 1975), p.61. This edition was developed from the previous edition of Harrison Hayford and Merton Sealts Jr. (Chicago, 1962). Neither was of course available to Britten, Forster and Crozier, who were more likely to have used an edition such as *The Shorter Novels of Herman Melville* (New York, 1928) or *Melville's Billy Budd*, ed. F. Barron Freeman (Cambridge, Mass., 1948). The matter is of more than merely bibliographical interest because there are major changes in both Stern

great sonorous orchestral tutti in favour of a separation of the various sections, with emphasis rather on the brass and woodwind than on the strings; and the effect of Britten's experience with chamber opera is also evident in the orchestral writing. It is in some ways a very delicate score, with a wonderfully conceived sound-world all its own.

Another challenge was how to give musical purpose and unity to the opera while suggesting the mist, fog and moral confusion (the Forsterian 'muddle') that are so essential to the librettist's conception. The opera was originally cast in four acts, and had a symphonic character. Act I covered Billy's introduction to the *Indomitable*, ending with a captain's muster in which Vere addressed his men, whom Billy then led in singing his praises. Act II was a 'slow movement', depicting the vessel at night. The chase of the French ship acted as a scherzo, and the last act began with the ballad 'Billy in the Darbies', and concluded with the hanging and the Epilogue. Britten revised this scheme in 1960 by tightening up the sequence of events into two acts without cutting anything essential (though the loss of the captain's muster is regrettable dramatically since Billy now swears to die for a man he has never seen). The atmosphere of moral uncertainty is suggested as soon as the curtain rises on the reminiscing Vere: an eerie string passage embodies a characteristic opposition between B flat major and B minor that haunts the whole score. So much of the melodic material of the opera is ultimately derived from the opening statement (Ex.1). This tonal ambiguity, however, is

Ex.1

projected on to a solid tonal framework that gives the opera a sense of progression as well as allowing certain key areas to be associated with certain crucial events. In Act I, the key scheme moves upwards from

---

and Hayford and Sealts from earlier editions. The chief ones are: the relocating of what used to be the 'Preface' and several other leaves; the reordering of the title from *Billy Budd, Foretopman* to *Billy Budd, Sailor (An Inside Narrative)*; and the change of the ship's name from *Indomitable* to *Bellipotent*.

this early and ambiguous B flat major with a few significant diversions—to E major for Billy's first aria, and to F minor for Claggart ('Was I born yesterday?') and the novice's touching scene. It reaches C major by the end of the first scene, stays there for Vere and his officers, then proceeds up to E flat major for the third scene, at the beginning of which the happiness of the men singing their shanty 'Blow her away to Hilo' seems literally to blow away the doubts and fears of the ambiguous tonalities of the previous interlude in a glorious gust of E flat—one of the opera's great moments. There follows Claggart's monologue, ending in his characteristic F minor, which then turns to F major to depict Billy asleep (the same motif as when later he is lying in chains), and the act concludes in G major with the duet between Billy and Dansker accompanied by an ostinato derived from Claggart's motif, to which Dansker sings 'Jemmy Legs is down on you'.

The tonality of the opening of Act II is again ambiguous, but in a more forceful way than that of Act I. The opening melody is in B flat, but the ostinato which animates the scene reiterates the G which closed Act I, and G major is adopted as soon as the ship is called to action. From here the key scheme gradually winds down again—sometimes reverting to the B flat major–B minor opposition as in the interlude depicting the mist and Vere's confusion—finally reaching C minor for Vere's aria ('Scylla and Charybdis') after Billy has killed Claggart. The court scene reverts to F minor, which turns to a radiant F major as Vere goes to tell Billy the verdict, and remains there for Billy's final scene. The hanging takes place in the remote key of E, and this incipient mutiny against the fated scheme of things both on stage and in the music is firmly quelled by an insistent B flat which rings out with the voices of the officers. In the Epilogue the B flat major–B minor opposition is finally reconciled by Vere's singing Billy's final ballad-like tune, which is firmly in B flat, to the words, 'I was lost on the infinite sea, but I've sighted a sail in the storm. . . . There's a land where she'll anchor for ever.'

Another problem for Britten was to suggest those aspects or passages of the story that had perforce to be left out of the libretto. In Melville, to take a down-to-earth instance, we learn of the love and harmony Billy spreads among his shipmates from a speech by Captain Graveling of the *Rights of Man*.[14] In the opera this slightly aggressive side of Billy's goodness is expressed in a series of rising arpeggios on

[14] *Billy Budd*, ed. Stern, pp.7–8.

triads a tone apart, first heard when the boat containing him and the other impressed men nears the *Indomitable* in Act I scene I. This motif subsequently forms the accompaniment to Billy's first aria ('Billy Budd, king of the birds!'), and when in his last scene Billy lies in chains, it punctuates the phrases of his ballad, played on the piccolo, still chirpy but lonely and forlorn. At the opening of Act II, however, it is transformed into the melody the whole crew sings in pursuit of the French ship, thus suggesting psychologically that this moment of unity is a product as much of Billy's influence as of the excitement of the chase (Ex.2). The unrest of the crew at other times,

Ex.2

indeed the whole atmosphere of incipient mutiny in the aftermath of Spithead and the Nore, is suggested by a musical motif first heard in the Prologue, where it is set to Vere's 'O what have I done?' (thus effectively showing his complicity in the state of affairs), and subsequently developing into the shanty 'O heave away, heave', that runs throughout the first scene (Ex.3), It is heard every time the

Ex.3

subject of mutiny occurs, and a variant of it forms Claggart's official accusation. At the climax of the opera, after the hanging, it turns into the wordless fugue which brilliantly suggests the famous passage in Melville:

> Whoever has heard the freshet-wave of a torrent suddenly swelled by pouring showers in tropical mountains, showers not shared by the plain; whoever has heard the first muffled murmur of its sloping advance through precipitous woods, may form some conception of the sound now heard. The seeming remoteness of its source was because of its murmurous indistinctness since it came from close by, even from the men massed on the ship's open deck. Being

inarticulate, it was dubious in significance further than it seemed to indicate some capricious revulsion of thought or feeling such as mobs ashore are liable to, in the present instance possibly implying a sullen revocation on the men's part of their involuntary echoing of Billy's benediction.[15]

Being a suggestive force, rather than a specific symbol, a musical motif can reflect such subtle changes of mood and meaning, the 'murmurous indistinctness' Melville describes, and Britten was able to achieve such nuance in his depiction of the other main characters. Claggart, for instance, is characterized by a motif that contains two falling fourths. It is first heard against the ambiguous B flat–B minor chord in the Prologue, but reaches its most powerful expression against a stark F minor chord bereft of its fifth, in such moments as the climax of the Act I aria (Ex.4). It is sad that Forster's Victorian ears could not hear the brilliance of Britten's music here, for it suggests a quality he had attributed to Melville in his *Aspects of the Novel*: he 'reaches straight back into the universal, to a blackness and sadness so transcending our own that they are indistinguishable from glory'.[16]

Ex.4

The motif of a perfect fourth, without the downward plunge of Claggart's depravity, effectively expresses the emotional charge behind the abstractions that both the Master-at-arms and the Captain use when they contemplate Billy: 'O beauty, handsomeness, goodness', they both sing to the same melody, sharing alone among the ship's crew a special sense of and connection to the natural wonder

[15] *Billy Budd*, ed. Stern, p.128.
[16] *Aspects of the Novel* (1927; Edward Arnold, 1974), p.98.

Philip Brett

of the Handsome Sailor, whose single flaw, his stammer (musically expressed by a trilling trumpet, the wood block and abrupt woodwind arpeggios), is a sign of the flaw of creation, of Original Sin.

Possibly the strangest and most daring moment in the score is the interlude after the trial and Vere's aria ('I accept their verdict'). It evidently expresses the intent of the chapter in which Melville tells nothing definite about what takes place when Vere communicates the verdict to Billy, but gives some hints and speculations which Britten and Forster worked up into the theme of salvation. What we hear are thirty-four clear, triadic chords, each of them harmonizing a note of the F major triad, and each scored differently. They are vaguely reminiscent of the chords that occurred earlier whenever Claggart addressed Billy: in the sailor's last aria they appear at the moment when he begins to feel his full strength, and finally and triumphantly they underpin the climax of the Epilogue when Vere, singing Billy's B flat melody, utters the crucial Forsterian lines, 'But I've sighted a sail in the storm, the far-shining sail, and I'm content.'[17]

These chords lie at the heart of the musical treatment of the metaphysical overtones of *Billy Budd*. They seem to suggest that in Platonic terms, the love of Ideal Beauty can lead to wisdom, knowledge and forgiveness; and that in Christian terms, goodness and love have the power to forgive. This moment of unalloyed optimism is perhaps the crux of the opera, and the richest result of the collaboration between these two remarkable men. Interestingly enough, such optimism was not characteristic of either of them, and they both retreated in the following years. When in 1957–8 Forster wrote his last and finest short story, 'The Other Boat', the two central characters, a young English officer and a young black man, destroy each other. This, Forster told his biographer, 'was more interesting than the theme of salvation, the rescuer from "otherwhere", the generic Alec [Scudder]. That was a fake. People could help one

---

[17] Cf. the 'Letter to America': 'Melville believed in Fate, but kept seeing out of the corner of his eye a white sail beating up against the storm. Doom was fixed, the trap clicked, the body splashed, the fish nibbled. But he kept seeing the obstinate white sail.' To be fair to Forster, then, it seems he was trying to suggest something more like hope than salvation, as other passages in the 'Letter' indicate. The closest he comes to the latter is in the following sentence, the last before his signing-off paragraph: 'The hero hangs dead from the yard arm, dead irredeemably and not in any heaven, dead as a doornail, dead as Antigone, and he has given us life.' But opera, even in Britten's sensitive hands, is no match for the fine distinctions of the Forsterian vision, which that final B flat chord, welling out of the orchestra, all but obliterates.

another, yes; but they were not decisive for each other like that.'[18] For Britten, too, there was a retreat from the idealism of *Budd*. When he came to write another work in which an upright, repressed man meets a vision of beauty, the result is less idealized. In *Death in Venice*, the composer's last opera, beauty enchants and then destroys: it leads as far as self-knowledge but does not reach the full distance to salvation.

[18] Furbank, *Forster*, vol.2, p.303. 'The Other Boat' appears in *The Life to Come and Other Stories*, pp.166–97.

13

Turning the Screw

WILFRID MELLERS

Britten discovered his essential theme in visiting North America and creating his first opera on a basic American myth, the transition from Nature to Nurture.[1] In the United States a dichotomy between the savage and the civilized state was pointedly manifest because America developed so rapidly from barbarism to industrial technocracy, and because industrialization brought a power that fulfilled, but of its nature also destroyed, the innocence it sprang from. The theme, latent in all Britten's operas, became patent again in the opera that, completed in 1954, stands midway in his career, *The Turn of the Screw*. Significantly, it is based on a story by an American author who was voluntarily expatriated. Leaving behind the giant technocracy that America had spawned, Henry James settled in Europe, where he wrote of the American as an innocent remade in the Old World. Britten's first opera, *Paul Bunyan*, concerns the American innocence, its 'advance' into civilized sophistication, and its corruption. *The Turn of the Screw* starts from our modern hyperconsciousness, linked with what James called 'the black and merciless things that lie behind great possessions', and explores its impact on the child within us all. The two operas are opposite but complementary poles.

James's *conte* is highly ambiguous and has been subjected to a variety of interpretations. Forty years ago it was accounted for in then fashionably Freudian terms, and one has to admit that only on this basis do the facts make sense. Since there never was a less adventitious writer than James, I find it difficult to credit that, were not the Freudian interpretation basic, he would have stressed the Governess's infatuation for the Guardian, who is presented as a figure of

[1] See above, chapter 7.

unattainable sexual glamour. Neither the Guardian nor the Governess's infatuation play any essential part in the story; moreover, although Quint's tower *might* be dismissed as a nineteenth-century Gothick trapping, one can hardly dispose thus readily of Flora's lake and her screwing of a pointed stick into a round hole! I cannot believe that a writer as 'conscious' as James, with a psychologist brother, introduced these incidents fortuitously. We have only the Governess's word that the children see the ghosts, and only dear Mrs Grose (whose name might be spelled with a second 's' instead of an 'e') in any way to corroborate her story. Mrs Grose's simplicity may be rendered susceptible to evil by the Governess's neurosis, but there is no evidence that she herself sees the ghosts. It would seem to be the Governess, the only consciousness through whom the dire tale comes to us, who drives Flora into hatred and sickness, and who kills Miles.

Yet although the psychological explanation fits the facts and must be part of the truth, it is not the whole truth. In uncovering psychological motivations one explains nothing *away*, for the human psyche is infinitely mysterious. It would rather seem that James's point is that the Governess's neurotic obsession opens her senses to psychic realities that are normally hidden, especially in the socially respectable world to which she belongs. James's tale certainly implies that the children had some intimate communion with the *living* Quint and Miss Jessel, and remain in some sense haunted by them. Quint, the low servant, and Miss Jessel, the well-born previous governess, were creatures ravaged by passions and terrors alien to anything Mrs Grose could comprehend, and remote from the social masks that people such as the Governess present to the world—except when, in going mad, they may have intimations of a deeper sanity. For although such passions and terrors may be 'bad', to use Miles's word, they are not necessarily and only bad since in representing the daemonic they embrace the heights along with the depths of human potential. The impact of Quint and Miss Jessel on Flora and Miles is comparable with the daemonic Beethoven's assault on an eighteenth-century drawing room. There are more things in heaven and earth, not to mention hell, than are dreamt of in the Governess's philosophy, or in Mrs Grose's lack of one. The children see these things out of the very 'perfection' of their childishness. Growing up, they might have learnt, like Beethoven, to deal with them—as Mrs Grose, innocent by natural limitations, never could. The innocent Governess sees them too, from the maelstrom of her neurosis. She, unlike Beethoven, is a victim of the daemonic's transmutation into the demonic, and destroys life in the attempt to save it.

This complex tissue of possibilities and impossibilities is latent in the libretto which Myfanwy Piper devised for Britten, though she gives the events an objective reality that can tell in theatrical terms. Thus in her version there is never any doubt that the two children and the Governess see Quint and Miss Jessel, as do we as audience. This does not deprive the ghosts of their subjective function; and so intelligent a librettist must have been aware that she had one advantage over James, in that the music may add the psychic dimension which her words lack. Unlikely though it may seem as basis for an opera, James's story proves an ideal vehicle for Britten's (strictly speaking) transcendent genius; as Myfanwy Piper tells the tale, Britten's music reveals the inextricable warp and woof of the natural and supernatural. In presenting the action in a series of cinematic flashbacks, sandwiched between instrumental variations on a single theme, he encloses the story within a single obsessed psyche; at the same time he objectifies the depths which that mind thinks it sees with a precision pertinent to us all, in that we have most of us had momentary glimpses of them. Watching the opera we ourselves suffer the awe-ful, fright-ful, unfathomable interplay of innocence and corruption which those differentiated innocents, the children, the Governess and Mrs Grose, undergo, until they find nemesis or expiation.

Britten, like James, opens with a Prologue. A narrator, holding in his hand the Governess's testament, 'written in faded ink', speaks in a recitative that minutely follows the inflections of speech. He is accompanied only by a piano, an instrument which in the nineteenth century, and even today, stands for domestic propriety. Thus we start in the 'real' world, from which the inner life of the psyche emerges as the piano is absorbed into the orchestral sonorities. That the Prologue is sung by the same voice that plays Quint cannot be fortuitous, for it suggests that Quint's terror and ecstasy are latent even beneath the prim Victorian façade. This is manifest in musical terms also, in that the piano's arpeggios prefigure the fourths, thirds and fifths that crystallize into the orchestral theme which tightens the screw within the Governess's mind. This theme, though given tonal manifestations, embraces every note of the chromatic scale, being a row which is transmuted in interludes between each scene. One would expect the theme and its variations to be monothematically serial since they

Turning the Screw

auralize an intensifying obsession within a single consciousness. Still more subtly, the row colours the thematic material of each scene, since the Governess's neurosis dominates all, and creates much, that happens in the world outside. No opera of Britten, or perhaps of any composer, is so claustrophobically close-knit.

Scene 1 is balanced equably between the outer and the inner life. The Governess, riding in a carriage towards Bly to take up her duties, sings a recitative as naturalistic as that of the Prologue. Talking to herself, she admits to doubts and fears, while soft timpani, thudding in the motivic fourths, simultaneously imitate the noise of coach and horses and hint at the psychic threat inherent in the theme. In Variation I the row's rising fourth, falling third and falling fifth are suspended in time and space, accompanied by flickering chords in parallel fourths. A frisky 6/8 carries the music into E major, in which traditionally Edenic key the children and child-like Mrs Grose welcome the Governess. The innocence of childhood games combines with the social elegancies that 'civilization' imposes on them; there's something faintly creepy about the harp glissandi and fourth-founded arpeggios to which the children make their bows and curtsies. When the Governess 'timidly' introduces herself to Mrs Grose she is accompanied only by a stepwise-moving theme on high violin, unstable in rhythm, chromatically vacillating. This becomes insidious throughout the opera, in association not only with the Governess but also with the ghosts, who may be projections of her nightmare. But the scene ends calmly, the children chanting and frolicking in 6/8 and Mrs Grose extolling their virtues in a speech-inflected version of their runes, while the Governess sustains a chorale in grave minims, expanding from the row. Her chorale expresses, perhaps, the 'ideal' perfection, free of the contagions of sin and mortality, which she would like to find in the children (and thereby anticipates a theme to be more deeply explored in *Death in Venice*).

In Variation II the chorale-like minims are transferred to the bass, which enunciates the row like a passacaglia. Woodwind fourths chatter in the rhythm of the children's games, but disperse when, in the next scene, the Governess, aghast, tells Mrs Grose of the letter she has received dismissing Miles from school. She is again accompanied by her chromatically serpentine theme on high viola, sprinkled with the dew of what is later to be revealed as an uncelestial celesta. The children's chanting of 'lavender blue' disarms; and the Governess and Mrs Grose decide to disbelieve, and do nothing about, the letter's innuendos. In Variation III dusk descends, as the row's initial fourth, third and fifth are metamorphosed into pentatonic arabesques on woodwind which, over sustained strings, emulate the (angelic) twittering of birds. The Governess, at peace, wanders in the grounds and, in Scene 4, spies through the twilight Quint on his tower. Significantly, she at first mistakes him for the Guardian for whom she nurses her frustrated passion. As she realizes that the figure is not he, Quint's magic celesta grows obtrusive. It cannot be fortuitous that it was first heard in relation to the Governess's dubieties, before she or we were aware of Quint's actual or potential existence.

Variation IV transforms the row into a grotesque march, with nagging note-clusters and fourths which are fused, in the next scene, with innocent E major diatonicism, as the children sing 'Tom, Tom, the piper's son'. When the children have danced away, Quint's apparition glares at the Governess through the window, to celesta-garlanded music in chromatically quivering fourths. Starker permutations of the row tread through the orchestra as the Governess, in agitated dialogue with Mrs Grose, discovers the ghost's identity. When she realizes that Quint is *dead* the orchestra is pervaded by a dotted-rhythm version of the wavering motif associated both with Quint and with her neurosis. Almost yelling rather than singing, she describes Quint as 'depraved', to a version of the row around E flat, a pitch already identified with Quint. Mrs Grose says she has no notion of what the Governess is raving about—and speaks sober truth.

Variation V brings us back to the everyday world. Bustling in academic fugato the row introduces Scene 6, wherein the clever children toss off their Latin and history lessons, exemplars of the knowledge civilized man labours to acquire. But it cannot keep the wolf at bay: the disturbance within Miles's mind becomes overt at the end of the scene, when he croons a pathetic snatch of a tune, based on the row's thirds often in false relation, to the words '*Malo* I would rather be, *Malo* in an apple tree'. This reference to 'badness' and to the Fall, ironically extracted from a Victorian primer, is paralleled in the next scene by the incantatory lullaby that Flora whispers to her doll. This summons the second, female, ghost, Miss Jessel: whom Flora pretends not to see, and perhaps doesn't see. The Governess wails, to dislocated permutations of the fourths, that the children are 'lost'.

Variation VII and Scene 8 form the opera's climax. The interlude evokes nocturnal mystery, the row sounding on distant horn in double-dotted rhythm, with reverberant gong and a halo of innocent pentatonics around E flat. From this note germinate Quint's melismatic siren-calls to Miles, and at this point the richness of the music's ambiguity becomes inescapable, for although Quint's arabesques are insidious and might be evil they are also fabulously beautiful, recalling flamenco music and Moorish cantillation. They have a dimension one cannot avoid calling religious; they open magic casements, revealing realms wildly mysterious, remote from the pieties of the Victorian country house, yet as inspirational as they are malevolent—if, in musical terms, they can be called malevolent at all. Thematically, they wondrously expand the Governess's chromatic vacillation; whatever subconscious awareness she may have had is now inexorably manifest. Quint is indeed 'all things strange and bold'; Miss Jessel is subservient to him, as the Governess is subservient to the Guardian, but she now joins in the ululations, calling to Flora in a more agitated line, with leaping sevenths. Cumulatively, the children and the ghosts build to a climax of orgiastic *ecstasis*, in which the Governess and Mrs Grose, searching for the children lost in the night, desperately participate. Throughout this sextet, in more than one sense the high point of the opera, Quint's melismata searingly penetrate, while the celesta embroiders pentatonics around E flat. The scene ends with Miles's assertion, to sharp-rhythmed fourths, that he is 'bad'. Though this may be true, he is also saying that he is aware of 'realities' which Mrs Grose knows nothing of, and which the scared Governess can admit to only by going lunatic.

Act II, balancing Act I, likewise falls into eight flashbacks. It is preceded by Variation VIII, which is based on the ghostly permutations of the row and leads into a double scene, divided into a colloquy between the ghosts and a soliloquy of the Governess. Possibly colloquy and soliloquy really take place simultaneously: in communing with herself the Governess 'bodies forth' the ghosts, revealing subconscious knowledge of their motivations. There is no precedent for this in James's story, where the ghosts are voiceless. But Britten was justified in thinking that for operatic purposes they had to sing; and Piper's dialogue gives them psychological justification, since we learn that Quint had cruelly betrayed Miss Jessel. In the Governess's fevered imagination Quint and Miss Jessel are thus identified with the Guardian and herself; the former identification had been made at Quint's appearance on the tower, the latter is shortly to become explicit. Certainly the marvellous line from Yeats, 'The ceremony of innocence is drowned', which the ghosts chant in agonized awareness that they have destroyed one another, is as applicable to the Governess as it is to them; and they sing it to another version of the Governess's chromatic oscillation, gravitating towards the obsessive E flat. When the ghosts fade into the Governess's monologue, her line still writhes through the chromatic undulation, now centred on C sharp, with snakey string scales depicting the 'labyrinth' in which she is lost.

In Variation IX and Scene 2 natural and supernatural worlds overlap. The row resounds polytonally on church bells, reverberant in overtones. Though this is a realistic musical image, it wonderfully expresses the chaos of a distintegrating mind, the more so because the children, processing 'like choirboys', sing a *Benedicite* ('may she never be confounded'!) through the bells' clamour and against the dialogue of the Governess and Mrs Grose. Reassured by the ambience of the churchyard, Mrs Grose praises the children's virtue. The scene ends, however, with the Governess's admission, in a darker permutation of her chromatic vacillation, that the house is 'poisoned', the children 'mad'. At the end of the scene Miles, perhaps remembering that his *Benedicite* has blessed dragons as well as higher creatures, brings darkness to light. Admitting that he *has* secrets, he challenges the Governess to do anything about it. She, to further extensions of the undulating chromatics over a thudding pedal, decides that she must leave Bly.

But, returned to her room by way of Variation X's extension of her labyrinthine music, she finds Miss Jessel in her own chair—the ultimate identification. When human and ghost converse it is clear that the Governess's anguish is equated with Miss Jessel's: both women are obsessed with Quint. Now the present and the past Governesses wail to the same drooping appoggiaturas, seeking possession of the children. She and Miss Jessel are one in that both are victims of love that has turned into hate; and in so far as Quint is her obsession with the Guardian she recognizes that he too is an agony that must be confronted and appeased. She decides that she must write a letter to the Guardian, despite his admonition that he would have nothing to do with the children's destiny. This is the fundamental failure of love, from which the later disasters spring. She writes her letter to a busy accompaniment of semiquavers based on the oscillating thirds of Miles's '*Malo*' ditty. As she reads the letter over to herself her lyricism radiantly admits to her suppressed love for Quint-the-Guardian. This moment of truth precipitates catastrophe.

Variation XI returns to the original version of the row, in canon between bass clarinet and bass flute. Nocturnal thirds in semiquavers flutter through the inner parts and persist through the next scene, entwined with the (also third-founded) '*Malo*' theme. Miles croons the tune to himself as the Governess approaches his bedside, hoping to extort some kind of confession. Quint, 'the hidden life that stirs / When the candle is out', ululates on his E flats, encouraging Miles to resist; and when the Governess expresses her determination to 'save' Miles, blows out the candle. Miles, after a shriek, says that it was he who extinguished it, as perhaps it was; the scene ends in sinister quietude with the '*Malo*' theme on cor anglais, in a haze of semiquaver triplets. Scenes and variations then succeed one another in phantasmagoric rapidity. In Variation XII the music becomes stark alternations of the '*Malo*' thirds on piano, punctuated in Scene 5 by Quint's spoken exhortations that Miles should steal the Governess's letter. In Variation XIII and Scene 6 Miles is playing the piano to the enraptured Governess and Mrs Grose. His music incorporates the row even in emulating rococo Mozart, but the simple diatonicism grows polytonal and rhythms are weirdly dislocated. Flora's game of cat's-cradle also goes awry; and the grown-ups, bemused by Miles's trance-inducing piano, don't notice when she slips away. In Variation XIV Miles hammers triumphant piano triads over an extended version of the row, embracing the stepwise undulations.

In Scene 7 Flora is with Miss Jessel by the lake. The child will not admit to the ghost's presence, and Mrs Grose, out of her depth, agrees with her. The Governess thinks this is because Mrs Grose has 'failed' her in running away from horror, but neither in James nor in Piper and Britten is there evidence on which to decide the matter. So when Flora works herself into a fury of hate directed at the Governess, one cannot be sure that it isn't justified. At the end of the scene the Governess's admission of her own failure is total, as her chromatic vacillation collapses into a long drooping scale that ends, in the next and last scene, in the abysmal depths of the solo double-bass.

Dubiety persists, for Mrs Grose confesses that Flora's nocturnal mutterings have convinced her that something is amiss and that she must take Flora away as the only palliative for her sickness. Again there is nothing to prove that the sickness may not have been induced by the Governess; Mrs Grose's account of Flora's delirium is accompanied by the undulating motif first heard when she recognized Quint from the Governess's description of him on the tower. In any case Flora leaves Bly, whereas Miles remains for the Governess to make a last attempt to 'save' him, singing 'passionately' over a bass that converts the first part of the row into an ostinato. The unremittingness of the passacaglia suggests her determination; the bright A major tonality and the dotted rhythm evoke the innocence she would pitifully recapture. When Quint coos his melismata, again anchored to his E flat throughout the A major tonality, the scene intensifies to frenzied conflict. Quint's E flat arabesques grind against the Governess's E and A naturals, as she demands that Miles reveal his secrets. In a bitonal duet Quint variedly repeats the song of seduction he sang from the garden, always around E and A flats, while the Governess urgently questions Miles in A major–minor. As the complete row unfolds in the bass, Miles admits to his theft of the letter and names Quint as his tormentor. Though he is thereby 'freed', the Governess's and Quint's roles as heroine and villain remain ambiguous. Significantly, Quint and the Governess *together* sing the *same music* (the motivic falling fourths) over Miles's dead body, and Quint's melisma of farewell, as ironic benediction, swells not from his E flat, but from the Governess's E natural. When she ends the opera by singing Miles's '*Malo*' ditty—in A major but with sharpened fourth and flat seventh so that an E flat major third sounds enharmonically within it—it is evident that her requiem for Miles is a confession that *she* is 'bad'. It is also a threnody for herself, and for Miss Jessel and Quint who are her projections. Thus Britten's musical, encompasses James's poetic, vision.

14

Through *Noye's Fludde*[1]

WILFRID MELLERS

Britten is by nature a lyrical composer—too easily so, Stravinsky would probably have maintained, though it's perhaps inevitable that the two most materially successful composers of our time should regard one another with a degree of suspicion. Those of us who consider both Stravinsky and Britten to be great composers (if less great than a Bach or Beethoven) may recognize that the key theatrical works in their respective careers are complementary. Stravinsky's *Oedipus Rex* transmutes humanism, by way of an oriental abnegation, into a Christianity reborn; Britten's church operas, *Noye's Fludde* and *Curlew River*, start from Christian assumptions, but use their medieval and oriental techniques to purge the Christian heritage of guilt. Both the Stravinsky and the Britten works represent a fusion of West and East, and in both cases the fusion is re-creative, not evasive.

Britten began his career with a rebirth, a work specifically called *A Boy was Born*, written when he was still a boy himself. Despite the archaism of the texts and of some of the musical procedures, the essence of this work is its theatrically re-creative immediacy; a boy is born indeed, and in the thirty years that have followed Britten has never forgotten that Boy and Birth. The wonderful Hardy songs [*Winter Words*] deal directly with the birth of consciousness which is also the death of innocence, and almost all his operas have the same theme. The limitation of range is part of the evidence of his genius, for in dealing with innocence and persecution he knows what he knows.

The grandest statement of this motif is in Britten's first opera, *Peter Grimes*. The unhero is here a genuinely tragic figure: the Savage Man

[1] From Wilfrid Mellers, *Caliban Reborn: Renewal in Twentieth-Century Music* (Gollancz, 1968).

153

who, given different circumstances, might have grown to civilized consciousness. Deprived of love, however, he destroys the Boy who is his own soul, and is hounded to his death by the World. Similarly, *Billy Budd* is specifically about the agony of growing up. Billy is a child destroyed by his childishness, which becomes the *mea culpa* of his stammer; the opera tells us that we can't dispose of evil by a blind blow, provoked by the inarticulateness of the good within us. Among the chamber operas, *The Rape of Lucretia* introduces an overtly Christian note into its fable of innocence corrupted, and *Albert Herring* has the same theme, almost the same story, as *Grimes*, but with a comic instead of tragic apotheosis. *The Turn of the Screw* offers Britten's most direct and painfully involved statement of the childhood and corruption motif, while in *A Midsummer Night's Dream* it finds perhaps its most maturely resolved form.

All this being so, it is hardly surprising that Britten should, throughout his career, have devoted time to the creation of music for children, nor that his most extended children's piece, *Noye's Fludde*, should deserve to rank among his supreme achievements. The choice of a text itself, as so often with Britten, is evidence of genius, of a self-knowledge that finds what is needful for each occasion. Thus, the Chester Miracle Play is medieval and the common people with whom it deals are, despite the intellectual sophistication of medieval civilization, childlike at heart. On the other hand, the story is unambiguously a conflict, so that the piece can grow from folk ritual into music-drama, if not into full-fledged opera. Indeed, it starts from a direct admission of 'humanistic' contrarieties; the congregation, including you and me, sing the well-known hymn 'Lord Jesus, think on me'. This hymn is an appeal to Christ to restore to us purity and innocence, which if we're adult we've lost, or if we're children we're about to lose, in travelling through 'darkness', 'perplexity' and the Flood. We start, that is, with the consciousness of sin and earth-born passion, which we have to encompass before we can see 'eternal brightness'. Although the Flood is in one sense a destructive force, it is in another sense (as it was in biblical myth) a necessary return to the unconscious waters.

So Britten sets the hymn as a rather wild march, a song of pilgrimage in which the pilgrims are the children, as well as everyone else who may be present in the church. The hymn's descending scale becomes a motif of affirmation ('think on me') throughout the opera, but the bass's mingling of perfect, god-like fourths and fifths with the

devil's imperfect ones imparts a slightly savage flavour to the simple
diatonic harmonies. The devilish, bitonal F naturals initiate the
conflict—between good and evil, between guilt and redemption—
which the drama is. When, in the third stanza, the words refer
directly to the Flood, the harmonies become more chromatic.
Possibly Britten intends these rather corny harmonies to remind us of
the turnover in the stomach and the chill down the spine that the
reverberating organ gave us, in the parish church, when we were
young. Possibly it still does the same, for children who go to church;
in any case, it tells them, as it reminds the grown-ups, of the Flood
they must pass through, to reach maturity.

This is manifest at the start of the opera's action, for the
congregational chorale introduces the Voice of God who declaims (not
sings) over fourths that are both perfect and imperfect. He may be the
maker of all things, but man, through the sin and guilt that pagan
music has no knowledge of, has thrown God's blessings away. The
theme of redemption is then introduced, because mankind may be
saved through the agency of Noah's Ark, which will breast the Flood.
Noah, who is man, sings to summon his children to an act of work and
worship. The modal E minor of the hymn (which we may think of as
the key of pilgrimage) changes to a pentatonic simplicity, full of godly
fourths and optimistic major thirds and sixths. This leads into a work
song as everyone gathers for the building of the Ark: an Orff-like
music of ritual action which becomes drama. The dancing tune which
Noah's children sing is derived from his original call, and is still
pentatonically innocent, at once medieval and jazzy in its syncopated
rhythm, marvellously suggesting youth's equivocal eagerness and
apprehension. So even in music as simple as this there is theatrical
projection and character portrayal, while the rapid modulations, or
rather shifts of key, are also a dramatic device to convey excitement.
Similarly, a primitive contrapuntal ensemble becomes a vivid musical
image for corporate action; this music is inseparable from physical
gesture and mime, which is one reason why children enjoy
performing it. Suddenly and dramatically the music breaks off, at
what seems to be a climax of solidarity, when everyone is about to
work together, hammering and sawing and caulking to make the Ark
that will save us all.

What disrupts this collective helpfulness is indeed the snake in the
grass, the fly in the ointment. Sex rears its lovely head as Mrs Noah,
singing major sixths (D sharps) that create sensual (Wagnerian!)

ninth chords, refuses to play any part in the labour of salvation. Instead, with her gossiping crones, she breaks into a parody of the work song in rapid 6/8 tempo. Of course she's a comic character, but Britten's music makes evident that the attempt of the Middle Ages to laugh away the dualism of sex didn't lessen its impact. Noah tries to assert his authority, making one of the stock medieval jokes about shrewish wives. He doesn't expect her to take any notice, and in fact she disassociates herself from the building by sitting with her gossips, at the side of the stage. The key abruptly changes from Mrs Noah's mingled F sharp minor and A major to F, and Noah initiates the building 'in the name of God'. The building song begins with God's rising fifths and is supported on an ostinato of fifths as bass, alternating between tonic and flat seventh. There is virtually no modulation, because this is ritual rather than drama. As a refrain between each stanza, however, Noah's children refer to the coming of the Flood, singing in four-rhythm instead of the ritual's triple pulse, and in increasingly full, emotionally involved harmonization which changes the F major ostinato to minor. In this action-ritual, children are involved instrumentally, playing open strings on violins and twiddles on recorders while the ostinato pattern is repeated; this beautifully suggests how the act of work and worship concerns us all, through the ages.

When the Ark and the action song are finished, Noah invites his wife, the perennial Outsider, to come in. She refuses, in a line that is more humanistically energetic than her husband's. In a canonic chase she parodies Noah's words, which, to medieval people, seems not far from blasphemy, and is enough to provoke God to a second utterance. He orders Noah to take the creatures into the Ark, two by two, and little boys summon them with a fanfare of bugles. Again, Britten exploits, imaginatively, the music of our everyday lives. The first congregational hymn had been a noise such as we've heard in church, time out of mind; similarly, the bugle procession is a noise we can hear in the streets on a Sunday morning, a noise in which our own Willies and Johnnies may well participate. The march, in the bugle key of B flat, is all tonic, dominant and subdominant, and reflects with realistic authenticity (like the marches in the music of Charles Ives) the tang and tingle of the noise we'd actually hear, wrong notes and all. Of course the wrong notes are right, because they are part of the innocence, and it is right too that there should be no modulation, which the bugles' simplicity cannot accommodate, apart from a brief shift to D flat for some of the wilder creatures ('beares, woulfes . . . apes and . . . weyscelles').

Between each statement of the march tune various beasts and birds emit *Kyries* of praise and thankfulness (oscillating simply between the fifth and fourth). The creatures are 'natural' but not 'conscious', so there is a kind of celestial farce in the bugle march and the squeaking of mice and gibbering of monkeys. Only when Noah and his children and their wives (representing mankind) join in a jubilant ensemble as they enter the Ark is there a change of mood and mode. The *Kyries* gradually grow from comedy to liturgical awe, from the rocking two-note figure into a beautiful pentatonic melisma. This melisma is rooted on G, which seems to be the key of harmony between man and God, and is the 'relative' of the more disturbed E minor, which is the key of pilgrimage.[2] There is no more than a touch of G major here, though when Noah once more orders his wife to come in 'for feare leste that [she] drowne', he reminds her, and us, of the first hymn that had asked for Jesus' pity on our sinfulness. In apparent paradox, she too sings the same phrase in protesting that she 'will not oute of this towne'. But if there is man's (and woman's) stupid pride in her defiance, there is also a kind of courage. This may be why she is not finally beyond redemption; it's the Mrs Noah in all of us that makes us human. Persistently, she sings sharpened sevenths against the hymn's modal flat sevenths. As humanist, she demands harmonic consummation, and throughout this dramatic exchange trills on a low D sharp (major seventh of E minor) repeatedly deny the tune its resolution into G. Mrs Noah says, to D sharpish arpeggios over an E minor triad, that she'd rather have her gossips than salvation, and sings, with the gossips, the Flood song, wherein the D sharps are aggressive over a lurching E minor ostinato. Between the stanzas of the song, Noah tries to call her home, with the hymn's descending scale, to G major. But the D sharp trills drive us back to the 'lumpy', D sharp-dominated ostinato. This, again, is a ritual piece that turns into drama.

The gossips say they'll sit there 'regardless', and get drunk, their justification being the typically human imbecility that they 'ofte tymes . . . have done soe'. Habituation is all, and human pride becomes indistinguishable from hysteria. The sons take over from

---

[2] G major is traditionally a key of benediction, from the baroque period onwards. In the B minor Mass Bach specifically associates E minor and G minor with crucifixion and redemption: a fact that Britten may be unconsciously or consciously recalling.

Noah, appealing to their mother in radiant parallel 6–3 chords, and with a humbly flattened, Phrygian version of the hymn phrase, drooping down to G by way of B flat and A flat. This flatness further counteracts the sharpness of Mrs Noah's sevenths, and although her denials then grow frenzied, mingling D sharps with fiercer leaps and tenser intervals, she willy-nilly finds herself singing the hymn theme of redemption, as her sons bundle her into the Ark. She struggles, of course, and boxes Noah's ears, but the tide is turned and the hymn phrase sounds in *fortissimo* unison, not yet in the resolution of G major, but in the original E minor. With a sudden miraculous shift to a sustained C minor chord on the organ—a further subdominant flattening of the Phrygian G minor of the last reference to the hymn tune, the D sharps finding rest in being metamorphosed into the E flats of the triad—Noah says that 'it is good for to be stille'. It is indeed, after the fury and the mire of human veins, and the stupidities of the human will; now the redeeming storm can work its way.

The Flood takes the form of a passacaglia, with a chromatic, rhythmically restless theme in which a falling third expands to a fourth and then to a godly fifth, only to wind itself back to the original drooping third. Though it generates the storm's excitement, the passacaglia theme is also God's Law which is beyond change, and again the piece is action as well as music. The drama is epic, concerning not individual men, but man's fate through successive generations. Child recorder players and open-string fiddlers place the epic in its present context, as they emulate wind, waves and flapping rigging. The animals panic to rising and falling chromatics, until gradually everyone begins to sing, over and through the passacaglia, the hymn 'Eternal Father, strong to save'. This Victorian tune includes the falling-scale figure of the first congregational hymn, but also a rising chromatic scale to express the urgency of our appeal to God. Britten manages to suggest that this chromaticism is both a part of our heritage (we've thrilled to it as long as we can remember), and at the same time something that has been discovered during the slow chromaticizing of the storm. The passacaglia bass persists as the congregation joins in the hymn, but disappears during a triumphant repetition with full organ and descant of boy trebles. After we've achieved, with God's help, the victory over darkness, the storm can subside. The various storm incidents are heard in shortened form, in reverse order over the declining bass theme, now dominated by pedal Gs on drums. The passacaglia closes in a profound calm, with an ostinato of spattering raindrops played on slung mugs and piano, the tonality poised between G and the subdominant C.

We still don't know precisely what the calm signifies; nor does Noah, who sends out the Raven and the Dove, the black bird and the white, to spy out the land and the waters. The point of the Christian mythology would seem to be the interdependence of good and evil; only through the Raven is the Dove apprehensible, and we must pass through the Flood to attain redemption. The music of the two birds is, anyway, closely related. The Raven dances to a fast waltz, played on the humanly emotive cello; it is chromatic and rhythmically unstable, veering now this way, now that. There is an E-ish flavour to its tonality, for the Raven is still a pilgrim; yet his line is lyrically songful, and we hear the passacaglia theme again as he flickers off into the distance. This recollection of God's will carries the tonality flatwards towards the dominant sevenths of A flat. This hovers on the brink of G major peace as the Dove, represented by flutter-tongued recorder, flies after the Raven in a graceful waltz that seeks to resolve the Raven's chromatics into rising diatonic scales. Tremulous dominant sevenths, repeatedly harking back to A flat, exquisitely suggest a mingling of ecstasy and awe, even fear, in the approach to G major bliss. When the Dove returns, alighting on the Ark, he brings our redemption in the shape of an olive branch; a transformed version of the passacaglia theme (in G with an E-ish flavour) becomes a melody not a bass, while Noah sings simple but noble fourths and fifths as he tells us that 'it is a signe of peace'.

God's voice speaks quietly in forgiveness, bidding the creatures to go forth and multiply. Sleepily, the tonality sinks to a subdominant pedal C, reminding us of that earlier subdominant triad that made it 'good for to be stille'. Over the pedal C, the bugle-call key of B flat softly intrudes, and the animals and humans leave the Ark, two by two, singing B flat alleluias. The syncopated theme reminds us of the first work song, of which it is, indeed, the spiritual consummation. Gradually, it is metamorphosed into a joyous ensemble, until the music changes back from drama to ritual, with tolling bells and modal flat sevenths accompanying God's benediction. G major finally comes into its own as the key of peace, uniting man with God in the last hymn, 'The spacious firmament on high'. This tune includes the first hymn's scale figure in rising, and in its original falling, form, both now in unsullied diatonicism. Ritual bells and bugles continue to sound in B flat, the major relative of G minor, which would seem to be

Nature's (preconscious) key. They remain unaffected even when everyone sings Tallis's hymn in G major canon, for the creatures are what they are, eternally unchanging in their relationship to God's cosmos, whereas man alone can progress from E minor to G major. The final pages are magic ritual in the ringing of B flat bells and the blowing of B flat bugles, and at the same time are the end of a human drama in the final resolution into a quiet, low-spaced, infinitely protracted G major triad.

15

Entertaining the Young:
The Little Sweep[1]

IMOGEN HOLST

Britten has given audiences of children an opera of their own in *The Little Sweep* (*Let's Make an Opera*). As with *The Young Person's Guide to the Orchestra*, this 'Entertainment for Young People' is rapturously enjoyed by the young of all ages, who insist on going to see and hear it over and over again. He has given the seven children in the cast just the right songs to sing and just the right story to act; and he has given the hundreds of children in the audience a chance of joining in the singing. Instead of feeling frustrated and cut off by a dark, impenetrable barrier from the excitement of the lights and the colours and the sounds, they find themselves caught up into the very centre of things. It is the members of the audience who provide the overture which sets the scene for the drama: it is they who send Black Bob and his son Clem and the little sweep-boy Sammy riding through the Suffolk lanes one winter morning in 1810, to sweep the chimneys at Iken Hall. By the time the curtain goes up there is no longer any dividing line between audience and performer or between amateur and professional, so there need be no fear of any self-consciousness, either on or off the stage. And as soon as the story begins to unfold, one realizes that there is no dividing line in Britten, whether he writes a tragic opera for grown-ups or a light-hearted entertainment for children.

When Black Bob and Clem threaten the 8-year-old Sammy, the moment is as fraught with tragedy as the bullying scene in *Peter Grimes*. Five bars are enough to convey the sense of desolation as

[1] Edited from 'Britten and the Young', in the Britten Symposium, 1952.

Sammy is left alone in the narrow chimney, with his rope dangling in the fireplace of the empty nursery:

Ex. 1

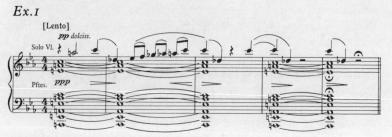

The children's voices are first heard offstage: their distant cries of 'Where are you?' bridge the narrow gap between speech and song. The rescue of Sammy, who is stuck in the chimney, bridges the still narrower gap between singing and dancing, for the children's 12/8 tune, to the words 'Pull the rope gently until he is free, Pull O! Heave O!' brings its own action with it. When Sammy has been rescued, the falling semitones of his pathetic appeal, 'Please don't send me up again!', follow the dateless tradition of all operatic laments. The children plan to hide him in their toy-cupboard; in an excited *vivace* they lead him across the room, deliberately planting his sooty feet down on the clean dustsheets in order to make false tracks between the fireplace and the window. There is a dramatic moment when they hear someone coming and have to hide under the dustsheets that are shrouding the chairs. Black Bob and Clem are hustled back into the room by the irate housekeeper, Miss Baggott, whose entry has a paralysing effect on the *vivace* tune; it staggers into an astonished augmentation. But Sammy is safe, and as soon as they get a chance to emerge from their hiding-places, the children prepare to give him a bath. The audience sings a rapid, syncopated description of this transformation scene, undeterred by the noisy splashings and the chromatic showers of soapsuds provided by the strings' accompaniment to the third verse. When the curtain rises again, a gleaming white Sammy is thanking the children for their help. They are distressed to think that he has to work for such a cruel master; the almost unbearable pathos of 'home is a hundred miles away' is saved from any suggestion of sentimentality by the extreme dignity of the children as they stand patiently waiting for their solo lines in the ensemble. Their unruffled resignation, as they watch the conductor for their lead, is unconsciously appropriate and deeply moving.

Entertaining the Young: The Little Sweep

Comedy returns with the indignant approach of Miss Baggott. Sammy is once more hidden in the toy-cupboard and the other children gleefully stick their tongues in their cheeks as they drape themselves into a sedate imitation of a Kate Greenaway tableau, the eldest boy leaning nonchalantly against the mantelpiece as he reads from a leather-bound volume, and the smallest girl sitting demurely on the floor as she inspects her toys. When the intolerable Miss Baggott threatens to open the cupboard door, a panic-stricken gasp of dismay can be heard throughout the theatre. But one of the children on the stage saves the situation by pretending to faint. 'Help! help! she's collapsed!' exclaims Miss Baggott, in a ridiculously fussy sequence of *marcato* crotchets. The children, in the approved style of many an operatic ensemble, take no notice whatsoever of the violent commotion going on all round them, but chant 'Poor Juliet! Can she be dying?' in a wickedly lugubrious *legato*, kneeling in an early nineteenth-century row, and lengthening their faces to an expression of mock piety. Miss Baggott retires, defeated, and the scene ends with the children's boisterous dance of triumph. It is left to the members of the audience to convey the passing of the hours with the haunting 6/8 of their 'Night Song':

Ex.2

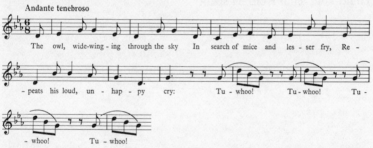

At the end of the song, as the last 'Tu-whoo!' fades away, the silence that receives it has a quality seldom found in a theatre.

It is morning. The coach is coming to take three of the children home, and Sammy is to be smuggled into their trunk and taken back to his own family. The children run in, one after another, to wish him good morning, the rapid entries in their *allegro* ensemble being free from all peril of anxiety owing to the pianist's *sforzando* octave leap which gives the new note to each soloist exactly two bars before it is wanted. Sammy's mood of courageous, but somewhat embarrassed,

gratitude is enhanced by the fact that he has to count his silent first
beats before coming in:

Ex.3

The children just have time to conceal him in the trunk before they
hear sounds of the comic arrival of Tom the coachman and Alfred the
gardener who have been sent to carry the luggage downstairs. But at
the very last moment there is a dramatic setback to their adventure,
for the two men complain that the trunk is too heavy: either it must be
unpacked, or it must stay where it is. 'Oh no!' the children exclaim,
with a hint of genuine tragedy in the sudden darkness of their C minor
chord. But all is well: they offer to help carry the trunk, and Sammy
escapes. There is a blaze of light on the stage as the audience sings the
chorus of the last song. The children have improvised a coach with the
nursery rocking-horse and a couple of chairs: the 8-year-old twins are
twirling brightly coloured parasols round and round to the rhythm of
the wheels, while the whole theatre is filled with the trotting and the
cantering of the percussion. The *con slancio* in this final *allegro* is
unmistakable, and not even the weariest of middle-aged observers
could hold aloof from its spell.

16

Small Victims: *The Golden Vanity* and *Children's Crusade*[1]

DONALD MITCHELL

We can regard *The Golden Vanity* and *Children's Crusade* as two sides of the same coin. The *Vanity* is clearly and intentionally an entertainment, immensely diverting to witness and great fun for children to perform. The *Crusade* is as dark as the *Vanity* is bright—I deliberately avoid using the word 'light'—and also marvellously devised for children to sing and play. But in no sense is it entertaining for performers or audience: the total experience is desolating, as intentionally devastating as the *Vanity* is intentionally exhilarating. The *Crusade* sets a tragic, desperate narrative of our time by Brecht, the *Vanity* an ingeniously dramatized version of a famous old English ballad which offers all the pleasures of a superior musical charade based on a story of the sea from long ago.

But once we look beyond these contrasts, qualifications begin to accumulate. For a start, we find that we cannot treat the *Vanity* as a glorious romp from beginning to end; for the end of the work, the Cabin-boy's death, brings us up short. This is the crucial moment, the moment of truth; and the *Vanity* here follows not the laws of convention, of entertaining make-believe, but the laws of its composer's artistic personality. Of course the incident is beautifully proportioned and within scale, and it does not demand more of its performers, musically speaking, than they can be expected to give. But the scene of the Cabin-boy's death by drowning, and the ensuing solemn funeral march, shift to a plane of feeling and musical invention decisively distinct from the preceding high-jinks of, say, the battle at

[1] Edited from the sleeve-note for Decca recording SET 445 (1970).

sea (with its sly musical reference to the abortive battle in *Billy Budd*, Act II)² or the sinking *Turkish Galilee* ('Gurgle, gurgle, gurgle'). In fact Britten brings to his Cabin-boy in the *Vanity* the inspiration and sense of compassionate involvement that we encounter in his operas proper, whether the heroes or heroines be Lucretia or Billy Budd, Albert Herring or Miles (in *The Turn of the Screw*)—or, one should not forget to add, Sam in *The Little Sweep*. In the big stage works the scale and complexity are necessarily different, but the impressive thing about Britten is the consistent level of his inspiration, *no matter what scale he is working on*. The *Vanity* is a small work; but we shall miss an important part of the composer's personality, if we too superficially equate the physical dimensions of a piece with the 'size' of its inspiration. Britten composes, whether for children or for adults, out of his total experience and his total commitment as an artist. We are moved by the death of the brave Cabin-boy because of an expressive weight behind the image which derives from long-standing pre-occupations of the composer: it needs no emphasizing that the sacrifice of an innocent victim—in essence, the tale the *Vanity* tells—is a theme persistently articulated in many of his major works. This degree of involvement on the composer's part is in turn the guarantee of our involvement, and also surely indicates the specific quality which appeals to the children for whom he writes. He does not cheat by writing music for them that is isolated from the music he writes for adults. He will skilfully take account of their talents as performers and, as the *Vanity* amply proves, no composer has a keener awareness of what a crowd of small boys will enjoy presenting on a stage with the minimum of props and the maximum of schoolboy relish. But Britten treats his young performers as professionals, and at least part of his real respect for them shows in his insistence on being no less himself in the *Vanity* than in a work of grander proportions. And if that means being serious, then he will be serious, and carry his cast and audience with him, such is the power of the images which are central to his art and distributed freely across the whole range of his music.

If the dramatic topic of the *Vanity* is characteristic of Britten, so too is the form of the work. In this sphere also we meet the same consistency, the same highly personal approach with its roots in Britten's own past. We note the masterly and wholly typical manner

² Cf. a similarly light-hearted self-quotation—of *The Rape of Lucretia* in *Albert Herring*—cited above, p.121 [C.P.].

in which the *Vanity* is bound together by what can be seen as a theme and variations (a favourite formal scheme of Britten's). The theme is the original ballad tune itself, which carries the main burden of the narrative throughout the work. At the same time, through ingenious rhythmic, harmonic or melodic manipulation, or a combination of all three, the tune is perpetually varied, with striking virtuosity, to match the changing dramatic events. The tune and its variations provide the overall unity, while *within* them are interpolated the vital scenes which allow for the statement or development of character, e.g. the Cabin-boy's approach to the Captain, 'What will you give me if I sink the *Turkish Galilee?*', and the miniature duet that follows, 'I will give you silver, I will give you gold', which contains some subtle characterization in the Cabin-boy's stubborn downwards inversion of the Captain's ascending and beguiling scales. Even when Britten is organizing a work of these dimensions he brings into play means of formal organization which are not distinct in kind from those he uses elsewhere.

We also hear the born musical dramatist at work in the *Vanity* in the skill with which he finds the right memorable phrase to delineate character or incident; and here the *Vanity* certainly joins hands with the *Crusade*. One of the most remarkable aspects of the *Crusade* is the sharply etched musical depiction of the incidents which make up Brecht's searingly poignant narrative of the lost, wandering 'five-and-fifty' children, harassed by war, blinded by blizzards, homeless and directionless, trying only to find a land 'where peace reigns'. The *Crusade* is a cantata, but the music is felt throughout with a dramatic intensity which brings to vivid life not only the principal figures in the band—such as the anxious leader, the little Jew ('Velvet Collar'), the drummer-boy or the boy from the Nazi legation—but the events by which they are overtaken and the pitiful efforts they make to alleviate their plight. The succession of scenes, dark for the greater part but occasionally illumined by the children's own humanity (their impromptu concert by a waterfall; the child lovers), unfolds with graphic realism in music far removed from mere 'illustration' and yet of an uncompromising *directness*: this is the only possible style, one soon comes to realize, that could contain (in two senses) the painfulness of the subject. Yet it is scarcely possible to think of the *Crusade* in a stage production, dramatic though its conception and gestures may be, because no staging could equal the drama which the music itself enacts and evokes in the imagination. (Its impact on one imagination can be seen in the series of paintings by Sidney Nolan which it inspired.)³

The design of the *Crusade* is more elaborate and complex than that of the *Vanity*, but again it is wholly typical of the composer. We encounter once more a continuous structure; this time, however, an extended sequence of dramatic episodes and character interludes forms the centre-piece of the work and the unifying idea massively frames (not punctuates) the central section. The first statement of the 'frame'—which sets forth the work's singular percussive sonority and exposes its characteristic building materials—runs from the opening ('In Poland, in nineteen thirty-nine') to the end of the sixth verse ('They wanted to fly from the fighting'). Then follows the big central section, in which the episodes and interludes, while widely contrasted and each retaining an independent character and texture, none the less flow and merge so adroitly that we are finally impressed by a large span of brilliant, teeming invention, not a mosaic assembly. This centre-piece is rounded off by the other leg of the frame, i.e. the final account of the dog is interrupted by a hushed echo of the frame, 'Please come and help us'; the rest is silence.

There is no make-believe in the *Children's Crusade*. In the *Vanity* we can accept the fact that the Cabin-boy rises to his feet with the rest of the cast for the cheerful march off, for such a resurrection is wholly appropriate within the work's own frame of reference. But no resurrection, no happy ending, is possible in the *Crusade*. The difference, as I have already suggested, is largely owing to the question of scale—of feeling, not only form. In the *Vanity*, while Britten certainly does not exclude his feelings, they are kept within the bounds of the piece. They do not step outside the children's world, where, of course, 'resurrection' is commonplace (compare children's life-and-death games). But how far can we regard the *Crusade* as a 'children's world', for all the fact that youthful performers are involved?

Not at all, one might think—except in a profoundly ironic sense (if the *Crusade* is a children's world, it is certainly not a world of their making). Here, though Britten uses children as performers and brilliantly exploits their musical abilities, the musical experience the work reveals is of an order quite distinct from the actual nature of the forces employed. With hindsight we can see that it would scarcely

³ Reproduced in facsimile (Faber Music, 1969).

have been possible to set Brecht's harrowing text in any other way; artistic necessity dictated that, if the work were to materialize at all, the performers could only be children. But this is not to underrate the inspiration Britten brings to the assembling of his forces, above all the audacious stroke of the percussion band, with its combined military *and* children's instruments associations. It is self-evident how different the character of the invention of the *Crusade* is from that of the *Vanity*, even while (like the *Vanity*) it remains within the scope of young singers and players. But perhaps more important is another difference, a possibly more significant contrast. Whereas in the *Vanity* the composer, though never less than himself, never actively intervenes but leaves the children's world intact, in the *Crusade* there is a crucial passage where the composer as it were occupies the centre of the stage. I refer to the important formal juncture, the return of the 'frame' after the central section, where for the first time the poet emerges as personal commentator: 'Whenever I close my eyes I see them wander. . . .' Up to this point in the work the composer has let his forces speak for themselves, but with the superbly calculated return of the opening idea, now transformed musically into a climactic vision of overwhelming intensity, a vision of a world other than the one that the children are leaving—'No more fire, no more thunder'—Britten speaks to us *about* them, though still *through* them. This intervention makes us realize that from the outset he has been inventing on a plane which would allow of such a transformation. It is a moment of revelation which transcends all questions of medium and it confronts us simply with an experience which is explicable only in terms of major art, to which category Britten's *Children's Crusade* undeniably belongs.

17

Public and Private in *Gloriana*[1]

DONALD MITCHELL

What one might think of as the central text of *Gloriana* occurs in Act III scene 1. The Earl of Essex has been found guilty of treason. His friends, foes and the Council of State wait on the Queen's decision. Will she, or will she not, sign the warrant sealing his death? Elizabeth expresses her agitation and anguish in a brief, highly charged aria, 'The Queen's Dilemma', which ends: 'I am, and am not; freeze, and yet I burn; / Since from myself my other self I turn.'

'Myself' and 'other self': the tormented Queen is torn between the self that must rule, govern and suppress treason, and the other self that loves the fiery ambition, touching impetuosity and lack of pomposity of the noble Earl of Essex. Establishment versus anti-Establishment! There is something of that too in the relationship of Essex to the Court; but in the main it is the Queen who occupies the forefront of our attention. In her is concentrated the battle between the public and the private, the conflict which is not only the kernel of the drama but also the prime agent of the shaping of the music, both its broad structure and its detail. As in any major Britten opera—and in my view *Gloriana* is a major work by any reckoning—there are immense rewards to be gained from study of the overall structure and the wealth of imagination with which it is filled out.

The opera is built outwards from the centre—a highly poetic and dramatic centre, the passionate relationship of the Queen and Essex. Two hearts, Gloriana's and Robin's (the Queen's use of the diminutive is a sign of her affection for Essex), pulse at the opera's midpoint; and one may be pretty sure that it was the possibilities of their dialogue that set the composer's inspiration (and his own heart)

[1] This text first appeared in *Opera*, October 1966, pp.767–74.

ticking over. The two great pillars that support the dramatic arch of *Gloriana* are the two duets of the Queen and Essex, the first in Act I scene 2, the second in Act III scene 1. The Gloriana–Essex relationship brings further evidence of the scope of Britten's gift for musicalizing a wide variety of passions; it is an astonishing spectrum that can include Sid and Nancy (from *Albert Herring*) and Elizabeth and Essex. The Elizabeth–Essex relationship is a brilliant study of the ambiguities that can surround a great passion. No need to doubt a basic mutual admiration. But how far does Essex love (and therefore flatter) the Queen because she is also the instrument of his ambition? How far does Gloriana love Robin because he represents for her a vanished youth and freedom?—for the ageing of the Queen is an important element in the portrait that the opera offers (see Act III scene 1).

All this is indicative of the complexity of levels that one encounters as soon as one approaches the heart of the opera. In short, it is in the private face of *Gloriana* that the essence of the work resides. This is in no way to disparage or underestimate the opera's public face. The spectacle is magnificent. But the grand accumulation of pageant, pomp and ceremony that forms so important a part of the work is an outward projection of the inner dramatic situation; hence the strength and relevance of the spectacle. The opera has two selves, the public and the private, which reflect the very constitution of the Queen herself and her relation to Essex, which is in itself a symbol of her dilemma. And I would suggest that one of the most profitable ways of approaching *Gloriana* is to trace its mingling of public and private and to observe the mastery with which Britten makes a unity of the conflict in which the opera has its roots.

A superficial glance at the vocal score might lead one to think that Britten has solved the structural problem by an elementary strategy: the confinement of public and private to separate scenes. But this, of course, would be far too rudimentary a device for a composer who is sophisticated in the best sense, i.e. one who makes immensely complex demands of our musical sensibilities. What we find in *Gloriana*, in fact, are many scenes and situations where the dividing-line is blurred; and these give rise to some of the tensest and most elaborate music in the score. A case in point is the wonderful second scene of Act II, in the garden of Essex House in the Strand, which culminates in a conspiratorial quartet of superb quality; the plotting, vengeful Essex is cautioned by his wife but supported in his ambition by Mountjoy and Lady Rich. The fantastic counterpoint of this ensemble represents an extraordinary double image: the intertwining of personal motives and, at the same time, the gravity of matters of State. Here it is useless to distinguish between public and private. The very counterpoint of private and public is the image that this quartet unfolds.

Gloriana is peculiarly rich in ensembles; I cannot think of another opera of Britten's, *Albert Herring* apart, which offers us such rewards in this sphere. The very first scene of Act I sets a precedent, closing with the radiant 'Ensemble of Reconciliation' in which Gloriana heals the breach between the ruffled Essex and Mountjoy, and imposes a stately unity on her temperamental courtiers. This is a big, spacious, majestic ensemble (with chorus), as public as, say, the quartet in Act II scene 3 is private. Here, the jealous Queen has publicly humiliated Lady Essex by purloining her dress at a Court dance and appearing in it herself, to grotesque and insulting effect. Lady Essex is consoled in a ravishing quartet, 'Good Frances, do not weep', which is a momentary oasis of intimacy in an otherwise brilliant and spectacular scene. The quartet is predominantly a tender inspiration but, even so, room is found in it for expression of Essex's outraged sentiments on behalf of his wife. We are reminded again that the operatic ensemble is the ideal vehicle for the counterpointing of dissimilar personal motives of contrasting reactions to a dramatic event. The unusual wealth of ensembles in *Gloriana* reflects a basic feature of the work that is still far too little appreciated: that the drama is not depicted in a series of historical tableaux but conceived as an interplay of conflicting passions among private persons who also wield public power.

Although there is no rigid distinction between exterior and interior scenes in *Gloriana*, five of the eight scenes clearly represent the public vein in the Queen's life: Act I scene 1, 'Outside a Tilting Ground'; Act II scene 1, Gloriana 'on progress' at Norwich; Act II scene 3, the ball at the Palace of Whitehall; and Act III scene 2, a street in London, which ingeniously conveys the news of Essex's rebellion and his subsequent proclamation as a traitor through the stop-press narration of a ballad singer. None the less, the composer and his admirable librettist, William Plomer, skilfully infiltrate unforgettable interiors into their exterior scenes. Even in the generally colourful first scene of Act I, the dark impetuosity of Essex is established in his jealous quarrel with Mountjoy. In a flash, a shaft is sunk into the turbulent depths of Essex's character. But by and large these are scenes devoted to the spectacle and public homage which were an obligatory part of the Queen's functions.

We should note the quality of Britten's invention in these scenes. He has never found it difficult to respond to just those social needs which form part of the opera's action. Indeed, in these public scenes we see him acting as composer to the Court of Queen Elizabeth I, and how brilliantly he fulfils his state commissions! One wonders what other composer could have brought off a chain of choral dances of such unparalleled freshness as those that adorn the Norwich scene. No marking time or padding out with ceremonious gestures: on the contrary, his inspiration works at top pressure, and it is small wonder that the music of the Masque has become celebrated as a choral suite in its own right. Similarly inventive is Act II scene 3, where a sequence of onstage instrumental public dances provides a back-ground to the cut-and-thrust of the private intrigue. Perhaps one ought to write background and foreground, because the mobile dialogue between the orchestras on stage and in the pit offers a continual shift of dramatic perspectives. Pastiche is scarcely an adequate term for the weight of re-creation that Britten brings to bear on his material.[2] These dances, like the choral dances in the Norwich scene, show a virtuosity of composition that lifts them out of the sphere of the merely incidental, decorative or dramatically functional. The opening pavane, brooding, sombre and moody, is characteristic: a dance charged with the tension that is to erupt later in the act. And if we attend to its detail, we discover a small and economical masterpiece of contrapuntal composition. Its intensity is a reflection of that virtuosity I have just mentioned. This is not imitation, but inspiration: and no more than an open pair of ears is required to make sure that we do not mistake one for the other.

This scene in the Palace of Whitehall is rich in private incident and public event; we move freely between different planes of action, and between two orchestras. And through the whole scene the dances thread their way, serving their various functions as exterior spectacle or personal comment: highly personal, indeed, when a distorted version of the hectic volta accompanies the Queen's burlesque of Lady Essex. This kind of development should make us doubly conscious of the potentialities Britten uncovered in the dances and

[2] See p.48 above, where Imogen Holst describes the research Britten required her to undertake for this scene [C.P.].

exploited to such surprising and novel effect. The interplay of the two orchestras in this scene allows the act to end with an astonishing *coup de théâtre*. After the Queen's appointment of Essex to overthrow Tyrone, which is celebrated in a big ensemble (again full of conflicting personal motives), a final dance is commanded to end the proceedings. The onstage orchestra begins a quick D major coranto, but before long the theme of the preceding ensemble—'Victor of Cadiz, / Overcome Tyrone!'—is softly introduced by the pit orchestra in unison, grows in volume, and finally obliterates the gay coranto. This massive assertion of A minor leaves us in no doubt that Essex's peak of exalted ambition is also the moment of his downfall. It ends an act which is truly spectacular, yet at the same time presents a highly worked-out web of personal ambitions.

While this most complex of the big, public scenes shows also the impact of human passions, the most private scenes, in turn, show the pressure of public cares on personal destinies. This is true above all of the Queen herself, whose central dilemma is the image refracted throughout the whole opera. Her feeling for Essex is the private ache which continuously nags at her dutiful consciousness of her solemn obligation to rule not only her subjects but herself.

I have outlined one example of the interaction of State and individual destiny in the conspiratorial Act II scene 2. The two scenes which go to the heart of the matter are, of course, those which involve the Queen and Essex virtually alone: Act I scene 2 and Act III scene 1. Both take place in the Queen's apartments at Nonesuch, the first when the relationship, though fraught with peril, might still yield at least Essex's public triumph and the continued intimate favour of his Queen, the second when all is dust and ashes, his career and his loyalty at serious risk, and the Queen disillusioned.

Essex's entry in Act I scene 2 is preceded by the Queen's conversation with Cecil, in which Ex.1a keeps us aware of the heavy

Ex.1a

cares of State always burdening the Sovereign. When he interrupts Cecil's audience, Essex's impetuous, yearning motif, 'Queen of my life!', an intrusion of the private on the public, is combined with the 'Cares of State' idea (Ex.1b). Thus the conflict underpinning the central dramatic concept is immediately exposed. It is some little

Ex.1b

while before the duet itself is under way, and some time before Essex finds the right music for the Queen's mood; his first lute song, says Gloriana, is 'Too light, too gay'. The second, 'Happy were he', an unforgettable inspiration, discloses the melancholy that lies at the centre of his turbulence. The dissonant pedals sustained throughout the first song tell us in advance of the Queen's comment that Essex has not yet struck the right note; and it is only after a wide-ranging sequence of soft brass chords—predictions of the song to come—that he alights on the C minor that unlocks his heart. The duet itself skilfully rounds out his character, his romantic, tender attachment to the Queen, his ardour, his ferocious suspicion of the Establishment. The Queen's feelings are also revealed: her admiration of Essex's fiery spirit and the animation brought by his recognition of her as prince and woman, which alleviate her consciousness of her declining years. None the less, the duet ends with a reminder of the 'Cares of State' (see Ex.1a), which prompts Gloriana to an affirmation of her sovereign responsibilities (the Queen's 'Soliloquy and Prayer').

The second duet is placed in Act III scene 1, where we also enjoy some of the most ravishing music for women's voices (a semi-chorus of Maids of Honour) that Britten has written since *The Rape of Lucretia*. Again we are in the Queen's apartments, but this time the dramatic situation is reversed. Essex has faltered in his loyalties, and the Queen is aware not only of her Robin's painful instability but of her own age (Essex has surprised her while she prepares to dress). The reversals are registered in the music. How dejected, for example, is Essex's 'Queen of my Life!' when transposed to a lower octave (Ex.2), so very different from the springy rapture of Ex.1b. But Ex.1b still has a role to play. It appears, charged once again with the energy and fervour of its original guise, as Essex makes a last attempt to turn the tide of the duet back in his favour. But his appeal fails and the motif sinks into a C minor, funeral-march-like section in which both the

Ex.2

Queen and Essex recognize that the past is irretrievable. C minor, we recall, was the key of the second lute song, which preceded the first duet; and it is with an infinitely poignant recollection of 'Happy were he'—now, 'Happy were *we*'—that the second duet comes to rest. Then there is a final orchestral reference to Ex.1b as the Queen commands Essex to depart, and, mingled with it, the pervasive 'Cares of State' motif (Ex.1a). Robin goes out of the apartment—and physically out of the opera—to a hushed, fateful juxtaposition of the motifs which marked his entry in Act I scene 2.

In the last scene the Queen has to decide whether or not to sign Essex's death warrant. But her decision—that Essex must die—leaves the conflict unresolved. The irreconcilable remains unreconciled. In the opera's closing pages, the great Queen, near to death, surveys her past, and amidst the grand verbal recollections of her public life there runs the private thread of the second lute song, now in majestic orchestral dress and elaborately worked. At the end of her life and her reign Gloriana is still faced by these two conflicting selves: 'I am, and am not; freeze, and yet I burn; / Since from myself my other self I turn'. The music tells us that she still holds Robin firm in her thoughts, which is perhaps a triumph of a kind; but achieved at what cost, at what cost.

18

The Composer's *Dream*[1]

BENJAMIN BRITTEN

Last August it was decided that for this year's Aldeburgh Festival I should write a full-length opera for the opening of the reconstructed Jubilee Hall.

As this was a comparatively sudden decision there was no time to get a libretto written, so we took one that was ready to hand. I get a lot of letters from young people asking me how they should use their talents, and I always reply that they should try to fit them into their surroundings. This is what has happened with my new opera. It is an example of how local conditions can determine what you do.

I have always loved *A Midsummer Night's Dream*. As I get older, I find that I increasingly prefer the work either of the very young or of the very old. I always feel *A Midsummer Night's Dream* to be by a very young man, whatever Shakespeare's actual age when he wrote it. Operatically, it is especially exciting because there are three quite separate groups—the lovers, the rustics, and the fairies—which nevertheless interact. Thus in writing the opera I have used a different kind of texture and orchestral 'colour' for each section. For instance, the fairies are accompanied by harps and percussion; though obviously with a tiny orchestra they can't be kept absolutely separate.

In writing opera, I have always found it very dangerous to start writing the music until the words are more or less fixed. One talks to a possible librettist, and decide together the shape of the subject and its treatment. In my case, when I worked with E. M. Forster or William Plomer, for instance, we blocked the opera out in the way that an artist might block out a picture. With *A Midsummer Night's Dream*, the first task was to get it into manageable shape, which basically

[1] From the *Observer*, 5 June 1960.

entailed simplifying and cutting an extremely complex story—one can only hope that one hasn't lost too much, but since the sung word takes so much longer than the spoken word, to have done the complete *A Midsummer Night's Dream* would have produced an opera as long as the *Ring*.

Peter Pears (who sings Flute, the bellows-mender) and I had endless trouble with the references and the proportions of the play. We stuck faithfully to Shakespeare's words, actually adding only one line: 'Compelling thee to marry with Demetrius'. We worked from many texts, but principally from facsimiles of the First Folio and the First Quarto.

I do not feel in the least guilty at having cut the play in half. The original Shakespeare will survive. Nor did I find it daunting to be tackling a masterpiece which already has a strong verbal music of its own. Its music and the music I have written for it are at two quite different levels. I haven't tried to put across any particular idea of the play that I could equally well express in words, but although one doesn't intend to make any special interpretation, one cannot avoid it.

The opera is more relaxed than *The Turn of the Screw*; it has far more scenes, and is much less uniform. In form, it is more like *Peter Grimes*. I have felt it to be a more difficult task to write than these, partly because the work in hand is always the hardest, partly because of the tremendous challenge of those Shakespearean words. Working at it, one was very conscious that one must not let through a single ill-considered phrase because it would be matched to such great poetry.

I actually started work on the opera in October, and finished it on, I think, Good Friday—seven months for everything, including the score. This is not up to the speed of Mozart or Verdi, but these days, when the line of musical language is broken, it is much rarer. It is the fastest of any big opera I have written, though I wrote *Let's Make an Opera* in a fortnight.

Writing an opera is very different from writing individual songs: opera, of course, includes songs, but has many other musical forms and a whole dramatic shape as well. In my experience, the shape comes first. With *A Midsummer Night's Dream*, as with other operas, I first had a general musical conception of the whole work in my mind. I conceived the work without any one note being defined. I could have described the music, but not played a note.

It was a particularly bad winter for me, writing it. Normally I work

perfectly regular hours, in the morning and again between four and
eight in the evening. Around Aldeburgh, the weather seems always to
be better in the morning; it clouds over about midday and I don't
work then. I cannot work at night. In Suffolk the air is strong, and by
nightfall I want to do nothing but sleep. This winter I became quite
ill, but had to go on working. A lot of the third act was written when I
was not at all well with flu. I didn't enjoy it. But I find that one's
inclination, whether one wants to work or not, does not in the least
affect the quality of the work done. Very often it is precisely after one
has had what one feels to have been a wonderful morning, that one
needs to watch out—perhaps one's critical faculties may have been
asleep.

I haven't tried to give the opera an Elizabethan flavour. It is no
more Elizabethan than Shakespeare's play was Athenian. Perhaps one
or two points may seem strange. The fairies, for instance, are very
different from the innocent nothings that often appear in productions
of Shakespeare. I have always been struck by a kind of sharpness
in Shakespeare's fairies; besides, they have some odd poetry to
speak—the part about 'you spotted snakes with double tongue' for
instance. The fairies are, after all, the guards to Tytania:[2] so they
have, in places, martial music. Like the actual world, incidentally, the
spirit world contains bad as well as good.

Puck is a quite different character from anyone else in the play.
He seems to me to be absolutely amoral and yet innocent. In this
production he is being played by the 15-year-old son of Leonide
Massine: he doesn't sing, but only speaks and tumbles about. I got the
idea of doing Puck like this in Stockholm, where I saw some Swedish
child acrobats with extraordinary agility and powers of mimicry, and
suddenly realized we could do Puck that way.

The opera, since it was written for a hall which holds only 316
people, is small-scale. The forces one uses must necessarily be small,
which has great advantages: one can work in a more detailed way with
them and get a greater degree of discipline. The singers do not have to
sing with such uniform volume, so that the voice can be used
throughout its full range of colour. Besides, on a small scale, we can
choose singers who either can act or who are prepared to learn to do
so. Some opera-goers seem to prefer singers who cannot act: there is a

[2] The spelling adopted by Britten and Pears, approximating to the Elizabethan
pronunciation. Shakespeare's source for the Queen of the Fairies' name was Ovid's
Metamorphoses, where both Diana and Circe are referred to as 'Titania' [C.P.].

curious inverted snobbery current in this country which even prefers operatic acting to be as bad as possible. They do not want opera to be serious at all. They like singers who merely come down to the footlights and yell.

For my part, I want singers who can act. Mozart, Gluck and Verdi wanted the same thing. There is one singer in this production who has never been on a stage before in his life;[3] but his strong concert personality fits naturally on to the operatic stage and his acting is developing very well. How many singers know how to move? I think it's essential for every potential opera singer to have a course of movement in an opera school. I must say one hoped, after the war, that audiences would revolt at seeing opera performed with bad acting, bad scenery and in a foreign language.

We are taking *A Midsummer Night's Dream* to Holland immediately after the Aldeburgh Festival. If it is any good it will get many different interpretations in many different places and all with translations. I have even heard *Peter Grimes* in Serbo-Croat. But the new opera was really written as part of the Aldeburgh Festival, for the reopening of the Jubilee Hall. Ultimately, it is to me the local things that matter most.

[3] Alfred Deller, who played Oberon [C.P.].

19

The Truth of the *Dream*

WILFRID MELLERS

In so far as Britten's operas gravitate around the relationship between innocence and experience they are also concerned with the relationship between reality and dream. It is too simple to say that in 'growing up' we are entering reality and leaving illusion behind; our unconscious motivations may be truer than conscious truth, and only in dreams may we be born again. Something of this is implicit in the interrelationship between natural and supernatural worlds in *The Turn of the Screw*, wherein subconscious realms touch, even while being inimical to, the heart's core. Whatever 'reality' may be, it is not totally contained within the social conventionalities and moral proprieties of Bly; and the opera concerns the Governess's necessary, but in her case bemused and disastrous, search for deeper veracities.[1]

After that crucially potent opera, Britten wrote a number of works that explored dream as a gateway to truth. The most profound is explicitly called *Nocturne*; a song-cycle for tenor, obbligato instruments and strings, it starts where its companion piece, the *Serenade* for tenor, horn and strings, leaves off. The *Serenade* deals in daytime experience, while ending with Keats's wonderful invocation of sleep. The *Nocturne* deals entirely in the world of night, but sees dreams as the source of the deepest reality known to us. The final song, a setting of Shakespeare's sonnet 'When most I wink, then do mine eyes best see', fulfils the cycle's theme, for Britten reveals the mystical depth beneath Shakespeare's conceit about the lover who sees his love 'bright in dark directed'. It is no longer merely the human beloved we are seeking in the blackness of the night; it is also the Beloved, the wellspring of life that mysteriously renews the human spirit.

[1] See above, chapter 13.

Britten calls on Shakespeare again for an opera closely associated with the *Nocturne*, and uses Shakespeare's text virtually without modification, except that for operatic purposes the script of a full-length play has to be reduced by about half. Shakespeare's *A Midsummer Night's Dream* is, as its title tells us, specifically about the relationship between reality and dream, and between natural and supernatural beings. The action functions on three planes: the conscious, or would-be conscious, world of the sophisticated young Athenians; the preconscious world of the fairies; and the world of the 'rude mechanicals' which is halfway between the two, human yet brutish, and therefore intuitively in touch with natural and supernatural realms. Being an early comedy, the play is not directly concerned with tragic experience, though the material of tragedy is latent in the human egoism inherent in Athenian law and in a father's harsh decree, and in the lovers' multiple self-deceptions. The play is thus about youth and the various kinds of illusion to which youth—and innocence in general, for the low types are not all young—is susceptible. Entering the magic wood, the humans encounter the supernatural beings, whose relationship to the humans parallels that of Greek immortals to mortals. It would seem that the human mind cannot conceive of a divine hierarchy as much less muddled than our own. The difference lies in the faculty for wish-fulfilment: the fairies can occasionally put things right by magic, we can't. So the mortals suffer for their mistakes and the fuddled fairies help them to start afresh, which may be a synonym for learning by experience. But nobody believes in solutions; both the humans and the fairies will commit the same idiocies and perversities as before, and neither human will nor fairy magic can be infallible.

Britten omits Shakespeare's Act I in the 'external' world in order to concentrate on the effect of dream on mortal creatures. At his beginning the twilit mystery of the magic wood is incarnate in a series of *pianissimo* major triads, linked by string glissandi. These diatonic concords cover all twelve notes of the chromatic scale and, despite their euphony, are in 'false' and enharmonic relation with one another, so their mystery is ambiguous from the start. The first characters to appear are four fairies who 'wander everywhere' to a falling and rising scale in 6/4, oddly elided across the bar lines so that we don't 'really' know where everywhere is. Tonality too is ambiguous: a Lydian G major with hints of D and F sharp. The voices are accompanied by magic instruments which, in this opera as in

The Truth of the Dream

The Turn of the Screw, tend to be percussive—harp, vibraphone, xylophone, glockenspiel. Although it is sung by children, the music is sharp, almost acid; their innocence, being preconscious, carries a threat, if only because it is beyond our would-be civilized awareness. This is explicit in the figure of Puck, a sprite who, linking mortals with immortals, is indeed 'beyond good and evil'. Britten indicates his moral neutrality by having him played by a boy acrobat who speaks rather than sings. His instrument is a trumpet, bounding in Brittenesque thirds, with a tabor-like drum that underlines his connection with the plough cycles and folk dramas on which Shakespeare also draws.

Like the fairy children, Oberon and Tytania, their King and Queen, are separated from normal operatic convention in that he is a counter-tenor and she a coloratura soprano. She is closer to normality and more capable of 'human' emotion than seraphic counter-tenor or children, and she falls in love with a human masquerading as a beast. That she crosses the barriers between human and non-human worlds may be why she and Oberon are at odds. He covets an (orphaned) human boy over whom she has established possession, and because they quarrel, Nature is in chaos: spring, summer and winter 'change their wanted liveries', to vividly naturalistic aural imagery. The basic tonality of this opening scene is A major, usually associated by Britten with Nature and often with childhood; but the key's radiance is disguised by bitonal accretions and undermining enharmony. The scene suggests that whatever supernatural destiny may rule us it is at best arbitrary, at worst malignant. And chance affects the immortals no less than us. Left alone, Oberon decides to spite Tytania by putting a spell on her whereby she will be unable to distinguish truth from falsehood, and sends Puck (who is also luck, good or bad) to seek a spellbinding herb. Oberon's instrument is the celesta, which intertwines in parallel major seconds, hinting at whole-tone instability. Puck frisks off to the sound of his arpeggiated trumpet and tabor, and the empty wood's glissandi and concords re-emerge. Throughout Act I they separate the appearances of the mortals and the immortals, enclosing both within sleep. That they contain the twelve chromatic semitones suggests that sleep forms a cosmos encompassing all aspects of our being—much as the twelve-note series that opens *The Turn of the Screw* is instrumentally varied in the interludes that represent the tightening 'turns' within the Governess's mind.

When Lysander and Hermia, the first pair of human lovers, appear they are 'lost in the blind mazes of this tangled wood' yet are at the same time imprisoned in, because frustrated by, their lost state. Rhythmically, their dualogue is dominated by an agitated ostinato of crotchet triplet–two quavers–quaver triplet; thematically, their music grows from permutations of a descending semitone followed by falling minor third and rising semitone—a humanly expressive motif within which we hear the alternating major and minor third of 'blue' false relations, though the major third is usually notated as a diminished fourth. They are in love; but since their love is aborted by human pride and wilfulness they resolve, as their duet flows into a more spacious if meandering line, to run away, through the wood, to a place where the 'sharp Athenian Law' cannot pursue them. Throughout the duet, tonality wanders too; though the key signature suggests E flat, which is the tonality associated with immortal Oberon and Tytania, this goal is not attained until, at the end of their dialogue, they swear mutual fidelity in a repeated-note incantation over their ostinato rhythm. Even so, repetitions of the oath flit through unrelated concords recalling those of the magic wood, the music of which recurs as the lovers stray more deeply into the forest, and Oberon reappears, to his secundally undulating celesta. The interdependence of mortals and immortals is revealed in the fact that his theme is a chromatic permutation of the alternating fourths and thirds to which the humans had meandered. It sounds spell-like in being self-enclosed, its second two bars being an inversion of the first two.

The other pair of potential lovers enters to an extension of the earlier love music, the intertwining minor thirds and diminished fourths being pervasive. They are only potential lovers since Demetrius is a hater who, chased by Helena, thinks he's in love with Hermia. Helena's simplicity is evident when, with tonality clearing to innocent A major, she self-abasedly compares herself to a fawning spaniel; the sixths of the scale are persistently flattened, and the diminished fourths between F natural and C sharp sound spaniel-like, simultaneously comic and forlorn. The human pair distractedly disperse as Puck returns to present the spellbinding herb to Oberon, who rapturously sings his set piece, 'I know a bank where the wild thyme blows'. It floats out of his undulating seconds on celesta, over the habitual pedal E flat, and thematically opens with the motif of alternating fourth (this time perfect) and third. Vocal melismata follow verbal inflection in a sublimated Purcellian arioso, garlanded with liquid harp scales as well as celesta. The spell itself, chanted over a fifth of G to D, tensely diminishes both the third and the fourth; the snake, with his 'enamell'd skin', is as seductive as Eden's serpent. The thematic motif gradually fades into almost spoken recitative on E flats repeated through the oscillating seconds. When the wood's dream chords and glissandi again take over, the 'rude mechanicals' enter to plan their play within the play, thereby giving another dimension to the theme of appearance and reality.

Though their 'Rurall Musicke' is grotesque, Britten's emulation of it is at once farcical and touching; he no more guys it than does Shakespeare. Indeed his music makes immediately evident what Shakespeare's words reveal only later: for the rustics' perky dotted rhythms are riddled with Oberon's parallel seconds, suggesting that the dim-witted yokels are in closer rapport with Nature, and even with the supernatural, than are the offspring of civilization. When they rehearse their play of Pyramus and Thisbe, which is about the destruction of true love by chance's malice, both the story they tell and the music they enact it to are ironic commentaries on the fortunes and misfortunes of the civilized: musical references to clichés of Italian romantic opera and to music-hall ditty and pub ballad are hilarious, yet also affecting in that they indicate how vulnerable are the masks which man as a social being presents to the world. The human hearts of the 'mechanicals' are revealed by Britten's music with an acuity that rivals Shakespeare's; in a trice knockabout farce may be metamorphosed into pathos, as when the bumpkins fearfully admit in *pianissimo* sextet that any offence to propriety would 'hang us all . . . every mother's son'. When they disperse, their adieux have a comparable tenderness; they seem to belong to the wood's triads and glissandi, into which their choric ululations dissolve.

The action switches to the first pair of lovers, still wandering in the woody maze, to music still dominated by their ostinato rhythm, now the other way round (quaver triplet–two quavers–crotchet triplet), and by the motivic minor third and diminished fourth, which sometimes sounds like a major third, or is stretched to a perfect fourth. The key signature again contains three flats, though there is no resolution into 'divine' E flat major, or even into C minor. When in weariness they fall asleep, they do so in canon, to a chromaticized version of the motif, ending on unison F sharps that ambiguously suggest F sharp minor, A major and D major. They thereby approximate to the tonality of Puck, who returns to the sound of his bounding trumpet, tinselled with his master's celesta. Although he is supernatural, he anoints the wrong eyes. Chance is blind indeed, though there may also be method in madness since it is through mis-take, mis-fortune and il-lusion that rebirth becomes feasible.

When the four lovers meet they are tortuously locked in their delusory identities; like most of us, they lack self-knowledge and therefore knowledge of one another. Britten brilliantly conveys this confusion by allowing the vocal phrases to expand into rising scales, and to modulate continuously. Yet the music cannot release itself from the prison of the motivic fourth and third, and is stabbed by syncopated quavers in whole-tone seconds, and later—as Hermia recounts her serpent-infested dream—by dissonant semiquaver quintuplets. The magic wood's concords and glissandi return as accompaniment to an arioso of Tytania, balancing Oberon's song about the bank with the wild thyme. She drugs herself with her voluptuous and virtuosic arabesques, and the fairies lull her to sleep with their 'spotted snakes' ditty. The verses are hardly comforting, for their spiky textures and broken rhythms are inspired by the snakes, hedgehogs and newts they're supposed to be banishing. But the Philomel refrain recalls Oberon's secundal oscillations, while the lulling itself reverts to the floating scales they had sung at the beginning of the opera. The harmony is tart; this dream, like *The Turn of the Screw*'s nightmare, fuses the light and the dark. Oberon squeezes the herb's juice into Tytania's sleeping eyes and croons his incantation over her, undulating in the motivic fourth and third over the E flat pedal; string tremolandi are splattered with glockenspiel and celesta. Committing her to waking illusion 'when some vile thing is near', he ends with the fourth–third theme mirrored in glassy inversion. The act dissipates into the forest noises.

Act II deals with the effects of the spell on mortals and immortals, and Britten devises for it another exquisitely precise musical image. Four concordant but unrelated chords embrace every note of the chromatic scale and so, like the original forest murmurs, may be said to embrace a cosmos—that of the psyche in sleep. Each chord is allotted to a different instrumental group: D flat major to muted strings; D major with added sixth to muted brass; E flat major first inversion to woodwind; and a C major third to harps and 'magic' instruments. That the mind is multi-faceted is suggested by the way Britten opens the act, with four variations on these chords, incorporating barely perceptible hints of the lovers' motifs, of

Oberon's seconds, and even of the Mechanicals' 'Rurall Musicke'. Perhaps it is not fortuitous that the bucolics first break the spell, clumping in for their rehearsal. Again their antics are suddenly illumined with pathos—for instance the *pianissimo* diminished fourth to 'present the person of Moonshine'. As Puck flies in, derisively watching, we cannot miss the affinity between his bouncy thirds and the rustics' galumphing bassoon and trombone. At the spectacle of Bottom 'translated' into an ass by Puck the yokels at first yell in ignorant terror, but then break into a fourth-founded homophonic quintet expressive of awe and wonder. They may be illiterate, but they recognize a marvel when they stumble on it: which is more than could be said for some more ostensibly civilized beings.

Left alone with the sleeping Tytania, Bottom tries to cheer himself up by bellowing a pop song. Britten's tune for 'The woosell cock' sounds raucously earthy, yet is tinged with human incertitude, since it incorporates the oscillating fourth and third. Awakened by Bottom's hubbub, Tytania is magicked into loving him. Her 'immortal' E flats, haloed with harp and glockenspiel, gain ascendancy over Bottom's all too mortal, trombone-based ditty, which is silenced when the four fairies are summoned to attend to Bottom's needs. Their music preserves its acerbity, with Puckish fanfares on muted brass; but Tytania's brisk waltz, inviting the fairies to reward beautiful Bottom with the lavish fruits of the earth, is merely pretty because merely illusory. The fairies pay homage to Bottom in a 'bowing' song in the dotted rhythm beloved of the high baroque; interlocking thirds and fourths pervade their tunes. Though the prankish fairy children are comic, their music has here a piquant gravity which prepares us for a radical change in mood when Bottom settles himself to sleep. For over harp triplets, clarinet and flute weave a lovely cantilena, moving stepwise or by minor thirds in tenderly voluptuous arches. There is a further ironic reversal when the fairies play Bottom a bucolic music on 'the tongs and the bones' (recorders, small cymbals, blocks): a music as childish as his own limited consciousness, in 'white' C major, related, perhaps, to Tytania's little waltz in the same key. But when Bottom has dozed off the cantilena recurs in a remote B major, and Tytania herself, taking her love in her arms, warbles to him the most ravishing music in this wondrously sensuous score. There's a poignant irony in the fact that this moment of ultimate beauty is provoked by false-seeming; is it that the Queen of the Fairies loves Bottom because, metamorphosed into a beast, he is closer to her world than he was in his human state? Certainly on the evidence of her *music* Tytania's love for Bottom misconceived seems deeper than whatever it is she feels for Oberon. The four magic chords recur at her overt admission of her love, and are again submitted to four instrumental variations.

At the last C major third Puck flits in to report to Oberon of Tytania's doting; in remarking that 'This falls out better than I could devise' Oberon confesses that he is no omnipotent godhead. That his power is a matter of chance is proved by the entrance of Hermia and Demetrius, human lovers hopelessly muddled by Puck's mismanaged magic. The diminished fourth–minor third motif, originally associated with human passion and its disruptive effects, is stated directly on tremolando strings, pierced by dissonant quintuplets on woodwind. Oberon, having reprimanded Puck for his stupidity and possible malice, sends him to find the other lovers, in the hope of righting a few wrongs. When Demetrius has succumbed to a sleep provoked by nervous exhaustion Oberon anoints his eyes with the 'love-juice', to his original fourth–third spell, centred again on E flat but with a B flat pedal sustained through wavering harp and celesta.

Waking up, Demetrius confronts Helena, and of course now loves her. They are simpler, perhaps even cruder, creatures than the other pair of lovers; released from the fog of misapprehension, he sings vigorously of his new-found love, with the motivic fourth expanded to a fifth, in a tonality close to C minor (relative of E flat) with flattened seventh. The hint of persuasive rhetoric in his line is appropriate, since Helena naturally finds his protestations difficult to credit. When Hermia enters, Helena upbraids her too, wondering how she could have been so cruel to her old school-friend. At this point her line not surprisingly grows pentatonic, and finds its way to 'childish' A major. But the savagely stabbing quintuplets soon shatter this Edenic retrospect, and the act reaches its climax in an ensemble of perplexity wherein the pairs of lovers sing, in an agitated 3/8, out of the confusion of mutual incomprehension. The bandying of insults between the girls, triggered by Hermia's 'dwarfish' stature, is as funny as it is in Shakespeare, yet at the same time sharpens the edge of the prevailing nervous tension. The medley of agony and absurdity, pity and terror, fury and farce is a not inaccurate simile for the human condition. When the two young men challenge one another over their love for Helena they sing unisonally a permutation of the seminal motif frozen into rigid minims; pride dams the flow of human feeling.

The girls rush off, and Oberon enters, in a rage; gods and mortals alike get it all wrong. Puck confesses that 'I mistook', and over his ostinato E flat Oberon encourages him to try again. Puck's 'false' voice confuses the would-be aggressive young men so that, worn out by their wanderings in the wood, they again droop into sleep, to a recurrence of the spellbinding chord sequence. This time each chord is long sustained, supporting themes derived from the motif. Lysander has the fourth and third over the D flat major triad; Demetrius has it over the D major with added sixth; Helena has it, more simply, over the E flat first inversion. Puck momentarily takes over in bitonality between E flat and his habitual F sharp–D–A complex; while the fourth chord, the high C major third, is reserved for Hermia, emotionally most intense of the human characters. She has the most lyrically sustained version of the latent theme thus far. The act ends with the fairies singing a therapeutic lullaby over the sleepers, the chord sequence being reiterated several times both forwards and backwards, while the vocal incantation swings gently in parallel thirds. The static spell is thus imbued with some harmonic momentum; its remedial function is now operative.

At the opening of Act III we are still in the wood, but night has been dispelled by early morning. Britten's musical image for this is itself aural magic. Oberon's whole-tone seconds are expanded into minor sevenths, floating in a diaphanous texture in the Dorian mode on G, devoid of chromatic alteration. Oberon promises to restore the sleepers to their former selves, renewed; and begins with his Tytania, whom he forgives, having (it seems) got his way over the orphaned human boy. This may mean that a bit of Tytania's tentative 'humanity' spills over, with the dawning day, on to the god-king; certainly Oberon's magically chromaticized seconds release Tytania to an exquisite unfolding of the diatonic music that opens the act. The King and Queen then awaken the four lovers by dancing a sacral sarabande in a gently double-dotted rhythm. Though the key signature has two flats, the melody gravitates around Oberon's E flat pedal, so the tonality is probably Lydian—a mode traditionally associated with healing, as the slow movement of Beethoven's opus 132 sublimely indicates. At the end of the sarabande a lark-emulating piccolo provides an ecstatic obbligato to the human–divine dance at dawn. But the lovers' awakening to their true selves is prompted not only by the lark but also by distant horn-calls, which echo from the 'real' world—the Court where Theseus and Hippolyta are to celebrate their marriage. Surfacing from sleep the lovers utter their true mates' names to permutations of the fourths and thirds, perfect and imperfect (Hermia's version, we note, is the most awestruck). The opera's marvellous climax occurs as the thirds and fourths ('mine own, and not mine own') swell into a slowly rising scale that irons out the 'meanderings' the lovers had gone through in Act I, and which had been prefigured in the fairies' wanderings 'over hill, over dale'. Letting in the light of understanding along with the light of day, the quartet is significantly supported only by sustained major triads similar to those which, in the first two acts' preludes and interludes, had contained the cosmos of the dreaming mind; musically as well as psychologically renewal has grown from submission to sleep. The lovers conclude their quartet by singing the original version of the motif—falling semitone, falling minor third, rising semitone, rising third—in canon by inversion. Mirrorwise, they at last see 'through a glass darkly'.

Bottom's retranslation effects a second, hardly less poignant climax. As he comes to consciousness he babbles snatches of the play of Pyramus, unable to distinguish between reality, theatrical illusion and visionary dream. Bits of his bawdy jig are interfused with Oberon's seconds, and with the clinging tendrils of Tytania's siren song. He returns to his peasant-like, child-like self to sing about his wonderful dream, again in C major, which seems to be a key of wish-fulfilment in this opera. He is once more the old Bottom, whose self-love is harmless, even amiable, compared with that of more pretentiously 'conscious' beings: so we are not surprised when his final apostrophe, beginning comically in falsetto, expands with true nobility into a 'tumbling strain' of falling thirds, over the four magic chords. Though he must return to his clownish condition, being incapable of grace, he has had his moment of vision, which distinguishes him from more mechanical mechanicals.

We are transported to Theseus' Court, which purports to be the 'real' world, by way of a quick march permeated by the horn-calls, over a passacaglia-style bass. Before the characters enter, the motif expands into the most sustained lyrical theme of the opera. The Duke annunciates his own marriage, and also that of the younger lovers, now restored to themselves and one another, the uncharitable Athenian law having been repealed by Theseus. The spacious theme that had grown from the motif rings in the bass, supporting ceremonial fanfares; but grandeur is deflated by the tootlings that introduce the play the yokels present in celebration of the royal wedding. The play's illusory nature is pointed by the civilized characters' bantering comments in secco recitative, but the irony is two-faced, since the play within the play, though uproariously funny, has a strength impervious to cynicism. It is tightly constructed in fourteen brief scenes arranged in mirror formation; and its musical-theatrical parodies are as beautiful as they are comic. Watching these antics in Britten's artefact we have no temptation to snigger at them as does the elegant audience at Theseus' Court.

Perhaps in real life we *might* snigger; if so, Britten offers the ultimate justification of art, which instils love by breaking barriers between dream and reality, innocence and experience. This is why he ends his opera as a genuine masque would have ended in the sixteenth century, merging theatrical artifice into the 'revels' in which the audience, both aristocratic and demotic, would have participated along with the actors and musicians. The mortals go off to bed while the fourth–third motif swings grandly in dotted rhythm; the immortals sing a night song that is by no means unequivocally reassuring, being tonally ambiguous, rhythmically nervous and melodically spiky, so that we remain aware of 'things that go bump in the night' even whilst they're being exorcized. Oberon and Tytania's final benediction begins in Puck's uneasy medley of F sharp, A and D, but settles into a 'slow and solemn' march in the radiance of F sharp major. Even here, however, the lilting Lombard rhythm is at odds with the verbal stresses, so a sense of startlement is still latent in the beatitude. The occupants of the house may be 'ever . . . blest', but it is Puck-Luck who speaks the epilogue, still to his prickly fanfares. So though he asks for and receives our approbation, we recognize that blessing is not an absolute, and tomorrow is another day. *A Midsummer Night's Dream* is a genuinely *comic* opera which none the less opens magic casements on '*perilous* seas, in faery lands *forlorn*'. If it is an accident that E flat is the key both of the immortals in *A Midsummer Night's Dream* and of Quint's evil in *The Turn of the Screw*, it is the kind of accident that happens only to genius. In the dark light of it we may understand why the comedy of the *Dream* is an achievement complementary to, and no less profound than, the tragedy of *The Turn of the Screw*.

20

Catching on to the technique in Pagoda-land

DONALD MITCHELL

Ubud, Bali (Indonesia)

17 January 1956
The music is *fantastically* rich—melodically, rhythmically, texture (such *orchestration*!!) and above all *formally*. It's a remarkable culture. . . . At last I'm beginning to catch on to the technique, but it's about as complicated as Schönberg.

(Britten to Imogen Holst)

The Prince of the Pagodas, Britten's only ballet score (his only mature score originally composed *for* the ballet, that is)[1] and that comparatively rare bird in the twentieth century, a *full-length* ballet, was first performed at the Royal Opera House, Covent Garden, in 1957, on the first day of the new year, with the composer conducting. The choreographer was John Cranko and the scenery was designed by John Piper.

Pangs rather than pleasure had attended the birth of the work, for Britten had found the whole business of writing the ballet an exceptionally arduous task. It was not so much the quantity of music involved, though this was daunting enough, but his being confronted with the difficulties, intransigencies and vivid temperaments (and tempers!) of the ballet world. The 'language' of ballet did not come easily to him: thus communication was a problem. It was an experience that left him feeling bruised and debilitated;[2] and almost

[1] Though one should bear in mind the Choral Dances from *Gloriana* and the dance element of *Death in Venice*.
[2] For example we find him writing to Erwin Stein (his publisher, at Boosey & Hawkes) on 13 November 1957: 'I was delighted with your sweet letter, but please don't think I

up to the time of his death he could rarely be persuaded to return to his score, either to look at it with a view to publication or to discuss a possible new production.

All this would be principally of biographical interest were it not for the fact that the experience of the première so profoundly coloured the composer's attitude to the work that to this day no full score, and indeed no score at all that he saw through the press himself, is generally available, and this a major composition that was first performed in 1957![3] A further ironic twist to the tale is provided by

---

was cross with anyone particular about the Ballet proofs. I was only just cross in the abstract to have to go back to that beastly work, of which at the moment I am heartily sick. The maddening thing is that after we have all spent hours reading it there will quite clearly remain dozens of mistakes. I frankly don't know what we can do, but I am clear at the moment I don't want any more to do with it! But I must not be silly, and your nice remarks about it make me feel that the work was not just a waste of a year's work.'

[3] Britten was also reluctant to approve the idea of a suite, to be drawn from the ballet by another and sympathetic hand, on the grounds that this was something he eventually wanted to do himself. But, though he may have contemplated it, he never got round to doing it. This meant that it was, in the main, only the *Pas de six*—the final set of dances from Act III scene 2—that was heard in the concert hall, and that infrequently. It was given a separate opus number, Op.57a, but was available only on hire, presumably because everyone was waiting on the appearance of the composer's own, or other authorized, suite, which was never to materialize. Not long before his death in 1976 Britten at last authorized the publication of a suite, taken from the ballet by Norman Del Mar. While this is more extensive than opus 57a, it is, in a sense, more 'Prince' than 'Pagodas' since, for practical reasons—the extra percussion required—it excludes the Pagodas' music. The 'Del Mar' Suite was given a first broadcast performance on 7 December 1963 by the BBC Scottish Orchestra conducted by Norman Del Mar. The first concert performance took place at the Edinburgh Festival on 29 August 1964. A study score of the 'Del Mar' Suite, *Prelude and Dances from the Prince of the Pagodas* (Op.57b: Boosey & Hawkes, 1980 (HPS 919)) constituted the first publication of any of the music from the ballet. (The first recording of this suite was issued in 1982 by EMI (ASD 4073).) Mr Del Mar has described the circumstances in which Britten heard the suite and the extent to which the published score of the suite neither represents entirely the composer's wishes (the *Pas de deux* is excluded) nor Mr Del Mar's own (so far as the finale is concerned). He writes in a 1980 programme note: 'Shortly before his death . . . Britten invited me to perform my suite in his presence at an Aldeburgh Festival and after this performance he finally sanctioned publication since he saw that he would clearly no longer consider tackling afresh the problems of a new and original suite. He regretted only two things: in the first place I had included nothing from Act II which described Bell Rose's journey through air, water and fire to Pagoda-land, and her first meeting with the Prince; and secondly he found my ending too abrupt.

'Where Act II was concerned a simple solution lay to hand in the form of the *Pas de deux* from the second scene describing the dance of the mystified Belle Rose with the Prince, temporarily released from his enchanted metamorphosis into a salamander, and this will be added to tonight's performance between Nos.4 and 5 of the [published] suite. . . .

the character of the music: it is not only one of the most exuberantly inventive of Britten's orchestral scores but also—if one can commit oneself at all to a sweeping generalization—one of his 'happiest' and most extrovert in spirit. We are lucky that the distempered view he came to take of the *Pagodas* did not prevent him from recording in 1957 a slightly shortened version of the complete score, and did not affect his spirited conducting of it.[4]

The Prince of the Pagodas remains an undeservedly little-known work, so I give here a synopsis[5] of the complete ballet as it was originally conceived for the first production of 1957:

ACT I

A brief orchestral introduction discloses first the fanfares (see Ex.15) that herald important events throughout the ballet and second a preview of Pagoda-land. Each of the *dramatis personae* in the ballet is depicted in a theme which remains a constant factor throughout while undergoing all manner of transformation and variation: the theme, like the human personality, retains its essentials but continually appears in a new light according to circumstance. Ex.1 is the motif

Ex.1

'But with regard to the ending, a problem remains. I had indeed omitted the final apotheosis as being too elaborate and diffuse to conclude a short suite of extracts, whilst failing to find a substitute, since only the composer himself could provide the necessary new music of the requisite proportions. The now published score, in deference to the composer's qualms, scrupulously documents the closing pages of the ballet without cuts or alterations of any kind, thus including both the grandiose apotheosis and the final gesturing of the Court Fool whose music appears nowhere else in the suite and has no relevance away from the stage. I therefore continue to end the suite exactly as I performed it to Britten on that happy and moving occasion at the Maltings, Snape, in June 1974.' A much more comprehensive suite, which *does* include the Pagodas' music, has been devised by Michael Lankester, who conducted its first performance, at a BBC Promenade Concert, on 21 July 1979. The materials for this suite can be hired from the publishers, Boosey & Hawkes. There is also at least one other concert suite, compiled by André Previn, and other conductors may have made individual compilations that have reached performance but have not otherwise been documented.

4 Originally issued by Decca on two discs, LXT 5336–7; now available in a boxed set, GOS 558–9.

5 Edited from my contribution to *The Decca Book of Ballet*, ed. David Drew (Decca, 1958).

associated with the Prince-as-Salamander. The curtain rises on the
Court of the Emperor of the Middle Kingdom. The compassionate
Fool prepares the room for the arrival of the Court. His characteristic
scurrying music is interrupted by a threatening trombone motif
associated with the malevolent Court Dwarf, who is bent on
obstructing the Fool as he goes about his duties (Ex.2). The Fool and

Ex.2

the Dwarf come to blows, but the Emperor enters and stops the fight
(alto saxophone and characteristic figuration). He separates the
opponents, after which a brilliant festal *March* introduces the
Courtiers. The *March* gives way to an elegant *Gavotte* (life at Court)
whose middle sections yield a solo dance for the Emperor (alto
saxophone), the major–minor theme registering the precariousness
and pathos of the aged Emperor's position (Ex.3). The *Gavotte*

Ex.3

returns and ends with the physically frail Emperor's collapse.
Fanfares, punctuated by distortions of the *Gavotte*, herald the arrival
of the four Kings who have come to seek the hand of the heiress to the
crown of the Middle Kingdom. The 'royalty' motif accompanies the
entry of their four Pages and, later, of the Kings themselves (Ex.4).

Ex.4

The Kings declare themselves in a series of character dances. The
King of the North dances a kind of Gopak; the King of the East is
immersed in a quivering but virtually static harmonic texture; the
King of the West is satirized in a malformed quasi-Polka(?), the
unmelodious melody of which is a grotesque twelve-note invention;
the King of the South polyrhythmically rocks and rolls to native
drums (see Ex.13a). The dances over, the Emperor sends for his elder
daughter, Princess Belle Épine. His questing figuration is succeeded

by her proud solo number (Ex.5), with a middle section (Ex.6) which later proves to be of great significance. The Kings bow to Belle Épine

Ex.5   Ex.6

(to Ex.4), but the Fool, to his own music, interrupts them and runs off to find Princess Belle Rose. The Dwarf tries to stop him (to Ex.2), but without success, and Belle Rose enters on the wings of an oboe, which bears the burden of her melody (Ex.7). First she dances alone, a

Ex.7

melancholy dance that expresses her status as a neglected younger daughter. But, as in a vision, the Prince appears to her, to his own princely tune (Ex.8). They dance together through a chain of

Ex.8

variations on Ex.8, at the height of which the Prince vanishes (cymbal), leaving Belle Rose alone. The Kings kneel ('royalty' motif, Ex.4) before Belle Rose—an action that angers the Emperor who, to yet another eruption of his nervous figuration, demands a choice of heiress. The Kings choose Belle Rose (Ex.4 again), and the now furious Emperor holds the crown over Belle Épine's head (tense brass climax, trumpets and trombones over side-drum) to stimulate the Kings' wandering affections. Belle Épine is triumphant (Ex.5), and the humiliated Belle Rose runs off, to the impetuous motif to which she ran on. Belle Épine dances with each King in turn: reminiscences of their diverse character dances are now confined within a uniform 3/4 and 'married' to motifs from Belle Épine's solo (Ex.5). But this is as far as her marital intentions go. To the Kings' disgust, she rejects each of them. At this there is consternation in the Court and royal spleen (a furious version of Ex.4). The Emperor tries to pacify the jilted suitors (Ex.3); fails (Ex.4); attempts to placate them with a recall of Belle Rose (Ex.7); but fails once more (Ex.4 again). Their Majesties' sole interest is the crown. The confusion is brought to an end by fanfares, broken into by derivations of Ex.4, now expressing astonishment, rather than rage. The doors of the palace open and four green Frogs enter, bearing a large emerald casket. The unexpected intervention of these emissaries from Pagoda-land is accompanied by a further transformation of the 'royalty motif'. Belle Épine tries to open the casket (to Ex.5, *pizzicato* strings), but without success. For Belle Rose, however, the casket opens of its own accord and she takes out a rose (celesta). The Courtiers laugh (*Gavotte*) but the Frogs silence them (Ex.4) and invite Belle Rose to step into a huge golden net. To turmoil in the Court and the Prince's tune (Ex.8) in the orchestra, Belle Rose is borne aloft, bound for Pagoda-land, with the Frogs as accompanying couriers.

ACT II

Scene 1 consists of three broad sections in which three of the natural elements—air, water, fire—are depicted in finely contrasted textures that give the 'feel' of each element in turn. The thread that binds the sections together is the urgent 'travel' music which accompanies Belle Rose's flight in search of her vision (Ex.9). Appropriately enough,

Ex.9

Ex.9 is both in her own key (G minor, compare Ex.7) and is also a variation of the tune associated with the object of her search (Ex.8, the Prince). *Scene 1* opens with Ex.9, after which we encounter the *corps de ballet* impersonating clouds and stars (their respective textures are unmistakable). Ex.9 recurs, and then the clouds and stars settle down to an ingenious *Waltz* which culminates in an attempt by the clouds to extinguish the stars. The strife is interrupted by the appearance of the moon (tolling trumpet motif with clarinet arpeggios). The moon vanishes, and the clouds and stars resume their waltzing. At the climax of the dance the moon reappears, triumphant, and then fades. The clouds cover the stars, and Ex.9 dashes Belle Rose into 'Water'—'a great Wave', whose salty intervention throws up sea-horses and fish-creatures and initiates their darting *Entrée*. Then follow a vigorous number for the sea-horses (dotted rhythm prominent) and a trembling, watery(!) nocturne—a miracle of invention and instrumentation—for the fish-creatures. A smart coda rounds up the sea-denizens in a *Galop*, after which Ex.9 plunges us into 'Fire', in whose *Entrée* we meet first the Male Flame (tuba) and then, after a brief continuation of Ex.9, the Female Flame. Both Flames are then 'developed' together in a *Pas de deux*, apart in two ensuing solo dances (Male, then Female). A dynamic coda for the principals and *corps de ballet* of Flames brings this section to an end, but Ex.9 remains to drop Belle Rose on to the threshold of Pagoda-land.

In *Scene 2* Belle Rose explores this strange territory to a solo violin cadenza (a free variation of Ex.8), discovers the Pagodas, and touches them, whereupon they revolve and emit their distinctive music (Balinese percussion band). The Pagodas are not unfriendly and offer her gifts. The dialogue between violin and percussion band continues until the fanfares sound once more, to which the Pagodas respond with an important characteristic rhythm (Ex.10). At this very

moment Belle Rose is blindfolded by the Pagodas—none too soon because, to Ex.1, a huge green Salamander now appears. The creature wriggles towards Belle Rose (who has tried unsuccessfully to remove her bandage) but, as his music moves to a climax, he sloughs off his skin. Ex.8 is heard, predominant in its rightful key (C major) but still combined with Ex.1—the thematic complex presenting Belle Rose's Act I vision of both Prince and Salamander—and the Prince emerges, tail-less and resplendent (see Ex.14), unperceived by the blindfolded Princess. The Prince and Belle Rose dance a tender *Pas de deux* (Ex.11), at the height of which the Princess's curiosity overcomes her

Ex.11

and she tears off her bandage. The Prince hides, and when Belle Rose finds him he is a Salamander again (gong) and so, too, is his characterizing theme (Ex.1), with which, punctuated by rustling from the spinning Pagodas, the act ends.

Catching on to the technique in Pagoda-land

ACT III

In *Scene 1* we return to the Palace of the Middle Kingdom. A brief orchestral prelude (based on Ex.5) establishes Belle Épine's precedence. She is now Empress. The Court is corrupt—a D minor section (D is Belle Épine's tonality) is suggestive of the prevailing atmosphere: its tune is none other than Ex.6, its accompaniment a vicious distortion of Ex.5. Thus the themes of the principal and middle sections of Belle Épine's first solo combine to produce a brilliant picture of power-drunk decadence. (The Dwarf *is* drunk: note his staggering gait in the brass, a motif appropriately derived from his mistress's Ex.5—Empress and Dwarf are thematically allied in evil intent.) The Empress summons the guards and has them fetch in the old Emperor, who is imprisoned in a cage (Ex.3). The Courtiers mock him: a variant of their *Gavotte* alternates with Ex.3. He is released, and forced to dance (alto saxophone): in a hushed middle section (muted brass) he remembers his former glory, then resumes his tottering steps. His torment is abbreviated by the agitated entry of an exhausted Belle Rose (Ex.7), together with the Salamander, who is at first not noticed by the Court, though his watching presence makes itself felt in the music. Belle Rose upbraids her sister for ill-treating their father. After a further (varied) reference to the Emperor's dance and dream of faded majesty, the music becomes yet more animated: the Empress orders the guards to seize Belle Rose. The Salamander moves to her rescue, whereupon he too is seized and prepared for execution. Belle Rose implores them to stop and— a crucial moment marked by a return of Ex.11—tenderly embraces the Salamander. He rises to his full height, sheds his skin, and in a clap of thunder (gong) the palace disappears. The Prince stands erect.

In *Scene 2* an extended orchestral transition, mounting to an enormous climax, leads us to the Pagoda Palace: the transition consists of the Prince's two tunes (Ex.1 and Ex.8) welded as continuous melody and surrounded by motifs, including Ex.10, drawn from the Pagodas' music in Act II scene 2. From darkness to light: the Prince, Belle Rose, the Emperor and the Fool appear and the inhabitants of Pagoda-land are liberated. A second orchestral transition gradually decreases in dynamic intensity, leaving the way open for the ensuing *Divertissement*, in which Love and Freedom are saluted in a set of dances:

Donald Mitchell

1 *Entrée Pas de six* Quick and energetic, 2/4
2 Variation[6] I *Pas de deux* Broadly, 2/4
3 Variation II Girl's solo Quick, graceful, 6/8
4 Variation III Boy's solo Quick, waltz, 3/4
5 *Pas de trois* Flowing, 7/8
6 Coda[7] Quick, 2/4
7 *Pas de caractère* The Emperor and the Fool Gracefully, 2/4
8 *Pas de deux* Belle Rose and the Prince Majestic, 2/2
9 Variation IV The Prince Impetuous, 5/4
10 Variation V Belle Rose Quietly, 3/2

The *Finale* to the *Divertissement* begins with a brisk fugato based on Ex.8 and leads into a *Waltz* whose principal refrain is again a derivative of Ex.8: x assumes special prominence in this context. During this *Finale*, which, as the concentration on Ex.8 implies, is focused on the Prince, we meet reminiscences of previous dances. It ends with radiant affirmations of its main tune and culminates in the ballet's apotheosis—first the fanfares and then an overwhelming processional, the ultimate transformation of Ex.1 projected across an ostinato bass and embedded amid fanfares and flourishes. But the kind, compassionate Fool has the last word. He joins the hands of the Prince and Princess and, to the scampering music to which he made his first appearance in Act I, he leads them forward in the sprightly epilogue that precedes the final curtain.

I have already spelled out[8] the idea of the changing perspective; and

6 'Variation' in its choreographic, not strictly musical, sense. But while it is indeed diversity that the *Divertissement* dazzlingly unfolds, there is room too for inter-dance sharing of some powerful melodic gestures and above all for some thematic transformation which directly relates to the dénouement that the *Divertissement* actually celebrates. For example, there can be no doubt, in my view, that in the *Entrée* we *are* (*pace* Peter Evans, *MMB*, p.234) expected to hear the motif which the oboe

gaily introduces at Figure 27: [musical notation] as a new diatonic

version of the Salamander motif (Ex.1). After all, the Salamander has just shed his green skin; and what could be more appropriate—or symmetrical—than the appearance, at the very beginning of the concluding *Divertissement* that signifies the Prince's final release, of his old motif, first revealed in the Prelude to Act I, in a new—*his* new—guise? No more clusters, no more heterophony: all that has been jettisoned along with the Salamander and the Pagodas. 'Transformation' is precisely what we have immediately experienced; and this familiar motif, given a fresh format, is a delicious and effective way of making the point.

7 The coda heard at the first Covent Garden performances was later deleted by the composer and a new number substituted.

8 Above, pp.21–2.

there is no doubt that the way we hear the *Pagodas* in 1983 is very different from the way we heard it in 1957. Then, the Pagodas' music seemed to represent an enthralling, presumably one-off, dash of exotic colour, the result of Britten's visit to Bali in 1956. Now, we hear a whole future embodied within their glittering revolutions. But there is something else too: not just anticipations of something to come but methods of organization, ways of compositional thinking, that with hindsight we clearly perceive to have had their roots in the techniques Britten encountered and assimilated on his Far East trip. One example comes early in the work: the treatment of the Prince-as-Salamander motif (Ex.1) which appears first at Figure A.[9] It is projected above an ostinato (bass trills!),[10] and as it develops through rhythmic contraction and motivic superimposition one has a substantial glimpse of the particular techniques that were to become prominent in Britten's music after 1964 (the watershed year of *Curlew River*).[11] Indeed the texture at this juncture—how it is compiled—is already conspicuously heterophonic in character. It is no accident that out of this preview of the Salamander music emerge the repeated chord-clusters that later are to characterize the Pagodas' music proper.[12] In retrospect, then, the *Pagodas* stands revealed as one of the first substantial manifestations of the new compositional methods that were to evolve in Britten's art over the last decades of his life.

But though we may not fully have received this dimension of the Pagodas' message in 1957, what we did hear was the tribute the work paid to Tchaikovsky, whose full-length ballets Britten took as a model. The score of the *Pagodas* is rich in salutations, not only in sonorous Tchaikovskian detail—the moments when we respond with delight to an unmistakable bit of witty or affectionate mimicry are too numerous to mention: they are of course deliberate and part of the composer's tactics—but in the work's larger formal organization. This was typical of the way Britten's mind worked: he would have thought it distinctly odd *not* to have 'consulted' the outstanding

[9] I refer throughout to the rehearsal letters and figures that appear in the piano reduction of the full score and in the full score itself.

[10] An ostinato seldom encountered. But there is a precedent in the last song of Mahler's *Kindertotenlieder*, well known to Britten.

[11] The only writer who, to my knowledge, has noted the implications of this passage is Peter Evans (*MMB*, p.225). But then he is virtually alone in having written anything serious at all about the music of the *Pagodas*.

[12] Cf. Act II Figure 74f., where the clusters reappear and play a very important role, and where the Salamander music itself is incorporated into a fully fledged gamelan texture.

creator from the past in the same field. If he was going to write a full-length ballet, then one aspect of its authenticity would be guaranteed by an audible pedigree.[13] There was also Britten's own intense admiration of Tchaikovsky's ballets, which was of long standing and based on an intimate knowledge of the scores.

When I was teaching at Sussex University, I had hoped to tempt Britten into a lecture room by inviting him not to teach or attempt to analyse but simply to talk about *any* piece of music that meant something special to him, from which he had learnt, and from which he thought students might learn. The response was immediate, though, alas, the project never got any further than that. The work he said he might be persuaded to talk about was one of the Tchaikovsky ballets. Why? Because of the marvellous orchestral imagination, of course; but also, more significantly, because of *the perfection of the small forms*, and because of Tchaikovsky's inventiveness within the formal constraints of the genre. I remember Britten's precise illustration of this last point: it was the *Pas de deux* (No.14) from the complete *Nutcracker*, and what gripped him was what Tchaikovsky was able to extract from his scale (Ex.12).[14] Tchaikovsky's importance as a principal model for the *Pagodas* inevitably brings to mind another marvellous twentieth-century score in which he was again saluted: Stravinsky's *Le Baiser de la fée*. In Stravinsky's case, Tchaikovsky's ideas stimulated him to a kind of simultaneous running commentary: we end up with a brilliant double perspective, a double image. In Britten's case, what *he* takes from Tchaikovsky were not the senior composer's own ideas—apart from those affectionately 'realistic' details which were part of the authenticity he sought to achieve—but what he had learnt in creative practice and principle from *Swan Lake*, *Sleeping Beauty* and *Nutcracker*. It was the renewal and extension of that great tradition that was Britten's ambition and he did not so much comment on Tchaikovsky as consult him, and make sure that we were aware that the process of consultation had taken place by the conscientiousness of the Tchaikovskian detailing.

Ex.12

[13] See also above, pp.33–5, for discussion of this characteristic feature of Britten's thinking in a slightly different context; and see his own comments on the *War Requiem*, above, p.96.

[14] It is hardly surprising, given Britten's own obsession with scales, that it was this number that so powerfully appealed to him.

Catching on to the technique in Pagoda-land

Of course it was not only Tchaikovsky who was consulted by Britten, but also Tchaikovsky's major successors in the field. Hence, for example, a number such as the *Variation for the Female Flame* in Act II (Figure 56f.), which unambiguously shows how well Britten knew his Prokofiev. Stravinsky too is a presence in the *Pagodas* in his own right. Everyone has remarked upon the tribute paid him, and particularly *Apollon Musagète*, in the music for Belle Épine (Act I Figure 36f.), but this is by no means the only salutation to him.[15] Less widely observed, if at all, is the witty, tongue-in-cheek reference to Stravinsky in Act I, in the third of the characteristic dances of the four Kings. One needs to be aware that the preceding dance (for the King of the West) is a mild satire on an aspect of Modernism, on what was, in Britten's view, the doctrinaire application of the twelve-note method: hence the peculiarly contorted and graceless twelve-note theme for the dance. Incidentally, the satire is given a further twist by a mechanical canon (see the entry of the xylophone at Figure 28)[16] which is there to emphasize and ridicule the *academicism* that Britten, or at least a part of him, associated with the serial method and its more mirthless practitioners. If Schoenberg is entertainingly scrutinized in the King of the West's dance—and none of this should be taken too seriously—it is Stravinsky's turn with the King of the South (from Africa), the middle part of whose dance (pianos and drums) offers a kind of kindergarten but highly effective simplification of a very famous passage indeed from *Le Sacre de printemps*: compare the rhythmic scheme at Figure 31 (Ex.13a) with Stravinsky's drumming in the concluding *Danse sacrale*, which likewise alternates threes and twos (Ex.13b). Thus in these two dances Britten gently guys in sequence both the elaborate *cerebration* and the no less elaborate *primitivity* which constitute two of the most important manifestations of 'modern music'. This was satire that was not meant to draw blood, but how Britten went about it was typical as well as great fun.

Ex.13a Britten

Energetic

Native Drums (Pfte. omitted) etc.

[15] A rather amusing though no doubt unconscious quotation is to be found in Act III at Figure 16f. (cf. also its repetitions 16 bars later and most extensively at Figure 18f.) where Britten shows that for all his well-known looking down his nose at *The Rake's Progress*, he had stored away a memory of Stravinsky's brilliant prelude to Act III of the opera.

[16] The only significant stretch of canonic writing I have found in the *Pagodas*.

Ex.13b Stravinsky

Tchaikovsky, Prokofiev, Stravinsky: all of them great *Russians*. These were the right ancestors for a full-length ballet and shared a common tradition. The very exclusivity of the genealogy, its Russian-ness, was once again part of the 'authenticity' of Britten's approach. But of course Britten himself was one of his own primary sources; and it is to his own musical personality that we should now turn, and in so doing take the widest view, i.e. not only of Britten past but of Britten future.

The past in fact need not detain us long. We may note briefly such things as the celesta's figuration, one bar after Figure 74 in Act I, which evokes *The Turn of the Screw* while being stripped of its association with Quint. (Though there is some connection, in that this is a *supernatural* moment—a casket, offered to Belle Rose, opening of its own volition: Britten was ever consistent in his instrumental imagery.) Then there are things of more general significance: for example we can be sure that Britten would never have been able to turn his hand to such a memorable, menacing and convincing tango in Act III (Figure 1f.) if it had not been for his experience in the thirties, when he turned out so many brilliant stylizations in a popular vein as part of his work for the theatre.

But it is the indications of the Britten yet to come which are now exceptionally intriguing. There are many relatively trivial, yet fascinating, glimpses of works still waiting to be born: for example, it is impossible now, when one hears the tom-toms 5 bars before the curtain at the end of Act II, not to be transported into the sound-world of the church parables and especially of *Curlew River* (cf. the use of the drums in *Curlew River*, Figure 43f.). But there is one late work that the *Pagodas* score often brings to mind in a quite particular way: *Death in Venice*. Again, one can divide the anticipations into categories of lesser or greater significance. Into the first perhaps falls the use of the tuba as a distinctive voice in the *Pagodas* (e.g. Act I Figure 61f.): one feels the instrument to be well on the way towards the extraordinary emancipation it achieves in *Death in Venice*. Or there is the tiny, tailpiece solo for the vibraphone (4 bars before Figure 72 in Act II) which so precisely replicates this particular

feature of the gamelan music of Bali and reminds us of its further use
in *Death in Venice*.[17] Speeded-up versions of the solo—shades of *Paul
Bunyan* (cf. Prologue to Act I Figures 11–12)—follow just before the
repeat sign after Figure 72 and again two bars before Figure 74.

An anticipation of a rather subtler order, and an altogether
weightier one because it is bound up with a complex, quasi-dramatic
manipulation of dissimilar categories of music, occurs in Act II, in the
scene where the Princess's eyes are bandaged and the Prince dances
with her in human form (*Pas de deux* for the Prince and Belle Rose,
Figure 78f.). It is a highly dramatic moment of confrontation,
between both the *dramatis personae* and the two types of music
involved: the Prince's, which belongs to the Pagodas and Bali, and the
Princess's, which belongs to Europe. It is a juxtaposition that we are
to meet again in *Death in Venice*, and again for dramatic reasons,
introduced to articulate the different experiential worlds. What is
even more striking is that the Princess's little game of hide-and-seek
with the Prince-as-Salamander (Act II Figure 85 to end) is conducted,
albeit in embryonic form, in precisely the terms in which Aschenbach
conducts *his* hide-and-seek with Tadzio through the alleys and *piazze*
of Venice in Act II of *Death in Venice*:[18] the repeated percussion
clusters,[19] derived in both instances from the Balinese gamelan,
are used in precisely the same way to identify Tadzio and the
Prince-as-Salamander in the circumstances of a *pursuit*, a *hunt*.

The full-length ballet of 1957 was a report on the experience of
visiting Bali the previous year.[20] There were further reports to

17 See above, pp.43–5, where I point out that Britten would have assimilated this
particular Balinese practice in the first instance from his acquaintance with Colin
McPhee's two-piano transcriptions of *Balinese Ceremonial Music* (1940), even before
hearing it for himself on the island.
18 Cf. Pagodas Act II, 1 bar after Figure 74f., and *Death in Venice*, Scene 16, Figure
301f.
19 I have already pointed out (above, p.201) that the chord-clusters initially emerge
from the Salamander music as it first appears in the Prelude. They are the vertical
manifestation of the impact made on Britten by Balinese music, of which just such
clusters are a prominent feature. They are also the direct predecessor of the similar
cluster which identifies Tadzio in *Death in Venice*.
20 As for any possible Balinese influence on the *Pagodas* scenario, I am much indebted
to Dr Roger Savage (Edinburgh) who has drawn my attention to the description of an
arja play—a 'modern operetta based on traditional theatre, with songs in old
Javanese metres'—in Colin McPhee's *A House in Bali* (O.U.P., 1947), p.170, some
features of which—e.g. 'the Princess who married Green Frog'—strike up an
association with the *Pagodas* fairy tale (not to speak of our own *Cinderella*). There
may well be other Balinese plays or tales to which the scenario of the *Pagodas* is more
closely related, but even this example suggests that Cranko, when devising the

Donald Mitchell

come—*Curlew River* and its successors and, ultimately, *Death in Venice*; and yet it was an experience that had actually begun in New York in the 1940s. The 'authenticity' of Britten's *Pagodas* would surely have given pleasure to his old friend Colin McPhee. McPhee would certainly have noticed with satisfaction the authenticity of the model upon which Britten had based his gamelan music in the ballet. As Douglas Young has pointed out, an excerpt from the original Balinese music which was Britten's inspiration and point of departure also appears in transcription in McPhee's major study, *Music in Bali*.[21]

---

ballet, acquainted himself with Balinese sources; and the most likely source of those would have been McPhee. The idea of a Prince born in some other form—a tiger, a frog—seems to run through Balinese mythology: see also McPhee, op. cit., pp. 65–6. There is an opportunity here for basic research into the origins of the story of the *Prince of the Pagodas*. John Percival, in his biography of John Cranko, *Theatre in my Blood* (The Herbert Press, 1983), gives an account of the collaboration between the choreographer and the composer (pp. 113–18). It is not without interest. For example, Cranko apparently referred to his scenario as a 'mythological fairy-tale' and hoped that people might leave the theatre saying 'I'm sure I've heard that story *somewhere* before'; and we may be sure they would have mentioned *Cinderella* among other remembered tales. On the other hand, Mr Percival makes no mention of Balinese sources whatsoever. I find it scarcely credible that these would not have been investigated by Cranko, to some degree at least. When Mr Percival remarks that Britten 'made some research into oriental music—Japanese and Balinese—for exotic colour', in seeming ignorance of Britten's historic 1955–6 trip to the Far East, which preceded the composition of the ballet, we become conscious of the pressing need for a properly researched account of the conception of the joint creation. Although somewhat oddly put, Mr Percival's reference to Britten studying 'a complete edition of Tchaikovsky's music' in the context of the *Pagodas* only goes to confirm what I write about Britten's consultation of his great predecessor on pp.201–2 above.

21 New Haven: Yale University Press, Ex.337, pp.348–9. See also Douglas Young's sleeve-note for *East–West Encounters*, Cameo Classics GOCLP 9018(D), a most valuable source of information about McPhee. Britten must have met McPhee not long after his arrival in New York in August 1939. At the back of his pocket diary for that year we find scribbled there: 'Colin McFee [*sic*] 129 East 10. Algonquin 4–4980'. The registering of that address and telephone number undoubtedly marked the beginning of their friendship. McPhee died in Los Angeles, where he was teaching at the University of California, on 7 January 1964. It is possible that the original gramophone recording of the ballet came to his attention. Further evidence has come to light of the close association of the two men during Britten's years in the United States. It was McPhee who prepared an ingenious and skilful transcription for two pianos of Britten's *Variations on a Theme of Frank Bridge*, which was used for performances in New York in 1942 of a ballet, *Jinx*, presented by the Dance Players at the National Theatre and first performed on 24 April. (We must remember in this context McPhee and Britten as performers at two pianos of the *Balinese Ceremonial Music*.) The manuscript of this transcription, now in the Britten–Pears Library at Aldeburgh, is dated 'Feb–March 1942'. A dyeline of a copyist's copy (also in the Library) was clearly used for performance: on it appear cues related to the dancers. (George Balanchine and Francis Mason, *Festival of Ballet* (W. H. Allen, 1978),

Catching on to the technique in Pagoda-land

But McPhee's book was not published until 1966, and of course where Britten found his model was in Bali in 1956, where he made his own notations of the various gamelan ensembles he heard and the various styles of performance.[22] Thus was the 'authenticity' of the gamelan

pp.326–7, give a detailed account of the story of the ballet. It was revived by the New York City Ballet in 1949.) There is also an intriguing undated letter of Britten's from these years, drafted for him by Elizabeth Mayer and addressed to David Ewen, an American popular encyclopaedist. Ewen had evidently asked for information about Britten and his music, to which the composer replied:

'Of course I shall be delighted to co-operate with you in your new book. Unfortunately I have so far been unable to obtain copies of the best articles written about me. They were published in periodicals in England some time ago & I am afraid I have not got them with me. But Mr Colin McPhee is engaged in writing a comprehensive survey of my work at the moment, which Arden Music is considering using sometime—but at any rate not before the fall—& anyhow there would be no objection to you using it I know.'

Presumably, and regrettably, McPhee's study was never completed and never published; perhaps Britten's departure from the States in 1942 killed off the project.

[22] Britten's manuscript notes of scales and fragments of typical Balinese gamelan figuration and textures, including indications of instrumentation, are preserved in the Britten–Pears Library. At the top of one page is written 'Kapi Radja (Overture)'; then follows this notation of the scale on which the particular piece Britten had heard was based. (See also *MBB*, p.234, where Peter Evans has correctly deduced the scale.)

Britten also wrote out as part of the same sketch scraps of motifs and rhythmic figuration and indications of the basic pulse or beat. At a later date, clearly, he looked through these notes in order to locate something appropriate for the ballet: under the notation given below appear the underlined words 'This for beginning of Pagoda scene'; and it was indeed by the scale and the subsequent outline of motif, rhythm, instrumentation and texture that the music for the Pagodas was generated. Cf. Figure 71f. with this transcription of Britten's on-the-spot, seminal sketch.

Xyl. Metal. Soft high gongs. Cymbals.

There is little probability that Britten would even have known of McPhee's *Music in Bali*. It is exceptionally interesting, however, that McPhee's 1966 excerpt from and commentary on the Balinese *gambang* style relate back to his two-piano transcription of the same *Gambangan* that he had published in 1940—one of the very transcriptions he played at that time with Britten. While there can be no doubt that Britten consulted not the almost forgotten transcription from 1940 when composing the *Pagodas* but his own manuscript notes from 1956, there can be little doubt that it was his unconscious memory of playing the 1940 *Gambangan* that influenced him to choose the very same music again from his own 1956 notations. I am much obliged to Douglas Young who has shared his thoughts with me about the history of this fascinating passage.

music in the *Pagodas* guaranteed in just the same way that the 'references' to Tchaikovsky *et al.* guarantee the mainstream tradition of which the *Pagodas* forms intended part.

I think I have said enough about the oriental dimension of the score to establish both the *Pagodas'* continuity with the past and its anticipation of the future in Britten's *oeuvre*. But there are one or two comments I should like to add which suggest how the *total* fabric of the music is permeated by the impact made on Britten's ears by the Balinese gamelan. I have discussed the clusters that characterize the Prince-as-Salamander and are conspicuously part of Britten's gamelan music (Ex.14). It seems to me now that the concept—the

sonority—of the cluster very significantly fertilizes long (occidental as well as oriental) stretches of the *Pagodas* and is indeed latent in the very first bars of the Prelude, whose diatonic fanfares, we come to realize, incorporate the two narrowest, most economical forms of the cluster, major and (as echo) minor seconds (Ex.15).[23] The seed we

[23] One recalls Erwin Stein's famous remark about Britten's discovery of 'the sonority of the second' in his discussion of the *Sinfonietta* (*BS*, p.249). The piled-up clusters one finds in oriental music must have made a special appeal to a composer who had long been devoted to the smallest type of cluster. Thus in the *Pagodas* two favourite sonorities—one fresh, one of long-standing—are integrated. Chains of seconds abound, most of them matching up to Stein's description of Britten's exploitation of them as 'beautiful and tender'. Furthermore, the very first initiating chord of the work, with added sixth, might be thought of in this context as particularly appropriate—a chord, as it were, with a built-in cluster. See also Peter Evans's comment in his review of the full score of *Death in Venice* in *Music & Letters* 62

Ex.15

discern there in the Prelude retrospectively proves to be the generator of so many formulations of the cluster principle throughout the ballet (one prominent and climactic example being Ex.14 above) that it is impossible not to conclude that the cluster is one of the leading and characterizing features of the unique soundscape of the *Pagodas* as a whole. It is not possible to list every example here, but in support of my contention I draw the reader's attention to the following passages, which include some of the major instances of the systematic use of clusters of many different kinds and yet all sharing to some degree a common sonority:

Act I

Prelude (complete); Figure 16f.; Figure 23f. (tremolando clusters); Figure 34f.; Figures 48 and 48aff.; Figure 50f.; Figure 64 to end of act.

Act II

Figure 32f. (tremolando clusters); Figure 56f. (seconds!); Figure 60f.; Figure 74f.; Figure 77f.; Figure 78f. (seconds!) to end of act.

Act III

Figure 19 to end of scene; Figure 60f.; Figure 73f.; Figure 89f.; Figure 97 to end of act.

(1981), pp.112–14: 'Britten's conversion, for long stretches of this opera, of harmony from an agency of movement into one primarily of motivic amplification ensures that one's ears soon become acutely sensitive to the harrowing ubiquity of certain intervallic complexes; and when the same nuclei are operating melodically, often in tenuously related two-part writing or a single part *heterophonically tensed against itself (the logical final stage in Britten's lifelong addiction to the "sonorous second")*, then "analysis", whether or not verbalized, appears an unusually immediate, and a required, part of the listening process.' [My italics.]

Donald Mitchell

One might even claim that it is through the idea of the cluster that the human beings of the Court are brought into relation with the magic world of the Pagodas. Just at the point (Act II Figure 74) when the offstage fanfare (the world of the Court) is juxtaposed with the Salamander's repeated chord-clusters (the world of the Pagodas) one hears that it is in fact the cluster that unites the two opposed ideas: the juxtaposition spells out the relationship between them. The cluster is one of the principal means through which Britten integrates his score—a bridge not only between his *dramatis personae* but between the musical world of East and West.

I have said nothing about the orchestration, which is virtually a subject in itself. It is in its way a veritable textbook of orchestration—or, perhaps better, the complete guide to Britten's exceptional orchestral imagination.[24] *Pagodas*, from this point of view alone, is surely one of the most remarkable scores to have been produced so far in the second half of the century. If nothing else it suggests that, given a composer of genius, there was a good deal of life left in the 'standard' symphony orchestra. It might be thought to be Britten's 'Concerto for Orchestra', though not so titled. Dazzling orchestration,[25] perfect small forms: what better model could there be for teaching?

[24] It seems beyond belief—certainly beyond *my* belief—that Michael Kennedy (*BMM*, p.214) can commit himself to the opinion that *Pagodas* 'of all Britten's large-scale works' is 'the least characteristic in sound'. Almost any bar of the score demonstrably shows this to be the reverse of the truth. And this from a *student* of Britten's music! Scarcely less disconcerting is Stephen Walsh's suggestion (*Observer*, 20 June 1982) in a review of the first recording of the 'Del Mar' Suite (see above, n.3) that in comparison with Britten's work from the thirties the ballet 'is merely a work of effortless talent . . . more like a well-rehearsed high-wire act; the creative muscles are so attuned to it that it barely stretches them any more'. It seems a curious conclusion to arrive at, especially in view of the Pagodas' innovative music. But perhaps this is what Mr Walsh means by writing, as he puts it, 'tongue in cheek'.
[25] I am thinking not just of the gamelan music, extraordinary though that is, both in its own right and as a marvellous example of Britten's 'photographic' ear: it seems hardly possible that so authentic a gamelan-like sound could be conjured out of the modern symphony orchestra. I also have in mind—but how does one choose amid such riches?—Variations I and II from the *Pas de six*, both of them built around very particular instrumental timbres and agilities (horn and piano in Variation I, solo violin in Variation II), both of them representing opposed extremes of colour and density (the one dark and heavy, the other light and weightless), both products of a common *un*common imagination.

21
The Church Parables (I):
Ritual and Restraint[1]

DONALD MITCHELL

Britten seems to me a peculiarly thematic composer. I am not thinking of the fertility of his melody or of the prominent role that themes and thematic organization play in his music, but of themes in a broader sense—concerns, commitments, attitudes and sources of stimulation which have been his long-standing preoccupations and which are variously reflected in his art.

There are too many themes of this kind to examine even cursorily here, but one thing emerges strongly from the briefest survey: the extraordinary consistency of Britten's personality. This may seem an obvious enough statement when made in connection with the music of his maturity, in which we find, whatever the chosen medium, an inimitable voice, style, manner. But consistency has been a feature of his music since his youth. We can look back to the early works—the Piano Concerto of 1938 for example—and discover there, perhaps to our surprise, not a musical personality awaiting or seeking formulation, but an established personality with whose language we are familiar through our experience of the later works. One of the pleasures of investigating the 'young' Britten is to discover so many features of the mature artist—of characteristic achievement, not the 'anticipations' we so often read about in programme notes.

Perhaps this is to say no more than that Britten, like most creators of eminence, has strong roots in his own past. We can see clearly now that works like the United Nations anthem *Voices for Today* (1965) and the *War Requiem* (1961) spring out of sympathies, out of

[1] Edited from the sleeve-note for Decca recording SET 438 (1970).

Donald Mitchell

passionately held convictions and profound beliefs, which were already manifest in what could be called Britten's socially committed works, composed during the politically turbulent and momentous 1930s—e.g. the *Pacifist March* (1937), *Advance Democracy* (1938) or the *Ballad of Heroes* (1939). In his works of the 1960s, naturally enough, the whole basis of the composer's attitudes has broadened: a political platform has, as it were, developed into a universal stage. *Voices for Today* speaks for international amity; the *War Requiem* and the *Cantata Misericordium* (1963) for peace, compassion, and common humanity; *Children's Crusade* (1969, to a text by Brecht) for children, always the innocent and voiceless victims of war. But the seeds of these late works were already germinating in the thirties, and it is of no little interest that some of the vivid musical imagery we encounter in the profoundly humanistic statements from the sixties was prefigured in the earlier works, which have been too often assessed simply as documents of the thirties. They may be that, but they are also characteristic documents of their composer and have an important place in the total profile of his art.

At the same time Britten continually surprises us by striking out in new, unpredictable and unsuspected directions. A thought-provoking instance is provided by the three church parables, *Curlew River* (1964), *The Burning Fiery Furnace* (1966) and *The Prodigal Son* (1968). If I am right about Britten's consistency, it should be possible to draw a meaningful line of development between his first full-blooded and full-scale opera, *Peter Grimes* (1945), and the ritual and restraint that comprise the chief distinguishing features of the church parables. Is the proposition tenable? Or does the division between opera house and church constitute an unbridgeable gulf?

I am the last person to deny or try to diminish the exciting strangeness and originality of the church parables, which in a wealth of ways offer a wholly unusual experience. Yet if we look back across the years we find, fascinatingly, an edging towards the style and conception of the parables in works which at first sight may seem totally alien to their exotic world. There is not space here for a detailed history of the origins of the parables, but if we are seeking for a work which significantly blurs the distinction between the kind of musical events we expect to find in church on the one hand and in the theatre on the other, we must travel back twenty years along the course of Britten's development, to his cantata *Saint Nicolas* (1948) in which the thrilling revival of the Pickled Boys is re-enacted not only for our

212

ears but also for our eyes. *Saint Nicolas* indeed, which freely introduces the dramatic gesture—'opera', if you like—into an arena from which the dramatic convention has been excluded in recent (but not in distant) centuries, already formulates a principle which is vastly enlarged and developed in the parables. One could call the incident of the Pickled Boys a *parable in miniature*—from twenty years ago!

In stressing *Saint Nicolas*, I have not overlooked *Noye's Fludde* (1957), which was a clear and obvious milestone on the road to the parables. But the cantata particularly shows that Britten's creative mind has long been concerned with the kind of dramatic possibilities he comprehensively exploits in *The Burning Fiery Furnace* and *The Prodigal Son*. The influence on the parables of oriental music is not something entirely new either: on the contrary, Britten's interest in the music of Bali was alive in the 1940s,[2] and first made a major intervention in his own music not in *Curlew River* of 1964 but in the wonderfully rich score of his full-length ballet *The Prince of the Pagodas*,[3] composed in 1956. And for further evidence of the thematic—in my sense—integrity of the parables in relation to Britten's music as a whole, I recommend a comparison of the demented hero of *Peter Grimes* (1945) with the Madwoman in *Curlew River* (1964). How revealing it is that these works, even though they occupy opposite ends of the theatrical scale, have so much in common. The theme of the social outcast, long one of Britten's preoccupations, is pursued in both—though, interestingly, the dénouement in the later work is the exact reverse of the outcome in the earlier: Grimes dies mad, but at the end of *Curlew River* the Madwoman has her sanity restored. It is perhaps characteristic of the way in which Britten's art has developed that reconciliation rather than disintegration is what he brings us in the 1960s. But *Curlew River* is a continuation of the same singular creativity that gave us *Peter Grimes*, not only in dramatic theme, but musically too. It is surely the example of Grimes's great solo cadenza towards the end of Act III which stands behind the characteristic intensity of the vocal style in *Curlew River*.[4] As for *The Prodigal Son*, startling though the juxtaposition may be, the *theme* of the work was adumbrated long ago in *Albert Herring*, Britten's comic opera first performed in 1947. Of

---

[2] See also above, pp.39–45.

[3] See also Chapter 20.

[4] It is not only the intense vocal style of Grimes's cadenza that provided a model for *Curlew River* but also the economy and sparseness of the accompanying orchestral texture, a different but no less relevant form of expressive intensity.

course, the one is a social comedy, the other a celebration of one of the greatest biblical tales. Yet the comedy of *Herring* is shot through with the profoundest and most compassionate of insights into the character of the emancipated-to-be Albert; and there will be few who do not respond to the deeply human and humane characterization of the parable's central figure, who, like Albert, wins his emancipation and is ultimately enriched by his experience. Britten's tender and compassionate treatment of the Prodigal Son reflects the same tenderness and compassion with which his characterization of Albert is so richly endowed. Of course, we have to recognize two strongly contrasted styles of invention, but they share the consistency of the composer's approach, which makes *Herring* so much more than comedy and *The Prodigal Son* so much more than ritual. Come to that, there is a real link, musically speaking, between Albert's distraught Mum in *Herring*, Act III, and the demented mother, the Madwoman, in *Curlew River*. But this need not disconcert us. The relation does not diminish the pity and awe we feel in the presence of the Madwoman in *Curlew River* and at the same time it shows *why* we respond so immediately and passionately to Mum's sorrow in *Herring*.[5] Britten in fact cannot help being *himself*, whether it is a comedy or a church parable in which he is involved.

A final link: much has been made of the free contrapuntal textures in the church parables, into which a very carefully controlled but none the less genuinely 'random' element is injected. Perhaps this does represent a new principle in Britten's art, at least in this mature formulation. However, it is worth recalling that it was in *Herring*, now more than twenty years ago, that Britten introduced those elaborately free ensemble recitatives, in which a conversational polyphony was achieved by the spontaneous and unmeasured repetitions of a given set of vocal lines. We may conclude that Britten has not fashioned his parables after a wholly new image, but composed himself *into* them, over a long period.

[5] Mum's grieving in the great quartet in *Herring*, Act III, and the Madwoman's in *Curlew River*, Figures 83–4.

22

The Church Parables (II):
Limits and Renewals

ROBIN HOLLOWAY

'A time there was' when music consisted simply of diatonic melody resonating in sympathetic spaces that gave delicate bloom to its austerity. Unsullied eternity was penetrated by the curious serpent, unbinding music's hitherto dormant power to *move*. Harmony and rhythm, once stirred into life, are both engine and fuel. But it's downhill all the way. As motion and emotion grow ever more comprehensive, innocence is left behind in an age of gold beyond recall. Childish directness is blighted by weary knowingness; deceit, baseness, corruption, lay siege to head and heart. The slippery road broadens as it descends. Expression once pristine easily becomes sentimentality, exaggeration, cheapness, coarseness, turgidity. The end is nigh—a maelstrom of total anarchy where every note (there are millions) is simultaneously whipped on by a perpetual extreme of intensity and weighed down with an urgent burden of inherited function. Hence a yearning to be cool and still and quiet; to escape the orgiastic debasement of excess and the excruciating exposure of feeling; to jettison the accretion of layer upon layer of sound and meaning; to recover primeval simplicity and freshness.

Traditionally efficacious to quench and console the exasperated spirit is the sound of the harp. And no one since its emancipation from mere arpeggios and glissandi has understood the genius of this instrument as Britten, who makes its technical character so influence his compositional thought that the music grows directly out of what the instrument can and cannot do. Total chromaticism is beyond its diatonic structure; the possibility of *these* will always make *those* notes unplayable; which necessitates ingenious choice in planning every harmonic change. Such narrow limits exactly suit an ear exceptionally sensitized to every inflection of every note, and a usage latent in his earlier harp-writing (brilliantly idiomatic from the start) increasingly permeates his later music whether or not the harp is literally present. For harp-tuning is an analogy for the way his harmony moves and a metaphor for the way his mind works.

The other instruments in the church parables are chosen out of exigency: a base of percussion and an organ drone to catch and hold the blur of voices; for characterization, the Ferryman's horn, the Madwoman's flute; for a special pervasive colour, the trombone in *The Burning Fiery Furnace* and the trumpet in *The Prodigal Son*; for more neutral omni-purpose, the viola and double-bass. In the resulting ensemble the harp is a vital element. It doesn't predominate, however; indeed, with a tone resonant yet fragile and an attack somewhat undefined, it remains rather submerged, its very lack of colour serving to bind the voices and disparate instruments loosely together without heaviness. But the principle of harp-tuning is fundamental to the whole sonority. The harp's 'limitations' allow Britten to control the harmony of the parables as a loom can be threaded to produce different patterns. Their harmonic fabric is woven on the harp-strings.

The result is like a return to the source and a new start. What Stravinsky called 'the brief but brilliant history' of harmonic ascendency seems to melt into a remote past as this music is heard; and, along with harmony, metre and measurement also dissolve, allowing the fluid eternals of diatonic melody to be rediscovered. The great romantic 'new starts' (from Beethoven and Schubert to Mahler by way of the *Rheingold* Prelude and Bruckner) are invariably harmonic; above the deep fundamental an *Ur*-shape gradually unfolds or boldly sounds forth, outlining an arpeggio with strong tonic–dominant emphasis. But Britten's 'new start' is quite different from such conscious primevalization; it is rather the natural extension of tendencies implicit in his brilliantly wayward mastery of traditional harmony, which, when pressed, can run quite counter to it though still alongside. His comment during his Far Eastern tour of 1956 that the music of Bali 'makes our tonics and dominants seem like ghosts' has a long ancestry quite apart from his own earlier involvement with Javanese scales. He writes after many decades of what can loosely be called orientalism in western music, from Debussy and the gamelan to Boulez and *Le Marteau sans maître*. Tenuous parallels for the aesthetic and sound of the church parables can be made with Satie, late Fauré and middle Bartók. More distinct forerunners come in Stravinsky— *L'Histoire du soldat* for the band and *Les Noces* (especially the end) for the sonority; in such things in Holst as the bitonal canons and the songs for voice and violin; with the recitatives for voice and flute over a drone bass in Mahler's 'Der Abschied': while very close, in quality of emotion as well as actual texture, is Debussy's Sonata for flute, viola and harp.

More widely suggestive, though difficult to define, is a comparison with music, of whatever epoch, that goes well in large resonant spaces. This obviously includes the entire era of plainsong to polyphony in up to forty parts. In more modern times instances are rare and special. For during the centuries when harmony and rhythm were hugely expanding into ever more sophisticated possibilities for tonal organization, only music of limited harmonic movement, basically non-modulating in tendency (even in a strict sense anti-tonal) and of broad rhythmic outline, could survive any degree of complicating acoustic fuzz. After the Venetians only Handel (because of his harmonic plainness) achieved this, until the nineteenth and twentieth centuries, when a few figures outside the central tradition— Berlioz, Mussorgsky, Stravinsky, Varèse, Messiaen—once again by accident or design write music accommodated to the capacities and restrictions of enormous resonance. To these can be added certain important aspects of Bruckner and Sibelius, who both belong basically elsewhere. Apart from Bruckner, this is all music where the learned refinements of harmonic function are not of primary importance; apart from Handel, music where tonics and dominants are well on the way towards disembodiment. Generalizing further, these composers (to whom Debussy must now be added, though his music would certainly not sound well in a big echoing space) are rootless figures, without much of a tradition before them or after. Their musical character is non-developmental; they build by repetition and ostinato, in blocks, whether large or small, separated or molten together. The warmly expressive is usually avoided; there is a tendency towards formalization, observance, ritual; they evoke places of theistic awe—Catholic interiors, forests and mountains, seascapes and cloudscapes, deserts, canyons and stars, *atmosphères*, *Sirius*, Judgement Day itself.

Strange though it seems at first glance, Britten's church parables belong with this kind of music. They render unending time and imply vast space and place, by dissolving the bounds of harmony and rhythm until it seems that music itself will drain away leaving nothing behind. Strange because Britten is by no means an egotistic sublimer or a professional visionary, but on the contrary an artist whose themes are humanistic, and who shows a particular feeling for the prosaic, the deprived, the victimized; whose desire is to be accessible and of service to a community, and whose gifts are in complete accord with this desire. His best and most frequent vehicles are song-cycles and operas, whose time-scales are distinctly less superhuman than sociable. Yet simultaneous with this conspicuous humanity a sort of oriental emptiness has evolved, unconscious or preconscious, 'before good and evil', utterly passive and detached; the nescience so longed for in *Winter Words*. That the two aspects are compatible is easily shown. The church parable time-scale is as slow as possible granted that this strictly practical composer will not make preposterous demands on his audience's time, attention and comfort; while endless space and place can be successfully evoked without a choir of a thousand, four brass bands, and St Paul's or S. Sulplice.

The wherewithal for these works, rather, is astonishingly modest; the still small voice is right on target. The *donnée* is a story, an appropriate plainsong, a troupe of acting singers, and a little band recalling distantly the Japanese inspiration and based, more nearly, on the needs of the story in characterization and colour, and on suitability to the church acoustic for which the parables are intended. The musical substance grows out of the endless variety of closely related melodic shapes derived from the initial plainsong, falling into blurring, echoes, drones and heterophony, and perpetually retuned by the harp (literal or metaphorical). The harmonic series alone would set the space vibrating with natural response. A plainsong will set up a blur of diatonic notes in close proximity that hangs in the air and slowly clears. A single note is retuned; then another and others following. We seem to 'see' the notes in all their relationships from the simplest to the more and more complex, audibly growing in unmissable progression, and always remaining absolutely lucid. Every retuning alters the relationships like an altering magnetic field—even the building seems to change in sympathy. However many the parts, we hear not harmony but intervals forming verticals and horizontals, not chords but 'aggregates' which seem to analyse themselves before our eyes as if for an acoustical demonstration. It is Britten's extraordinary achievement in the church parables to have integrated the discoveries of serial and post-serial pitch-organization into the fundamental unchangeables of the harmonic series.

In *Curlew River* everything already familiar from Britten's earlier operas is quintessentialized with harsh nakedness. Characterization in voice and by instrument ranges from the Ferryman with his sturdily agile horn and the Traveller with his trudging double-bass double-stops to the astonishing feat of stylization (out of Donizetti via Japan) in the ululations, flutters and swoops of the Madwoman and her flute. Sense of place, so fully evoked in the *Peter Grimes* Sea Interludes, is now set with the barest minimum of notes. Just as the acting area gives next to nothing to see, so this music gives next to nothing to hear; but this minimum suffices to render river, marsh and circling birds with startling vividness. Sense of movement—Britten's gift for depicting action (hauling the boat, spinning, laying the dinner-table, plying the lagoon)—is never so basic as here in hoisting the sail and poling across the river.

Though there is precedent too for the ensembles, it is in these that the newness of the church parable style is most striking. They are indeed remarkable; their mixture of fixed and free (always with the scrupulous sensitivity to pitch-inflection already mentioned) un-ostentatiously resolves the twentieth-century problem of voices moving against each other in anything but triads and scales. The first and most inspired, 'Birds of the Fenland', opens up a fully realized vision of a kind of music different from anything ever heard before, though its ingredients are all, when separated, extremely familiar and extremely simple. Set against the ensembles are the various 'arias' for the Madwoman; and again the exposure and intensity of such things as 'East, east, east . . .' and 'Hoping, I wandered on . . .' takes them into a sphere beyond their direct ancestry in Britten's previous portrayals of desolation, anguish and madness. Things that could be mannered to the point of self-parody seem here to enter an area where painfulness no longer gives artistic pleasure; such unclothed excruciation makes one almost grateful that he never composed the *King Lear* of his dreams.

Three moments of harp-tuning genius must be singled out: the flute's last entry in the 'Birds of the Fenland' ensemble, whose final B double-flat becomes the Ferryman's A natural as the action resumes; the electrifying effect of the harmonic change from the moment of universal recognition that she is the boy's mother to the

Madwoman's own recognition; and the wonderful way the piccolo solo representing the boy's Spirit takes his mother's characteristic dissonance out of A natural into A flat regions, the closing ceremonial heterophony then restoring C, and the final plainsong A natural. Such matters are virtually meaningless in words; the point is, they have been so composed as to make them completely audible and affecting to a listener who doesn't know what 'flat' or 'natural' means.[1]

The work gives a beautiful sense of grading its sonorous resources for maximum meaning. The percussion base and the deeper voices set the Madwoman in relief; indeed we tend to forget that she also has a man's voice, so isolated are she and her flute from the mid-range of other voices and instruments. The motion of crossing the river sets up a feeling of great spaciousness that persists long after the ferryboat completes its journey. Soon before the crisis of the action, the marvellous entry of the deep bell takes this sense of opening space on to a different plane, awakening the deepest and fullest range of reverberation, catching the little bells which in turn sympathetically attract the voice of the Spirit, itself thin and deliberately only just perceptible between the waves of the massed other forces, but none the less forming the 'acoustic climax' as surely as it does the dramatic. After this, the spaciousness is fulfilled; the work's most sonorous passage yields to its least; the boy's voice trails off and up into the piccolo, diminutive of his mother's curlew-flute, and is lost to sight; the echoes die, the building ceases to vibrate.

The importance of *Curlew River* as a crossing-place and synthesis can hardly be overstated. In some dream-conflation of harsh East Coast Anglia and milk-and-honey West Coast America, middle-age Christian culture lies down with ageless Japan and Bali, and native Englishry (folksong, Elizabethans and Purcell, Vaughan Williams and Holst, the earlier Britten himself) nuzzles the European avant-garde. Very difficult, vitally important questions of harmony and rhythm are dissolved and solved with breathtaking ease (the practicality of the performing notation in itself opens up enormous new possibilities for compositional procedure). None of this would signify were the work not also very beautiful, and quite peculiarly affecting. Indeed there really seems to be no parallel for its fusion of narrow concentration with infinite suggestion. This music goes

---

[1] For one who does, the admirable chapter on the church parables in *MMB* is warmly recommended.

straight to the most painful place in a totally disembodied martyrdom of St Narcissus (Canticle V)—the spiritual groin.

After this, *The Burning Fiery Furnace* is clearly something of a fun piece, sometimes unsuccessfully as in the arch little riddle scene, sometimes with uncertain results as with the would-be comic gravity of the young Israelites' reluctance to eat at Nebuchadnezzar's table. Modest fun is made from their three names, outlandish in two languages; and glorious fun with the 'cornet, flute, harp, sackbut, psaltery, dulcimer, and all kinds of music'. By far the best thing in the work is the march inspired by this list of instruments, and there is hardly a better instance in all Britten of his delight in gratifying our desire for a half-expected surprise than the moment when the players transport the delectable little invention all round the church.

But in spite of the brazen trombone and the new colours in the percussion, too much is a pale replay of the predecessor. Everything fresh and inevitable in *Curlew River*—the triple frame of plainsong, address, ceremonial heterophony; the characterization in voices and by instruments; the big set pieces—is here by formula, because the genre requires it. The twitterings of Nebuchadnezzar and his Astrologer are closer to mannerism than to real characterization; and during the earnest chanting of the three goodies our ears stray guiltily to the musicians as they prepare one by one for their 'unholy' procession. Dissatisfaction is focused in the other set pieces. The orgy of abasement before 'Merodak' is ice-cold, horrible, and completely stunning. But its complement, the miracle in the furnace, badly hangs fire. The greyness of the crowning *Benedicite* recalls Britten's United Nations anthem *Voices for Today* with its equally doleful vision of the age of gold. Even the return, with converted Babylonians joining the goodies and the finely composed instrumental enrichments, cannot ignite it into celebration. The triple frame closes in, but the climax has escaped.

With *The Prodigal Son* the sense of genre has become distinctly dutiful, and the musical impulse tired. The story is again serious, but without the inward concentration of *Curlew River*. In its absence we hanker for something to compare with the pleasure of the intricate and delicious little Babylonian march. The main set piece, the orgy in the City of Sin, goes rather for the coldly disgusting quality of 'Merodak', heightening it into something more complex in meaning, though just as horrid in sound. There are of course inspirations throughout, notably the Prodigal's frisky escape from boredom and the brilliant closer and closer entwining of Tempter and tempted as the city is neared. Also inspired is his homeward journey, an urgent fantasia on the work's germinal plainsong in four free parts over the percussion ostinato of his weary footsteps. But just before it, his lowest hour grubbing with the swine is set to a rehash of incomparably more poignant originals in the Madwoman's arias. And some of the music is frankly perfunctory, especially the elder brother with his landlubbery clusters, and the dance of welcome when the Prodigal returns.

There is a problem of monotony. The deliberate blandness of the father's farm is all too effective; at the reconciliation our strongest reaction to the return of the seraphic unchanging B flat chord from which the younger son fled is to remember the boredom that impelled him rather than be moved by his return. More difficult still is the final ensemble. The voices go up and down and round about, repeating 'was dead, and is alive; was lost, and is found' to the densest 'aggregate' in all three parables and the one closest to a discord that needs resolution; but nothing seems to focus or clinch, whether musically or dramatically. As in *The Burning Fiery Furnace* the climax is somehow missed (though everyone knows where it should be); moreover in *The Prodigal Son* the reserve upon which the genre depends for its expressive manner gives way in two crucial places to a direct appeal—to pathos in the father's forgiveness, to reconciliatory warmth in the final ensemble; and in both cases the result is ineffectual.

These shortcomings in *The Burning Fiery Furnace* and *The Prodigal Son* suggest limitations in the church parable convention unraised by *Curlew River*; moreover they touch upon wider limitations in Britten at large. In the depiction of Babylonian gold-lust and the debaucheries of the Big City a tone can be heard that is not so much ascetic as prim and even priggish. This music renders abandon with monkish distaste; there is no imaginative understanding of the ambiguity within 'sinfulness'. One has only to recall the comparable vignettes in *Mahagonny*—also the work of a moralist whose attitude to what he pictures with such seductive pleasure is unmistakably severe—to see how coldly Britten looks upon the frailty of the flesh. The effect in *The Prodigal Son* of setting the famine the morning after to the same music as the 'dark delights' of the night before is of lofty disapproval rather than spiritual insight. 'Sin' is only joyless, fearsome, loathly; therefore its music is made so; and as the framework closes on each story and the Abbot comes forward to preach, we feel a discomfort different from what is intended. After the story of the miracle in the furnace he tells us that 'Gold is tried in the fire, and the mettle of man in the furnace of humiliation' and prays that

> *God give us all*
> *The strength to walk*
> *Safe in the burning fiery furnace*
> *Of this murderous world.*

The aptness is undeniable; but what the composer's art has so extraordinarily opened up suddenly becomes thoroughly small and dry, and not a little banal. How serious, really, is the tone of this elaborate medievalizing? Do the spectators also dress up, in fancy, to become illiterate peasants receiving a 'sermon in sounds'? No answer; the musicians process out, taking their noises with them, leaving their audience too much in the dark.

Worries about the didactic strain in these explicitly moralizing works open up wider reservations still. The church parables officially exemplify Hope, Faith and Love: but it is difficult not to find such neatness a little laboured, especially when *Curlew River* seems to embody all three. Faith and Love remain abstractions in their respective parables, giving scant warmth for all the wagging finger. The same is true of *Curlew River*, but with positive effect. It is far less insistently didactic, working—overwhelmingly—by pity and terror; and it is propelled by something absolutely authentic, a yearning for 'someone . . . someone . . .' that goes altogether beyond an emblem of Hope in the abstract. If the three parables have a common theme it is the drabbest stoicism: make do, knuckle under, hold fast, carry your burden, forgive and forget, dutifully kill the fatted calf. This is cold comfort at best, and at the worst, not bread but a stone. And artistically the result is a severe impoverishment, even a denial, of the free spirit that could once set Rimbaud and Michelangelo, and write the *Spring Symphony* and *The Prince of the Pagodas*.

And so the very clarity of the renewal in the parables soon serves to expose limitations more clearly than before. The irresolutions that linger on after three ostensibly reconciliatory endings suggest a high degree of disquiet which indeed surfaces in Britten's next stage work,

Owen Wingrave, with a turbulence, almost an incoherence, unique in this artist. 'Peace' here is certainly not an inert abstraction, but whereas the cardinal virtues fail to quicken their respective parables, 'Peace' has a weight thrust upon it which it simply cannot bear. It is a truism that everyone hates war and wants peace, and equally that a tyrant has never been defeated or a people civilized without the military virtues. Why not write three parables on honour, courage and glory?—for it is another failure of imagination, another limitation, to dismiss them as base or hollow. To place all self-deception, brutality and blood-lust on the one side and all humane decency on the other is more than just simplistic and mean; it is *untrue*. And this, in a man of painfully sensitive conscience, must stand at a peculiarly vulnerable place. It is commonplace to pay pious tribute to Britten's pacifism. But Peace and its facile companion Compassion can hardly be reconciled to a preoccupation with subject-matter that sometimes seems closer to a nervous compulsion than to the spirit of 'peace on earth, good will towards men'. And in Owen's monologue praising peace we sense that the word's larger vibrations carry beyond the purely conventional associations invoked. His fervour and the music's glittery warmth amidst so much that is angular and crashing, suggest what dare not speak its name in work after work. 'Love is the unfamiliar word'—not love as an abstract, but the individual eros. Peace is the symbol of self-discovery, self-possession, self-realization: 'in Peace I have found my image'. The private, almost fetishistic quality of this word in Britten's output explains itself—warrants its full warmth—only if it is understood as the pass- or code-word for his sexuality.

The wonder is that he could ever as an artist get beyond this impasse, for the extent of repression that these unresolved tensions indicate is so great as to suggest the imminence of an explosion. *Owen Wingrave* indeed has about it something explosive, though characteristically muffled, for Britten's more fruitful way out is by relaxing, by easing off the tight tense area into a state of mind which in full consciousness can honour, and eventually glory in and die for, its devotion to its own 'sinful' predilections. *Death in Venice* has no sermons about sacrifice to idols, or admonitions to Carry on Hoping or to Love your Neighbour. Here beauty, not peace, is hymned; and beauty's devotee, far from dedicating himself to its destruction or being its unwilling agent, as once in the past, can give himself up to the human body who possesses it; rapt, intent, and relieved even

1 Percy Grainger, in the early 1920s

2 Dmitri Shostakovich, photograph inscribed for Peter Pears by the composer

3 Gustav Mahler, the newspaper photograph from which Thomas Mann modelled the features of Aschenbach in *Death in Venice*

4 Frank Bridge, probably about 1910 when he was composing *The Sea*. Britten heard Bridge conduct *The Sea* at the Norfolk and Norwich Triennial Festival in 1924 and was 'knocked sideways'

5 Eric Crozier and E. M. Forster working on the libretto for *Billy Budd* at Crag House in 1950

6 Peter Pears and Myfanwy Piper at the New York (Metropolitan Opera) première of *Death in Venice* in 1974, with George Sturm (left) and Hans W. Heinsheimer (right)

7   Michelangelo Buonarroti
(*Seven Sonnets of Michelangelo*)

8   Christopher Smart
(*Rejoice in the Lamb*)

9   John Donne
(*Holy Sonnets of John Donne*)

10   Friedrich Hölderlin
(*Sechs Hölderlin-Fragmente*)

11   Alexander Pushkin
(*The Poet's Echo*)

12   William Blake (*Songs and Proverbs of William Blake*)

13   Herman Melville
(*Billy Budd*)

14   Paul Verlaine (*Quatre Chansons Françaises*) and Arthur Rimbaud (*Les Illuminations*) in London, 1872. Drawing by Félix Regamey

15 William Soutar (*Who are these children?*)

16 Wilfred Owen (*War Requiem* and *Nocturne*). This photograph, taken at Dunsden Vicarage in 1912, was given to Britten by Wilfred Owen's brother, Harold, at the time of the première of the *War Requiem*

17 Thomas Mann (*Death in Venice*)

18 Henry James (*The Turn of the Screw* and *Owen Wingrave*)

19 Thomas Hardy (*Winter Words*)

20 Edith Sitwell (*Canticle III: Still falls the Rain*). Drawing by Wyndham Lewis, 1923

21 William Plomer (*Gloriana* and three church parables)

22 W. H. Auden (*Four Cabaret Songs, Our Hunting Fathers, On This Island, Paul Bunyan, Hymn to St Cecilia*, among other works)

Act 4 DS.

Chorus: You've no idea how dull it is
Just being perfect nullities,
The idols of a democratic nation;
The heros of the multitude,
Their dreams of female pulchritude;
We're VERY VERY tired of admiration.

(~~LULLABY SUNG BY CHORUS~~)

(LULLABY AGAIN BUT SUNG OFF BY CHORUS)

new (1)

(CURTAIN)

Paul Bunyan:

Now let the complex spirit dissolve in
                                   the darkness
Where the Actual and the Possible are mysteriously exchanged

For the saint must descend into Hell; that his order may
                                   be tested by its disorder

The hero returns to the ~~womb~~ humble womb; that
                                   his will may be pacified and refreshed.

Dear children, trust the night and have faith in to-morrow
That these hours of ambiguity and indecision may
                                   be also the hours of healing

End of ACT I Sc.2.

23 A page of the working text for *Paul Bunyan*, annotated by Britten and
W. H. Auden. When Britten revised *Paul Bunyan* in 1974–5, this part of the
text was used for the new 'Bunyan's Goodnight' (No. 17)

24 The two Lucretias:
Kathleen Ferrier and Nancy
Evans

25 Montagu Slater

26 Britten with Montagu Slater in deepest Suffolk (Snape), *Grimes*-time,
1943–4

27 An early meeting of the English Opera Group, Christmas 1946. Left to right: John Piper, Eric Crozier, Joan Cross, Peter Pears, Benjamin Britten, Erwin Stein and Anne Wood

28 A page from the full score of *Billy Budd* (beginning of Act II in the original four-act version) in Britten's autograph

29 Britten with Julius Katchen during the
Decca recording of *Diversions* in 1954

30 The two Nicolases: Peter
Pears and David Hemmings
during the Decca recording
of *Saint Nicolas* at Aldeburgh
Parish Church, 1955

31 Britten, Norma Procter, Peter Pears and John Culshaw at a
Decca recording session

32 The Purcell Singers outside Blythburgh Church, 1956. Peter Pears, Benjamin Britten, Basil Douglas and Imogen Holst are at the left of the group: Rosamund Strode is at the far right of the front row

33 Britten with members of the *Noye's Fludde* menagerie at Orford Church, 1958

26   *A Midsummer Night's Dream*

Then let us teach our trial patience,
Because it is a customary cross,
As due to love, as thoughts, and dreams, and sighs,
Wishes and tears: poor fancy's followers.
LYSANDER: A good persuasion; therefore hear me
  Hermia:
I have a widow aunt, a dowager,
Of great revenue, and she hath no child:
From Athens is her house remote seven leagues,
And she respects me, as her only son:
There gentle Hermia, may I marry thee,
And to that place, the sharp Athenian Law
Cannot pursue us. If thou lov'st me, then
Steal forth thy father's house to-morrow-night:
And in the wood, a league without the town
(Where I did meet thee once with Helena,
To do observance to a morn of May)
There will I stay for thee.
HERMIA: My good Lysander,
I swear to thee, by Cupid's strongest bow,
By his best arrow with the golden head,
By the simplicity of Venus' doves,
By that which knitteth souls, and prospers loves,
And by that fire which burn'd the Carthage Queen,
When the false Troyan under sail was seen,
By all the vows that ever men have broke,
(In number more than ever women spoke)
In that same place thou hast appointed me,
To-morrow truly will I meet with thee.
LYSANDER: Keep promise love: look here comes Helena.
      Enter Helena.
HERMIA: God speed fair Helena, whither away?
HELENA: Call you me fair? that fair again unsay,

6.

LYSANDER   A good persuasion; therefore hear me Hermia:

I have a widow aunt, a dowager,

Of great revenue, and she hath no child:

From Athens is her house remote seven leagues,

And she respects me, as her only son:

There gentle Hermia, may I marry thee,

And to that place, the sharp Athenian Law
Cannot pursue us. If thou lov'st me, then

There will I go with thee.

HERMIA   My good Lysander, (I swear.... lov'st me)

I swear to thee, by Cupid's strongest bow,
By his best arrow with the golden head,

LYSANDER   By the simplicity of Venus' doves,

HERMIA   By that which knitteth souls, and prospers loves,

LYSANDER   And by that fire which burn'd the Carthage Queen,
When the false Troyan under sail was seen,

BOTH   By all the vows that ever men have broke,
'In number more than ever women spoke)......

      Enter Quince the carpenter, Snug the joiner, Bottom the

34 Peter Pears's annotated copy of the Penguin edition of Shakespeare's *A Midsummer Night's Dream*, and an early typed draft of the libretto, annotated by Britten, of the same passage. Note the addition of the only non-Shakespearean line—'Compelling thee to marry with Demetrius'—in Britten's hand, and the acknowledged need for a new line in Pears's working text

35 Benjamin Britten aged about ten years at Lowestoft

36 Britten in his twenties

37 Britten and Pears in the 1940s

38 Grimes: chaos and cosmos

39 Britten and Pears with Mstislav
Rostropovich in Armenia, 1965

40 Britten on the beach at
Aldeburgh, with Clytie,
mid-1960s

41   One of the last photographs with Peter Pears, at Snape, 1974

to ecstasy by uttering what has been so long constrained. This explicitness (absolutely delicate, unprovocative, unlibidinous) of Britten's last opera opens up a more humane moral sphere than the moralizings of the church parables. Their sermons appear sour, their presentation of the virtues impoverished. *Death in Venice* is neither mean nor covert; it knows what it is doing, and its moral understanding has put aside childish partiality. Yet the opera would not have been possible without the parables; the strait has contributed generously to the open. The masterly fluidity and flexibility, the minimum of notes and maximum of suggestion, evocation and implication everywhere in *Death in Venice* are a triumphant vindication of procedures that, beginning in the utterly strange and new, had run, in the two later parables, into perilously shallow water.

This extraordinary flowering out of the church parables shows by contrast that they had indeed moved towards the very edge of musical interest. For worse as well as for better they are necessarily thin. Negatively this implies undernourishment—works of art that, as Henry James put it, 'ask more of the imagination than they can be detected in giving it'. Positively it implies 'nothing in excess'; 'less is more'. Britten is obviously an archetypal thin (in modern times the thin have been leaner still in reaction to the epoch of unbridled fatness). The balance can be delicate; there is a point where the paradox of less-because-more becomes strained; pregnant parsimony miscarries; the hungry sheep look up and are not fed. Much in his later music crosses this threshold: the conspicuous loss of sensuous surface in the later song-cycles, the grit and grind of the cello suites, the sourness of *Children's Crusade* and much of *Wingrave*. Such music certainly seems to require more of us than it gives. But the parables are poised at the crux. It is clear that this style's parsimony is its strength; that it wears its starvation like a rose; that renewal is born from a scrupulous and humble attention to native limits. It is hardly surprising that the miraculous fusion of monotony with intensity happens only once.

What thinness cannot do is obvious enough; but positive thinness has the power to have us forgo what it misses, and concentrate upon the special range of effects that it alone can achieve. In the end what Britten can and cannot do are equally conducive to the resulting music. Thus the familiar 'inability to let go' that arguably fudges the climactic emotional moments in *Peter Grimes*, *The Rape of Lucretia* and *The Turn of the Screw* becomes a source of great intensity when not letting go is of the essence. This is why we demur when Britten ventures in the parables to re-allow direct pathos even in *Curlew River*;[2] and the problematically 'sinful' orgies in the other two can be related to the relative tameness of the Dionysiac element (indicating recoil rather than abandon) at the end of the main action in *Billy Budd* and in Aschenbach's nightmare in *Death in Venice*.

Knowing from Nietzsche that 'the degree and kind of a man's sexuality permeate the loftiest flights of his intellect', we read without surprise, in the famous letter[3] to Britten where Auden urges upon his friend the 'demands of disorder', of the correlation of his attraction to 'thin-as-a-board juveniles' with prelapsarian innocence. The mature Britten's characteristic thinness, of which the parables are the crucial examples, is inseparable from the theme that inspires all his most individual work. Their unexampled severity presents with startling clarity the feeling for innocence and the nostalgia to return to simplicity and unconsciousness. Their method enmeshes the theme in the work's very substance, making it possible to hear every troubling element—the Madwoman's anguish, the Babylonians' idolatry, the temptation and fall and humiliation of the Younger Son—as a mistuning, a disturbance of the eternal diatonic drones. As the story unwinds, its crises are sympathetically caught in ever more tortuous distortions; as it comes out well, so alien notes are restored to normal; and thus the rebirth of nescience is woven into the actual sounds themselves, providing the very reason for the notes being the way they are.

[2] There is just one, very brief, unconvincing touch—the passionate descending phrase in octaves at Figure 76.
[3] *BA*, pp.161–2.

23

Owen Wingrave: A Case for Pacificism

JOHN EVANS

> I have absolutely no patience with Pacifism as a political
> movement, as if one could do all the things in one's
> personal life that create wars and then pretend that to
> refuse to fight is a sacrifice and not a luxury.[1]

So wrote W. H. Auden to Stephen Spender in 1941. This is a point of
view to which Britten, a close artistic collaborator of Auden's since
1935, was directly opposed. Since his youth, Britten had been an
individual of strong opinions and ideologies. In his final year as head
boy of his Lowestoft preparatory school, South Lodge, he had done
much to stamp out the bullying of younger boys and had left the
school under a cloud for writing a combative essay on animals that
condemned all forms of cruelty and persecution. At Gresham's, his
Norfolk public school, he had refused to join the school Officers'
Training Corps. For Britten, pacifism was, and remained, not a
'political movement' but an essential requirement for a civilized
existence.

During the 1930s Britten was able to articulate many of his more
passionately held views, and principally his pacifist convictions,
through continued artistic collaboration with some of the most
brilliant minds in music, the theatre, broadcasting and left-wing
politics. The immediately pre-war period was of course especially
political, with its strong undercurrents of Communist activity in
Oxbridge circles, the rise of Fascism in Europe, the outbreak of the
Spanish Civil War, and the growing threat and eventual confirmation

---

[1] Quoted in Charles Osborne, *W. H. Auden, The Life of a Poet* (Eyre Methuen, 1980),
pp.206–7.

of Nazi aggression. Britten's personal diaries from this time contain much political comment, and his views were undoubtedly stimulated and encouraged by his colleagues in the GPO Film Unit and the Group Theatre, organizations for which he acted as resident composer after completing his period of study at the Royal College of Music. The fruits of his labours with the film documentary pioneer John Grierson (e.g. *Coal Face* and *Night Mail*), the Group Theatre writers Wystan Auden and Christopher Isherwood (*The Ascent of F6* and *On the Frontier*), and the Left Theatre writers Randall Swingler and Montagu Slater (the *a cappella* chorus *Advance Democracy* and *A Pageant of Empire*) have been documented by Donald Mitchell in *Britten and Auden in the Thirties*. But pacifism was undoubtedly the cause closest to Britten's heart and he contributed to pacifist propaganda through the *Pacifist March* (1937) written for the Peace Pledge Union and through the incidental music for Paul Rotha's pacifist film *Peace of Britain* (1936).

When war was declared, Britten was on tour with Peter Pears in North America. Following the example of Auden and Isherwood, who had emigrated to the United States in January 1939, Britten and Pears considered the possibility of American citizenship during their prolonged stay. By now Isherwood, like Britten and Pears, had declared himself a pacifist. Auden, on the other hand, had no time for pacifism, as is clear from his letter to Spender, but had none the less washed his hands of a Europe that seemed intent on destroying itself. The decision to return to the United Kingdom in March 1942 was not an easy one for Britten and Pears, both now pacifists at a time of war and returning to a country committed to war. Brave gestures against school authorities, friendly discussions with his composition teacher Frank Bridge (an equally devout pacifist), and propaganda through the theatre and documentary film were things of the past: Britten was now required personally and publicly to argue *his* case for pacifism before a Tribunal for the Registration of Conscientious Objectors. In later years this case was argued again on a massive scale in the *War Requiem* (1961) and with unreserved passion in the opera for television, *Owen Wingrave* (1970).

The BBC commissioned Britten's fifteenth work for the stage, and his first for television, in 1966. As was often the case with him, an operatic subject had been on his mind for some time before the commission. In a letter to Eric Walter White written on 5 November 1954, just after the première of *The Turn of the Screw*, he asked, 'By

Owen Wingrave

the way, do you know another short story of James' called "Owen Wingrave" with much the same quality as the Screw?' The story concerns Owen's rejection of the strong military traditions of the ancient Wingrave family. Destined for an army career since birth, Owen chooses to rebel against a profession that his developing pacifist convictions have made abhorrent to him. At the centre of the action James placed Spencer Coyle, at whose cramming establishment Owen and his friend Lechmere are being coached for Sandhurst. Eventually Coyle and his wife, who 'favours' Owen, sympathize with and stand by the boy against the combined forces of his family at Paramore— General Sir Philip Wingrave (Owen's grandfather), the formidable Miss Jane Wingrave (Owen's aunt), the 'faded, inoffensive' Mrs Julian (who, James informs us, was 'domesticated there by a system of frequent visits as the widow of an officer and a particular friend of Miss Wingrave'), and her daughter Kate (Owen's fiancée). Like Peter Grimes, Owen is in complete conflict with, and totally isolated from, the society in which he is 'rooted'; and like Grimes, and indeed Billy Budd, he is ultimately to be sacrificed to the common good. He is disinherited for refusing to conform and, goaded by his fiancée, he agrees to sleep in the haunted room at Paramore where two of his ancestors died after bringing disgrace to the family under similar circumstances. Kate relents later that night, but too late to save Owen, who is found dead. The implication is that he has been victorious in his own private battle. This may seem a remote supernatural tale to us now, but one suspects that the subject seemed disturbingly relevant to the composer in the late 1960s, with the escalation of the war in Vietnam. History appeared once more to be repeating itself. Britten cannot have failed to be aware of the parallels in the situations facing Owen at the end of the nineteenth century, Britten himself as a young man in the late 1930s and the young in America in the 1960s.

For a translation of this supernatural tale into a libretto Britten turned to Myfanwy Piper, who had provided the libretto for his first James opera, *The Turn of the Screw* (1954). James's 'Owen Wingrave' was written for the 1892 Christmas issue of an illustrated magazine, the *Graphic*. It was subsequently included in an English edition of his short stories published in 1893, and in 1907 he made it into a one-act play entitled *The Saloon*. Myfanwy Piper ignored this dramatization and concentrated on the original short story. 'Owen Wingrave' falls short of the suspense and subtle ambiguity James generated in 'The

Turn of the Screw'. The corporate hostile force at Paramore is somewhat indeterminately characterized by James, and it was left to the librettist to mould and develop the individual personalities. Through their musico-dramatic characterization, and particularly through the often devastating use of parody, Britten was able to elaborate upon the obsessional quality of the Wingrave family tradition and the sinister nature of Paramore.

Above and beyond the supernatural element that both stories exploit, a close parallel exists between Britten's interpretation of them: Owen's 'innocence', like Miles's, must be surrendered to a 'responsible' morality, and both Owen and Miles are required to conform to the 'maturing'—and corrupting—influence of 'experience'. Indeed one almost expects Kate to echo the Governess's 'What have we done between us' over Owen's body at the end of the opera, so closely parallel are the dramatic situations. The reprise of the Wingrave Ballad at the end further reinforces the parallel, imbued as it is with the same degree of pathos as the Governess's heartbreaking cry of *'Malo, malo'*. But the quality in 'Owen Wingrave' that undoubtedly aroused Britten's sympathy was the uncompromising expression of the pacifist views that James had held ever since the days of the American Civil War. Britten's opera is just as uncompromising in its message and in this respect the television opera is as much a 'parable' as anything he composed in the 1960s.

Owen Wingrave was drafted and composed while Britten was also much occupied with two major projects: the composition of the third church parable, *The Prodigal Son* (1967–8), and the television film recording of *Peter Grimes* at Snape Maltings (February 1969). He and Myfanwy Piper began preparatory work on the scenario for *Wingrave* in spring 1968; the composition sketch was begun in summer 1969. Work continued in Aldeburgh, Venice and Wolfsgarten, and it was his first major composition to be partly composed in his newly acquired Suffolk retreat at Horham. The composition sketch was finished in February 1970 and the full score was completed by August. The opera was written for a specific English Opera Group cast: Benjamin Luxon (Owen), Janet Baker (Kate), Jennifer Vyvyan (Mrs Julian), Heather Harper (Mrs Coyle), Sylvia Fisher (Miss Wingrave), Peter Pears (General Sir Philip Wingrave), John Shirley-Quirk (Spencer Coyle) and Nigel Douglas (Lechmere). There is no chorus, though the Wingrave Ballad that frames Act II (devised

Owen Wingrave

by the librettist to retell the family legend of the boy brutally killed by his father for refusing to fight when challenged by a friend) is scored for tenor (sung by Pears in the original production) and a distant chorus of boys' voices. From these vocal specifications one might expect orchestral forces similar to those of *The Rape of Lucretia, Albert Herring* or the *Screw*. However, Britten scored the opera for an orchestra of some forty-six players, almost identical with that of the Cello Symphony (1963) but with a larger and more prominent percussion band: hardly a chamber ensemble, although it could be described as a number of potential chamber ensembles, such is the nature of much of the orchestration. Britten conducted the English Opera Group cast and the English Chamber Orchestra for the original production, which was filmed and recorded at Snape Maltings in November 1970 and given its television première on BBC2 on 16 May 1971.

The opera is in two acts: the first, a Prelude, seven scenes and four interludes, lasts just over an hour; the second, a Prologue (the Wingrave Ballad) and two large-scale scene-complexes, each of six continuous sub-scenes, lasts just over forty minutes. Apart from the Wingrave Ballad and quotations from Shelley's 'Queen Mab'[2] (substituted by Myfanwy Piper for the poems of Goethe that James has Owen read in Hyde Park) the libretto is in heightened prose. Within this structure the closed forms of aria and ensemble predominate to an extent that is perhaps surprising for Britten at this stage of his career.[3] The musical language of the opera is altogether individual, representing a fresh departure, after a decade devoted to the liturgical-theatrical medium of the church parables, and heralding a renewed interest in the potential of full-scale opera, which the composer had not explored since *A Midsummer Night's Dream* in 1960. Not surprisingly, then, *Wingrave* is a hybrid of chamber-musical colours from *Lucretia* (harp and strings in the Hyde Park scene), parody techniques from *Herring* (in the treatment of the hostile forces at Paramore), musico-dramatic schemes as subtle as those of *Grimes* and *Budd*, motivic and twelve-note elements as in the *Screw* and the *Dream* (eight different rows, employed at crucial stages of the drama), techniques of metrical flexibility and textural non-alignment from the church parables, and heterophonic techniques that belong to a

[2] Britten had made use of 'Queen Mab' before, in the film *Coal Face*.
[3] See above pp.88–90, where the composer discusses the impact of the filming of *Peter Grimes* on the musical forms in *Owen Wingrave*.

John Evans

completely different culture but had already found expression in *Paul Bunyan* and *The Prince of the Pagodas*.[4]

But *Owen Wingrave* is not less rich for drawing on a wide range of resources. Indeed, it is one of Britten's most economic, tightly organized and finely wrought scores, second in these respects only to *The Turn of the Screw*. The textures are sparse and the forms compact and integrated by a technique of effortless yet highly compressed transition, a musical equivalent of television's cross-fade. The principal motifs of the Prelude to Act I and the Wingrave Ballad are in effect the counterparts of the principal orchestral and vocal themes of the *Screw*. However, the expository function of the *Wingrave* Prelude is very like that of the Prologue to *Billy Budd* and the opening scene of *Death in Venice*, and, as in the latter case, twelve-note elements exercise absolute control on the formal structure in a way that owes its example, if not its technique, to Schoenberg. From the very opening of *Wingrave* the characteristic percussion scoring (with piano and harp) of a three-bar martial figure establishes the percussion orchestra as an autonomous group associated throughout with the ancient Wingrave military tradition (with one important exception in Owen's 'Peace' aria). Like the *Screw* theme, the three chords on which this figure is based are constructed from a twelve-note series (Ex.1a), here in vertical rather than horizontal alignment as two dominant sevenths in first inversion and a *Grimes*ian minor ninth (Ex.1b). Like the music of the wood in Act I and the opening chords of Act II of *A Midsummer Night's Dream*, this sequence recurs refrain-like throughout the opera, articulating the structures within the score. But in the

Ex.1a

Ex.1b

---

[4] See above, p.41 and pp.205–10.

Owen Wingrave

Prelude Britten isolates the diminished triad contained within the first two chords (marked **x** in Ex.1a) for a sequence of instrumental cadenzas, each related to a Wingrave ancestral portrait. Each portrait adds a new pitch to an accumulating twelve-note cluster that underpins the texture: the fifth is a double portrait (for piccolo and trombone) of the ferocious old Colonel and the boy whose fate is lamented in the Wingrave Ballad; the tenth portrait, representing Owen's father, is a twelve-note theme, a *Klangfarbenmelodie*, over an accumulation of eleven pitches from the pedal series; and Owen himself appears as the last portrait, with a sublime resolution on to the twelfth pitch, D. So in the Prelude alone Britten introduces three different twelve-note sets. A further five are employed at various stages in the score, but no system is devised for their translation into a 'method' of composition, and tonal hierarchies and functionally directed harmonies are never abandoned to any degree. More important than the way in which Britten employs these twelve-note elements is the way in which he constructs his tone-rows; and it is interesting to note that with only one exception—the rising sequence of two hexachordal whole-tone scales that underpins the dinner procession in the last scene of Act I—every tone-row is constructed entirely from interlocking diminished triads. Indeed, the diminished triad becomes the dominant motif of the entire opera, and its peculiar quality of tension and irresolution is clearly what Britten was determined to exploit.

As the centre-piece of the opera, the Wingrave Ballad (see Ex.2) gives a driving impetus to the compact, throughcomposed structure of Act II. It introduces three important motifs that complement the diminished triads of the Prelude: the three-note figure of the opening phrase (**x**), the seventh figure 'Paramore shall welcome woe' (**y**), and the distant trumpet fanfare (**z**). Both **x** and **z** have, however, been foreshadowed in Act I. In the interlude that precedes Scene 4 (and Owen's return to Paramore to face his family 'the living and the dead'), views of Paramore are accompanied by a new development of the opening twelve-note statement of the Prelude as 'ground' beneath slowly unfolding string melody which anticipates **x** and is punctuated by **z** of Ex.2.

The tonal fabric of the opera owes as much to the expository Prelude as do the thematic structures, and more specifically to the last portrait cadenza—the horn theme associated with Owen himself (Ex.3). Here we discover the first substantial challenge by perfect

Ex.2

Ex.3

triads to the diminished triads of the martial pulsation. As perfect and
diminished triads are juxtaposed, Britten highlights the major and
minor modes of the theme's tonal centre of D. The minor mode
ultimately gives way to the major, complete with pivotal dominant
preparation, and the same major/minor ambivalence is projected into
the opening scene of Act I. This major/minor conflict is the conflict
within Owen, and its various inflections dictate the tonal and dramatic
alliances of the opera. Owen's closest allies, the Coyles, more often
than not express themselves on the sharp side of Owen's D major:
notably the Lydian A major of Coyle's compassionate arioso in Act I
scene 1 ('Straight out of school they come to me') and in its reprise in
Act I scene 6 ('I own to a deep interest in the boy') and the E major of
Mrs Coyle's first appearance in Act I. The Paramore contingent, on
the other hand, express themselves through keys to the flat side of

Owen Wingrave

Owen's D minor, and the first substantial tonal contrast in Act I scene I is effected by Lechmere's mindless glorification of war with an exuberant rendering of 'The Minstrel Boy' and a shift from D major/minor towards B flat. Lechmere's characteristics are very much Wingrave characteristics, and he shares the tonal regions of B flat and E flat with the Wingrave paterfamilias Sir Philip, whose senile trumpeting exploits the same dotted fanfare-like motif. The hostility of the ladies is more ambiguous and the music characteristically associated with them usually involves a variety of tonal juxtapositions within tightly organized forms. Miss Wingrave's music is declamatory and regal in tone, with woodwind trills nervously punctuating the vocal line. Kate has a brief and exquisitely organized recitative and arioso, heavy with youthful self-regard. Her mother proves to be first-class raw material for a vivid Britten portrait, with music reminiscent of the Governess's 'labyrinth' aria in its intense highly charged quality and compulsive word repetitions. But Mrs Julian is older and worldly wise, and her music boasts a bitonal canon by inversion in an agitated texture of pizzicato strings. Taking Owen's D major/minor as the central pivot, the sharp/flat alliances are clearly defined:

Mrs Coyle	E			
Spencer Coyle	A			
	D	Owen d	G/g	Mrs Julian
			g/G flat	Kate Julian
			F and G/g	Miss Wingrave
			B flat	Lechmere
			E flat	Sir Philip

The most substantial and certainly the most passionate aria in the score is Owen's *and Britten's* great apostrophe to peace after Owen's disinheritance in Act II. In a staggering transformation of the role of the percussion orchestra Britten creates a sensuous, shimmering, gamelan-like cloud of tuned percussion hovering high above a succession of radiant, widely spaced chords that punctuate Owen's thoughts. (The roots of these chords are formed from yet another twelve-note series in which diminished triads predominate.) As Donald Mitchell has pointed out, the 'Peace' aria recalls an earlier, ecstatic aria about peace, Billy's B flat major aria in Act II of *Billy Budd*—'a sail in the storm, / The far-shining sail that's not fate', which is taken up by Vere in the opera's Epilogue when he too affirms his inner peace: 'I was lost on the infinite sea, but I've sighted a sail in the storm. . . .' Mitchell explains:

> Britten finds (unconsciously, I'm certain) a consistent musical imagery which for him is associated with the idea of pacification, of reconciliation. One senses something almost uncanny about the precision of the imagery of what is so often considered to be an abstract ideal. But for Britten, 'peace', whether public or private, is not an abstraction: for him it is as real as its opposite—violence, war.[5]

Despite a host of glowing notices (notably from John Warrack, Eric Walter White, Winton Dean, Peter Evans and Noel Goodwin) after the television première in 1971, *Owen Wingrave* has failed to establish itself in the operatic repertoire. Since its stage première at the Royal Opera House, Covent Garden, on 10 May 1973, it has received only two new productions outside the United Kingdom and one student production, at the Royal College of Music in 1980. The original television and stage productions were of course seen by an audience of millions all over the world, yet, if anything, one would expect that to encourage the staging of new productions and generate considerable interest with opera audiences. Clearly this has not been the case. One problem posed to opera producers is the flair with which Britten and Myfanwy Piper have exploited the television medium. Mrs Piper's clear, succinct text is brilliantly suited to the complicated technical demands of television opera; and it is characteristic of Britten that the operatic conception is enhanced, rather than hindered, by a thorough understanding of televisual techniques. In realizing and exploiting these methods Britten benefited from his apprenticeship with the GPO Film Unit in the 1930s: the structures of the opera are compact, bridge passages brief, transitions swift and scenes mixed—all of which poses technical problems for a production team within the limitations of an opera house.

The first and probably the most difficult of these pitfalls is Act I scene 2, where the action is cross-cut between Owen, in Hyde Park, and Coyle and Miss Wingrave at her Baker Street lodgings. As Coyle informs Miss Wingrave of Owen's decision to give up his military training, the tension between Owen's reflective music and Miss Wingrave's ever more agitated outbursts reaches a climax as the

---

[5] *'Owen Wingrave* and the Sense of the Past', in the booklet accompanying the complete Decca recording (SET 501–2) of the opera conducted by the composer.

Owen Wingrave

Horse Guards come trotting through the park. For Miss Wingrave these are 'the glory and pride of England', but for Owen they are translated into 'a scene of military carnage'. The scene is superbly conceived for the screen, and it was very convincingly realized for television; but it remains a problem in the opera house. So does Act I scene 5, which demands the elision of the events of an entire week during which Owen is under constant attack. Very often interludes between scenes are abandoned altogether; and in the final scene of Act I we hear the private thoughts of each character at the dinner table. In the television production the Wingrave Ballad was illustrated by slow-motion mime in sepia, the use of monochrome strikingly evoking an earlier historical period. It is obviously not possible, and anyway surely not desirable, to attempt to reproduce these effects in the opera house. Britten was an exceptionally practical, professional and, above all, pragmatic creative artist, and I believe it would have been impossible for him to compose an opera for television without keeping at least one eye on the operatic stage, for it is there, after all, that the future of the work lies. It is not my job to tell producers how to overcome these technical difficulties, but it strikes me that while they persist in creating problems for themselves (and often for their singers), they might, for once, tackle some of the problems posed by a composer.

Britten's message in *Owen Wingrave* is uncompromising: a total denunciation of war and a passionate plea for peace. Opera audiences, on the whole, wish to be entertained, moved, excited—but not harangued. The countless ardent admirers of the *War Requiem* are offered the distance and shelter of religious ritual, whereas this fiercely argued condemnation of the unthinking glorification of war on the operatic stage offers no such comfort. There are those who will agree with Debussy that music exists to be served and not exploited ('Il faut servir, pas se servir de, la musique'). But those who choose to neglect *Owen Wingrave*, Britten's fourth parable of the 1960s, are neglecting one of his finest scores from any period and for any medium.

24

Death in Venice:
The dark side of perfection[1]

DONALD MITCHELL

In its original form this 'introduction' was a radio script broadcast by the BBC on the night before the second performance of Death in Venice *at Snape Maltings on 22 June 1973; in other words, the judgements in it were made at a very early stage in the life of the work. The composer, needless to add, would have preferred there to be no 'introduction' at all and especially not in advance of the first broadcast performance. Indeed it became clear to me on this occasion that Britten's well-known distaste for critical commentary on his music—adverse or positive—was much more intense when the appraisal preceded the musical event. (He was unable to attend any of the performances because of the major heart operation he had undergone in May, but heard both the broadcast performance (or part of it) and the 'introduction'.)*

[D.M.]

A new major work by Britten, particularly a new one of the calibre of *Death in Venice*, can at first hearing present some puzzling aspects. One feels oneself launched into new musical and dramatic territory, with only a minimal map to consult. But as almost always with Britten, one does find landmarks from the past that help one to locate one's present bearings and give one a foothold from which to begin the climb towards a more complete understanding. I say 'climb' because I am convinced that *Death in Venice* does represent a pinnacle of achievement, and one that must be rare for any composer, however fertile and prodigiously gifted.

[1] Edited from the original radio script and the subsequent sleeve-note for Decca recording SET 581–3 (1974).

Death in Venice

Let me start with an obvious point, about the idyllic scene on the beach towards the end of Act I, where a still balanced and still partly detached and observing Aschenbach, the renowned man of letters, watches the boys' games (Scene 7, 'The Games of Apollo'). Through his naturally classically orientated eyes—and in retrospect how ironical his poised classicism appears—the boys take on the guise of young Greek athletes sporting in a pentathlon, watched by an admiring crowd. They dance, accompanied by chorus (the onstage crowd) and, principally, percussion (the instrumental sound that is always associated with them). These are choral dances, in fact; and in a flash one is transported back to 1953 and to Act II scene 1 of *Gloriana*, where a masque danced for the Queen on progress also took the form of choral dances. As in the Coronation opera, a high solo voice functions as the master of ceremonies, in the case of *Death in Venice* a counter-tenor, the Voice of Apollo (see Ex.1a); and as a generating idea which lends Apollo's music its particular contour, atmosphere and colour, Britten uses a fragment of a Delphic Hymn, c.138 BC (Ex.1b).[2] The music of these choral dances in *Death in Venice* is unlike any other music in *Death in Venice*—aptly, because it is a half-visionary scene, half out-of-time, whose independent, even

Ex.1a Death in Venice

Ex.1b Delphic Hymn

formalized, slightly aloof and 'classical' style is quite deliberate. It is also the last moment of repose in the opera, before the serene vision of games in the sun fades and Aschenbach is seized by the passion that will destroy him. While the choral dances in *Death in Venice* have a wholly different and indeed far more complex function to play than those in *Gloriana*, it is plain that the principle first adumbrated in the Coronation opera has been picked up again twenty years later,

---

[2] See No. 7(a) in A. T. Davison and W. Apel, *Historical Anthology of Music* (Cambridge, Mass.: Harvard University Press, 1950).

developed, and lent new significance. One will never now hear the *Gloriana* dances in quite the same way.

Dance and mime have vital roles to play in this particular opera. One might argue that the idyllic beach scene is a far-reaching transformation and indeed transfiguration of the old concept of the *divertissement* that was once very much part of opera as spectacle, as entertainment. Britten's beach scene shows us what a long way we have travelled from that tradition, from the spectacular to the visionary. The idea of dance, of movement, is central to the concept of the new opera, not a subordinate part of it. As a result, one may think, ballet is raised in *Death in Venice* to a new formal, dramatic and expressive status—a typical instance of the revolutionary innovations Britten so quietly and surprisingly effects.

One of the many-layered ironies in Mann's novella[3] is that Aschenbach, the most literate and literary of literary heroes, a writer so articulate about himself, whose elegant literary artefacts, his communications, have reached a wide public—he is, above all, a man with a public—never exchanges a word with the boy. It is not because the occasions cannot be contrived, but because he can't do it, can't say it—in short, can't communicate. He has, rather like Schoenberg's Moses, *no words*. Words fail him, because he has no language, no style, in which to make articulate the feelings that overwhelm him. That lack is the very heart of his problem, the paralysis at the centre of his creativity. When the terrible, ecstatic, but tortured self-realization is torn out of him, after the choral dances (see Ex.8a below), he falls back on what *he* thinks is a cliché—which is, of course, another irony—'I love you'.

That there is no verbal communication between the two principals in *Death in Venice* certainly creates a situation ripe for music, and is doubtless one of the reasons why the story had a powerful appeal for the composer. Music, as it were, can do everything that cannot, in this case, be spoken. At the same time, it was a dramatic problem that had to be solved; and it has been solved with conspicuous brilliance and originality by Britten and his librettist, Myfanwy Piper, by casting the boy and his family as dancers. This means that the composer and his colleagues have an additional dimension at their disposal, a visual language which is non-verbal but made up of a vocabulary of movement, mime, gesture and dance. Thus the idea of beauty, which

[3] I strongly recommend T. J. Reed's introduction to his edition of the original German text in the Clarendon German Series (Oxford University Press, 1971).

the boy represents, is articulated in ritualized movement and music, while the rest of the opera is unfolded in the traditional association of words and music.

I say 'ritualized' because, although there are scenes in which the boy and his family move in a relatively naturalistic manner (though still never communicating through words), at all crucial moments, for example at their very first appearance (Scene 4, 'The first evening at the hotel'), they are distinguished by a rite of gesture and movement, a remarkable amalgam of mime and dance that separates them from their fellows, making them strange and apart. And I have no doubt that the importation of ritual at this level into an otherwise relatively naturalistic framework or context shows the influence on Britten's imagination of his extraordinary works from the 1960s, the church parables *Curlew River*, *The Burning Fiery Furnace* and *The Prodigal Son*, in which a highly elaborate language of gesture and mime was developed in a unique way.[4] In *Death in Venice* one encounters for the first time a profound influence from the ritual world of the parables being exercised on a mainstream theatre piece. (I am thinking of the mode of dramatic presentation rather than purely musical techniques, though there, too, as I shall suggest, the parables' influence is substantial.)

Of course, we must witness the strangeness, the otherness, of the boy not only in his gestures, but also in his music. And here again Britten alights on a novel solution. It is to a large percussion band, with all this means in terms of a distinct sonority and a distinctive kind of invention, that he entrusts the music for Tadzio, his family, and his young companions. The music for vibraphone that indelibly marks the first entry of Tadzio the first time we, and Aschenbach, see him, in Act I (Ex.2), has a wholly distinctive sound and character—it is

Ex.2

4 See above, chapter 21 [C.P.].

overpoweringly present and yet at the same time emphatically remote—that sharply separates it from the score of which it forms part, where, of course, the 'conventional' orchestra is used. Though let me spell out that there is absolutely nothing conventional about the orchestral sound Britten creates in *Death in Venice*. It is wholly surprising, even by his own surprising standards, and its extraordinary refinement emphasizes the particular quality of the work—which is one of those pieces that mysteriously summons up new sources of creative energy and the precise means of expression to articulate them.

The use of the percussion band for Tadzio and his associates complements and crystallizes in sound the strangeness, the otherness, the beauty of the boy that—literally—sounds a *new note* in Aschenbach's life. Yet just as there is a precedent in *Gloriana* for the choral dances of *Death in Venice*, so there is a precedent for this percussion band and its exotic, gamelan-like character, a precedent which also involves dance and which dates from 1956. This is Britten's full-length ballet, *The Prince of the Pagodas*, in which appeared a component of his art that has now become of great technical, dramatic and expressive significance for him. In the fairy-tale ballet, the percussion band is an emblem of an exotic, non-human world, not an underworld, but an *other* world, clearly marked off from the human world by its distinctive 'Pagodas' music[5] (see Ex.3). The evolution of this particular component in Britten's

Ex.3

[5] See above, p.198 [C.P.].

Death in Venice

music could be the subject of a whole study.[6] After a long span of time, the 'Pagodas' music reappeared in a formative role in the deliberate musical and dramatic distinctiveness of the church parables, of *Curlew River* especially; once again calculated strangeness, otherness, was embodied in techniques and sonorities of exotic origin.

It is interesting that this concept of 'otherness' consistently appears in Britten's more recent art in the guise of the independent percussion group, providing in all kinds of contexts a glimpse or hint of a world infinitely desirable, maybe, but also infinitely remote from the world as we know it. There is a remarkable instance in *Owen Wingrave*, in Owen's fervent address to public and private peace,[7] when the delicately radiant, yet again unmistakably exotic, contribution of the percussion group surely symbolizes what Owen yearns for so fervently: peace, the very element which is so foreign to the whole Wingrave world, just as Tadzio is foreign to the world Aschenbach inhabits (Ex.4).

Ex.4

So the unique characterizing quality of the music for the boy and his family in *Death in Venice* by means of the percussion ensemble has a long tradition behind it in Britten's own music. The exoticism is perhaps given a new twist in the new opera by the parallel between the importation of 'alien' elements into a western musical language and the cult of the alien god Dionysus which supposedly swept through ancient Greece—not to speak of the further parallel with the cholera

[6] It is partly traced above, pp.39–45, and see also chapter 20 [C.P.].
[7] See above, pp.231–2 and 235–6 [C.P.].

epidemic that reached Venice in 1911 (a principal event and image in Mann's text), which is thought to have had its origins in India. Thus the percussion music in *Death in Venice* embodies not just one image, functions not just as one metaphor, but presents a whole complex of images and metaphors in a dense web of musical thinking and construction that is quite the equal of Mann's elaborate literary construct. The percussion band is Tadzio's world, but it is also everything that is strange, an encompassing symbol of all the diverse kinds of strangeness that disrupt the ordered, super-civilized, rational world of Aschenbach.

While the percussion lends the boy his aura of special, alien beauty, as observed by Aschenbach, the conventional orchestra, however unconventionally handled, evokes the seascapes and landscapes that are the other varieties of beauty seen through Aschenbach's eyes. They are not at all exotic in the Tadzio sense, for they comprise the European scene that is the long-established backcloth to Aschenbach's life. A notable generator of these beautiful orchestral inventions is the Barcarolle which represents, in substance and in many forms, Aschenbach's journeys by gondola. It also serves the Overture, haunting, lapping music with characteristic features of the barcarolle, the nocturne and the lullaby—rhythms, textures and images much favoured by Britten throughout his life. We may feel we are not so far distant from Rome and *The Rape of Lucretia* as we approach Aschenbach's Venice.

To take another example, the spacious contours of the music that embodies Aschenbach's first view of the beach suggest the ecstatic release of feeling as he surveys the amplitude of the beach and the brilliance of the sea after his arrival in Venice (Ex.5).[8] It is an upsurge of lyricism, from a constricted heart, that plays a prominent role in the opera. It is not just an image of beach and seascape. It becomes inextricably intermingled with and modified by Aschenbach's feelings—it is an *interior* view. And by the end of the opera the view, like everything else seen through Aschenbach's eyes, has changed almost out of all recognition. As Aschenbach walks on to the deserted beach for the last time, the 'beautiful view' has diminished, has

[8] Britten told me that the 'view' music came to him complete—out of the air, so to speak—when he was abroad, thinking about and planning the opera but not yet composing it. He wrote the theme down on a scrap of paper. It was not uncommon for him to have ideas in this way, but he found (he said) that he seldom used them once the compositional process actually started; more often they were rejected; but not in this case.

Ex.5

contracted. It is not only a melodic contraction; the former warmth
and generosity of the orchestral sound has been touched by a terrible
frost, and what was in bloom has withered (Ex.6).

Ex.6

Aschenbach's changed perceptions of the physical world about him
are represented by the modification of certain basic musical materials.
As the opera progresses, the distortions intensify. The beauty of
'ambiguous Venice' becomes ever more ambiguous as the cholera
disrupts the city and Aschenbach's insensate passion increasingly
consumes him. The music that is *not* modified is, naturally, that of
Tadzio and his comrades, which remains throughout bright, static,
remote and rhythmical—unchanging. The beautiful Tadzio leaves
the opera as beautiful and as untouched as he entered it,[9] whereas
Aschenbach undergoes the ultimate modification: from life to death.

That radical transformation, accomplished over two acts, is
embodied in an unceasing transformation of the work's basic musical
materials. It is not possible in this context to scrutinize in anything
like the appropriate detail the brilliance and resource Britten brings to

[9] Perhaps not quite so. His fierce struggle with Jaschiu at the end of Act II develops
from the norm of a familiar beach game into overt hostilities, with the tuba
contributing its characteristic infection to the climax (Scene 17, 'The Departure').
The music reflects the disillusioning impact of Experience on Tadzio's Innocence (to
use Blake's terms). But he is intact again, in possession of himself and his own
unmodified theme, for his walk out to sea and final summons to Aschenbach.
However, one may think that the world leaves its mark even on Tadzio.

the variation of his principal thematic and motivic materials, but here is one example of the process of distortion and contortion at work. First (Ex.7), in pure, diatonic ascending scales early on in the opera,

Ex.7

Aschenbach announces his intention to offer up his days to the sun and the south, in softly glowing string textures. Then, in the catastrophic moment of self-revelation at the end of Act I after the poised classicism of the choral dances, when Aschenbach surrenders himself to Eros, those ascending scales, now massively distorted and thickened out in dissonant lines, ascend to the truth about himself and his feeling for Tadzio: 'I—love you', he cries. With 'love you', in the very last bars, Aschenbach finds the truth about himself and, with superb musical irony, in alighting on the truth, *also alights on his own key*, E major. Ex.8a shows the moment of piercing self-perception that precipitates the steep plunge into the abyss which is the dramatic substance of Act II. If we now look back to the start of Act I, we realize that Aschenbach's self-declamation, 'I, Aschenbach, famous as a master-writer' (Ex.8b), has adumbrated the E that is asserted with such telling irony at the very end of the act.

Aschenbach's music alters, but Tadzio's does not; for example, if we look at the very end of Act II, after Aschenbach's collapse, we hear Tadzio's theme (vibraphone) unfolded, quite distinct and separate from the long orchestral melody that is a threnody for Aschenbach, an elegiac orchestral version of Aschenbach's own Hymn to Apollo at the end of Act I (compare the orchestral threnody with Aschenbach's ecstatic 'When thought becomes feeling, feeling thought . . .'). Thus in the postlude to the whole opera—the concluding Mahlerian Adagio for orchestra—Tadzio and Aschenbach are thematically counterpointed, and yet remain worlds apart, because both principal sonorities are there too, the bright, aloof percussion (Tadzio) and the

Death in Venice

Ex.8a

Ex.8b

warm, yearning orchestra (Aschenbach), and the two 'worlds', as we know from the drama we have witnessed, don't mix, don't relate. There is no more of a relationship between the boy and the writer at this ultimate stage in the opera than at any other. The postlude brings Tadzio and Aschenbach into their closest musical relationship (compare the long, ascending, and still aspiring string melody—which inverts the direction of Tadzio's music—with Aschenbach's) but the composer remains faithful to the end, as he must, to the clear

Donald Mitchell

separation of his central characters. This final 'union' marvellously sums up what the whole opera has been about. It does not resolve the drama, because the only possible resolution would have had to be a false one. Britten does not falter, and maintains the separation that is the heart, the ironical heart, of the opera, to the very end, until Tadzio vibrates into stillness and Aschenbach expires in the highest register of the strings (harmonic).

I mentioned above the profound influence of the church parables on *Death in Venice*, not only on the mode of dramatic presentation but also on specific musical techniques. For example, some of the writing for the brilliantly conceived chorus—a real chorus of soloists—is related to the choral techniques first revealed in the parables; and the pronounced metrical freedom, the flowing *un*measuredness, of so much of the music in *Death in Venice* clearly has its origins in *Curlew River*. Again, as in the church parables, especially *Curlew River*, there is often a feeling of suspended tonality. (There are tonal areas, certainly, such as Aschenbach's E and Tadzio's A—which are themselves related—but one feels these, perhaps, as dramatic and characterizing rather than as functional in a form-building sense. I do not know, as yet. Further study of the opera may well result in new ideas and information about its long-range tonal organization.) What many people might think of as characteristically 'operatic' tunes belong to those parts of the opera—e.g. the scenes in the Barber's shop (Scenes 8 and 15) or the Strolling Players' scene (Scene 10)—where Britten deliberately exploits a popular vein, with popular snatches of melody, though the harmony, not surprisingly, is often unpredictable, contradicting or unseating the expectations aroused by a familiar melodic pattern. In many textures elsewhere, as in the parables, the 'harmony' is drawn from the notes that make up the vocal line. And of course the general spareness and austerity of the textures has its precedent in the instrumental economy of the parables. Yet, though the sound of *Death in Venice* may be calculated with exceptional refinement, even by Britten's own standards, the score is exceptionally rich and varied in colour. 'Less is more' (Mies van der Rohe) is certainly the case in *Death in Venice*.

There are other key works and sources besides the parables. One source is Peter Pears's art as a singer, not least his performances as the Evangelist in the Passions of Bach and Schütz. Indeed, the specific influence of Schütz on the compositional method of the recitatives for Aschenbach in *Death in Venice* is unmistakable. Two further works by

Death in Venice

Britten should be mentioned, the orchestral song-cycle, *Nocturne* (1958), and the opera *Billy Budd* (1951). The *Nocturne*'s flowing, seamless form and swift alternation of dramatic scenes and moods are very close to Britten's recent theatrical techniques, but it also has a more specific relevance here. Behind its marvellous evocation of sleep lies a profound reflection on the nature of the real and the unreal, of true appearances and false, worked out in multiple images of night and day, sleep and wakefulness, dream and nightmare. The poetic images are, as it were, an articulation on the surface of the metaphysical preoccupations which are the real content of the work, and which are worked out in purely musical terms through the use of a highly elaborate language of musical symbolism. Britten has a musical language for metaphysics at his disposal—an aspect of his art that has so far received perhaps less attention than it might have done. It is a profound presence in *Billy Budd*, another crucial work in Britten's output, in which, one remembers, there is a protagonist, an upright man like Aschenbach, who finds himself in a terrible moral predicament; and it is surely no accident that we hear from time to time in the noble accents of Gustav von Aschenbach an echo of Edward Fairfax Vere, Captain of the *Indomitable*. We may also remember that in *Billy Budd*, now nearly a quarter of a century ago, Ideal Beauty in the form of Billy was viewed in dramatic relation to, one might say, a composite Vere–Aschenbach–Apollo and Claggart–Dionysus. Moreover, without wanting to force similarities where there are none, we cannot but recall, in the light of *Death in Venice*, that another Angel of Death is encountered in *Billy Budd*; and without wishing to impose crude patterns and talk about a composite Billy–Tadzio, which might be something of a critical fabrication, there is clearly a sense in which in both Billy and Tadzio we witness the paradoxical enchantment and destructive power of Beauty— whereupon we realize that *Death in Venice* is not a fresh departure, but fresh evidence, rather, of a long-standing preoccupation of Britten's.[10]

In *Death in Venice*, he has created a *chef d'oeuvre* of the first rank, which subtly alters our perception of the world, and which, I predict, will have a major influence on the shape of musical theatre for decades to come.

[10] Cf. above, p.142, and below, p.266 [C.P.].

25

Towards a Genealogy of
Death in Venice

CHRISTOPHER PALMER

One mellow autumn evening in 1892 a gondola drifted through the lagoons of Venice. Its owner, a middle-aged English writer, lay back absorbed in the melancholy reflections appropriate to his romantic surroundings. Suddenly his attention was riveted by the extraordinary beauty of the figure sturdily rowing a passing tourist boat, a bronzed *faccino* in the broad black hat and white costume then fashionable among gondoliers. Slowly the boat drew away, the youth disappeared from view, and the man was left with a sense of deprivation. His biographer notes that

> It was typical of John Addington Symonds to seize upon a fleeting encounter like this as a revelation of significant truth . . . the symbol of a lost ideal. . . . The boy . . . became intricately fused with Symonds's feeling for Venice and his response to the landscape of the lagoons. . . . His precise mood of melancholy had to be recaptured, 'one of those sad moods, in which all life seems wasted, & the heart is full of hidden want, & one does not even know what one desires, but a sense of wistfulness is everywhere—one of these moods has been upon me several days'.[1]

In June 1926 A. E. Housman wrote to his sister Kate:

> I was surprised to find what pleasure it gave me to be in Venice again . . . certainly there is no place like it in the world: everything there is better in reality than in memory. I first saw it on a romantic

[1] Phyllis Grosskurth, *John Addington Symonds* (Longman, 1964), p.1.

250

evening after sunset in 1900, and I left it on a sunshiny morning, and I shall not go there again.[2]

Meanwhile, in May 1911, another writer had been to Venice ('the incomparable, the fabulous, the like-nothing-else-in-the-world', as he called it), and immortalized his visit in his novella *Death in Venice*. Thomas Mann, his wife Katja and his brother Heinrich had planned a holiday on Brioni, off the Dalmatian coast. That turned out badly and, on an impulse, they went to Pola and took a steamer for Venice, where they spent a week at the Hôtel des Bains, on the Lido. Here Mann encountered the original of the beautiful boy whom the elderly writer Aschenbach fatally loves in *Death in Venice*.[3] In May 1932, when his children Erika and Klaus were staying in Venice at the same hotel, Mann felt he had to write to them,

. . . because the place is so important to me and I am glad to think of your being there. In spirit I am with you leading that unique life between the warm sea in the morning and the 'ambiguous' city in the afternoon. Ambiguous . . . is wonderfully relevant in all its meanings, and for all the city's modern silliness and corruptness . . . this musical magic of ambiguity still lives. . . . You mention that it must have been lovely in the middle of the last century. But Platen was already saying: 'All that is left of Venice lies in the land of dreams'. . . . For certain people, there is a special melancholia associated with the name of Venice . . . my heart would be pounding were I there again.[4]

'Platen', August Graf von Platen-Hallermünde (1798–1835), a late romantic poet with strong classical affiliations (and, like Housman and Symonds, homosexual), was one of those for whom Venice had a 'special melancholia'. In *Death in Venice* Aschenbach, approaching Venice from the sea, thinks of the 'melancholy and susceptible poet who had once seen the towers and turrets of his dreams rise out of these waves': the poet is Platen. According to W. D. Williams 'his passionless objectivity, his extreme cultivation of formal values, is a cloak thrown over his natively romantic sensibility; indeed it is

[2] *The Letters of A. E. Housman*, ed. Henry Mass (Rupert Hart-Davis, 1971), p.238.
[3] In the early 1960s a Polish count aged 68 proved from photographs and recollections that he had been that boy. Mann himself stated, in *A Sketch of My Life*, that all the people and incidents of the story were drawn from life.
[4] *The Letters of Thomas Mann*, selected and translated by Richard and Clara Winston (Secker & Warburg, 1970), vol.1, p.187.

more, it is a necessary form of self-protection against the threat of disintegration'.[5] He chisels out statuesque, marmoreal verses, perfectly proportioned, but devoid of human feeling and sensuous appeal. Such are his fourteen sonnets on Venice: verbal reflections of the ornate and grandiose palaces, the still canals, the plethora of classical paintings and sculptures. Yet he is also everywhere conscious of the worm within the rose, the all-too-perfect ripeness poised on the brink of decay. This is the 'ambiguousness' of Venice to which Mann refers and which accounts for its appeal to all 'double-natures' (as Ernst Bertram describes them in his Nietzsche book) like Platen, Nietzsche and indeed Mann himself. Platen's Venetian sonnet which ends

> *Dann stört mich kaum im schweigenden Reviere*
> *Herschallend aus entlegenen Kanälen,*
> *Von Zeit zu Zeit ein Ruf der Gondoliere*[6]

reads like a classical pre-echo of Nietzsche's better known

> *An der Brücke stand*
> *Jüngst ich in brauner Nacht.*
> *Fernher kam Gesang;*
> *goldner Tropfen quoll's*
> *über die zitternde Fläche weg.*
> *Gondeln, Lichter, Musik—*
> *trunken schwamm's in die Dämmerung hinaus. . . .*
>
> *Meine Seele, ein Saitenspiel,*
> *sang sich, unsichtbar berührt,*
> *heimlich ein Gondellied dazu,*
> *zitternd vor bunter Seligkeit.*
> *—Hörte jemand ihr zu?*[7]

Here we are aware of the intense *musicality* of Nietzsche's poetic gift. In the lines immediately before the introduction of this poem in *Ecce*

---

[5] 'August von Platen' in *German Men of Letters*, ed. Alex Natan (Oswald Wolff, 1969), vol.5, pp.135ff.

[6] Then the gondoliers' cries, intermittently ringing from distant canals, scarcely disturb my silent reverie.

[7] Just now I was standing on a bridge, the evening brown around me. Singing came from the distance; it flowed away in drops of gold over the trembling surface. Gondolas, lights, music—it swam, drunk with rapture, far out into the twilight.

My soul seemed a lyre, invisibly moved, trembling with radiant bliss, it sang a gondola's song secretly to itself. Was anyone listening?

Towards a Genealogy of Death in Venice

Homo, he says: 'Were I in search of a synonym for music, I would say Venice. For me tears are music, music tears; and I know what bliss it is not to be able to think of the South without trembling in anticipation.' For Nietzsche and for Mann (one of his most ardent disciples) music meant above all Wagner, and Wagner meant above all *Tristan und Isolde*. And here we return to Count Platen, for his most famous poem also bears the name of Tristan.

> *Wer die Schönheit angeschaut mit Augen*
> *Ist dem Tode schon anheimgegeben.*[8]

In effect: he who experiences essential beauty no longer belongs to life. In his essay on Platen, Mann discusses the poem in terms which bear directly on his own *Death in Venice*. The soul-world entered by Platen, he says,

> . . . is a world in which the imperative to live, the laws of life, reason and morality are nothing; a world of drunken, hopeless libertinage, which is at the same time a world of the most conscious form, the most deathlike rigidity; which teaches its adept that the principle of beauty and form does not spring from the sphere of life . . . . [What conditions this world] is the idea of beauty and death, the idea that the arrow of beauty is the arrow of death and eternal pain of yearning: only there does it find full expression. Death, beauty, love, eternity: these are language symbols for this at once platonic and intoxicatingly musical soul-miracle so full of fascination and seduction. . . . And those who on earth wear the order and are the knights of beauty are knights of death.[9]

This is the world of *Tristan*, Mann's *Death in Venice* and Britten's *Death in Venice* (and, in a sense, *Billy Budd*), all poems of unquenchable, endless love which issues in death, which *is* death, because it can find no release, fulfilment or expression on earth.[10]

[8] He who once has looked on Beauty has lost himself irretrievably to Death.

[9] *Essays of Three Decades* (Secker & Warburg, 1947), p.261.

[10] That Platen was one of Thomas Mann's models for Aschenbach is made abundantly clear by the passage from the same essay describing how the poet, with immense patience and devotion, 'had wrought out of the golden shield of language the most splendid and enduring things; he had . . . performed miracles of stylistic and intellectual perfection, single-handed, all in order to become worthy to fall asleep to the gods on the knee of the little Theoxenos'. Platen himself proclaimed, 'Der Kunst gelobt' ich ganz ein ganzes Leben, / Und wenn ich sterbe, sterb' ich für das Schöne.' ['I have spent my entire life in ceaseless devotion to Art; and when I die I shall die for Beauty.'] Platen was, like Aschenbach and, one suspects, perhaps a little like Britten

Christopher Palmer

Wagner and Britten may seem an unlikely juxtaposition, but perhaps their meeting on other than technical levels is brought about through Thomas Mann as intermediary. Wagner's personal links with Venice were as strong as Britten's. He orchestrated the *Tristan* love duet there and died there; a few weeks before his death, while staying with him at the Palazzo Vendramin, Liszt wrote his two extraordinary solo piano pieces entitled 'La lugubre gondola', early archetypes of Impressionistic water music. In *Death in Venice* Aschenbach feels himself impelled to write, in Tadzio's presence, a piece on a certain 'cultural phenomenon' with which he is familiar and which means much to him. This fits an essay Mann wrote when he was in Venice in 1911, which was on Wagner: 'Auseinandersetzung mit Richard Wagner' ('About the Art of Richard Wagner'). Some of the manuscript paper bears the letterhead 'Grand Hôtel des Bains, Lido—Venice', and it is tempting to think that it was written in the real-life Tadzio's presence, on the beach.

It is certainly more than coincidence that water and the sea play so large a part in the work of both Wagner and Britten. Nietzsche was one of the first to associate the 'Dionysian' music of *Tristan* with diving, swimming and drowning, and later writers, notably Baudelaire ('la musique souvent me prend comme une mer'), Swinburne, D'Annunzio and Mann,[11] followed suit. Wagner himself constantly used water metaphors in relation to *Tristan*; for example when the latter was incubating he was much occupied in studying Liszt's symphonic poems, and told the composer that each time he read through one of the scores he felt as though he had dived down into some crystal water. Later he observed that in *Tristan* he had 'poured himself out in music'.[12] In *Death in Venice* the sea is omnipresent. To it Mann attributes the same 'dangerous fascination' (Nietzsche's phrase) as to music. Aschenbach's love of the ocean has its source, we

---

himself, in a similar case to Melville's Captain Ahab in *Moby Dick*: 'gifted with the high perception, I lack the low enjoying power. Damned most subtly, and damned most malignantly! Damned in the midst of Paradise!'

11 In her introduction to the Blackwell's German Texts edition of *Tonio Kröger* (Oxford, 1943, p.xlv) Elizabeth M. Wilkinson points out that 'the sea, its rhythms, its musical transcendence, vibrates in the language of all [Mann's] books, even when there is no talk of it; and no German since Heine . . . has written of it so that we not only hear its rush and roar, but feel the spray and the salt tang on our lips and crush the shells beneath our feet.' The same is true in England of Britten's music.

12 See Elliott Zuckerman, *The First Hundred Years of Wagner's Tristan* (New York: Columbia University Press, 1964), p.10

Towards a Genealogy of Death in Venice

are told, in a 'yearning . . . for the unorganized, the immeasurable, the eternal—in short, for nothingness'. This Nirvana-urge, which Wagner described as one of the sources of *Tristan*, is found in many *Tristan*-derived scores in which the sea or water is a ruling force: in d'Indy's *L'Etranger*, in Delius's *A Village Romeo and Juliet* in which the young lovers drown themselves, and in Debussy's *Pelléas et Mélisande*, where the sea is symbol of the womb and choas of things whence we arose, and whither we return. So too in Mann's and Britten's *Death in Venice*: Aschenbach watches Tadzio bathe and then run out of the sea against the water,

> . . . churning the waves to a foam, his head flung high. The sight of this living figure, virginally pure and austere, with dripping locks, beautiful as a tender young god, emerging from the depths of sea and sky, outrunning the element—it conjured up mythologies, it was like a primeval legend, handed down from the beginning of time, of the birth of form, of the origin of the gods.

The end comes on the beach too: Aschenbach dies, slumped in his chair, watching Tadzio,

> . . . a remote and isolated figure, with floating locks, out there in the sea and wind, against the misty inane. . . . It seemed to him the pale and lovely Summoner out there smiled at him and beckoned . . . pointed outward as he hovered on before into an immensity of richest expectation.

The sea, as symbol of the nothingness which is everythingness, is the ultimate appeaser of Eros, that simultaneous longing for the senses' fulfilment and their extinction; and in Britten it is the be-all and end-all not only of *Death in Venice* but also of *Peter Grimes*[13] and *Billy Budd*. Here is the crux of the affinity between Wagner and Britten.[14] 'The only fulfilment is that of personal passion; this cannot be achieved except by separation from the conditions of the material world (society, civilization, domestic loyalties) . . . finally . . . it cannot be achieved within Time at all.' Wilfrid Mellers's account of the literary-dramatic aspect of Wagner's adaptation of the *Tristan* myth[15] applies equally, *mutatis mutandis*, to *Death in Venice*, *Grimes*

[13] PETER: What is home? Calm as deep water. Where's my home? Deep in calm water. (*Peter Grimes*), Act III scene 2).
[14] See also above, p.111–13.
[15] *Caliban Reborn* (Gollancz, 1968), p.36

and *Budd*. All three are set on or by the sea, their heroes all go down to a watery grave, and in all the sea acts ambivalently both as Alma Mater and as aggressor or agent of destruction. And when we recall that Wagner in *Tristan* was the first to explore through in-depth musical expression the related areas of night, sleep and dreams—related not only to each other but also to the *sea* as symbols of infinity, of the ultimate spiritual reality—and when we recall how frequently the idea of redemption recurs in both Britten's operas and Wagner's, then we can begin to make out a case for describing Britten as a Wagnerian composer. He is certainly an artist of the Wagnerian kind, in whom the creative impulse originates in a need to understand himself and reveal his self-understanding to the world, however he may thus paradoxically be *mis*understood by the world. It is important to note too that sex in one form or another is clearly a basic preoccupation of all the works mentioned in the preceding pages; apropos which Mann in his Platen essay quotes Nietzsche to the effect that the degree and kind of a man's sexuality permeate the very loftiest heights of his intellect.

Surveying the scene from the purely aesthetic point of view we find that sensibilities have always been ravished by the waters of Venice. Shelley noted the fairy-tale qualities of its sunsets; Symonds in his chapter on Venice in *The Renaissance in Italy* speaks of the 'vaporous atmosphere' which makes the city a unique theatre for sunsets, and describes the elemental conditions of Venetian art as light, colour, air, space; Henry James refers in his *Foreign Parts* to the 'inscrutable flattery of the atmosphere' which renders everything pictorial and harmonious; and all connect this quality of light with the presence of water.

For hundreds of years artists and writers have been attempting to capture the magic of Venice in colour and word. Music had to wait until the late twentieth century for those descriptive or rather evocative passages in *Death in Venice* which are among the finest in the work: the music of the open sea as Aschenbach approaches Venice on the boat, in which the feel as well as the sight of the 'low-lying clouds, unending grey' is conjured up in the heterophonic, diatonic string texture (whose heterogeneous homogeneity is partially achieved through free bowing); the sea motif, heard for the first time as the Hotel Manager shows Aschenbach the view of the sea from his room; Aschenbach's contemplation of the prospect when he is left alone: the *Grimes*-like thirds interweave and overlap in woodwind solos—an aural equivalent of the sound, shape and colour of the 'long low waves, rhythmic upon the sand (Ex.1); the gondola music, with its lolling, lapping rhythm and 'Serenissima' motif refracted in dipping figures; the gondoliers' cries, hauntingly re-created from authentic

Ex.1

sources; the moment when Aschenbach pursues the Polish family in a gondola, with the tuned percussion that signals Tadzio's presence sounding the 'Serenissima' motif while, deep down below, in the lagoon (as in Billy's lullaby), the oozy liquidity of bass clarinet and harp keeps the music in water-motion (Ex.2).

If we return to the beach we find those *Grimes*-like thirds participating not only in the music of wind and water itself but in the

Ex.2

siren-like chorus of offstage women's voices calling not so much to Tadzio as for and on behalf of him, and, indeed, in this case helping to lure an innocent man to his doom.[16] Tadzio is identified with the elements. In Britten's musical catechism 'elements' mean the 'elementary' triad, compounded of major and minor thirds, and for him chains of thirds seem to be associated with the elements: not only with water and the sea—as in *Grimes*, *Death in Venice*, the ballet of sea-horses, fish-creatures and waves in Act II of *The Prince of the Pagodas*, 'Afton Water' in *A Birthday Hansel*, and the sea-girt *Golden Vanity*—but also with sunlight (Act II scene 2 of *The Rape of Lucretia*). Here, in *Death in Venice*, the third is insidiously 'sweet and wild', a perfect musical incarnation of Tadzio's name which 'with its softened consonants and long-drawn *u*-sound, seemed to possess the beach like a rallying-cry . . .' (Mann). The music seems to sweep like a great wave or surge of water over the beach—or rather over the star-struck Aschenbach, whose 'heart and soul and senses, / World without end, are drowned'[17] (Ex.3).

Ex.3

---

16 The effect of the offstage chorus, heard at varying proximity, is not unlike that of the last act of *Grimes*; and indeed there is a basic similarity, for each is a chorus of predators searching for their victim. The parallel is reinforced in the last scene of *Death in Venice* when the warning voice, the danger signal, of the tuba enters the scene. In *Grimes* the tuba represents a foghorn, both danger signal and siren song.
17 Housman, *A Shropshire Lad*, XIV.

Towards a Genealogy of Death in Venice

But in Venice, it seems, darkness, dis-ease and death are never far away. James in *The Aspern Papers* (1888) evokes the city's façade of glamour and enchantment: 'See how it glows with the advancing summer; how the sky and the sea and the rosy air and the marble of the palaces all shimmer and melt together.' But the narrator is an unscrupulous scholar determined to charm the letters of a dead American poet out of two desiccated spinsters whose lives are crumbling away along with the old *palazzo* they inhabit. In Arthur Symons's *Extracts from the Journal of Henry Luxulyan* (1905) the eponymous hero begins, like Aschenbach, by yielding to the city's seductiveness: 'I must sink into this delicious Venice, where forgetfulness is easier than anywhere in the world . . . it is all a sort of immense rest, literally a dream, for there is sleep all over Venice.' Soon, however, signs of distemper begin to declare themselves:

Does the too exciting exquisiteness of Venice drive people mad? Two madhouses in the water! It is like a menace . . . every day I find myself growing more uneasy. If I look out of the windows at dawn, when land and water seem to awaken like a flower, some poison comes to me out of this perhaps too perfect beauty. . . . I have never felt anything like this insidious coiling of water about one. I came to Venice for peace, and I find a subtle terror growing up out of its waters. . . .

Three years later Symons succumbed to a nervous breakdown in Venice. And Helen Waddell, after seeing the dungeons in the Doge's Palace, wrote to her sister that 'you open a door and come straight into the great court, blazing with light . . . and thank God you don't live in the fifteenth century. It is the combination of the two things—the perfect sensuous imagination of beauty, and that dank cruel horror existing side by side. . . .'[18]

So Venice is an embodiment in both its physiognomy and its inner being of the antithesis between beauty and ugliness, good and evil, darkness and light and all the extremes experienced throughout his history by ethical man. It was, therefore, a perfect setting for Mann's variation on the archetypal theme of the corruption of sense by the senses, the mind by the body, man by the animal. Others who had developed the theme before him included Goethe, in *Elective*

[18] Quoted in Monica Blackett, *The Mark of the Maker* (Constable, 1973), p.42. Cf. also Byron (*Childe Harold*): 'I stood in Venice, on the Bridge of Sighs; / A palace and a prison on each hand.'

Affinities, and Mann's own brother Heinrich, in *Professor Unrat*
(1905), about the downfall of a respectable schoolmaster at the hands
of a night-club tart (later a famous film with Marlene Dietrich, *The
Blue Angel*). If in tracing the lineage of *Death in Venice* we look further
afield, to Norway, we find a striking parallel, to which Donald
Mitchell has drawn attention,[19] in Ibsen's *When We Dead Awaken*
(1899–1900), his last play, consciously written as a final statement—
like Britten's *Death in Venice*. In Professor Rubek, Ibsen draws a man
who has sacrificed Irena, his true love and inspiration, for the sake of
what he persuades himself is his art. Irena in real life was Rosa
Fitinghoff, with whom Ibsen, at 70, had fallen in love—a 'später
Abenteuer des Gefühls', like Aschenbach's. Like Aschenbach's too
are the sentiments voiced by Rubek when, at the height of his fame,
talk about the artist's vocation and mission begin to strike him as
hollow and meaningless. Instead he wants life. 'Isn't life in sunshine
and beauty altogether more worthwhile than to go on till the end of
one's days in some damp clammy hole, tiring oneself to death
wrestling with lumps of clay and blocks of stone?' He confesses to
Irena that, in his youth, he had been filled with the conviction that if
he touched her, or desired her sensually, his vision would be so
desecrated that he would never be able to achieve what he was striving
for—the work of art came first, flesh and blood second. 'In those days
my great task dominated me completely—filled me with exultant joy.'
Aschenbach all over.[20]

Even more remarkable as a harbinger of *Death in Venice* is Walter
Pater's short story *Apollo in Picardy*, first published in 1893. Here we
find 'a cold and very reasonable spirit disturbed suddenly, thrown off
its balance, as by a violent beam, a blaze of new light, revealing, as it
glanced here and there, a hundred truths unguessed-at before, yet a
curse, as it turned out, to its receiver, in dividing hopelessly against
itself the well-ordered kingdom of his thought.' This 'receiver' is
a monk, Prior Saint-Jean, the author of a dry, strict treatise on
mathematics, astronomy and music, his vocation being the abstract
sciences; poets he regards as miscreants and demons. But his health
becomes affected by long and rigorous intellectual application

[19] 'A *Billy Budd* Notebook', *Opera News* (New York), vol.43, no.19 (31 March 1979),
pp.12–13.
[20] A similar late realization of the loss of human warmth for the sake of formal
perfection is recorded of her father by Imogen Holst in *Gustav Holst* (Oxford
University Press, 1938), p.141.

(compare Aschenbach), and he is sent to an *obédience* in Picardy. A friend warns him that there 'the mere contact of one's feet with the soil might change one' (as in Venice). Disturbed by thought of the coming journey, the Prior dreams of hell-fire (compare Aschenbach's vision of the jungle). He takes with him a young novice, Hyacinth; and immediately they arrive 'the atmosphere, the light, the influence of things, seemed different from what they knew' (as in Aschenbach's first contact with Venice). Climbing up one night into the *solar* of the Grange, Prior Saint-Jean finds a youth asleep, and seems

> . . . to be looking for the first time on the human form, on the old Adam fresh from his Maker's hand . . . could one fancy a single curve bettered in the rich, warm limbs; in the haughty features of the face, with the golden hair, tied in a mystic knot, fallen down across the inspired brow? And yet what gentle sweetness also in the natural movement of the bosom, the throat, the lips, of the sleeper! Could that be diabolical, and really spotted with unseen evil, which was so spotless to the eye?

(Compare Tadzio.) Then the Prior, his moral constitution undermined by the 'luxury of the free, self-chosen hours, the irregular fare, the doing pretty much as one pleased' after the severe discipline of the monastery ('self-discipline my strength' Aschenbach mocks himself), becomes more and more infatuated with the boy, Apollyon, encountering in him, for the first time in his life, 'the power of untutored natural impulse, of natural inspiration'. Vocation, scholarship, reputation—all go for nothing (Aschenbach: 'all folly, all pretence'). The narrator wonders if the Prior, on his way from the convent, 'passed unwittingly through some river or rivulet of Lethe, that had carried away from him all his so carefully accumulated intellectual baggage of fact and theory?' The metaphor would fit perfectly in *Death in Venice*: in fact Aschenbach passed through just such a river, rowed in the coffin-black gondola by a Charon-like gondolier who did as he pleased, left no name and took no money. The weather at the Grange (as in Venice) becomes 'fiery and plaguesome', the 'first heat of veritable summer come suddenly'. The implication is that a triangular situation develops between the two young men, Apollyon and Hyacinth, and the Prior. A catastrophe becomes inevitable, and when it arrives is both gory and erotic. Apollyon challenges Hyacinth to a naked, moonlight game of quoits. A sudden icy blast of wind takes control of Apollyon's quoit, it lodging in

Hyacinth's skull and killing him instantly. Mann's Aschenbach sits in the park and watches Tadzio at play,

. . . and at such times it was not Tadzio whom he saw but Hyancinthus, doomed to die because two gods were rivals for his love. Ah yes, he tasted the envious pangs that Zephyr knew when his rival, bow and cithara, oracle and all forgot, played with the beauteous youth; he watched the discus, guided by torturing jealousy, strike the beloved head; paled as he received the broken body in his arms and saw the flower spring up, watered by that sweet blood and signed for evermore with his lament.

And similarly in Picardy, the blood of Hyacinth, mingling with the rain, colours the grass around his body, and the following morning the Prior beholds a marvel of blue flowers. Apollyon makes off, and the Prior is arrested on suspicion of murder and dies mad. Apollyon and Tadzio are both Angels of Death.

While I am not trying to claim *Apollo in Picardy* as a hitherto unrecognized source of *Death in Venice*, the parallels are consistent and striking. Possibly the link is to be found in classical scholarship. In *Plato and Platonism* Pater touches on the Spartan festival of the *Hyacinthia* and describes Plato in terms which suggest not only Pater himself but also Aschenbach: 'Austere as he seems, and on well-considered principle really is, his temperance or austerity, aesthetically so winning, is attained only by the chastisement, the control, of a variously interested, a richly sensuous nature.' And as T. J. Reed has shown in the introduction to his Oxford University Press Clarendon German Series edition of *Death in Venice*, Mann used two Platonic dialogues (the *Symposium* and *Phaedrus*) and Plutarch's *Eròtikos*, in his novella.

Here we might suppose this particular branch of the genealogical tree to come to an end; yet not quite so. For both Pater's *Apollo in Picardy* and his thematically similar *Denys l'Auxerrois* were once considered as possible opera libretti by Szymanowski, who greatly admired him. Here the long arm of coincidence apparently grows to phenomenal proportions; for in the early summer of 1911 Szymanowski made a memorable journey to Sicily and Italy. On 30 April he was in Palermo announcing his intention to reach, during the ten days following, Naples, Rome, Florence and finally Venice. He was in Vienna by the time Mahler died (18 May), so at some time between the end of April and the middle of May 1911 he was in Venice. He may even have seen 'Tadzio', his fellow countryman. His path could not have crossed Mann's, since the latter did not arrive in Venice until the end of May (he had followed the newspaper accounts of Mahler's last hours on Brioni). Yet how extraordinary that these two artists, much akin in spirit, should have just missed each other in Venice in the month of Mahler's death: for if Mann's Italian trip engendered *Death in Venice*, Szymanowski's travels in the south, particularly in Sicily, produced his opera *King Roger* (1918–25)—which is virtually identical in theme with *Death in Venice*. The twelfth-century king is irresistibly attracted by a handsome young shepherd who preaches a cult of beauty and sensuous delight and who later reveals himself as Dionysus; whereas the king, of course, thinks to bear the 'Apollonian' insignia of law, order and decency. The king yields to the shepherd, but—and here the story diverges radically from *Death in Venice*—comes to realize that the Dionysian religion of pleasure is ultimately just as constricting and *re*stricting in its way as the dogmatic rigidity of the Church, and he rejects both. The tensions are resolved in the last act which is set in a Greek temple overlooking the sea. A picture of dawn on the face of the deep leads to Roger's apostrophe to the sun (in the 'basic', 'Brittenish' key of C major) and the opera ends with the spirit of regenerated man merging with sun and sea in a burst of 'elemental' ecstasy.

There is not scope in this discussion for a comparison of Britten's *Death in Venice* with Mann's; in such a comparison Mahler would be a key figure, as Mann's model for Aschenbach's facial features[21] and as a lifelong source of musical inspiration to Britten. Britten worked on *Death in Venice*— the story of an artist's dissolution and death—at the end of his life with Mahler's portrait looking down on him from the wall of his study; and both Britten and Mahler died of a chronic heart condition. In Britten's *Death in Venice*, as in late Mahler, the music longs for, yearns towards, death, yet regrets intensely the leaving of life; messages of farewell are everywhere. (Actual reminiscences of Mahler in *Death in Venice* are neither more nor less frequent than elsewhere in Britten, but circumstances naturally make us more conscious of them, e.g. the drone-struck music of slow dawn and

[21] In 1921 Wolfgang Born's nine coloured lithographs for *Death in Venice* were published in Munich. Born knew nothing of the part Mahler had played in the genesis of the novella, and so Mann was amazed to discover that Aschenbach's head in the last picture, 'Death', unmistakably revealed the Mahler type. See *Selected Letters*, pp.100–2. The photo of Mahler from which Mann worked is reproduced as plate 3.

dispersing shadows, of waking from heavy slumber to a sense of ultimate reality, which unveils Act II; and, of course, the final Adagio).

But in considering the relation of Britten to Mann I propose to bypass Mann's *Death in Venice* and turn to its aftermath. In his letter of 4 July 1920 to Carl Maria Weber, a kind of apologia for *Death in Venice*,[22] Mann sets forth his attitudes to eroticism in general and homosexuality in particular. He quotes his own *Betrachtungen eines Unpolitischen* on the relationship between mind and life, and then asks

> but what else have we here if not the translation of one of the world's most beautiful love-poems into the language of criticism and prose, the poem whose final stanza begins: 'Wer das Tiefste *gedacht*, liebt das *Lebendigste*'. This wonderful poem contains the whole justification of the emotional tendency in question, and the whole explanation of it, which is mine also.

This 'wonderful poem' is none other than Hölderlin's 'Sokrates und Alcibiades' set by Britten as the third of his *Sechs Hölderlin-Fragmente* (1958) to music of the serenest, sweetest triadic simplicity; it is another rainbow-arch of chords (as Eric Walter White describes the music of Vere's interview with Billy in *Budd*),[23] except that the determining melodic line is not this time formed from the constituent notes of any one triad but is a repetition of the same melody which had accompanied (unharmonized) the first part of the poem, which calls Socrates to account for the court he pays to Alcibiades. Metaphorical harmony is the result of adding literal harmony, chords, to a melodic line which in its unaccompanied state is questioning, unfulfilled. It is perhaps significant, in the light of Britten's use of the triad in those two instances as a symbol of beauty, that very few bars in *Death in Venice* actually make use of the pure triad, two of which comprise Aschenbach's (initially) happy acceptance of his love for Tadzio: 'So be it!'

A similar and profounder coincidence in this chapter of co-incidences involves Mann's last major work, *Doktor Faustus*. This epic story of a fictitious contemporary composer (Adrian Leverkühn), set against the backdrop of the rise and fall of the Third Reich, was begun in May 1943 and finished in January 1947. During the summer of 1944 Mann worked on chapter 20, which describes the first

[22] *Selected Letters*, pp.93–7
[23] *BLO*, p.162.

compositions Adrian completed after making his pact with the Devil. Among them were settings of Verlaine and Blake—'Chanson d'Automne' (which had been one of the 14-year-old Britten's *Quatre Chansons Françaises*) and, uncannily, 'The Sick Rose', which Britten had composed as part of the *Serenade* for tenor, horn and strings in 1943, at the very time Mann was beginning his novel. The sexual metaphor of this latter poem is ironically appropriate in Leverkühn's case, whose pact with the Devil manifests itself as syphilitic infection; but the poem is also a verbal distillation of 'ambiguity' of the kind which Mann saw in Venice. That Mann was conscious of an underlying affinity of theme between *Faustus* and *Death in Venice* is shown by the warmth of his response to a seventieth birthday article by George Lukács which described *Death in Venice* as 'signalling the danger of a barbarous underworld existing within modern German civilization as its necessary complement'.[24] Nor is the connection between Blake and Venice missing from Britten's music, in which the major/minor antithesis—the variable third—is an archetypal symbol for good versus evil, and is as all-pervasive in 'The Sick Rose' (Ex.4a) as in *Death in Venice* (Ex.4b); in both cases the idea is that of a cancer which has spread through every part of the organism.[25]

Ex.4a The Sick Rose   *Ex.4b Death in Venice*

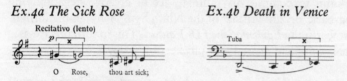

It is uncanny that these two creative artists, who never met or worked together, should turn to the same poetic text at virtually the same moment. Furthermore, another Blake poem which Mann has Leverkühn set—'A Poison Tree'—was actually set by Britten, both earlier (an unpublished setting dates from 1935) and much later (in the 1965 *Songs and Proverbs of William Blake*). Mann's comment on Leverkühn's treatment can be applied to Britten's: 'The evil simplicity of the verse was completely reproduced in the music.'

[24] Quoted in Thomas Mann, *The Genesis of a Novel* (Secker & Warburg, 1961), p.115.
[25] In an address given during the period of his writing *Doktor Faustus* (published in *Thomas Mann's Addresses* (Washington: Library of Congress, 1963)), Mann claimed for romanticism a 'peculiar and psychologically highly fruitful relationship to sickness. Even in its loveliest, most ethereal aspects, where the popular mates with the sublime, romanticism bears within its heart the germ of morbidity, *as the rose bears the worm*. Its innermost character is seduction, seduction to *death*.' (My italics.)

Christopher Palmer

A final point to be made in connection with *Doktor Faustus* is the wholly Brittenish character of the 'Echo' episode. Echo is an enchanting small boy, half Hermes (like Tadzio), half Christ, a vision of 'adorable loveliness which was yet a prey to time, destined to mature and partake of the earthly lot', such as Britten would surely have warmed to as readily as Leverkühn. But part of Leverkühn's convenant with Satan is that he is not permitted to warm to anyone; and because he does, Echo dies, horribly, of cerebro-spinal meningitis, but not before he has inspired in Leverkühn some settings of Ariel's songs from *The Tempest*.[26]

Echo is in fact one of those young sacrificial victims, agents of salvation, that people Britten's scores—Lucretia, Billy, Isaac, Miles, the Madwoman's son in *Curlew River*, the Cabin-boy in *The Golden Vanity*, Owen Wingrave—all Angels from Heaven, but, as Vere says, 'the Angel must hang'. Tadzio is rather a destroyer, bringing Aschenbach to ruin and death in abject humiliation. But then so in their way are Billy and Miles—and Echo. Billy kills Claggart, dies and condemns Vere to a lifetime of self-laceration ('O what have I done?'); Miles dies, after (we imagine) driving the Governness insane and irremediably corrupting Flora. Echo dies—but his death causes Leverkühn to commit his ultimate act of creative negation, the 'taking-back' or 'un-writing' of the Ninth Symphony, in the form of his last work, the *Lamentation of Dr Faustus*. This in turn precipitates his final, complete mental and physical breakdown.

Over the years Venice seems to have offered a kind of common meeting-place of the mind to many artists whose temperaments involved them as closely with the life of the senses as with that of the intellect. Their age-old problem is stated with devastating simplicity in *Carmina Burana*:

> *So short a day*
> *And life so quickly hasting,*
> *And in study wasting*
> *Youth that would be gay.*[27]

---

[26] *The Tempest* was a project that Britten had often contemplated undertaking. At one time he had thought of writing the music for a film version of the play to be directed by Richard Attenborough and shot in Bali, with Sir John Gielgud as Prospero.

[27] Trans. Helen Waddell in *Medieval Latin Lyrics* (Constable, 1929), p.203.

Towards a Genealogy of Death in Venice

In Britten the problem is that of the child shut out of the Kingdom of Heaven or the Garden of Paradise: he cannot re-enter unless he discards the 'disease of feeling' (Hardy) which is an inevitable consequence of growing up.[28] Neither Mann nor Britten offers a solution to these problems, which are by their nature insoluble; but by stating or crystallizing the matter in a unique and memorable fashion and creating works of art *about* men who create works of art they modify our perception of the world about us. They open our eyes to aspects of human experience, to immemorial truths; they teach us that life as we know it as 'civilized' human beings is absurd, that men are interested in things they were never meant to be interested in, pursuing aims they were never meant to pursue. And if artists affect ordinary people in this way, must they not also exert a profound influence on each other, and determine and modify each other's ways of feeling, thinking and expressing? How else can we account for the appeal of the thoroughly 'sentimentalic'[29] Mann to the 'naïve' Britten? The result of this appeal was one of the masterpieces of twentieth-century music, one which, surely, Mann himself unwittingly adumbrated in his essay on Wagner written on the Lido within sight of the real-life Tadzio. He envisioned the masterpiece of the twentieth century as eminently un-Wagnerian; distinguished by its logic, form, and clarity; austere and yet serene; more detached, nobler and healthier than Wagner's operas; 'something that seeks greatness not in the colossal and the baroque, and beauty not in the ecstatic'. The musical substance of Britten's last opera corresponds to every one of these prescriptions, and it is a supreme (and happy) irony that it is based on the very work that was taking shape in Mann's mind as he wrote his Wagner essay. In an unpublished letter to Britten dated 14 September 1970 (mainly concerned with the Mann family's positive response to Britten's desire to compose *Death in Venice*) Thomas Mann's son Golo wrote, 'My father . . . used to say, that if it ever came to some musical illustration of his novel *Doktor Faustus*, you would be the composer to do it.'

---

[28] As Thomas Mann's son Klaus says in his autobiography *The Turning Point* (Gollancz, 1944), p.16: 'No matter how hard we try to capture the bliss of paradise, it is only our own longing for the paradise lost we succeed in finding . . . there is no happiness where there is memory. To remember things means to yearn for the past. Our nostalgia begins with our consciousness.'

[29] See n.7, below, p.312.

VOICES

26
Composer and Poet

PETER PORTER

Not since the days when musician and poet were the same person has there been a great composer whose art is as profoundly bound up with words as Benjamin Britten's. There are many special clauses which need to hedge this statement round, but it remains, I believe, true in essentials. Musical composition up to Josquin is, despite the growth of instrumental invention, a matter of sung notes, usually in the service of the Church. Notes need syllables; syllables come in words. There have always been composers whose need for words is satisfied by the liturgy, but even with them the direction of their art may be shaped by the ambience, often literary, of the words in the sacred texts they set. So, early on, the divorce of the poetical sensibility and the musical was not yet radical or divisive. Whatever the circumstances of the working lives of men such as Lassus, Gibbons and Monteverdi, they served an as yet undisturbed muse, whose purpose was truth and praise, and whose means was eloquence.

The Florentine opera inventors wished to use music to make poetry even more eloquent. They could not have imagined the world of Bellini and Verdi, where music ruled and libretti were largely ridiculous to literary men, valued only by fellow professionals for craftsmanship, and by the public for having led to the composition of beautiful music. There is no sneer here at nineteenth-century Italian opera: its achievements are among the finest in all musical history. Rather, the point is that a composer such as Britten, born into a world of professionalism in art (and he, misguidedly in my view, urged 'professionalism' on his colleagues, probably to combat endemic English snobbery), was faced, in the 1930s, with a profession profoundly wrenched from its natural alliances, an artistic atmosphere inimical to the recognition of the common source of poetry and music in the imagination. Britten's whole instinct was in the other direction: he had an antediluvian sense of the unity of musical and poetical vision.

The whole corpus of Britten's work is informed by a deeply poetical feeling. Vocal compositions predominate in his output, but this is not the whole or even the main part of the case. Instead, it can be said that what poets have prefigured in words, he has reworked in music. This recognition of the fact that even a superb piece of poetry leaves something more to be said is what makes many of his settings so masterful. Tone-deaf poets (and I am sad to say that many of my colleagues have either little ear for music or simply resent its being better placed in the public eye and so eclipsing their own achievements in the matter of love and fame) often resent such works as Britten's settings of Donne's *Holy Sonnets*. The musical rhetoric gets in the way of Donne's own eloquence, so their argument runs. There will always be opinions on such unprovable things. I prefer to put forward a different case. By fertilizing his musical mind in poetry, Britten gets back to the unfractured sensibility of the pre-classical past (that is, music before Purcell). There are composers greater than him who wrote a great deal of vocal music, some of it, such as Mozart's operas and Bach's cantatas, the most splendid in the long history of word-setting. But their inspiration is more universal than Britten's, and their mastery of instrumental music shows that the profoundest analogy which may be developed round their art is with philosophy. Poetry is unfriendly to philosophy, if not inimical to it, though it may live on equal terms with theology. The one great predecessor whose creative personality springs equally from an instinctively poetical nature is Schubert. Although he is a greater composer than Britten, he too can carry his most heartfelt work beyond words only into chamber music, though this for him includes solo piano pieces. Britten is a master of opera, which Schubert is not. His operas, however, are essentially chamber-music works, though this is not the place to develop such a notion. For both Schubert and Britten the world in which music grows is a poetical place—i.e., it is human, speculative, dramatic, aphoristic and spontaneous. From the world of philosophy springs the opposite achievement of the symphonic.

For someone not attracted especially to the technique of development, the setting of poems to music is an obvious and natural recourse. Right through his creative life, Britten gave direction to his genius and staked out claims on the inchoate by identifying himself with poets and poems. His humanism saved him from the turmoil which followed the break-up of nineteenth-century symphonism with its attendent idealism and demonism. It is notorious, of course, that his music makes no appeal to those members of the avant-garde who are still caught in the turbulence of late romanticism. It is interesting to compare the sort of poetry which fertilized Britten's mind with that which attracted Mahler, Berg and Schoenberg. The difference is not just between English and German literature, but between a still naïve imagination (in an unpejorative sense) and three sorts of Faustian apocalypse. For the Austrian composers, poems are perilously close to case-history. They are content to make use of the words, and invent the poetry for themselves in their music. For Britten, poetry is what the world is, and not what is made in and by music—though music can add to it. It is not surprising that Britten, like Schubert, is a great melodist: he finds shapes in notes as memorably limned as the shapes in verse he is using. Britten, as a true son of the twentieth century, has the advantage of educated literary taste hardly available to Schubert. This is something I shall discuss later, in comparing briefly his practice when writing songs to already existing poems and when setting especially written libretti. But it does not separate him from Schubert. Perhaps other musicians have had equally good taste in poetry, but Britten is most unusual among composers of the highest level of invention in making settings of so much great and near-great verse. The list is impressive: Auden, Rimbaud, Smart, Cotton, Quarles, Hardy, Owen, Hölderlin, Pushkin, Soutar and Eliot, as a sort of second eleven to Tennyson, Keats, Donne, Wordsworth, Shakespeare, and the authors of the Chester Miracle Plays, among others.

Naturally composers have a better chance of being widely read these days than they had in Beethoven's and Schubert's time, but Britten's depth of concern for literature is *sui generis*, something far more profound than his being a composer in a country whose greatest artistic achievements have been in poetry. How far his early friendship with Auden led him towards the more esoteric of the authors whose words he set is not easy to guess, though compositions such as *Friday Afternoons* and *A Boy was Born*, both pre-Auden, show an already highly developed and original taste in English verse. The poems Britten chose from de la Mare's extensive anthology *Come Hither* for *Friday Afternoons* show him not just seizing on works which will please schoolboy choristers, but selecting poems with a strong individuality, a definite idiosyncrasy, and no touch of the 'poetic' or half-timbered. The most beautiful tune in the set is fitted to the most mysterious poem, 'A New Year Carol'. Early on, Britten revealed that paramount ability which distinguishes him from many accomplished vocal composers—the finer the poem, the greater the composition it gives rise to. Opera libretti are a different matter; and there are a few rare occasions when he fails to rise to the challenge of magnificent verse (*Songs and Proverbs of William Blake* is, for me, a surprising example of this); but in general his imagination is so in accordance with poetic inspiration that he is able to find musical devices which amplify already achieved verbal utterances.

Perhaps I might use a personal argument to illustrate the power which Britten's music has to illuminate poetry. Several of the poets whose works now mean the most to me I first understood only after hearing his settings of their verse. This may be a slightly backhanded compliment, since it may suggest that I was poorly educated or responded to verse only sluggishly. Instead, I believe it shows that there is no substitute for imagination in the quickening of one's appreciation of any art, even the art of which one is to be a practitioner oneself. Thus I had read John Donne but had responded to his baroque exaggeration very imperfectly until I heard Britten's music for nine of the *Holy Sonnets*. There, in his equally extravagant declamation, with its quick-changing moods, its matching of imagery with musical virtuosity, and its reliance on a range of vocal devices from bitter parlando to the most saturated melisma, I found a way into Donne's world. From the helter-skelter of 'Batter my heart', the fanfare-baroquery of 'At the round earth's imagined corners' (so like a Bernini monument), the *morbidezza* of 'Since she whom I loved' (Schubert and Wolf very much present: 'Nacht und Träume' and 'Um Mitternacht') to the marmoreal 'Death, be not proud' (another Britten passacaglia), Donne's universe of auto-angst spoke to me for the first time. Britten's settings are not alien to Donne's poetry: on the contrary, they show the listener how poetical Donne is, and they underline that in linking itself to poetry music may be returning to its true home—at least, when the composer has a genius for song.

Britten, of course, is a composer in the Purcell mould—he is not interested in Wolf's Poetic Supremacy Act, no matching of one note to one syllable unless that is the best way to do it. His instinct for poetry prevents his being burdened by false reverence for the mechanics of versification. The tropes which poets put upon the page, often ignored when they read their poems publicly, are as much guides to creation as strict formal machines to be observed or critically scrutinized. People often forget that experience makes a shape in memory as well as on the page, and that subject-matter may be said to have at least a secondary shape by virtue of its selection from experience and its fictional concentration on some aspect of a whole continuum of experience. Thus poetry, by selection, becomes what Wallace Stevens calls 'a supreme fiction'. A musical genius, knowing where this supreme fiction lies, can serve it in terms of his own art. His technical requirements and the poet's are best matched when they achieve the closest approach to the original imaginative template. All this is perhaps a roundabout way of saying that living poetry produces living music and respect for the original is best shown by richness of invention. Such is certainly what happens in Britten's Donne songs.

Even more eye- (and ear-) opening for me was the discovery of Christopher Smart's Bedlam poem, *Jubilate Agno*, which I first met in Britten's festival cantata, *Rejoice in the Lamb*. I now know the whole torso (only about half of this extended antiphonal poem has survived) almost by heart, and it has become a key work in my own interior map. Britten's selection of passages for setting reveals an innate understanding of what will go well with music and what will not. He chooses verses from the celebrated passage about Jeoffry, Smart's cat, and Jeoffry's antagonist, the mouse, but he also picks lines which are by no means among the best known. 'Hallelujah from the heart of God, and from the hand of the artist inimitable' might be said to cry out for music, as also might the whole passage beginning 'For the instruments are by their rhimes', but it took a more original mind to discern what could be done with 'For I am in twelve hardships, but he that was born of a virgin shall deliver me out of all', and 'For I am under the same accusation with my Saviour—for they said, he is besides himself', and the sublime excerpt 'For at that time malignity ceases and the devils themselves are at peace. / For this time is perceptible to man by a remarkable stillness and serenity of soul.' *Jubilate Agno* was first published in the late 1930s after having lain, not unknown, but unregarded, for almost two hundred years. Britten had only Stead's text to go on, so that while he appreciated the antiphonal nature of the poem he had not seen W. H. Bond's disposal of some of the 'Let' verse and 'For' verse exchanges. Bond's matching of lines is very convincing, as far as it goes, but Britten's musical dramatizing of the poem serves Smart so imaginatively that direct antiphonal exchange is not missed. His selection from the poem becomes a microcosm of the whole of Smart's euphoric Pelagian outpouring. Knitted together in music of rhythmic exactness and great melodic simplicity, the text takes on a wholeness which is true to the unique vision Smart was serving. I can think of no other composer who would have perceived the musical potential of the poem, nor of anyone else undaunted by its oddity, its departure from canons of sense and taste.

Britten had already shown his originality of inspiration in selecting passages from Rimbaud's *Les Illuminations*, but Rimbaud was the centre of a posthumous cult. The passages selected again reveal Britten's excellent judgement in choosing what suits music. They are not necessarily the most striking parts of the collection, if one judges on purely literary grounds, but they are concrete and rhetorical at once, or they are aphoristic and prophetic. The heart of the cycle is 'Being Beauteous', a poem which needs music to make its greatest impact. Britten turns the strange tribal poetry of *Les Illuminations* into the musical equivalent of Douanier Rousseau paintings, most notably in 'Antique' and 'Marine'. And when the oracle speaks, its utterance is the purest lyricism, a sort of definition by strangeness—as in 'Phrase' and 'Départ'. Though people might have wondered at an Englishman looking to a hermetic French poet for his text, they could not have questioned Rimbaud's place in French literature.

It was quite otherwise with Smart when Britten wrote *Rejoice in the Lamb* in 1943. Smart, despite Dr Johnson's somewhat equivocal recommendation, was still considered the archetype of the mad poet, and nowhere more so than in *Jubilate Agno*. Canon Hussey's commission would have been much more orthodoxly discharged if Britten had set some of the stanzas from 'A Song to David', a neatly contrived piece of versification which rises to great heights at the end but which cannot compare with the exultant home-made doxology of *Jubilate Agno*. My point is not to claim *Rejoice in the Lamb* as one of Britten's greatest compositions: it is perhaps too slender a piece for that. But I am convinced that it enshrines some of the purest responses ever made by a musician to the very heart of that mystery which we know as poetry. Smart captures in his poem an innocence known perhaps only to children and the benignly insane, and in so doing shows the rest of us, labouring under the full weight of our super-egos, that heaven does indeed lie about us. Britten's lines from Smart are more than well chosen; they amount to a biopsy of the poem. There are many passages that he did not set which all Smart-lovers cherish, but only one line which I would have liked to see included in the cantata. This is the supreme 'For in my nature I quested for beauty, but God, God hath sent me to sea for pearls.' Now Smart has come into his own. Today's public has developed a taste for the wonderful rigmaroles of madness, though one might hope at least to distinguish between Smart, Blake and Clare on one side and R. D. Laing on the other. But Britten was there before us. It is inspiring to find an artist in another discipline showing the way to literary taste.

Britten's willingness to write music to texts in foreign languages other than Latin has often been remarked upon. Since his Rimbaud and Michelangelo settings date from his American period, a deliberate interregnum where he appears to have set about ridding himself of English unprofessionalism, his works with foreign language texts tend to be regarded as his most mechanical creations, as *exercises de style.* Such is Sir Peter Pears's view of *Les Illuminations* in his article on Britten's songs in the Britten Symposium.[1] The opposite seems the case to me: exotic texts lead to Britten's most intense visions. The foreign language brings out an answering hermeticism, a command to the oracular. This is nowhere more evident than in the *Sechs Hölderlin-Fragmente* of 1958. (I forbear to mention *The Poet's Echo* as I do not understand Russian.) This is an especially touching posthumous tribute to the poet with the finest sensibility in German literature from a practitioner of the sister art which has consistently fed on it, and brought fame to it—fame, that is, to a host of poets from Goethe to Rilke, but not to Hölderlin. The long procession of masters of *Lieder* simply passed Hölderlin by, partly no doubt because his characteristic works are extensive and written in difficult metres. Only Brahms in his *Schicksalslied* brought a brooding intensity to Hölderlin's verse, though the poem he chose is not one of the best. Britten recognized instantly what Hölderlin pieces would sit well with music, and without bypassing the poet's pervasive Philhellenism, sought out that same sense of strangeness which inhabits Smart's more circumstantial apocalyptics.

Not all six poems are properly called fragments—certainly 'Sokrates und Alcibiades' and 'Die Heimat' are highly organized works (Britten fragments the latter by setting only some of its

[1] BS, pp.65–6.

stanzas), but 'Hälfte des Lebens' and 'Die Linien des Lebens' stand in German poetry like uncut gems, pieces of dazzling brilliance from a mind driven mad by the unbearable ordinariness of life. *Sechs Hölderlin-Fragmente* is Britten's masterpiece about art. It is also the apotheosis of his aphoristic style—'Die Heimat', for instance, being an apophthegm about the German *Lied*, an example of Hans Keller's 'functional analysis', of explaining music in terms of itself. There is a temptation to assert that only a foreigner would dare to add music to so perfect a lyric as 'Hälfte des Lebens', but Britten's willingness to set equally famous poems from the inheritance of his own literature (Keats's sonnet 'To Sleep', Shelley's 'On a poet's lips I slept') show that his confidence in his ability to find notes for the most finished structure is undaunted. In 'Sokrates und Alcibiades' occurs a line which sums up Britten's artistic creed: 'Wer das Tiefste gedacht, liebt das Lebendigste'. However, it is to Hölderlin's madness, as to Smart's, that he turns for his deepest insights (and to desolate Hardy, whose poem 'Before Life and After' distils a love of nescience well beyond the ordinary compass of despair). The four-line epigram which the poet wrote on a piece of wood for his protector Zimmer towards the end of his long and gentle insanity, 'Die Linien des Lebens', is matched by Britten with music of the utmost severity and consolation. As Peter Evans points out,[2] Britten here has recourse to an *echt-Deutsch* technique, the chorale or cantus firmus. Yet the powerful tread of the piano accompaniment and the inexorable progress of the steely vocal line are Britten's own resource. A chorale for him is as idiosyncratic as it is for Stravinsky. 'Die Linien des Lebens' is one of those poems which, once encountered, can seem to irradiate the mind like some fissionable pile. Again, writing as a poet who has had his own invention triggered off by certain works, I am grateful to Britten for directing me to this Hölderlin quatrain. I might easily have found it for myself: it is not especially fugitive, and I had been familiar for many years with Michael Hamburger's complete Hölderlin translations when Britten wrote his cycle. But Britten's music lit up the poem for me, and now the two conditions of art, Hölderlin's verse and Britten's music, exist together and independently for me. Much that I have written and want to write starts with these seminal lines. This quotation is in Michael Hamburger's excellent English version.

[2] *MBB*, p.369.

Composer and Poet

The lines of life are various; they diverge and cease
Like footpaths and the mountains' utmost ends;
What here we are, elsewhere a god amends
With harmonies, eternal recompense and peace.

Two other Britten song collections must be mentioned here. (The term 'song-cycle', being a translation of the German *Liederkreis*, gives a slightly misleading impression. A distinction should always be made between a true cycle, dramatically organized and telling a story (*Die schöne Müllerin*) and a collection of poems by the same author or one illustrating a theme (*Dichterliebe*, Britten's *Nocturne*).) These are *Winter Words* and *Who are these children?*

Thomas Hardy's poetry has attracted many English composers, though not as many as the epigrammatic verse of music-hating Housman. Again, though, only Britten has seen the potential for music in the heartland of Hardy's genius, his realism. Britten has avoided all touch of the dreaded English pastoral, and reproduced Hardy's urban lyricism and particularly his Victorian or Darwinian doubt. I have myself made an anthology selection of Hardy's poetry and can testify to the originality of Britten's choice of poems. All are excellent as verse and wholly typical of their author, but none would occur as a first choice for setting to the mind of a less original composer. Only 'Proud Songsters' is from Hardy's last collection, published just after his death at the ripe age of 88, which gives Britten's work its title. Hardy contributed a wry prefatory note to *Winter Words*, remarking that it was unusual for a man of his advanced years still to be coming before the public with new works. Britten has glossed this by stressing the contrast between, but also the sly alliance of, youth and age in his songs. Most of the poems follow Hardy's musings about the transitoriness of existence, from the autumnal vision of 'At day-close in November' to the breathless renewal of 'Proud Songsters'. Youth and age confront each other in 'Wagtail and Baby' (also of course human deviousness and animal cunning) and in the encounter of the convict and the boy with the violin. 'The little old table' and 'The Choirmaster's Burial' are full of the sweetness of Hardy's despair, his sense of pain clinging to things. Then both the journeying boy in 'Midnight on the Great Western' and the numinous abstracts of 'Before Life and After' speak of Hardy's peculiar sense of tragedy, a view of free will which can be described only as post-Darwinian. 'Before Life and After' is a great poem, and an even greater song—the greatest single song Britten wrote, in my view. Only after meeting the inexorable yet cutting lyricism of this song is one's emotional focus directed back to Hardy. It is schoolmasterly dogma that poetry must be concrete, that it should deal with things not ideas. Yet Hardy uses nothing but abstractions, and makes a masterpiece with them. Who but Britten would have seen that this masterly poem still needs the bitter-sweet additive of music to make it complete? I have not found 'Before Life and After' in any selection of Hardy's poetry. Britten can have had no nudge from literary authority towards it when he was choosing his poems for *Winter Words*. 'The disease of feeling germed' writes Hardy, and the push towards the frontiers of the mind becomes the equivalent of a programme about a space-probe on Saturn. The Victorian debate on God's existence and His worth becomes lyric poetry and then lyric song. 'Ere nescience shall be reaffirmed / How long, how long?' *Winter Words* is far removed from the general world of English song. It is too circumstantial, too realistic, too uncomfortable to fit in with the tradition of pastoral and 'Linden Lea'. Yet it is the most unmistakably English of music, just as Hardy is so palpably English a poet. When I wrote, at the beginning of this chapter, that Britten's music was profoundly bound up with words I was thinking of his Hardy cycle particularly. For too long before Britten the English genius for music was separated from the more consistently developed English genius for poetry. Bringing them back together to inherit the tradition of Dowland and Purcell would be effected only by a composer whose temperament was poetic and whose love of literature was deep.

The last of my choices of Britten's masterpieces which is also an example of his pioneering taste in purely literary terms is *Who are these children?* written late in his career (1969–71). The commission came from Scotland, which may have pointed Britten's researches north of the border, but only his own instinct took him to William Soutar, the strange invalid poet who died in Perth in the early 1940s. Soutar was that rare thing, a caustic original, and one of the finest poets in the long course of Scottish literature. He wrote in both Scots and English, and his vision is toughened and deepened by looking out from the confinement of an upper room (Emily Dickinson's case). He has something in common with William Blake, writing proverbial poems, snatches of childhood rhyme and concealed prophecies, and is equally at home in formal verse and fierce demotic. The shape of Britten's cycle resembles that of his Blake songs, being a mixture of the proverbial and the lyrical, and alternating Scots and English as well. This is for me by far the most successful of Britten's late vocal (non-operatic) works, and I like to think that its quality is reflected from Soutar's special imagination. It further develops Britten's perennial themes of the clash of innocence and experience, and the malice of war. The last song is an epigram on that symbol of nobility, an oak tree.

> *The auld aik's doun:*
> *The auld aik's doun:*
> *Twa hunna year it stude or mair,*
> *(We were sae shair it wud aye be there,)*
> *But noo it's doun, it's doun.*

You can fit out your regret in your own terms as you listen to Britten's setting, so original and traditional at once. Is it civilization, western tonality, British certainty, human steadfastness, or uncompromising truth which is being honoured in its passing? Could it even be the power of poetry itself which has fallen?

I have deliberately left the libretti of Britten's operas out of the main debate, since I think that the requirements of specially produced dramatic texts alter literary expectations entirely. Despite the examples of Da Ponte, Hofmannsthal and Auden, the true 'poets' of the world's great operas are the composers themselves. Britten's taste in words for his operas is, indeed, a more uncertain thing than his taste in texts already in existence, but shares with that an openness and forthrightness which redeems the clumsiness of some of his collaborators. I have always found the poeticizing of Ronald Duncan's verse an embarrassment in *The Rape of Lucretia*, though I do appreciate that the special tone of that opera (each of Britten's operas has an ambience of its own) would not be same without Duncan's peculiar lambency.

Myfanwy Piper's libretti (*The Turn of the Screw, Owen Wingrave* and *Death in Venice*) are especially important, as they show composer and librettist evolving a new way of constructing operas—what might be called cohesion by amplification. The unfolding of an operatic event in short scenes, both spiralling out from a given state or tension, and curving inwards towards moral resolution, is Mrs Piper's and Britten's invention—the screw is turned in all three of these operas. There have been operas before theirs which are made up of short scenes (e.g. *Wozzeck*), but they have invented (in practice, the best way of inventing things) a new style of libretto, one ideal for the turning of stories or short novels into operas.

Peter Grimes, *Albert Herring* and *Billy Budd* have more conventionally constructed libretti, but highly effective ones. Both Montagu Slater and Eric Crozier gave Britten what he wanted in these works: singable texts where the words do not call attention to themselves but are the straw out of which the composer makes his bricks. A good librettist is one who lets the composer be the poet. This is what lies behind Verdi's insistence on *brevità* in his operatic books, and what makes Piave a better collaborator than Boito. Slater should be more commended than he usually is for his contribution to *Peter Grimes*. Too often people select apparent howlers and solecisms in the text (the composer regrettably led the way here) and overlook the brilliant portrait-gallery of characters which makes the Borough come so garishly to life. Slater's craftsmanship gave Britten Mussorgskian opportunities which he seized with alacrity.

Two special relationships with librettists must be at least mentioned. They are with Shakespeare and Auden. There could be no question of rewriting Shakespeare when Britten came to *A Midsummer Night's Dream*, as would have been possible for a composer working in another language. This is why British operatic adaptations of Shakespeare have previously been so unsuccessful. We cannot alter his words and the awe felt for his poetry so often overwhelms original creation. Verdi and Berlioz, even Gounod, were luckier. Nevertheless, I think it fair to say that Britten and Peter Pears rewrote Shakespeare brilliantly in their opera, and did so without adding more than one line to his play. The *Dream* is a quintessence, with Britten's music replacing the music of the verse in Shakespeare's full text. By filleting the play into its three levels of operation—the fairies, the lovers and the mechanicals—Britten was able to expand where the dream-status demanded it (the scene of the reconciled lovers' awakening, for instance) and compress elsewhere. In and out of the magic wood pass the denizens of the dream. Shakespeare's spirit is fully honoured, but the lineaments of musical theatre are substituted for the harangues and tableaux of the play. The fairies are the deepest layer, connected via Bottom to the mechanicals; the lovers and the Court are the thin soil of the upper world. It is not my brief to make musical judgements, but the fact that I consider this to be Britten's most beautiful opera (not perhaps his most perfect: I would count *The Turn of the Screw* to be that) is a measure of his tact and imagination in his relations with poetry, especially supreme poetry.

The full story of Britten's friendship with Auden may never be told. Much of it anyway is the concern of his biographer. Donald Mitchell's *Britten and Auden in the Thirties* is a fascinating study, but it hardly covers the most fruitful part of their collaboration—the time of *Paul Bunyan* and the *Hymn to St Cecilia*. It is also weighted too much against Auden. How far Britten's remarkable certainty when choosing poetry for setting was helped by Auden's tutelage is difficult to tell. Certainly, he never showed the slightest influence of Auden's cranky views of how music and poetry work together. But then these pronouncements date from later in Auden's life, from the American years when he had become an instant guru and mid-Atlantic Goethe. Donald Mitchell cites entries from Britten's diary of 1936 testifying to both the admiration and the sense of oppression which Auden's intellectual dominance aroused in him. He was not the only one to be bothered by this. Stephen Spender wrote of Auden in 1945 that he was the commanding figure of his generation, and Uncle Wizz affected many people as a bully, whether he intended to or not. Yet Auden's powerful personality worked usually in benign ways, and I can see, throughout Britten's career, vestiges of an approach to poetry which is distinctly Audenish. Clarity, unexpectedness, a fondness for litanies, aphoristic brevity, and a predominant enthusiasm for the crisp and the real are all qualities in Britten's vocal music, and in Auden's poetry and his productions as an anthologist. Britten's song-cycles of mixed origin show a poetic taste which reflects Auden's many popular compilations. The *Nocturne*, for instance, and the *Serenade* are excellent pocket anthologies, much more like Auden's vision of poetry than any other literary person's.

The revival of *Paul Bunyan* in the last year of Britten's life demonstrated that there was more good music and wise verse in the 'choral operetta' than either collaborator had remembered. Part of the trouble originally must have been the operetta's being born at the point of Auden's and Britten's splitting up, so that subsequently both parties were likely to be unjust to their creation. The American critics did not take kindly to two apparently cocksure Englishmen dressing up a bit of their own folklore for them. Then there were popular misapprehensions of Auden's style, which apply also to his verse plays, written with Isherwood. Mention of Brecht, Georg Kaiser, Ernst Toller and the rest of the exponents of epic theatre is quite out of place. The real influences are Gilbert and Sullivan, Broadway musicals and Shakespeare's chronicle plays. Yet, in *Paul Bunyan*, Auden came closer to understanding and dealing with America, both mythical and everyday, than he ever did afterwards. He had been there only two years when he wrote *Bunyan*. And Britten forged a popular style which underlies *Grimes*, *Herring* and even the late church parables. Besides *Bunyan*, Auden afforded Britten the chance to write two masterpieces—*Our Hunting Fathers* and the *Hymn to St Cecilia*—and several other haunting short pieces, including some of the songs in *On this Island* and 'A Shepherd's Carol' from *A Poet's Christmas*. To wish that they could have worked together in the years of Britten's maturity is pointless, and the verbose text of Auden's Christmas oratorio, 'For the Time Being', plus the oddities of the libretti Auden wrote for Henze, suggest that Britten might have rebelled at what Auden, as opera theorist, would have offered him. But *The Rake's Progress* shows what Auden could achieve when he served a composer of commanding intellect, and Britten, post-*Grimes*, might have received from him a superb opera book. It is, alas, empty conjecture.

I have hardly touched on the subject of Britten's use of literature in purely instrumental compositions. *Young Apollo*, *Sinfonia da Requiem*, *Lachrymae*, *Six Metamorphoses after Ovid* and perhaps the Second and Third String Quartets owe their inspiration and some aspects of their form to literary models. Britten's imagination pivots on nodes of value which if not necessarily verbal are sited in poetical humanism. And he never profanes the spirit of poetry, never uses it as merely a vehicle for more transcendent things. It is significant that, despite his knowledge of literature, he never supplied his own texts for any work. If the total commitment of a composition like *Parsifal* was beyond him, so was the sense of profanation by ego which that work carried with it. His use of words is never over-reaching, which may be why he turns so often to forms such as the sonnet, the epigram, the antiphon, and such sparse lyrico-dramatic exchanges as are to be found in the miracle plays. To recognize that a poem of such ripe perfection as the Keats sonnet in the *Serenade* could still be made to bear the further weight of music was a daring epiphany. He saw that such sweetness had to be made more sweet, and this he did. The result is paradoxically a purification of Keats's mawkishness.

There is so much of the created world in Britten's music. One is always discovering something new in his delineation of character and place. Smart's line 'For nature is more various than observation tho' observers be innumerable' is Britten's slogan as he adds music to his poetically recorded universe. It should also be the watchword of all who listen to Britten's music and claim to comprehend it.

27

Voice and Piano

GRAHAM JOHNSON

Benjamin Britten is almost unique in that the high quality of his operas does not diminish the stature of his songs with piano. The same could not be said of Bellini, Verdi or Wagner for example, nor on the other hand can anyone really claim that the operas of Schubert, Schumann or Wolf match the quality of their greatest *Lieder*. The majority of Britten's works for theatre or concert-hall were written for a number of versatile singers, artists who were as much 'opera singers' as 'recitalists', and whose example has done much in our country to defeat the notion that rigid barriers should exist between these two arenas of vocal art. Britten was an eminently practical musician, he conducted his stage works and accompanied his songs—the music was performed and created by the same hand. This is one of the reasons that his operas and song-cycles seem to grow out of each other and to be equally vivid. As composer, conductor and accompanist he made us feel that song and opera were *au fond* the same thing, differing only in scale, as if viewed from different ends of a telescope.

Of the 'well over fifty songs' he wrote while still at school,[1] it is easy to see why the adult Britten retained a particular affection for his setting of Longfellow's translation from the German, 'Beware'.[2] It is tempting to glance patronizingly at the unchanging Fs in the bass (tonic—subdominant 6–4—tonic) and diagnose (and dismiss) a childish hand. The astonishing thing is that the 9-year-old Britten has the courage to *stay* pivoted around F minor, allowing the shapely rise

---

[1] Britten's note to the published score of *Tit for Tat* (Faber Music, 1968) lists the poets he set as a boy, among them Kipling, Shakespeare, Shelley, Burns and Tennyson ('The Angels' Call', a companion piece to 'Beware' and possibly his first nocturne).

[2] The first eight bars of the manuscript of this song are reproduced in *PL*, plates 28 and 29. A fair copy of 'Beware' appears in *BR*, p.17.

Voice and Piano

and fall of the tune to mould the song. He refuses to play his harmonic trump card until the sense of the admonishing words 'Trust her not, she's fooling thee' demands it. Unlike most young composers Britten refuses to run before he can walk. He has a healthy respect for tune and the touching qualities of a good sequence. Above all, there is already a feeling for the human voice and the emotive power of portamento.

Britten's mother was a singer and no doubt it was her performances of songs like Cyril Scott's 'Lullaby' which shaped the boy's vocal sympathies and understanding. 'The Birds' (1929, text by Belloc) is dedicated to Mrs Britten and clearly shows a future opera composer's mentality. From very early on, Britten sees each poem as a battle-terrain carefully to be conquered and he plans his strategy well in advance. The opening of 'The Birds' is low-key and meek; it has a lucid clarity which suggests childlike devotion. Jesus receives marvellous gifts, 'and yet with these He would not play'. That unexpected 'and yet' is prepared by a modulation like a change of mind, and it makes the ear *hear* a separate *action* or new decision. The tempo quickens and the clay birds are blessed. They miraculously soar into life, and it is here that the vocal line explodes *esultante* into C major. And we actually *see* their flight, because Britten's music has an extraordinary ability to suggest movement and gesture. At the end, on the words 'bring my soul to paradise', the use of modulation creates an image of stretching out to reach the unattainable; something about the simple contained quavers in the accompaniment suggests a child's hand on the keyboard and a child's glance towards heaven. Britten's achievement here is already that of the born song composer: he has shaped poem and music into a single entity, an *event*.

The five Walter de la Mare songs of *Tit for Tat* were written between 1922 and 1930. When Britten came to publish them in 1969 it was natural that he should 'titivate them a little', observing that 'new musical styles had appeared on the composer's horizon too recently to be assimilated'. Despite the inevitable influences of Delius, Ireland, Vaughan Williams and Warlock, it is Frank Bridge who presides most noticeably over *Tit for Tat*—not the earlier, more popular Bridge, but the Bridge of the half-lit world of the Tagore songs and the magnificent setting of Humbert Wolfe's 'Journey's End'. The most original song in the cycle is 'Tit for Tat' itself, where the emotions behind the music are felt at first hand. The young composer is outraged by blood sports and the cruelty of man. The 'solemn and to the point' opening chords form a miniature dead march, and the loudest pianistic moment of the whole set depicts the human bully thundering through the undergrowth. Just imagine, Tom Noddy, poet and composer say, what it would be like to suffer like this yourself. The song might be a preparatory exercise for *Our Hunting Fathers*.

On this Island is, like *Our Hunting Fathers*, a product of Britten's association with W. H. Auden in the mid- to late-1930s. Auden's words cannot all be readily understood, and in some of the poems he seems to be communicating with a small group of close friends to whom allusions which would baffle the public make perfect sense.

In the opening song, 'Let the florid music praise', Britten paradoxically invests these private words (describing a failed love affair) with the baroque splendour of a Purcellian ode. The grandiose arpeggio figuration sketches the outlines of physical beauty which parades and struts before us, its breathtaking allure provoking the longest coloratura passage in any Britten song: all is ceremony and heartless pomp. As the music moves from D major to G minor the focus shifts from the beloved to the slighted lover; the ode changes to funeral music. Diatonic clarity gives way to a chromatic labyrinth of grief, mourning the 'secretive children' (perhaps shared ideas and projects—always an Auden preoccupation) doomed by the lover's intransigence. The remarkable coda achieves *Dido*-like intensity: the piano spreads its chords like a harpsichord underneath a heartbroken vocal line, while the trumpet-like trills and leaps show that despite everything the proud beloved still exerts an imperious fascination.

Auden tells the love story in language as ornate as Dryden's. With unerring instinct Britten looked into his English musical heritage and found an equivalent; he cheerfully bypassed all the stuffy rules of prosody, adhered to by many of his seniors, which did not permit melismas or any kind of vocal flamboyance. What was good enough for the seventeenth century was good enough for him, and Stravinsky's neo-classicism across the channel must have been an encouragement too. The whole cycle is a fascinating compendium of different styles; it is rather like a young man trying on five different suits and looking good in all of them. From the florid opening song it is a long journey to the cabaret-style 'As it is, plenty', another examination of disillusioned love, this time heterosexual, which concludes the cycle.

'Now the leaves are falling fast', the second song, places the cycle in its contemporary, political context. The running semiquavers of the vocal line and the pulsating piano quavers punctuated by ominous left-hand 'timpani' vividly convey the impression of time running out. The static last page describes a vision where world peace and personal fulfilment were only distant benumbed dreams. 'Seascape' and 'Nocturne' are the most accessible songs. In 'Seascape', fast semiquavers ebb and flow in support of a fine singable tune, which is never afraid to break into melisma, like decorative foam on the waves' edge. In 'Nocturne' Britten displays an audacious ability to write long phrases based on the common chord.[3] The tempo is an *andante* that does nothing to disturb the dreamer; the rising and falling phrases reflect his slow breathing, while the bass chords sink deeper and deeper into the subconscious and the voice part wanders upward into the unconscious void. The simplicity and regularity of these underlying chords give the song the effect of a stately chaconne accompanying the slow spinning of the world as 'Now through night's caressing grip / Earth and all her oceans slip'.

Auden's poem 'Underneath the Abject Willow', dedicated to Britten, reads like a brilliantly persuasive warning, something of a psychological sermon on the subject of sexual repression and the necessity of enjoying oneself. Britten's setting of it for two female voices is full of giddy fun: *vivace* and staccato and 'impetuous'. 'What is thinking for?' the poem asks, and the song, refusing to think, goes on its happy way. It is not what Uncle Wizz meant at all, and Britten's refusal to take the Instant Romance lecture seriously is a devastating, if unconscious, retort.

In complete contrast, the solo song 'Fish in the Unruffled Lakes', for voice and piano, finds Auden in a mood of gratitude

> *That you my swan, who have*
> *All gifts that to the swan*
> *Impulsive nature gave*
> *The majesty and pride,*
> *Last night should add*
> *Your voluntary love.*

The semiquavers in the upper reaches of the piano suggest both the gleaming stillness of water and the darting movement of the fish beneath the surface. The calm world of the non-feeling fish changes to

[3] Cf. 'Antique' in *Les Illuminations*; the daring simplicity of this setting is discussed below, pp.314–15 [C.P.].

the rumbling predicament of humans when the same semiquavers three octaves lower now mutter 'duty's conscious wrong', then tick like a time-bomb in 'the devil in the clock'. The whole catalogue of sorrow and envy is gradually softened by a sequence of descending modulations until the voice is left on its own for three bars. The unaccompanied vocal line rises in semitones which suggest the dawning of a marvellous realization. On the word 'you' the piano recommences its glistening, darting figurations while the swan-beloved glides in the vocal line above. The effect of that moment of the rejoining of voice and piano is as if dreams of love have now crystallized into reality and the singer finishes the song in unruffled gratitude and wonder.

Time and again Britten writes himself into his music, and the *Seven Sonnets of Michelangelo* are among his strongest statements, both musically and personally. The idealized vision of friendship we glimpse at the end of 'Fish in the Unruffled Lakes' is now a firm and permanent reality. This cycle ranks with Schumann's *Myrthen* as a garland of songs to celebrate a marriage of minds and hearts. The first sonnet (XVI) is a proud and powerful declaration: the opening gesture in the piano part sounds like the flourish of a quill pen certain of what it is going to write and far mightier than a sword.

All through the work Britten uses tiny devices which place the words in their geographical context. The second sonnet (XXXI), for example, uses double-dotted rhythms to suggest urgent pleading with a suggestion of an Italianate sob in the voice. The third (XXX) contains the same hurdles that an eighteenth-century teacher of bel canto would expect his pupils to negotiate with perfect legato. This is the Italy of Padre Martini rather than Puccini. All is classical proportion, with the Lydian harmonies providing shafts of sunlight which turn into moonlight and back again. The pianist's right hand crosses over his left, descends into the bass and then moves up again into the treble, all as inexorably as night yields to day. The setting is both sensuous and chaste, an alliance typical of Britten.[4]

For those who may need convincing that Britten could write red-blooded love music there are sonnets LV and XXXII, and a marvellous serenade (XXXVIII) which evokes the strumming of a guitar and the splashing of courtyard fountains, the tenuti in the vocal line adding just the right suggestion of hurt pride and improvised

---

[4] Cf. the setting of Coleridge in the *Nocturne*, discussed below, p.325 [C.P.].

gallantry. The last sonnet (XXIV) is the grandest of all and here we sense most deeply the monumental nature of Michelangelo's feelings, and of Britten's. The music is that of a grave and holy ceremony where the fanfares and flourishes are of quite another order from those of 'Let the florid music praise'. The piano and voice alternate in large paragraphs; they are complementary halves of a whole, one handing over to the other and gradually merging. The pentatonic chord at the piano's climax, before 'qual uso o qual governo', is a vivid pre-echo of Tadzio's music in *Death in Venice*. Britten's first love music links hands with his last.

The Holy Sonnets of John Donne were written at a time of spiritual and physical crisis. Britten had just returned from accompanying Yehudi Menuhin in concerts given to concentration camp survivors and had fallen ill. The seven settings were written within days of each other in August 1945 and have a feverish quality unique in his song output. He had already planned to write them before seeing the camps, but mental anguish and physical infection must have joined forces to generate music which, in Peter Pears's words, 'defies the nightmare horror with a strong love, the instinctive answer to Buchenwald from East Anglia'.[5]

Each song is bound together by a motif which runs through the piano part in ever-changing form. The first sonnet, 'O my blacke Soule', is a *tour de force* in this respect. The hammered double-octave F sharps in the opening page form an austere background to Donne's words. Their dotted rhythm, continuing through the whole sonnet, underpins the strength and expanse of the vocal line. On 'Thou art like a pilgrim' the F sharps rise to G: the tiny jump of a semitone seems gigantic, and suggests the beginning of the soul's pilgrimage. The journey continues with the same indefatigable dotted rhythm climbing to almost every note of the scale until the last section, where we reach B minor, only suggested in the opening. In these final four lines four colours are represented by four chords: the 'holy mourning blacke' is the chord of B minor/major, containing both a D natural and a D sharp; the red of the 'blushing . . . with sinne' is C minor/major with the same clash of thirds; the red of 'Christ's blood' is a consolatory rich B major—the first such chord we have had in the whole four pages; and finally the white of redeemed souls is B drained of colour, without a D natural or D sharp, bare and unblemished.

These are tiny touches of word-painting from a composer who had just written his first great opera, and who could bring to the song form large-scale intensity at the same time as care for the smallest detail.

The setting of 'Batter my heart' takes its rhythm from the triplet suggested by the prosody of the opening words, whose meaning is the starting-point for the relentless battering semiquaver triplets, all staccatissimo, which jump around the keyboard to represent the palpitations of ecstatic fear. Fiendish as the accompaniment is, it is, as always with Britten, superbly pianistic. The sonnets 'Oh, to vex me' and 'Thou hast made me' also take the breath away with the virtuosic demands made on singer and pianist, the former a mercurial and unsettled scherzo ending in a shudder of guilty fear, the latter a thundering étude of double octaves, the pianist's hands chasing each other and never catching up, the voice hanging on for dear life, defying death with a sustained and heroic line.

The faster sonnets are cleverly placed between the weightier pronouncements of the third, fifth and seventh, elegy, dirge and reveille respectively, which paint the suffering and sighs of 'holy discontent', the horror of doomsday and the glory of the last trump. The core of the cycle is the sixth sonnet, 'Since she whom I loved', a profoundly moving prayer written with Schubertian simplicity and a Schubertian ability to modulate at exactly the right moment. This is love music which is not of this world, and there is nothing else like it in English song. The last sonnet, 'Death, be not proud', is a passacaglia descended from Purcell, yet could such a song have been written for voice and piano without taking German *Lieder* into account? Throughout the cycle there are moments of illustration which remind us of *Lieder* ('Die Wetterfahne' of *Winterreise* in the opening bars of 'What if this present' and the majesty of 'O Tod wie bitter bist du' of Brahms's *Vier ernste Gesänge* in the last song, 'Death be not Proud'), yet it is pure underivative Britten, and represents one more step in the cosmopolitan widening of his language, a language that had already encompassed Rimbaud and Michelangelo.

Canticle I: My Beloved is Mine is the first of a series of five, all to religious texts and all embodying a new approach to a time-honoured means of presenting vocal music in a semi-dramatic context. The texts are much longer than is usual for a song, and Britten sets each as a miniature cantata which is in itself a sort of continuous song-cycle. Francis Quarles's poem is an ecstatic elaboration on the words 'My beloved is Mine and I am His' from the *Song of Solomon* (*Canticles*).

Voice and Piano

The movements of *Canticle I* are Andante alla barcarola, a linking Recitative, Presto, and Lento. The opening Barcarolle is as much water music as Schubert's 'Auf dem Wasser zu singen'. The opening words, 'Ev'n like two little bank divided brooks / That wash the pebbles with their wanton streams', give Britten his cue: the left hand of the piano part flows in unruffled 6/8 as one stream, the right hand represents the other, 'Which ranged and searched a thousand nooks'. The tonality or modality of each hand's music is as difficult to pin down as water itself. The treble seems to coincide harmonically with the bass for a moment and then goes off on a new path. The two streams are also images of courting lovers and of Christ drawing the human soul towards Him. At the moment that the piano strands at last come together the voice is set free, released from its brooding observation into ecstatic expression of unity. The syncopations, hitherto the province of the accompanist, have now affected the voice part, and the melismas burst into flame.

A declamatory Recitative proclaiming unswerving faith is accompanied by two heraldic trumpets (one in each of the pianist's hands) with the same triplet–duplet conflict between them. The Presto suggests a three-part mirror canon without actually being one. (It could easily be scored for bassoon, clarinet and oboe.) There is still an element of pursuit between the parts but the restlessness is no longer one of courtship but rather that of weathering a storm: the text at this point speaks of a determination to remain loyal amid the vicissitudes of life. The singer picks his way through the agile counterpoint and arrives safely, his jumping quavers changing to crotchets, dotted crotchets and finally resolute minims. This swift quasi-instrumental passage is just what is needed to save the continual protestations of love from cloying. The crowning glory of the work is the intimate vocal musing of the coda, supported by the luxuriant G major triads which have blossomed from austere two-part chords at the beginning of the section. The turbulent G minor tributary streams in the beginning of the piece have reached their destination and have undergone metamorphosis as part of nature's cycle, and the soul has reached fulfilment in divine grace ('He is my altar; I his holy place'): as Goethe says, 'Man's soul is like water, from heaven it comes, to heaven it rises.' The closing section's vocal line is arched like a rainbow; it requires in performance such ineffable legato and delicacy of feeling poised between the sacred and the sensual, that after Peter Pears one despairs of hearing it sung as the composer envisaged it.

Graham Johnson

With the formation of the English Opera Group Britten began a new phase of his career. As he ventured into the realm of chamber opera—*The Rape of Lucretia* (1946), *Albert Herring* (1947)—his works for voice and piano mirrored the tendency towards economy and concision, their texts chosen to match the new pithiness. This was not so much simplification as distillation, ensuring that music of increasing sophistication and subtlety should also be increasingly direct.

A Charm of Lullabies, written for the mezzo-soprano Nancy Evans, is a stepping-stone to the new style. The voice part is more straightforward than ever before, with no extended melismas. The piano part is pared down to essentials, with none of the virtuosic demands of the Michelangelo and Donne sonnets. This is also the first cycle without any elements of Purcellian or European stylization, though it does contain a charming Scottish lullaby. The songs achieve directness certainly, but they are a little earthbound compared with the vocal works with piano which followed in the 1950s.

Canticle II: Abraham and Isaac is new and original in conception, yet tells a story known to everyone. It has the excitement of opera and the economy of song. In setting his text from the Chester Miracle Play Britten organized a sequence of recitative, arioso and aria which gives the work the shape that could be fashioned only by an experienced man of the theatre.

A lesser composer would have required God to be sung by a third singer—probably a bass, and from behind a curtain. Britten's solution is to combine the voices of Abraham and Isaac, thereby suggesting God speaking *through* them, so from the beginning they are the involuntary tools of their maker's will. At the end of God's initial command the alto has a long-held E flat which fades away as the same note, softly sung by the tenor, takes over from it. There is thus a change of vocal timbre and a brightening of the vowel sound from the alto's 'be*fall*' to the tenor's '*my*', underpinned by the piano's striding quavers and an abrupt modulation shifting from the dominant seventh on F down to D flat major. These changes rapidly bridge the divide between God's words and human reality, and suggest Abraham's return to self-possession and consciousness as God's spirit leaves him. The emergence of Abraham's own voice is like a gauze being raised on stage, signalling the beginning of the human drama. A number of opera composers who have mixed the divine with the mortal would envy the speed and economy of Britten's scene-change at this point. Abraham's music as he and Isaac prepare for their journey achieves an almost Schubertian quality of tenderness and resignation. This music is the basis of the hymn of thanksgiving which closes the canticle and is also extensively paraphrased—indeed recomposed—in the 'Quam olim Abrahae promisisti' of the *War Requiem*, assuming there a far more menacing and ironic character, in accordance with Owen's recasting of the story.

In Isaac's prayer, 'Father, do with me as you will', the boy's plight moves the composer to write a farewell duet of such eloquence that an analysis of the bare constituents (a bass line rocking between D flat and A flat for twenty bars, and sequences of notes falling to simple cadences) can do little to convey its power in performance. Here *Canticle II* declares its relationship to *Billy Budd*: the 'Billy in the Darbies' soliloquy is also poised between the tonic and dominant, again portraying the humility and goodness of an innocent victim about to be sacrificed.

Throughout *Canticle II* the piano functions as commentator and master of ceremonies. The magnificent and tension-building funeral march which prepares us for the moment of sacrifice is in the hands of the pianist. The voices in their terror and distress are transfixed on C sharp, the insistent bass of the piano music. When God eventually intervenes it is with a terrific thunderclap, a massive tremolando on the piano which dissolves into the same E flat arpeggio (minus the fifth, B flat) that opened the work. Once more both voices are absorbed into the spirit of God.

Winter Words stands at the centre of Britten's song *oeuvre*. The songs have about them a sanity and stability which is one of the hallmarks of English song, a certain equanimity which is lacking in the ardent wooings of Michelangelo and the fevered visions of Donne. As always, however, certain songs by Britten resonate with echoes that come from far beyond British shores. Britten's and Schubert's winter cycles are distant relatives. In the first song of *Winterreise*, 'Gute Nacht', we hear the desolate trudge in D minor of the wanderer beginning his journey. One of the most magical moments in all *Lieder*—a moment Britten and Pears managed incomparably in performance—is the modulation to D major in the fourth verse as the singer treads softly so as not to disturb his beloved's dreams. In the opening song of *Winter Words* we also have a D minor landscape, windswept in late autumn rather than snowbound, but evoked in music of impetuous and passionate feeling which calms as the singer looks back to greener, softer June days when the trees were in full leaf. As this reverie introduces 'the children who ramble through here', the music relaxes, an F sharp gradually creeping in here and there to soften the minor tonality, until on 'when no trees, no tall trees grew here' Britten places a melting D major chord which is almost as memorable as Schubert's modulation. In the fourth song, 'The little old table', we have something of an English domestic equivalent to 'Der Lindenbaum'. Schubert's accompaniment evokes the rustling of leaves as the wind plays through them; Britten's depicts the creak of a table when touched 'with elbow or knee'. The tonality of E major/minor is also common to both songs. Schubert's outdoor sensuous flowing triplets and Britten's indoor staccato left-hand creaks have the same dramatic function: both speak of a former beloved. The *sound* of something familiar transports poet and composer into the past. There are other echoes of Schubert's cycle, certainly unconscious and coincidental, but showing an affinity of approach to words and situations. The dotted rhythm and the irony of the convict's outburst, 'This life so free / Is the thing for me', in the seventh song, 'At the Railway Station, Upway', have something of the reckless sarcastic bravery of 'Mut'. In 'Proud Songsters' we see how Britten, like Schubert, has realized the value of placing a fast song between blocks of slow ones. 'Proud Songsters'[6] is a whirlwind of 'particles of grain and earth, and air and rain', and fulfils in *Winter Words* the function of 'Der stürmische Morgen' and 'Mut'. The last song, 'Before Life and After', ends the cycle with a question: 'Ere nescience shall be reaffirmed / How long?' This is a desolate emotional landscape, despite the singer's sweet nostalgic longing for the world 'before the birth of consciousness, / When all went well'. The poet's pain would be eased by returning to the time before 'the disease of feeling germed', by stepping into another world. This is also in a way the plea of the traveller in the last song of Schubert's cycle.

But the songs which have something of a *Winterreise* flavour are not the major part of *Winter Words*. If Britten had chosen a different

---

6 Nothing could be further from Britten's 'Proud Songsters' than Gerald Finzi's setting (1936) of the same text. A comparison illustrates the type of verve and audacity which Britten brought to English song. Finzi's 'Proud Songsters' (*Andante* ♩ = 69) is reflective, the work as it were of a gentleman ornithologist with all the time in the world. Britten's setting (impetuous, ♩ = 176) treats the poem quite differently. It catches the *pride* of these songsters ('brand-new birds of twelve-months' growing'), and the explosion of nature that brought about their creation.

selection of Hardy poems he could have created a cycle as bleak and tragic as Schubert's. But *Winter Words* is *not* tragic, and a very English sense of emotional porportion is preserved by inserting story-telling ballads between the more introspective lyrics, stories full of bitter-sweet humour and wry social comment. 'Midnight on the Great Western' is a masterful twentieth-century 'Erlkönig'. The journeying boy is carried not on horseback but in a third-class railway carriage. The chugging of the engine is less dramatic, but no less ominous, than the thundering of horses' hooves. There is no father with the boy and certainly no elfin spirit to snatch his life away, but still he is in danger. He does not yet belong to 'This region of sin that you find you in', but the train, with monotonous certainty, *is* carrying him to the big city and a future which no one can guess. Britten invented a piano motif to introduce and punctuate the song which exactly captures the mournful whine of a distant train whistle and the Doppler effect as it changes pitch in motion; and cunningly placed hemiolas indicate occasional changes of rhythm as the train moves from one piece of track to the next.[7] Yet this illustrative virtuosity never obtrudes on the compassion evoked for the young traveller. The 'satire', 'Wagtail and Baby', is full of charm: like *Canticle I* it is a barcarolle—'Auf dem Wasser zu singen' again. (Wherever a *Lied* seems to have entered Britten's music, it is one that he often performed himself.) Seeing the imperturbability of the wagtail when confronted with any member of the animal kingdom, and its terror at the approach of any human, even 'a perfect gentleman', 'the baby fell a-thinking'. In two lines of piano postlude Britten provides us with a musical depiction of an infant's mind searching about in various unlikely keys before coming to its inscrutable conclusion.[8]

'The Choirmaster's Burial' is a complete little scena with pompous vicar, peremptorily intoned funeral service and band of spirits singing and playing the choirmaster to his last rest. The song is bound together by Britten's ingenious use of 'Mount Ephraim' in the piano part, the psalm tune requested by the choirmaster for his burial service. The simple little melody flowers into an ecstatic triplet variation at the end of the song as the 'band all in white / Like the saints in church-glass' perform the music the vicar has forbidden. The

---

[7] Donald Mitchell (*BA*, p.95, n.16) has pointed to the similarity between the 'railway ostinato' of this song and that of Britten's 1939 cabaret song, 'Calypso' [C.P.].

[8] Only the end of Satie's song 'Daphéneo' with its final 'Ah' can match this song in depicting the processes of a child's logic.

music on the printed page (minims and crotchet triplets in spacious 3/2 bars) even has the look of the 'ancient stave' in this ceremony of spirits. The song is framed at beginning and end by short recitatives which introduce and 'sign off' the tenor man's story—a miniature form of the device used in *Billy Budd*, where the whole opera is a flashback in Captain Vere's memory. 'At the Railway Station, Upway' is another scena. Instead of the elaborate staves of ancient music-making, the accompaniment is reduced to one line, giving it the appearance of violin music. Many devices of fiddle-playing are transferred to the piano: open strings, double-stopping, détaché bowing, spiccato and even a final harmonic. The 'violin' twangs and is strummed, reflecting the puffing of the train, the empty smiles of the constable, and the 'grimful glee' of the convict, whose song about freedom is accompanied by arpeggios of demonic bravura. Together the vocal line, moving between recitative and arioso, and the violin create a vivid image of the boy, tentative at first—the lack of a 'big tune' suggests he is no virtuoso on his fiddle—but eager to comfort the convict. Within that moment of crossing paths in totally different destinies the boy and the convict are linked, despite the ingenuousness of one and the cynicism of the other, by music.

Canticle III: Still falls the Rain for tenor, horn and piano was written to commemorate the young pianist Noel Mewton-Wood. The piano, however, takes a subsidiary role, with much muted and rumbling writing in the bass clef during the horn interludes. The alternation of verses and instrumental variations gives listeners necessary time to digest Edith Sitwell's highly wrought imagery and lends an appropriately hieratical character through the solemn interchanges of voice and horn, which unite only in the last variation. Unlike some of Britten's music, *Canticle III* is not proof against bad performance: in the wrong hands it can sound anything from very dull to glibly melodramatic. Self-consciousness and artful vocal display, no matter how accomplished, yield diminishing returns to music like this. It is given to very few singers to forget themselves so entirely, to immerse themselves in the music with such selflessness, that they make us believe that they stand for an entire faith, that they mourn on behalf of a whole generation. Yet this was Pears's achievement in the *War Requiem*, as the Evangelist in the Bach Passions, as Elgar's Gerontius, and in *Still falls the Rain*.

Britten's foray into the setting of German verse in the *Sechs Hölderlin-Fragmente* was in part the result of his friendship with the

Prince and Princess of Hesse and the Rhine, whose home Schloss
Wolfsgarten, near Darmstadt, often provided him with a hospitable
and sympathetic atmosphere in which to work. Prince Ludwig keenly
admired the poetry of Friedrich Hölderlin (1770–1843), whose last
years were spent in the grip of schizophrenia. The Hölderlin settings
have a clear and unforced quality that is a musical equivalent of
Hölderlin's search for a hellenic means of expression. The distinction
between Britten's Donne settings and the new cycle is of the same
order as that between the copious richness of Wolf's Goethe songs and
the slim and concentrated writing of his *Italienisches Liederbuch*.

I had the good fortune to work on these songs with the composer. In
the first song, 'Menschenbeifall', he insisted on hearing the note
played by the left-hand thumb as clearly as the note an octave lower
played by the little finger. 'I'm not looking for the total evenness of a
Richter', he said, 'but you can do better than that if you listen
carefully!' The piece is full of rests and pauses and looks rather dry
and explosive on paper. Britten was adamant that I use the pedal in
the first two pages (I had been using none), changing the pedal on each
crotchet. He said that the pedal should be used in all his music, except
where he specifically forbade it.[9]

The second song, 'Die Heimat', uses a canon at the distance of a bar
between voice and piano. (Hanns Eisler by coincidence had also
chosen canonic imitation between piano and voice when setting this
poem in 1943.) Britten's music is full of the nostalgia of homesick-
ness, and it is his playing of this song at our lesson that I most vividly
remember, especially the subtle *rubato* in the inner quaver triplets (he
wanted them to be 'phrased in throbs') while the little finger of his
right hand etched in the melody. The immediate effect was of a ship
gently blown on the waves with what seemed like a siren song in the
distance. 'Sokrates und Alcibiades' is ingeniously planned so that
Socrates' argumentative questioner has the answer before his very
eyes (or ears) in the piano part but is too busy heckling to perceive the
truth of beauty. When Socrates sings his reply, its simplicity and
tranquil self-assurance are Britten at his most affecting, a pre-echo of
Aschenbach's Phaedrus aria in Act II of *Death in Venice*. Britten

9 Adjectives like 'glowing', 'shimmering' and 'luminous' were used in connection with
Britten's own playing partly because of his use of the pedal. By daring to retain certain
elements of preceding phrases whilst casting off others—i.e. changing the pedal, but
not completely—Britten kept a halo of atmosphere around phrases whose sound
would otherwise be dull and prosaic. Peter Pears has always given the advice
'Half-pedal!' to young accompanists, to make us sound like Britten.

discussed with me how each chord should be weighted and voiced, even how the chords might be scored in orchestral terms.

'Die Jugend' is Hölderlin's reworking of the Ganymede story, better known in Schubert's and Wolf's settings of Goethe's poem. Britten playful use of hemiola—the stresses in the vocal line are placed a crotchet later than the bar-line—gives the song the air of a flirtatious saunter. At the end the boy describes how he has become a man in the arms of the gods. The last page is nothing more than a G major scale in the vocal line climbing to D, trying again and reaching E, getting louder (supported throughout by throbbing chords and left-hand trills) and reaching F sharp, and finally gaining the top of the scale. The top G reached by four ascending attempts and finally sung *forte* unmistakably suggests that the ephebe has become a warrior. It is a virile musical climax to a very sensual song. Britten expected a wide variety of touch in this piece. His own staccato, mezzo-staccato and staccatissimo (not to mention his seamless legato) were all quite different sounds. In the middle of the song the two hands, the right legato and the left staccato, are so close that there is a danger of their getting caught up with each other. As Britten played this passage it was as if the two strands were coming from opposite sides of the orchestra.

The last two songs look forward to the future. The autumnal 'Hälfte des Lebens' has a vocal line suspended over ostinato piano figurations, and the alignment of voice and piano seems only approximate, though in fact it is exactly notated. This apparent rhythmic independence of voice and accompaniment occurs increasingly in later works. The closing song, the visionary 'Die Linien des Lebens', is austerely, cumulatively contrapuntal in texture in a manner which points forward to 'A Poison Tree' in the Blake songs, and to the opening song of the Pushkin cycle.

The church parable *Curlew River* (1964) marks a new beginning in Britten's output and his next song-cycle, *Songs and Proverbs of William Blake*, reflects the change in approach. Even if we were ignorant of the composer's interest in new sonorities, we would notice that the look of the music on the printed page is entirely different from that of, say, *Winter Words*. Passages in the Blake songs could almost have come directly from the vocal score of a church parable: the bass quintuplets in 'Ah, Sun-flower', for example, suggest the double-bass writing in parts of *The Burning Fiery Furnace*. The piano is more than ever an orchestral instrument, but this time it represents not a full orchestra, nor even a chamber orchestra, but an amalgam of special and very different sonorities, layered in exotic and new combinations. The pedal is employed to create an approximation to a church acoustic, with sounds clinging together in a haze of echo, and the use of the 'curlew' sign[10] gives the singer great rhythmical freedom—the voice floats on these sounds rather than trying to synchronize with them.

Peter Pears, keen admirer of Blake, selected the words, devising an ingenious sequence of proverbs and lyrics in which each proverb sets the scene and gives the clue for the following song. The proverbs are appropriately cast as weighty pronouncements, accompanied by flourishes from the piano. Initially they are chanted on one note, becoming more melodic as the work progresses. Dietrich Fischer-Dieskau was the dedicatee of the cycle and everywhere in the work we can see the imprint of that singer's artistic character and special abilities. The work requires terrific vocal stamina. 'London', for example, with its long phrases starting *forte* and fading into exquisite held *piano* notes in an awkward part of the baritone range, was made for the virtuosity, breath-control and lung-capacity of a Fischer-Dieskau or Shirley-Quirk.

Britten's settings of Blake's experiences of Hell recounted in the fervour of visionary innocence are unremittingly serious, dark and bleak. There is scarcely a trace of a smile anywhere in them, unless it is a smile of irony. Even 'The Tyger' (fast and exciting) and 'The Fly' (buzzing and hovering) are deadly earnest. 'London' paints the sordid horrors of the capital with claustrophobic intensity; 'The Chimney-Sweeper' points to the abuse of child labour, the sweep singing of the miseries of his plight while the piano comments in crystalline notes of icy indifference. 'A Poison Tree' begins in static minims, but resentment and anger build up and grow like a cancerous fugue, part piling on part, until the page is teeming with malignant sextuplets and tortured harmonies. The last song, 'Every Night and every Morn', leaves us in no doubt that this cycle is about 'those poor souls who dwell in night'.

Although these settings inspire respect and admiration rather than affection, few would dispute that the cycle contains one of Britten's greatest songs, 'Ah, Sun-flower'. The ponderous bass gives the impression of long-stalked grandeur 'weary of time'. The large golden

---

[10] The function of the 'curlew' sign is described above, p.56, n.1 [C.P.].

flower shudders on its stem, bowed down and wilting with the sun's departure but aspiring to the skies in the shimmering heat. Britten's own playing of the grace-notes and tremolandi of the accompaniment was other-worldly, like the rippling of that invisible solar energy which coaxed the flower to blossom and grow to its full majestic height.

Britten's music-making was rooted in East Anglia and yet throughout his life he felt a need to reach out to other cultures and languages. A part of his international appeal is that in certain works, without renouncing his individuality, he meets other cultures halfway—something that has not been a strong musical characteristic of our island race. In the 1960s it was as if the composer became increasingly aware of his responsibilities to use his musical gifts to build international bridges. He believed that friendship and music made a powerful combination, and that his personal and creative associations with Shostakovich, Richter and the Rostropoviches were the most important contributions he could make to détente.[11] A holiday in the Soviet Union in 1965 with the Rostropoviches was the final incentive the composer needed to set Russian verse and *The Poet's Echo* was written for Galina Vishnevskaya (Mme Rostropovich), whose voice had been in his mind when writing the magisterial soprano part of the *War Requiem*. The circumstances surrounding the composition and first informal performance of *The Poet's Echo*, when even Pushkin's clock chimed in seeming approval and blessing, are beautifully recounted in Peter Pears's diary, *Armenian Holiday*.

The Poet's Echo is much shorter than the *Songs and Proverbs of William Blake*. Instead of being throughcomposed with connecting recitatives (the role of Blake's proverbs), each number stands separately, although in the closing pages there is a Schumannesque cyclic return to the music and sentiments of the first song. The timbre of Vishnevskaya's voice is built into the entire work, and it is a voice which, to western ears, seems to embody the vicissitudes of the Russian soul, switching with volatile energy from inconsolable loneliness to expansive glee. The title of *The Poet's Echo* seems appropriate from the outset, and there are gaps of eloquent silence where the poet waits in vain for reciprocation or appreciation.

The opening song, 'Echo', is the reverberation of layer upon layer of sound across the lonely steppes; every canonic device of

---

[11] For Britten's interest in Russia and Russian music during his early years see above, pp.33–8 [C.P.].

augmentation and diminution is used to achieve the effect of sound-waves travelling into the distance. Britten finds intervals and harmonies which suggest Russia as surely as the vocal line of the *Seven Sonnets of Michelangelo* suggests Italy, but of all Britten's stylizations *The Poet's Echo* is the least open to charges of parody or eclecticism. It is written, not from the viewpoint of an outside observer of Russia, but from that of an honorary musical citizen. At the heart of the cycle is 'The Nightingale and the Rose'. The accompaniment consists of major seconds throbbing in punctuated bursts, representing not only birdsong, but also perhaps a heartbeat racing with expectation or dragging in helpless disappointment. In a close dialogue between the parts the piano shadows and mimics the wilting and swooning voice, which uses melismas that seem to catch in the throat with passion and grief. The tiny gruppetto of two semiquavers followed by a quaver rest flutters through the piece like the flapping of a nightingale's wing. When this is transferred to the voice the effect is that of a folksong lament, ornamented and improvised around age-old words.

Arranging folksongs from different countries had always been a strong interest of Britten's, inspired as he was by the example of Percy Grainger, and inspiring in turn composers like Aaron Copland to reappraise their national heritage with the sophisticated hand of an 'art-song' composer. In his last years folksong assumed even greater importance, giving rise to the orchestral *Suite on English Folk Tunes* and the late arrangements for Peter Pears and the harpist Osian Ellis.

The extent to which folksongs should be arranged at all has always been a controversial issue. It goes without saying that Britten's approach was not that of Cecil Sharp or Vaughan Williams. In bringing the folksong into the recital-hall, on his own terms, Britten claims only to present *one* version of the 'original', not a definitive version. Such an arrangement as his 'The Ashgrove', with its subtle moonlit harmonies and deliciously meandering accompaniment, is sometimes accused of being 'too clever'. Objections have also been made to his 'Polly Oliver', in which Britten the opera composer constructs with the utmost economy a series of scenes which bring the story vividly to life: we hold our breath as Polly tiptoes out of her house; we *see* the strutting drill sergeant; at the doctor's diagnosis the music shakes its head despairingly; and the last page conveys the tender loving care with which Polly nurses her captain.

The pathos and intensity of the greatest of the old unaccompanied folksingers is not easy for singers of our own age to recapture, cut off as they inevitably have been from hearing this music in its original context, handed down from generation to generation. At least Britten removed these songs from the schoolroom where they have long been turgidly accompanied by an upright piano dogging the vocal line, and where folksong has sadly become associated with compulsory music-making. The fact is that Britten's folksong arrangements are not folksongs at all and have to be appreciated (or not, as the case may be) on their own terms. His accompaniments help to ignite the singer's imagination, giving interpretative clues and a firm supportive base on which to build a characterization. It must be remembered that very few concert singers could cope with presenting folksong without the 'frame' that a Ravel, Britten, Canteloube or a Berio have provided. There will also be singers of different talents who will convince us of the unadorned beauties of the same melodies. Neither side should press its case with dogmatic single-mindedness.

The words of Britten's last song-cycle, *Who are these children?*, are by William Soutar (1898–1943), who wrote his longer poems in English but his poems for children in Scots. The cycle interweaves the delightful shorter rhymes with the more serious and anguished English poems, contrasting the horrors of the warring outside world with the innocent, unselfconscious world of the young. The use of dialect roots these youngsters to a specific locale: one of them is employed as a pantry-laddie by a member of the local gentry ('The Larky Lad'); another is unfortunate enough to get clouted by teacher, mother, father and brother one after another on the same day ('A Black Day');[12] and another finds joy in the natural beauties of the Scottish countryside in summer ('A Laddie's Sang'). The younger children sing riddles in the playground; one of them cuddles up to sleep in his 'wee-creepie bed'; the whole family meets for supper in a mood of sober reverence and gratitude to have food at all in these hard times.

Soutar wrote most of these poems in his diaries for the years 1940–3 and, in his ordering of them, Britten emphasizes the fragility of this invalid's world which is threatened and precarious and where the children above all are the passive victims of violence. He makes the long poems which constitute the 'second' cycle similarly threaten and encroach on the edges of the innocent 'first' cycle where the domestic issues, for those living them, seem so much more important than the political ones.

[12] Shades of Kenneth Loach's *Kes*—a film which Britten much admired.

Danger seeps in like a sinister poison: the third song, 'Nightmare', follows two short songs of carefree happiness and Britten reverts to the style of the Blake songs, creating a mysterious mood of dreamlike prophecy and foreboding. For the next two songs we return to the down-to-earth life of local Scotland, and then the composer unleashes 'Slaughter' in the heart of the cycle. 'Fate rides upon an iron beast and tramples cities down', wrote Soutar in 1941, and Britten makes the voice ride on a rampaging barrage of quavers as prickly and violent as bayonets, chasing each other in canon at only a quaver's distance. This is a recapturing of the accompanimental style which painted the apocalyptic visions of Donne. In 'Who Are These Children?' the two strands of the cycle are drawn together: the victims of a sky-borne violence come face to face with violence on their own doorstep. Blood sports always revolted Britten, and this song shows once again his lifelong anger and contempt for the hunt. Not even the catastrophe of a village laid waste by bombs can stop the foxhunt pageantry conducted with military precision. The men are elegantly clad, the women immaculately made up, determined that the old order will carry on regardless. At the end of this song, dominated by the piano's imitations of the implacable and strident hunting horn, the singer, who has been describing the uniformed arrogance, sees children at the corner of the picture. Britten sets the lines as if he has seen a frightening and chastening vision:

> *Who are these children gathered here*
> *Out of the fire and smoke*
> *That with remembering faces stare*
> *Upon the foxing folk?*

(Soutar wrote the poem in response to a haunting photograph in *The Times Literary Supplement*.) 'The Children' (1937) was a prophecy for Britain of what was already a reality in Spain, and Britten makes it the most original and disturbing song of the set. It is built up harmonically from the actual pitches produced by the air-raid siren. The opening ranks with 'Midnight on the Great Western' in showing Britten's genius for using the simplest pianistic means to mimic the mournful sounds of a mechanized twentieth century. 'The Children' is a spine-chilling evocation of the terrible calm that follows complete devastation. The 'all-clear' sounds on a decimated world, and as always it is the children who have suffered and whose blood 'corrupts the heart of men'.

I was present at a rehearsal of the cycle in the spring of 1971. At the end of the run-through Britten asked me, with disarming simplicity, if I thought the song 'The Auld Aik'[13] was all right; was 'doun' repeated too many times? Before I could reply, he defended the repetitions: 'It really *is* down, you see; it's the end of everything.'

Britten had often enough written effects from the Far East into his scores, but *Canticle IV: Journey of the Magi* borrows from the Middle East. The whole score has an eastern fragrance until the last pages, but even then the inclusion of a plainchant in this context seems more Byzantine than Anglican. Only *The Burning Fiery Furnace* can rival it for suggestions of pagan splendour later tempered by the advent of Christianity. An extraordinarily exotic vocal timbre is achieved by combining the three voices (the three kings) of counter-tenor, tenor and baritone. The swaying and lurching of camels ('sore-footed, refractory') is heard in the very first bars: this is the music of journey and search. There are memories of summer palaces and sherbet (a shared melisma for counter-tenor and tenor), and then comes that part of the journey where the senses are numbed by travel. Rippling chords and trudging notes played *pianissimo* under the words 'At the end we preferred to travel all night' give the impression of one hour merging into another as the kings, wearily finishing each other's sentences, see less and less of their surroundings. In their exhausted daze imagined voices tempt them to give up the search; they concentrate ever more intently on their destination. When the journey eventually comes to an end it is in a burst of plainsong arriving like a shaft of sunlight in a dark pagan world.

With Britten's death in 1976 we lost the composer who would have been most likely to find a means of maintaining the writing of English songs with piano as a living art. In a world that seems less and less interested in the delicate and civilized amalgam of poetry and music, we would have been surprised and enriched by Britten's uncanny ability to find new and appropriate solutions to problems which others found insoluble. And there was and is a problem about continuing to write songs. In the years that I knew him, the last seven of his life, I think even Britten sometimes felt the time for song-writing was over. Equally I am sure that just as when he changed direction operatically, transplanting Japanese drama to the East Anglian fens, he could have revitalized song. 'Ben will think of something wonderful,' was the confident statement of a whole generation of musicians.

13 One stanza of this song is quoted above, p.281 [C.P.].

I and so many others were so sure that Ben, like the old oak of Soutar's cycle, would always be with us, that with his loss it still seems that the musical landscape has been laid waste. In the field of vocal music his stature dominated the horizon. His roots were sturdy, digging deep into the past, his branches were many and his leaves were capable of infinite renewal. He gave shelter to many slender talents, mine among them. Without this shade and protection many seedlings would have come to nothing, and among these seedlings were some of the greatest British singers before the public today, some of whom he saw grow and flower, with paternal delight. And when these singers are succeeded by others, the lineage will continue to be traced back to Britten because of his music, because of the changes he has permanently effected in English music-making, particularly for the voice, and because of the school that has been established in his and Peter Pears's names at Snape. The difference between the 'auld aik' and Ben is that even if the composer was felled far too soon his work will continue to flower in greater glory with each succeeding season.

28

Embalmer of the Midnight:
The Orchestral Song-cycles

CHRISTOPHER PALMER

His is the night side of things, a nocturnal poetry uncanny and equivocal, compound of that gentle magic of moths, owls, and nightscented flowers so distinctively English. His developing technique emphasized this aspect of his art, but scattered among his works are a number of daylight ones too—in which the peculiar combination of thyme and distant sea, of the glitter of sun upon waves, is evident. . . .

These words were written not about Britten, although they might well have been, but about his teacher, Frank Bridge.[1] They remind us that Britten's response to nature and his development into one of the finest nature-poets of his generation owed much to Bridge's *The Sea, Enter Spring, Oration, Phantasm* and particularly *There is a Willow Grows Aslant a Brook*. These, however, are all purely instrumental works, while much of Britten's nature-and-night music involves the voice. In this chapter I want to consider the song-cycles with orchestral accompaniment of which this particular preoccupation is the principal *fons et origo*: the *Quatre Chansons Françaises, Les Illuminations* (which, as I shall explain, I regard as a nocturne), the *Serenade* for tenor, horn and strings and the *Nocturne*. Each logically follows the other and represents the composer at successive stages, as it were, on his journey from light into night, and back into the light again.[2]

The journey begins in the clear light of boyhood with the *Quatre*

---

[1] Peter J. Pirie, *Frank Bridge* (Triad Press, 1971), p.29.
[2] Two vocal works with orchestra, *Our Hunting Fathers* and *Phaedra*, are not dealt with here; see pp.395–402 for the former and 409–10 for the latter.

The Orchestral Song-cycles

Chansons Françaises, composed when Britten was only 14. We are astonished by how much of the mature composer has already evolved, in terms not just of musical language but of theme, style and overall conception. Of course there are weak and derivative passages. No 14-year-old could be expected to cope with Hugo's 'La douleur est un fruit; / Dieu ne le fait pas croître sur la branche trop faible encor pour le porter' in the third song, 'L'Enfance', which depicts a sweet innocent child obliviously singing and playing while his mother lies dying. Nevertheless, Britten's musical treatment reveals the opera composer in embryo, notably in the use of a French nursery song (always given to the 'sweet innocent' flute) as an ironic, quasi-independent counterpoint to the music of the mother's death-agony. The irony may even be double-edged, inasmuch as the second line of the song runs 'On ira chercher le loup'—the 'wolf' of the nursery-song suggesting the imminent arrival of death. However jejune the musical matter, the dramatic spirit is anything but. Even more remarkably, the 14-year-old Britten is already preoccupied with the theme of the vulnerability of innocence which is to pervade his whole life's work.

Other aspects of the *Quatre Chansons Françaises* are no less prophetic. The idea of a 14-year-old public schoolboy setting French texts was in itself revolutionary. Although the orchestra employed is not small (it includes three clarinets, four horns, harp, and piano—the latter an unusual touch, reminiscent of the scoring of Szymanowski's orchestral song-cycles), nothing approaching a conventional tutti is to be heard; even in 1928 '*all* Britten's music is chamber music' (Donald Mitchell).[3] A pronounced sensuousness of texture is also apparent, a feeling for beauty and fitness of sound, particularly in the first song, 'Nuits de Juin'—perhaps Britten's first nocturne—which incorporates some authentic night-music-like sounds (flutes at 'les astres sont plus purs'). The first of the two Verlaine settings, 'Le ciel est, pardessus le toit', seems to me the finest song, notable for the grace and transparency of its instrumental textures; for its subtle evocation of distant song and dance ('cette paisible rumeur là / Vient de la ville'); for its passionate climax, the dissonant G natural piercing the A flat minor harmony at 'Pleurant sans cesse' like a rapier-thrust; and for the economic but telling use of the semitonal birdsong motif (oboe), which comes to dominate both

---

[3] Colin Matthews notes (in the preface to the vocal score) that the orchestral parts required virtually no editing: everything sounded well.

orchestra and vocal line in the coda—music of heart-searching and weeping (Ex.1). Verlaine wrote the poem in a Belgian prison, from whose yard he could see 'the voluptuous, trembling leaves on the top of some tall popular in a neighbouring square or boulevard'.⁴ At the same time, he recalled, 'I used to hear the distant, muffled sounds of gaiety', which Britten evokes in his setting. Verlaine's term of imprisonment was the tragic outcome of his liaison with Arthur Rimbaud, whose *Les Illuminations* were to inspire Britten's second collection of settings of French poetry for voice and orchestra, one of his finest works before *Peter Grimes*.

Ex.1

Britten encountered Rimbaud's poetry when he was in his mid-twenties, through Auden. Someone of a more intellectual turn of mind would probably have spent long hours agonizing over the 'meaning' of *Les Illuminations*; not so Britten, whose response was immediate and enthusiastic. Around 1937 he told the soprano Sophie Wyss, who had given the first performance of *Our Hunting Fathers*, that he had spent the weekend with Auden's parents and had discovered some 'most thrilling' poems by Arthur Rimbaud which he

⁴ Quoted in Joanna Richardson, *Verlaine* (Weidenfeld and Nicolson, 1971), p.122.

The Orchestral Song-cycles

'had' to put to music. This suggests to me that Britten recognized
spontaneously, in a flash of 'illumination' as it were, a profound
affinity between the boy-poet and himself. He may have read, and
Auden probably told him, something of Rimbaud's background and
the forces which motivated his work; but he does not seem to have
been aware of the closeness of the parallels between himself and
Rimbaud, nor to my knowledge has anyone drawn attention to them
before.[5]

In the winter of 1870, during the Franco-Prussian war, the
16-year-old Rimbaud was wandering about Paris, homeless and
starving. There he seems to have undergone a very painful and bitter
experience, which Enid Starkie sees as the source of much of his later
maladjustment and distress, and which he himself recorded in the
poem originally entitled 'Coeur supplicié' with its haunting refrain in
the final stanza, 'Comment agir ô coeur volé?' Something also seems
to have gone wrong with Britten's apparently sunny childhood which
marked him for life (we do not know exactly what it was). The
outcome for Britten and Rimbaud was similar: a disgust with life in
the raw and an intense nostalgia for past childhood when all was
innocence and purity. (Though his home environment in provincial
Charleville, on the Franco-Belgian border, was unsympathetic,
Rimbaud returned thither for shelter whenever his life outside
became intolerable; for the implications of Britten's return to
Aldeburgh, see above, pp.70-1.) Rimbaud's poetic creed—his
'Théorie du Vagant'—manifests his yearning to return to the days
before Christianity, when the dilemma of right and wrong did not
exist: in the terms of the last poem Britten set in *Winter Words*, 'before
the birth of consciousness'. He discovered however—as did Britten—
that one is a slave of one's baptism, and that one cannot entirely
extirpate the tree of knowledge, for its roots have spread its
ramifications through one's whole being. Many of Rimbaud's *Les
Illuminations* are built round remembered experiences of childhood
and view the contemporary world through the eyes of a child. For
example, 'Parade', 'Metropolitain' and the two poems called 'Villes'
show us the modern metropolis in magic, monstrous technicolour,

---

[5] The first edition of Enid Starkie's masterly critical biography of Rimbaud was
published in 1938 (Faber and Faber) so it is possible that Britten was familiar with it
by the time he started work on *Les Illuminations* (Auden reviewed the book in *New
Republic*, 1 November 1939). Much of the information in this chapter is derived from
the revised edition, *Arthur Rimbaud* (Hamish Hamilton, 1947).

living and moving pictures in which the depicted objects, known and
unknown, real and imagined, merge in a kind of blended solidity and
vagueness unbounded by ordinary laws of logic.[6] Rimbaud, like
Britten, knew that as a child he had experienced extraordinarily vivid
sensations and impressions and had registered them without any
conscious or rational control, but that the onset of maturity had
blunted their sharpness and clarity. In *Les Illuminations*—and this
was surely the secret of their appeal to Britten—Rimbaud tried to
recapture and make permanent that first intuitive emotional state, to
reproduce childhood memories and sensations with that childlike
unquestioning wonder and amazement which is nearer to truth than
all the self-consciously studied 'wisdom' of books. The Garden of
Eden, however, once abandoned, does not readily readmit those who
seek to return to it as Prodigal Sons; and Rimbaud used several
factitious means, including hashish, to recreate his primal paradise of
the mind and senses. Hence the inscrutability of some of *Les
Illuminations*, such as 'Villes', 'Parade' and 'Being Beauteous', which
exemplify Rimbaud's concern to create a language in which ideas and
meanings are subordinated to the sound and the music of words, their
variety and juxtaposition. (Literal English translations read like
gibberish, and the practice of providing such translations for
recordings or concert performances of Britten's *Les Illuminations* is
unfortunate.) Only a composer who was 'naïve' in the Schiller–Keller
sense[7] would have risked the kind of inspired simplicity we find in
Britten's *Les Illuminations*; in fact an English composer who would
set Rimbaud at all would have to be 'naïve', since 'sentimentalic'
French composers, deeply conscious of the 'difficulty' of his work,
have for the most part studiously avoided him. But Britten was
sublimely unconscious of any such difficulty; the poems appealed
to him, he 'had' to set them, so he took them and made them his
own.

The poems' kaleidoscopic chaos of imagery might seem to demand
a full spectrum of orchestral resource, but Britten knew better.
Strings as against the full orchestra have the immediacy and vividness

[6] See Starkie, *Rimbaud*, pp.216–17.
[7] In his preface to *OBB*, Hans Keller applies to composers the distinction drawn by
Schiller between the 'naïve' artist—he who is 'in tune with nature, expressing it, its
laws, its truths spontaneously' and the 'sentimentalic' (= Schiller's *sentimentalisch*,
also a coinage) artist who is 'the perpetual striver, who thinks it better to travel than to
arrive'. Into the first category Keller puts Mozart, Bruckner and Britten; into the
second, Beethoven, Mahler and Wagner.

of a black-and-white photograph as against a coloured one, and the solo soprano projecting her brilliance and (single) colour on to a backdrop nominally neutral or monochrome but capable of infinite subtleties of expressive refinement and nuance creates a dramatic, dynamic effect of extraordinary strength and starkness. The light is the brighter for the environing night; everything seems lit up in preternaturally bright colours. In many ways it does make sense to consider *Les Illuminations* as one of Britten's nocturnes. In 'Fanfare' the great city flashes, flames and dazzles with its alluring siren lights; 'Villes' and 'Parade' are fantastic nocturnal processions, garish and stroboscopic; 'Phrase' pictures the night sky with its myriad stars; while the sunset colours of 'Départ' with its 'jaded nostalgia' (Pears)[8] are unmistakable. Edward Sackville-West, in his introduction to the vocal score of *Les Illuminations*, notes that 'it is always a picture, not an idea, that is evoked, and Britten's settings have rightly the *sharp outlines* and *vivid colours* of a missal' (my italics). A crucial colouristic dimension is lost, or at best distorted, when the singer is a tenor (even Peter Pears) rather than the intended soprano.

The choice of strings also enables Britten to indulge another of his childlike traits—that of causing one instrument or instruments to impersonate another or others. The title of the first song, 'Fanfare', provokes the sounding of not one but two trumpets, one in B flat (violas), the other in E (first violins), the keys being cunningly chosen to exploit the resonance of open strings (D and E respectively). The direction *poco sul ponticello* results in a startlingly realistic trumpet-like rasp and stridency. Over a trilling pedal point on cellos and basses which suggests the sight and sound of a distant metropolis, the dialogue becomes ever more animated, even disputatious, as we draw nearer the city, until the sky appears a mass of flickering, flaring tongues of fire. Only with the entry of the soprano, who 'alone has the key' (literally!) is the argument settled: she mediates in terms of C, which contains both E and, as the seventh partial, B flat (the latter conjured up in the magic-fairyland sounds of the cellos' and violas' glissandi in natural harmonics on the open C string). In 'Phrase' we are again in fairyland with harmonics evoking the distant tintin-nabulations of bells (surely the exquisite 'cloche de feu rose dans les nuages' in another 'Phrase'); the alighting in the last bar on a 'transfigured' (Peter Evans)[9] B flat turns the 'key' (in the specifically

Rimbaldian[10] as well as the generally musical sense) in the next song, 'Antique'. The transition is magical, an early example of Britten's ability, later more fully illustrated in the *Serenade*, *Nocturne* and *Songs and Proverbs of William Blake*, to find connections between poems not intended by their creators to be linked in a chain. For the text of 'Phrase' runs: 'J'ai tendu des cordes de clocher à clocher; des guirlandes de fenêtre à fenêtre; des chaînes d'or d'étoile à étoile, et je danse.' Britten arrives in B flat at 'danse': and the music of 'Antique' takes form as the music of a slow dance in B flat, no doubt derived from the verbal evocation of limbs in slow studied motion in the last part of the poem ('en mouvant doucement cette cuisse, cette seconde cuisse et cette jambe de gauche'). And since a dance is supposed to be primarily a visual rather than an aural experience, Britten contrives to give us something to watch: not only the lower strings' guitar-like pizzicato but also the spectacular effect of the first violins joining in by slow degrees, like more and more 'gracieux fils de Pan' entering the dance—one solo violin, two solo violins, second desk of first violins, third and fourth desks and finally tutti. (Gramophone listeners are perforce deprived of this extra dimension.) The second violins are silent, presumably because Britten wanted only the finest, purest tone in the high register. How simple, yet how effective; and it is part of Britten's child-like-ness that he is never afraid to do the obvious—because he doesn't regard it as obvious in a pejorative sense, but as the right and natural course to adopt under the circumstances. Then in 'Royauté', Rimbaud's touching poem of a mad or drunken couple who, because they really believed one afternoon they were king and queen, actually *were*, Britten, again the 'maître jongleur', turns his string orchestra into a military band, complete with snare-drum triplets and bass drum and, at one point, the E major trumpet flourish of 'Fanfare' ('où les tentures carminées se rélévèrent sur les maisons'). At 'il parlait aux amis de révélations, d'épreuve terminée' we should note the low close-spaced triads, a Britten sound-image for darkness, secrets and inscrutability which is to recur in such diverse contexts as the *Serenade* and Aschenbach's aria 'Mysterious gondola' in Act I of *Death in Venice*. The procession gradually disappears in the distance to the sound of some agile euphoniums and tubas (cello and bass pizzicati). As for 'Marine', the range, richness and depth of sonority make it difficult to believe a full

---

[10] In French the authenticated adjective from 'Rimbaud' is *rimbaldien*.

symphony orchestra is not playing. Britten chooses the bright-red key of A major, which enables him to make full use of the penetrating sonority of the violins' open A and E strings.[11] It is perhaps the most thrilling song of the series; fired by the idea of 'tourbillons de lumière', by the clash and convulsion of light on water, Britten projects in the music an ecstasy which is present in other Rimbaud *Illuminations*, but not overwhelmingly in this particular one. But 'Marine' is a seascape (or more probably a river or wharfscape inspired by the London docks), and we know something of the importance of the sea as an archetype for Britten.[12] Archetypal too are the basic melodic shapes of 'Villes', 'Antique', 'Marine', and 'Being Beauteous'—all built from the common chord, which in this case is derived ultimately, of course, from the reveilles of 'Fanfare'. I suggested above that a child receives all impressions and sensations with unquestioning wonder and amazement, the sense of *déjà vu* being as yet unknown to him.[13] It follows that a musical child will hear a C major chord as it might sound in the Garden of Eden. According to Pears an older American composer once told Britten he did not know how he dared write the melody of 'Antique'. He dared because to his childlike innocence of musical spirit there was nothing audacious about what he was doing—he liked the sound of the triad so he used it and, because he was a genius, the result was not banal but inspired. In the same way his setting of the National Anthem modulates in the middle from E flat (*pianissimo*) to B flat (*fortissimo*), from tonic to dominant: one of the most elementary progressions in musical syntax. Yet its effect in performance is indescribably thrilling. Many lovely touches in *Les Illuminations* are the result of this unselfconsciously novel use of commonplace, bread-and-butter formulae, for instance the singer's last line in 'Being Beauteous'—'le canon sur lequel je dois m'abattre à travers la mêlée des arbres et de l'air léger'—where streams of parallel triads moving in contrary chromatic motion eventually converge on a G dominant chord, a moment of arrival

---

11 Donald Mitchell, referring to *Young Apollo*, for piano and orchestra, and to Tadzio's music in *Death in Venice*, has identified A major as the 'Apollonian' key in Britten, i.e., the key of sunlight. (Sleeve-note for EMI ASD 4177.)

12 See above, pp.110–19.

13 As a performer Britten tended to give of his best in 'innocent' music or that which invoked a spirit of lost innocence. Among his and Pears's most memorable recordings are in my view not only their Schubert and Grainger but also their 'I Have Twelve Oxen' (Ireland), their ineffably poignant 'In Youth is Pleasure' (Moeran) and the roistering 'Yarmouth Fair' of Warlock.

exquisitely marked by a double-bass pizzicato, which then resolves on to C. The effect is that of a breath of soft summer night air (Ex.2). In the same way in 'Départ' Britten makes utterly fresh and poetic use of repeated chords in triplet groupings, one of the most tiresome accompanimental clichés in the nineteenth-century song-composer's repertoire; here they combine with a very slow rate of harmonic change to give the song its 'feeling of spaciousness and long farewell'.[14] We are moving on, inevitably, inexorably; but we have loved and learnt much and are loth to leave.

Ex.2

Britten later frequently chose to set texts by writers of a homosexual or part-homosexual orientation (Michelangelo, Melville, Mann, Forster, Hölderlin, Owen), and Auden would have made him aware of Rimbaud's relationship with Verlaine. Many of *Les Illuminations* date from the period the two poets spent together in London in 1872; this was Rimbaud's first experience of a modern industrial capital, and he reacted with fascinated disgust. Britten, who came to the same city some sixty years later as another innocent abroad, would have understood the feeling perfectly; once he was established at

[14] Donald Mitchell, BS, p.33.

Aldeburgh he shunned the capital as far as he could as a nightmare of sophistication, squalor, noise and stereotype. This of course was in his later years, after he had not so much compromised with the world at large as created his own world at Aldeburgh. Rimbaud was never able to make such an accommodation. His precocity was extreme: he wrote his masterpiece, *Le Bateau ivre*, at 16, and his last work, 'Une Saison en Enfer', at 19. Then the childhood vision deserted him, and he gave up poetry for ever. To Britten, according to Pears (in an undated programme note), Rimbaud was one of those 'bewildered but gifted young of whom he was fond: "lost sheep" as he called them'. It is easy to see why Britten was attracted to this mad child-genius; and he was similarly attracted to Grainger (mad, and a child who never grew up), Owen (who died young) and Smart and Hölderlin (both mad).

By the time of the *Serenade* Britten had been through his *Wanderjahre* or *Saison en enfer*, and a world of tranquillity and deep security is epitomized by the horn solo, first on- then offstage, which frames this 'exquisitely selected miniature anthology' (Eric Walter White) of poems about evening and night. The trumpet alarms of the Rimbaldian metropolis are a million miles away; here the environment is old-fashionedly pastoral, reminiscent indeed of Samuel Palmer's *Harvest Moon* (which adorns the first edition of the vocal score (Boosey & Hawkes, 1943)). In this Prologue and Epilogue the horn must use natural harmonics, which sometimes misleads listeners to blame the soloist for playing out of tune. The idea did not originate with Britten: Vaughan Williams, in the slow movement of his *Pastoral Symphony*, interpolates cadenzas for natural trumpet and natural horn respectively so that the seventh and ninth partials have their true intonation, i.e. sound out of tune to our corruptly well-tempered ears. Like Britten he was attempting to evoke an 'old-fashioned' landscape at sunset and to do so resorted to 'old-fashioned' sounds.[15]

[15] Much of Vaughan Williams's *Pastoral* was conceived in Flanders where the composer was on active service during the First World War, and the trumpet solo is a reminiscence of a bugler practising at dusk—war and peace, as it were, under the same sky. The horn-calls in the *Serenade* are handmaids of Venus, bringer of peace, goddess of love; in the *War Requiem* they perform a complete volte-face, transferring allegiance to Mars, the bringer of war: Heaven and Hell—two faces of the same coin. Donald Mitchell, in an essay written to accompany the complete Decca recording of *Owen Wingrave* (SET 501–2), has drawn attention to a similar ambivalence of connotation in the case of percussion instruments—at once children's playthings and accoutrements of war—which Britten puts to telling use both in *Wingrave* and *Children's Crusade*. See also Chapter 16.

Christopher Palmer

(This is not the only contact of this kind between Britten and Vaughan Williams. At the climax of 'Bredon Hill' in *On Wenlock Edge* (a work Britten recorded with Pears) the singer is directed to sing 'O noisy bells, be dumb' in his own tempo, independently of the orchestra—an anticipation of the type of lifting-of-restrictions in the related areas of tempo, metre and bar-lines Britten employed in his music of the 1960s. Like all 'children', Britten possessed a unique power of assimilation. His memory and imagination were richly stored with ideas, borrowed both consciously and unconsciously, from which he created something that was his alone. The vocal virtuosity of 'Rats away!' in *Our Hunting Fathers* is adumbrated in Bliss's *Rout*, with which Britten was familiar in his youth. The voices' free chanting of 'pleni sunt coeli et terra gloria tua' in the *Sanctus* of the *War Requiem* may be indebted to the spoken 'Glory to thee Holy Spirit' in Holst's *Hymn of Jesus* and, in the same work, to the 'free chanting' of the semichorus' 'Vexilla regis prodeunt' independently of the orchestral accompaniment, which is 'repeated ad lib until the chant is finished'.)

The first song of the *Serenade*, Cotton's 'Pastoral', is a paradigm of Britten's compositional skill. Its relationship to the Prologue is strong yet subtle. The tonic F of the Prologue becomes the third of the D flat of 'Pastoral', and the rhythm of the first bar of the former becomes that of the first bar of the latter. The notes of the soloist's descending first phrase, 'The Day's grown old', following the decline of the sun, are those of the 'natural' D flat triad: an obvious cue for the horn, which responds immediately in a manner explained by the first line of the second verse, 'The shadows now so long do grow'—for the horn 'shadows' and deepens the vocal part as if in the rays of the setting sun, refracts it at a new angle, in a new colour. When the ant 'appears a monstrous elephant', Britten wittily uses the capacity of the horn's low register to suggest the horrific (low C, *fortepiano*); the same is true at the end of the following stanza, when the small stripling following the 'very little, little flock' (the harmonic substance of stanzas 1 and 2 now split up into tiny woolly pizzicato molecules) appears 'a mighty Polypheme'. Here the horn hits a low D flat, where it remains comfortably lodged for the remainder of the song (it has followed the sun to the rim of the horizon and can sink no further without, as it were, falling off the world) until its final *pianissimo* echo of 'The Day's grown old'. This last stanza brings a momentary modulation into an E flattish tonality (while the horn pedal provides a firm anchor to the real 'home' key, the sunset key of D flat), which, together with the appearance for the first time of 'The Day's grown old' in the strings, breathes a delicious air of evening cool; underneath, the close-spaced low string triads denote the gathering darkness (cf. 'Royauté' in *Les Illuminations*, and the Keats 'Sonnet' discussed below).

That intimation of E flat in the last stanza of 'Pastoral' becomes the home key of another evening genre-picture, the Tennyson 'Nocturne'. If 'Pastoral' was sleepy and rustic, 'Nocturne' is spectacular and dramatic, 'full of starry glitter and the last flashes of the sun'.[16] Castle walls, snowy summits, lakes and cataracts, cliff and scar, purple glens—this landscape is Scottish rather than English, hence the scotch snap in the accompaniment. In each song of the *Serenade* the horn plays a different role: here it is silent in each verse but joins the voice in a free cadenza for the refrain in a manner prophetic of Britten's later work. In Blake's 'Elegy' it is very much the protagonist; its part is an intense and concentrated exploration of the interval of the minor second, e.g. G sharp moving downwards to G natural in an E major triad. This is an archetypal symbol in Britten of evil, of the ubiquitous imperfection in the divine image, and is related to the more conventional symbol of the tritone, the *diabolus in musica*, inasmuch as the latter is an 'unnatural' semitonal distortion of the 'natural' shape of the triad—for instance if in the chord of E major the lowest note moves up a semitone from E to F, the triadic purity is besmirched and a tritonal relation established between the F natural and the triad's top note, B. (Britten extensively exploits this tritonal disfigurement or corruption of the triad in *Owen Wingrave*.) In Blake's metaphor of corruption the semitones invade and infect the whole body of the music, like the canker spreading through the heart of the rose; even the central recitativo vocal section, when the horn is silent, begins and ends with them. And while the horn is thus going about its evil business in 'unnatural' semitones, the 'natural' triadic shapes with which it is normally and idiomatically associated become the strings' prerogative and can perhaps be taken as representing the healthy body asleep (the deep, heavy-breathing rhythm implies as much), obliviously unresistant to the encroachments of the enemy. The quasi-subterranean horn-calls of the double-basses' pizzicati, occasionally lapsing into semitones, are particularly intriguing.

That the semitonal ambiguity of 'Elegy' has a universal significance for Britten is made clear in the succeeding 'Dirge', whose vocal

16 Peter Pears, BS, p.67.

Christopher Palmer

ostinato begins with basically the same figure (now G natural–A flat [G sharp]–G natural). This vocal part is marked *come una lamento* and otherwise has no expression marks or dynamics, so the tenor has to sing throughout in a kind of *mezza voce*, at the top of his range. The result is a totally sexless, un-human sound (one of Grainger's 'moaning nature-voices'?), an eternally self-renewing refrain, a bleached and spiritless song of the vanity of all human endeavour, which continues to lament in some corner of the universe long after it has passed out of our immediate earshot. This much is, I think, implied in the written notes and in the way they are performed by Pears; to 'interpret' them as does Robert Tear, self-consciously and with studied 'expressiveness', is to miss the point. The voice is in a sense unregardingly, impassively independent of the orchestra, which represents the human element, man going to his long home. A fugally impelled funeral procession comes in sight from afar, approaches close enough to strike mortal terror into our hearts (horn hysteria) and then makes off, leaving the last word to the disembodied wail and whine of the singer, 'lost with all souls on the infinite sea' and beset by the same semitonal instability as Captain Vere.

After its virtuoso display of acrobatics in 'Hymn', with the two soloists weaving round each other an 'embroidery of stars' (Edward Sackville-West), the horn is *silent* in the Keats 'Sonnet'—allowing the player both to catch his breath and make his way offstage for the Epilogue. The 'Sonnet' is built on what is broadly speaking an ostinato of four chords—precisely the chords which, as Eric Roseberry was the first to notice,[17] were to reappear in Act II of *A Midsummer Night's Dream*, respaced and rescored and with the order of the first two reversed (Exx.3a–b).[18] The text in each piece is concerned with the properties of sleep, and so the similarity (of

---

[17] See *Tempo*, No.66/7 (Autumn/Winter 1963), pp.36–7.

[18] I cannot resist here drawing attention to a minor discovery of my own: surely the chord marked (d) in Ex.3a—C major but with the fifth of the triad missing—*must* be derived from another celebrated nocturne with which Britten was certainly familiar, namely Mahler's setting of Nietzsche's 'Mitternachtslied' in the fourth movement of the Third Symphony. Compare the following with (d) in Ex.3b:

Ex.3a Serenade

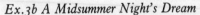

Solo Vc. *(a)*   *(b)*   *(c)*   *(d)*

Ex.3b A Midsummer Night's Dream

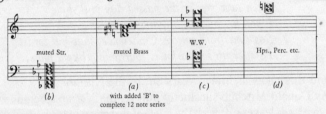

which, the composer assured Roseberry, he had not been conscious) is yet another example of the consistency of Britten's musical imagery. The entire song evolves from this basic *donnée*; even the canonic line that rises in some perturbation through the accompaniment to 'Then save me, save me' is derived from the opening three notes of the solo cello phrase in Ex.3a. A transposition of the chord sequence to the lower reaches of violas and cellos after 'lulling charities' reverts to the low-triad image earlier mentioned in relation to 'Pastoral' and to 'Royauté' in *Les Illuminations*. The 'lulling' vocal melisma at this point and the 'burrowing' figure in cellos and basses at 'burrowing like a mole' *are* obvious touches of word-painting, as certain critics have disparagingly declared, leaving less obvious and more interesting features of these two passages unremarked: the sudden void which yawns between the deepest low F of the basses and the high tremolo G flat violin chord in the first, a chasm some four octaves deep; and, in the second, the significantly *semitonal* constitution of the 'burrowing' motif, inescapably reminiscent of the worm burrowing into the rose.

Just as we find in the *music* of the Keats 'Sonnet' a clear prefiguring of Britten's *A Midsummer Night's Dream* night music, so the *words* contain the seeds of two of his later celebrations of night.

Christopher Palmer

O soothest Sleep! if so it please thee, close
In midst of this thine hymn my willing eyes

reads like an echo of the song by Dowland which is the basis for the *Nocturnal* for solo guitar:

Come, heavy Sleep, the image of true Death,
And close up these my weary weeping eyes. . . .

And, indeed, at the end of the *Nocturnal*, soothest Sleep does close the player's willing eyes in midst of her hymn, for his fingers drop from the strings in mid-phrase. Keats continues:

Then save me, or the passed day will shine
Upon my pillow, breeding many woes,—
Save me from curious Conscience, that still lords
Its strength for darkness, burrowing like a mole;

—and this takes us fifteen years on, to the *Nocturne*.

As Donald Mitchell succinctly puts it, the *Nocturne* begins where the *Serenade* leaves off: with the poet safely asleep in his bed. He is not allowed to sleep undisturbed for long, however; if the *Serenade* is like a collection of pictures in a gallery, each complete in itself although linked by a common theme, the highly unified *Nocturne* is more in the nature of a symphonic dreamscape—if 'symphonic' is not too ponderous a term for this gossamer web of imagined incident and image, and 'strings stretched from belfry to belfry, garlands from window to window, golden chains from star to star (*Les Illuminations*): a kaleidoscope of textures so subtle, so poetically attenuated, so individual in the brightness of their dark, that I'd claim Britten's feeling for beauty of sound as the finest in England since Delius's. The principal unifying agent (Ex.5x) is the motif of muted strings, divisi, breathing gently in and out in the same dactylic rhythm as the sleeper so tenderly depicted, years before, in the 'Nocturne' of *On this Island* (Ex.4). Here the opening words of the excerpt from Shelley's *Prometheus Unbound* provide the clue:

On a poet's lips I slept
Dreaming like a love-adept
In the sound his breathing kept. . . .

Throughout the piece Ex.5x serves primarily as connective tissue, linking one poem or dream to another and constantly reminding us of

Ex.4

Ex.5

the silent presence of the sleeper. Ex.5 is typical of the seamlessness of Britten's transitions. The spiky minor ninth in bar 1 has been a recurrent, irritant feature of the Tennyson 'Kraken' setting; in bar 2 it dissolves effortlessly into the 'breathing' motif (just as the Kraken's bassoon disappears into the violas) and, two bars later, opens out into the sensuous, euphonious *major* ninth which, in bar 10, sets the scene of Coleridge's moonlit wilderness.

The breathing-sounds are heard almost continuously throughout Middleton's 'Midnight's bell goes ting, ting, ting, ting, ting', for this is not so much a dream as a picture of the sleeper asleep surrounded by night sounds and the creatures that make them: conversely Ex.5x is altogether absent before, during and after Wordsworth's nightmare vision of the French Revolution (from *The Prelude*), since the poet here depicts an insomniac. Not until after Owen's 'The Kind Ghosts' do we re-enter the sleeper's bedchamber to find the evil, troubled parts of his dreams over and done with. Now flute and clarinet conjure up the sights and sounds of summer in a buzzing, humming scherzo that corresponds with the Jonson 'Hymn' in the *Serenade*, light after darkness. But the poet's real business is not summer but sleep, sleep which is richer than all the beauties of the daylight world combined. So little by little Ex.5x obtrudes: first a single chord merely (at 'Sleep?'), then a phrase, then two phrases, finally a complete texture as the vocal line flowers into lyricism. The listener may be struck by a sense of familiarity; he has already heard the phrase in the Shelley and in the Middleton ('And the cats cry mew, mew, mew'). It is the theme of 'nurslings of immortality', the 'forms more real than living man' that the poet can shape from his dreams, from things whose outward appearance he perceives less clearly than their inner essence. C major is the key of night, when this process is underway; D flat (so close to C and yet so far) the key of day, on which the final statement of Ex.5, after the great Shakespearean love song, must inevitably but regretfully settle: inevitably because the night is now spent and must issue in day, regretfully because so much of Britten's work belongs to a

> . . . *climate where they say*
> *The night is more beloved than day.*

The *Nocturne* is scored for seven obbligato instruments and strings; the latter on their own accompany the introductory 'On a poet's lips I slept', establishing the 'breathing' motif. The Kraken's instrument is the bassoon; one might perhaps have expected Britten to choose, say, the horn, which has more power, weight and volume; but the bassoon has agility in its murky lower register, a thin, bloodless, piping plangency in its upper, and a generally dark, sickly colour, all of which the composer exploits to great effect in his only underwater sea-picture. The music is based on a 'ground' which consists of the common chord of B flat minor—naturally, for Britten is here depicting a state of nature, the sea-bed and its denizens, and so, as in the *Serenade*, employs the 'natural' formula of the triad. Triadic thirds, now reflecting moonlight, are also prominent in the next song, in which Coleridge's 'lovely Boy' plucks fruits to the sweet-flowing liquefaction of the harp. According to the score this section is a 'slow waltz', but nowhere is there the slightest suggestion of the rhythmic three-in-a-bar of the conventional waltz; indeed at one point the vocal line describes an arc of such effortless, endless fluidity that the ear is wooed into imagining that the bar-lines have disappeared (Ex.6). The sheer *sound* of the texture is a miracle in this setting, a paradoxical blend of innocence and sensuality—which is no paradox when we remember that children are sensual in a quite innocent and unselfconscious way. A child, naked but for a twine of leaves, is the subject of the poem, and as I have suggested Britten himself in certain ways always remained a 'child'.

Ex.6

If the horn seemed a more obvious candidate than the bassoon for 'The Kraken', the bassoon's greater delicacy and subtlety would surely better qualify it for 'Midnight's bell goes ting, ting, ting, ting, ting' than the horn; but this is again to underestimate Britten's resourcefulness and his knack of using instruments in unfamiliar though always idiomatic ways, showing them capable of a greater range and variety of effects than even their players would sometimes believe possible. In this case the horn commands a fascinating empire of nocturnal onomatopoeia: distant chimes at midnight, dogs howling, nightingale twittering, owls tu-whit-tu-whooing, ravens croaking, crickets hopping, mice nibbling, cats mewing. But by now the night is far advanced, and the crisis looms: the Wordsworth setting is a portent of war, as 'The Kind Ghosts' is its aftermath. Midnight's bell becomes the beat of the timpani. Little by little the nightmare takes shape: a long-held pedal F sharp while it is still distant, the pedal dislodged chromatically (like ground giving way beneath the feet) as it approaches, finally the strings 'rearing and whirling'[19] as it becomes a tangible reality. The climax is imminent at 'And in such way I wrought upon myself', and Britten builds up, step by step, a towering inferno of dissonant tremolo strings—a clear anticipation of the Prelude of *Owen Wingrave*, in which the subject again is past wars and their reverberation in the present (another instance of consistency in Britten's musical imagery). The tenor's hysterical declamato malediction 'Sleep no more!' releases the tension, and the passage which follows is one of the most remarkable in the work. The timpani's *fff* cannon-fire, a regular four-in-the-bar, makes a quick *diminuendo* into hollow, distant re-echoings down the centuries, as it were into some dark tunnel of infinity such as might have housed the participants in Owen's 'Strange Meeting'. Owen is the poet here, and the poem is one of the greyest, bleakest and most hopeless of his elegies for cannon-fodder youth. The drum-beat becomes a ghostly pizzicato heartbeat, a barest flickering of life, but enough to give shape and pulse to the cold, sightless yet sobbingly expressive melancholy of the cor anglais. Imogen Holst relates this instrumental solo to Bach;[20] to me its sinuous, chromatic, wraith-like arabesques are more reminiscent of oriental music, and the dead (and deadly) pizzicati have a timeless, impassive quality. Perhaps this is a counterpoint to the 'Dirge' in the *Serenade*, a kind of cosmic lament. Only once are the strings, voice and instrument roused simultaneously to a *poco forte*, at the terrible line 'Nor what red mouths were torn to make their blooms'. A *diminuendo* immediately succeeds for 'The

---

[19] Imogen Holst, 'Britten's *Nocturne*', *Tempo*, No. 50 (Winter 1959), p.21.
[20] 'Britten's *Nocturne*', p.21.

shades keep down which well might roam her hall', but the 'roaming' cor anglais brings them to a kind of shadowy life. The ghosts' footfall (here, as with their roaming, the music visualizes what in the poem does not happen) is picked out in delicate duet of high staccato quavers for voice and instrument, reminiscent of the mouse's 'peep, peep, peep, peep, peep' in 'Midnight's bell'; the latter sound itself is recalled at the end of 'The Kind Ghosts', after the pizzicati have disintegrated upwards and out into dust and finally nothingness. Few will disagree with Peter Evans that 'it is possible to find this more chilling than anything in Britten's later treatment of Owen in the *War Requiem*'.[21] But even in dreams we cannot live permanently in limbo; life must go on, summer flashes and hums all around us (flute and clarinet) with a delightful touch of pomposo vocal humour at '[What] more full of visions than a high romance?'; little by little the blessed refreshment of untroubled sleep returns. Here for the first time the strings are silent, the more effectively to render their gently persistent interventions in response to Keats's invocation to sleep. Until now, in fact, the strings have played a more or less subsidiary role: they have self-effacingly illuminated each of the obbligato instruments in turn. But in the Shakespeare sonnet, the emotional consummation of the entire piece, they are the stars, uniting all their resources in a strong, singing, supple line of surgingly impassioned intensity and eloquence. Why? Because, surely, this is the only song in the *Nocturne* which deals with naked human emotion—love—and the strings of all instruments are those which correspond most nearly to the naked human voice.

In 1884 the young 'Fritz' Delius, amateur orange-grower in Florida and would-be professional composer who, like Britten, turned to the New World *as* a 'new world', and later, in *Paris—the Song of a Great City*, wrote his *Illuminations*, a cityscape that was also a 'départ dans l'affection et le bruit neufs', left his orange-grove for the wider world of men. His 'Frank Bridge'—one Thomas Ward, the only teacher from whom, in later years, he claimed to have learnt anything worth knowing—gave him a book of Byron's poems as a parting gift. In it Delius found the following passage from 'Manfred'. He never set the words, nor did Britten, but their spirit

[21] *MBB*, p.374.

Christopher Palmer

pervades much of the music by which they are both likely to be remembered:

> I linger yet with nature, for the night
> Hath been to me a more familiar face
> Than that of man; and in her starry shade
> Of dim and solitary loveliness
> I learned the language of another world.

29

The Choral Music

ANTHONY MILNER

Britten's first choral publication, *A Boy was Born*, consists of six variations on an original theme for unaccompanied mixed choir and boys' voices. It exhibits many features that recur in later works: a free tonality that can seldom be pinned down to a precise major, minor, or modal scale but is none the less always related to some melodic or harmonic feature that acts as a centre; markedly individual melody closely allied to sensitive word-setting; a flair for selecting and combining widely contrasted texts to provide a unified structure for musical forms; and an astonishingly economical yet versatile use of thematic material. The chorale-like setting of a (translated) sixteenth-century German carol that forms the theme is built from an opening motif of four notes, D–E–G–E, by transposed repetitions, sequence and inversion, yet, for all the ingenuity revealed by analysis, sounds completely spontaneous and uncontrived. Its apparently effortless directness and simplicity are paralleled in many of Britten's works, sometimes evoking the mistaken judgement that his music's charm rests on shallow foundations. Nothing could be further from the truth: Britten's meticulous craftsmanship is of the kind whose greatest art is to conceal art. While detailed analysis of every work is not intended or possible within the scope of this survey, a few observations on the techniques used in this early work may serve to illuminate some of its composer's basic methods of composition.

The theme is harmonized by seventh chords (built from super-imposed fourths derived from the span of the basic motif) alternating with thirds (the interval between the motif's second and third notes); the sevenths, at first minor, suggesting modal tonality, are later sharpened and by transposition gradually embrace a wide chromatic range, yet end with a clearly implied tonality of D. Unlike baroque and classical models the variations do not preserve the structure of the theme but freely expand its basic materials. Thus Variation 1, 'Lullay, Jesu', a dialogue between Mary (womens' voices) and her child (boys) over an ostinato-like repetition of falling fifths, has melodic lines spun from the basic four notes; as these lengthen the choral texture increases from two to eight parts. Variation 2, 'Herod', declaims the tale of the Massacre of the Innocents in jerky rhythms, mingling 3/4 and 6/8 patterns in melodic lines that alter and distort the motif's note order. A semichorus sings the text of Variation 3 (the simplest) to bare homophonic combinations of fifths and fourths, recalling the theme's opening harmonies, while the boys sing 'Jesu' four times to a melismatic expansion of the motif. The latter continues as a wordless flow of quavers throughout Variation 4, shifting from one line to another, forming the background to the narrative of the Three Kings' journey. In Variation 5, scored for the upper voices only, the women emphasize the 'bleak mid-winter' of Christina Rossetti's poem by slow harmonies of descending seconds and fourths (an inversion of the motif) that suggest falling snow. Above this the boys sing the ancient Corpus Christi Carol to a folksong-like dancing melody, thus producing an astonishing juxtaposition of different cultural worlds that is perhaps the most moving and certainly the most original device in the entire work. Variation 6 is a large rondo finale whose episodes are settings of three independent carol texts, the whole being bound together by 'Noel' and 'Wassail' refrains, both derivatives of the basic motif. It is not only the longest and most varied movement but also the most complex contrapuntally, much of it in eight parts. Its coda links the basic D–E–G–E to the words 'Glory to God' (recalling one of the earliest medieval incipits for the *Gloria*), and over developments of it the boys sing fragments from some of the preceding movements as a transition to a new melody setting Quarles's 'This night a Child is born'. This, still based (though more freely) on the fundamental note-cell, is accompanied and developed by the chorus in an elaborately contrapuntal close.

The work's close motivic structure and use of variation, paralleled in many works by Bartók, Stravinsky and Schoenberg, link Britten's music firmly to the basic mid-century European preoccupation in composition, even though his styles seldom have much in common with those of his contemporaries. At a first hearing the listener is hardly aware of the cycle's profound unity: what captures attention is the 19-year-old composer's virtuoso display of contrapuntal ingenuity in a widely contrasted range of forms and textures that illumine the mood and meaning of his chosen texts.

Though the compositional techniques of *A Boy was Born* are seminal to Britten's later development, his subsequent choral works are markedly different in textures and word-setting. Except in some sections of the *War Requiem* he never wrote such elaborate vocal counterpoint again. The nine years which preceded his next important choral work, the *Hymn to St Cecilia*, contained much that stimulated his dramatic powers and bore fruit in his first opera *Paul Bunyan*, but his treatment of words was more immediately transformed by the influence of W. H. Auden's verse, by his discovery of Purcell's music (which seems not to have begun till after *A Boy was Born* was finished), and by the increasing virtuosity his musical style demanded of its performers. The orchestral song-cycle *Our Hunting Fathers* is the crucial work that epitomizes Britten's new treatment of words, but little if anything of its character appears in the *Ballad of Heroes* for tenor solo, chorus and orchestra written three years later. While this memorial to the men of the British Battalion of the International Brigade who died in the Spanish Civil War is hampered by Auden's and Randall Swingler's poor texts, it contains several prophetic features: trumpet fanfares; recitatives punctuated by brief orchestral comments (foreshadowing passages in the *War Requiem*); and the first of Britten's many ground-bass movements in its Scherzo, in which a ten-bar bass accompanies a simple tune of the type employed for the audience songs in *The Little Sweep*. An even more significant device occurs in the finale, where the regular bar patterns for Swingler's choral hymn are counterpointed by the tenor soloist declaiming Auden's poem to a melody of expanding phrase-lengths—a technique Britten used in many later contexts, notably the Sunday Morning scene in *Peter Grimes*.

Of the four choral works written in the years 1942–4, three quickly became favourites with audiences and performers. All are distinguished by a new quality in the treatment of words, a directness and apparent simplicity that it would be exaggerated to term dramatic, although very probably it was stimulated by the experience Britten gained in *Paul Bunyan*. For the first time Britten's choral writing approaches that of Purcell in vigour, force and delicacy, in the way word-rhythms and weight of syllables decisively influence the shape of melodic lines as well as of musical rhythms. The *Hymn to St Cecilia*, composed to a poem written for him by Auden, is the second of his five works for unaccompanied choir. His infrequent use of this medium may have stemmed from a desire to avoid the associations it carried from English part-songs and church music of the nineteenth and early twentieth centuries. Each is remarkably different from the others, the Auden setting being one of his most beautiful works. The beguiling ease and charm of its opening section arises from the combination of women's voices in 6/4 dance rhythms over a slower rhythm shared between the tenors and basses, whose sequential melody springs from that of the upper voices, but soon diverges from it. Superficially the texture follows the ancient pattern of a regular melody moving over an ostinato-like bass, but the phrases of both constituents are five bars long (linked in the bass but not in the upper parts), and the resultant persisting asymmetry in the internal phrase organization provides a momentum that maintains an almost unceasing rhythmical ebb and flow. The parallel chords and sequences of falling fourths produce continual tonal ambiguity; the women's major triads swing from E through A, F and B, returning to A, but because the bass patterns soon move to notes that momentarily convert the triads into sevenths, the way is opened for a freely modulating expansion that touches on, without ever settling in, tonalities remote from the basic E major. At the beginning the mingling of E and C major triads to accompany a 'white-note' scale suggests the Phrygian mode, but this does not become a certainty till the final bars. The first section concludes with a unison-octave repetition of the opening bars that serves as a refrain.

In the middle section scale patterns in mainly five-bar phrases cross and recross in free imitation over an implied E major triad pedal to evoke a child-like paradisal simplicity. When the pedal E abruptly changes to C major at the words

> *I am defeat*
> *When it knows it*
> *Can now do nothing*
> *By suffering*

the effect is startling because for the first time in the work the meaning of individual words and phrases is musically emphasized. The section closes with a harmonized version of the refrain, moving from A major through E to settle on a C major cadence that ushers in the opening A minor of the third section. Above six statements of a descending ostinato in the basses, moving in crotchets and slurred pairs of quavers, the three upper parts, in broad semibreve and minim rhythms, develop motifs combining the fourths and fifths of the first section into long lines, which fulfil the expectations aroused by the sudden harmonic change in the preceding section. The listener's attention is thus more and more strongly drawn to important emotive words. As the bass ostinato gradually begins to fluctuate and modulate, the urgency of the text draws the upper voices into imitation of the ostinato while the contrapuntal combinations produce the sharpest and most intense dissonances yet heard in the work. These relax for a moment as the upper voices take over the ostinato in an A major variant, but begin to return in the lament for lost innocence ('O weep, child, weep, O weep away the stain'), centred on the C major harmonies that have been heard from the beginning but whose full implication is only now revealed—a masterstroke of long-distance preparation. The final combination of the ostinato motif and its inversion, punctuated by solo recitatives, quickly re-explores the shifting implied tonalities of the first section before closing in a leisurely, expanded restatement of the refrain.

A Ceremony of Carols, composed like the *Hymn to St Cecilia* during his voyage home from the United States in 1942, is Britten's first work for boys' voices, though it has been frequently sung by girls and women. Preceded and followed by the plainsong antiphon 'Hodie' from the Christmas Eve Vespers, this cycle of medieval and sixteenth-century poems is permeated by small melodic cells derived from the chant, but the melody is restated fully only in the central harp interlude, where it is accompanied in block chords over ostinato patterns. The striking sonorities produced by the combination of treble voices and brilliant harp figurations display the composer's gift for producing new effects by simple means. In vocal textures which are mainly homophonic, Britten underlines the essentially dance-like styles of the majority of the movements; only in the fifth, eighth and ninth movements is counterpoint employed, though the unison song 'This little Babe' expands quasi-heterophonically into close canon for its final stanza. The vivid and immediately memorable melodies blend elements of modal, major and minor tonalities, so that although their tonal centres are arranged in a key-scheme of descending thirds, each encompasses a wide chromatic range that seems both logical and original. Despite the necessarily limited vocal compass and the continual crossing and recrossing of the vocal lines, the variety encompassed in this fifteen-minute work is remarkable, ranging from the sparsely accompanied monophony of 'That yongë child' to the clashing note-clusters evoking bells in the final 'Deo Gracias'.

Both the following two choral works, written during the period in which Britten worked on *Peter Grimes*, show greater precision of detail in matching verbal and musical rhythms than any of his previous works; in both, regular barring is abandoned when the texts require it. The festival cantata *Rejoice in the Lamb*, commissioned by St Matthew's Church, Northampton, sets a group of passages from the lengthy *Jubilate Agno* of the intermittently deranged eighteenth-century poet Christopher Smart. For such a text, so violently varied in styles and rhythms and mingling poetry with prose, selection is as essential an ingredient of the compositional process as the choice of notes; Britten's ten-section structure aptly reflects the poem's wayward changes but none the less is firmly based on a satisfying musical plan. Unified by basically simple and tradition-saturated material of scalic motifs and triadic harmonies, the work's fresh unconventional style is particularly notable in the declamatory asymmetric rhythms of the litanic second section, the delicate interplay of solo voices and organ in the passages dealing with Smart's cat Jeoffry and the mouse's 'personal valour', and the harmonic progressions of the quasi-Purcellian 'Hallelujah'.

The *Festival Te Deum* for St Mark's, Swindon, emphasizes its precise textural declamation by constantly varying metres (5/8, 7/8, 4/4) for the voices over an organ accompaniment moving in steady dotted rhythm—a metrical counterpoint exceptional in Britten's works. While the *Te Deum* does not equal *Rejoice in the Lamb* in melodic charm, both pieces illustrate Britten's fundamental approach when writing for amateur singers: without abdicating his personal idiom, he employed basically uncomplicated material in ways that led the performers out of traditional habits into new awareness of the musical possibilities of the English language, thus persuading them to accept styles and treatment that they would previously have rejected. The same is true of his later small occasional pieces, such as the *Hymn to St Peter*, Op. 56a, *Antiphon*, Op.56b, and *Psalm 150*, Op.67, for children's voices and instruments. In such works, as in his larger works for children, Britten effectively educated and prepared the new English audiences which were needed for the making and sustaining of a native operatic tradition.

The title of the *Spring Symphony* aroused much unfavourable comment at the first performance (1949) and for many years after. But what *is* a 'symphony'? During the four centuries from Giovanni Gabrieli's *Symphoniae Sacrae* to Shostakovich's Fourteenth Symphony (modelled partly on the *Spring Symphony*) the meaning of the term has varied so widely that today a composer can apply it in the manner of Humpty Dumpty: 'When *I* use a word, it means just what I choose it to mean—neither more nor less.' In an article printed shortly before the first performance, Britten justified the title by stressing its 'traditional four-movement shape', while pointing out that the movements were 'divided into shorter sections bound together by a similar mood or point of view'. This recalls the group of choral movements that constitute the second part of Mahler's Third Symphony, but an even stronger link with Mahler's Second Symphony (and through Mahler with Beethoven's Third, Fifth, and Ninth) is implied by the composer's choice of texts 'not only dealing with the spring itself but with the *progress* of winter to spring and the reawakening of the earth and life which that means' (my italics). The work's 'centre of gravity' lies at its end (as is true also of the Beethoven and Mahler works), the whole forming a unity in which each section maintains a momentum that reaches its culmination in the finale. Another, equally important, influence stems from the odes of Purcell, Blow and Handel.

But what is perhaps the most striking single feature of the *Spring Symphony*, its harmonic and tonal organization, owes nothing to the music of the previous three centuries; its springs from Britten's decision to end the work with the famous thirteenth-century 'Sumer is i-cumen in'. In its original form this is a four-part round with a tune built on alternating chords swinging to and from a C major triad. Although Britten does not use these particular chords, their static repetition has parallels in much of his harmonic writing (especially in the third section of the first movement, 'Spring, the sweet spring'). Here, as in many of his earlier and almost all his later works, Britten's harmonies do not move inevitably towards a cadence. Chords alternate with or follow one another but do not 'progress' in the sense that classical and Romantic harmonies do. Stravinsky used an analogous treatment of harmonies in the section of the third movement of his *Symphony of Psalms*. As the culmination of the *Spring Symphony*, 'Sumer is i-cumen in' must sound inevitable, as if the whole work had led up to it. Since the harmonies are 'non-progressive', the shifts in tonality that lead to the Finale's C major take place between sections rather than within them, though each part of a 'movement' ends in such a way as to lead to the next, a process effected more often by melodic than harmonic means. The opening of the introductory section of the first movement, 'Shine out, fair Sun', stresses the note B so as to make the listener expect it to move to and establish the tonality of C; instead, after a dozen bars, it leads away from C. The whole work is built on a tonal arch stretching from this deferred resolution of the opening B to the C major of 'Sumer is i-cumen in' that ends the Finale. Moreover, the main direction of the first movement's tonal shifts is also established by the same section: the opening B, hinting at a move to C, after many divergencies *en route* finally leads to A major for the second section, 'The Merry Cuckoo': a pattern of successive tonal centres, each either a second or third apart from the preceding one. The other sections are based on G major, E major and F major. The slow movement's sections are centred on D minor, B minor, and G minor, a pattern of thirds; while the third movement uses B flat major, A major, and G major, a chain of seconds. It can hardly be a coincidence that all the intervals of the 'Sumer' tune save three are either seconds or thirds.

Apart from this tonal scheme there is no unifying musical theme; nor are the forms employed in the individual sections obviously linked, though within each movement the sections share motifs that are subtly flexible. The orchestration, though often sharply contrasted from one section to the next (and here the baroque tradition of Purcell's and Handel's odes is most apparent), also, if paradoxically, underlines the work's essential unity. In the Introduction the gradual addition of instruments in successive orchestral interludes, until in the last the whole orchestra is playing, provides an impetus which lasts throughout the work, even though the full orchestra is not heard again till the Finale. From the end of the Introduction there is a gradual reduction in orchestral weight and power until the middle section of the second movement ('Waters above'), where the soloist is accompanied only by violins. After this another build-up continues so that by the end of the third movement only the harps, timpani and percussion are absent from the orchestral tutti. Within the Finale the contrasting alternation of instrumental groups returns, producing a sense of recapitulation, but the entire performing body, instrumental and vocal, is simultaneously involved only when the 'Sumer' tune arrives.

Fundamental to the work's symphonic approach is the Introduction's long duration, which almost equals that of the entire fourth movement. The gradually increasing lengths of the alternating choral and orchestral paragraphs, the growing tonal ambiguity of the timpani's opening tritone B–F, the widening melodic intervals and longer motifs of the successive orchestral passages—all convey the sense of breadth and long-scale planning that a symphonic work requires. A contributing factor is the forward impetus provided by the shifting tonalities: although in all the sections after the first the tonal centres are clear, nearly all are coloured by bitonal implications. By the end of the first section the F of the opening has effectively changed enharmonically to E sharp, leading to the F sharp minor triad at the second section's opening which propels the tonality to A. But this fluctuates between major and minor (with hints of C and F majors, its mediant and submediant), so that when the central section of the first movement arrives ('Spring, the sweet spring') its alternating mingled chords of G and D major seem inevitable. The resulting stressing of C sharp not only provides a Lydian colouring to G major but, more important, re-emphasizes the fundamental role of the tritone which permeates the work in many different ways that cannot be detailed here. One further example must suffice. In 'Waters above', the 'still centre' not only of the second movement but of the whole work, both the tenor solo's arching melody and the shimmering rain patterns in the accompanying violins are based not so much on the ostensible B minor of the key signature but on the ancient Locrian mode (beginning on the seventh note of the major scale), whose fifth note is a tritone above its fundamental. (There is a foreshadowing here of the evocative use of this mode for the 'Tadzio' theme in *Death in Venice*.) The unanalytical listener perceives the work's unity even if he is unaware of the means by which it is achieved; the work is indeed a symphony, albeit of a markedly original kind, whose overall structure transcends its superficially cantata-like mixture of solo and choral sections.

Written ten years after the *Spring Symphony*, the *Cantata Academica* and the *Missa Brevis in D* are Britten's first published works to Latin texts. Since no one nowadays learns Latin as his mother tongue, it cannot be regarded as a living language (the ecclesiastical argot of Roman seminarians notwithstanding). Not having the experience of variable speech intonations and rhythms such as moulded his settings of English, French and Italian, Britten followed Stravinsky's example in *Oedipus Rex* and treated his texts as 'phonetic material', though he never, in either of these works or in the

War Requiem, imitated the older composer's frequent disregard of basic stresses and syllabic quantities. The pedestrian text of the *Cantata Academica*, commissioned for the quincentenary of the University of Basle, could only be so treated, for a composer can hardly be inspired by such statements as 'With equity in teaching and learning is united a friendliness towards strangers.' Britten uses the words mainly to provide a rhythmic foundation for a joyful extrovert work that blends student exuberance (especially in the frequent choral unisons, the 6/8 rhythms in the Scherzo, and the tenth movement's *canto populare*) with the devices of musical academicism: canon, fugue and ostinato. Another ostensibly 'academic' device is the use of a thirteen-note *tema seriale* (the first note is repeated as the last of the series), each of the thirteen movements being based on the corresponding note of the series, which usually takes the form of a pedal sustained more or less throughout the movement. This pattern is broken only by the seventh movement, which is based on the seventh and eighth serial notes, because the eighth movement presents the *tema* complete (the only time it is heard in the work). Apart from this there is no serial organization, and the cheerful tonality is worlds apart from the expressionist harmonies of the Second Viennese School. Britten's playful ingenuities produce music which is congenial to both vocal and instrumental performers and which transcends, as does Brahms's 'Academic Festival' Overture, the occasion for which it was written, meriting its continuing success with audiences.

The short movements of the *Missa Brevis* composed for the boys of Westminster Cathedral Choir and their director, George Malcolm, enhance the liturgical action rather than delay it (as so frequently happens with settings of the Mass Ordinary). In this, one of his most attractive yet poignant works, Britten exploits the almost wind-instrument timbre that was a notable result of Malcolm's training. The bright yet often harshly dissonant sounds derive much of their effectiveness from taut motivic organization. There is a new concentration of technique, rare in previous works, that seems to anticipate aspects of his style after the *War Requiem*. The fundamental unit, descending intervals of second and third spanning a fourth, derives from inversion of the *Gloria*'s plainsong intonation: a basic note-shape of European music that Britten had already used extensively in *A Boy was Born*. Parallel sixth chords accompanying this motif in the *Kyrie* juxtapose unrelated chords to produce at times a restless chromaticism, elsewhere a tonality based on triads linked by thirds (D, F sharp, A, and C). Everywhere the interval of the fourth predominates, whether in the dancing 7/8 dialogues between voices and organ of the *Gloria* or in the descending scale patterns of the *Benedictus*. The most chromatic vocal writing occurs in the *Sanctus*, where overlapping entries of a motif built from fourths produce a brief twelve-note series; but a D major triad pedal anchors this passage firmly to a tonal foundation. Much of this little masterpiece contains hints of the *War Requiem* already in progress during its composition, the *Agnus Dei* most strongly, especially in the urgently insistent 'Dona nobis pacem', whose final cadence (where alternating chromatic chords collapse on a second-inversion D minor triad) has no precedent in Britten's earlier writing. The scoring for boys' voices is an object-lesson in producing unusual sounds by the simplest means. Every line is easy to pitch and memorable in its brevity yet, in contrapuntal or homophonic combination against the organ's largely independent accompaniment, tests ears and timing to the utmost without ever straying into the realms of impracticability.

The *War Requiem*, one of the monumental masterpieces of our century, is rightly regarded as a watershed in Britten's career. It gathers together elements from all his past experience of writing operas, choral works and songs into a wholly original synthesis which is not, as has been said, a combination of oratorio and song-cycle, but a setting of liturgical texts with poetical commentary. The liturgical propriety demonstrated in the *Missa Brevis* is equally evident here, revealing an understanding of the liturgical forms and functions of the musical portions of the Mass Ordinary and Proper almost unmatched in the past three centuries. Though the work was not designed for the liturgy, an awareness of its liturgical structure is essential to a proper understanding of its unique nature. Wilfred Owen's poems can be regarded in the medieval sense as tropes to the liturgical movements, their choice and positioning being an essential element of the compositional process. Their special character is underlined by their being confined to the tenor and bass soloists with a chamber orchestra, whereas the Latin texts are distributed between two other groups: the boys' choir accompanied by chamber organ, and the soprano solo, chorus and full orchestra. These three groups do not mingle till the end of the final movement. The contrasts between the chamber group and the rest, the dramatically emphasized relevance of the poems to the liturgical texts, and especially the sense of urgency in the work's message, reveal the experienced opera composer. In this profoundly felt expression of passionate conviction, Britten avoids the elaborate thematic development of *The Turn of the Screw* and the motivic complexes of *Billy Budd* and *A Midsummer Night's Dream*. Moreover, though there are many melodic and rhythmic patterns that provide thematic cross-references and interrelations which deepen in meaning and impact with each successive hearing, there is nothing resembling symphonic treatment. The result is a direct and simple style appropriate to the work's apocalyptic blend of grief and warning.

The *Requiem aeternam* shows Britten's awareness of an introit's ancient processional function; its slow dragging string melody, whose successive phrases increase in length, dynamics and orchestration, provides a powerful opening that immediately strikes the listener as the commencement of a large-scale work. In sharp contrast with this melody's fundamental D minor is the bell's tritone, F sharp–C, an interval of paramount importance throughout the work, both unifying and ambiguous. Its notes are immediately taken up by the chorus for monotonic intonation of the Latin text. The boys' unison melody in mainly uniform rhythm for the psalm versicle 'Te decet hymnus' has the tritone notes for its beginning and end, but its re-entrant curves also emphasize another tritone, B–F; so that with the second phrase, starting on F sharp and inverting the first, the complete span mingles suggestions of F and F sharp tonalities. This ambiguity is heightened by the accompanying organ triads, which embrace all twelve notes. The calm and quasi-liturgical mood of this section is typical of all the boys' music and is what keeps it distinct from the rest. As the melody closes, settling on the two initial tritonal notes, it leads to a condensed repeat of the 'Requiem' section. This, like the first, ends on the tritone, but with bells suddenly displaced by harp arpeggios over a striding bass derived from the string theme at the beginning of the movement. These elements provide the material for the chamber orchestra's accompaniment to the first Owen setting, 'Anthem for Doomed Youth'. Here the tritone, pervading the orchestral harmonies and the declamatory phrases of the tenor line, is grimly ironic, its previous link with the *Requiem aeternam* belied by the orchestra's onomatopoeic suggestions of gunfire. Only in the sonnet's sestet, 'Not in the hands of boys', do its earlier associations return in the oboe's repetition of the 'Te decet hymnus' melody, whose figures are gradually incorporated in the tenor line. The concluding choral *Kyrie* crystallizes the tritonal figures from the earlier part of the movement into a series of chords whose threefold (slightly varied) statement leads the tritone to an F major triad. Here again Britten's feeling for liturgical function guides the musical form; the *Kyrie* being basically a litanic chant, its simple musical treatment not only emphasizes the verbal meaning but provides a moving coda to the movement. While earlier large-scale settings of the Requiem Mass had merged *Introit* and *Kyrie*, Britten, by placing the Owen setting between them, differentiates their separate functions and yet binds both in musical unity.

The *Dies irae*, despite the Owen interpolations, is more unified than most large-scale settings of this text. After the introductory 4/4 brass fanfares, the asymmetrical 7/4 metre of the opening chorus sets a basic mood of fear and uncertainty that colours to a greater or lesser degree all the movement's nine sections. Major and minor tonalities blur and blend throughout, following the implications of the initial trombone and trumpet motifs. These juxtapose G and B flat major triads, thus also reaffirming the basic tritone B–F; the D flat–G of the following horn motif links the tritone to the main tonal centre of the movement, G. Thematically all the sections employ in varied ways the material of these brass motifs, with the striking addition of a new figure (derived from the leaping string motif of the *Requiem aeternam*) at the entry of the soprano solo with 'Liber scriptus'. Many variants of this, both melodic and rhythmic, permeate the second and third choral sections, while the soprano solo in the 'Lacrimosa' is built on a freely melismatic inversion of it.

Britten brilliantly solves the problem arising from the text's continuous rhythm of trochaic tetrameters. (Purcell faced the same problem in Tate's libretto for *Dido and Aeneas*.) Though metrical asymmetry is the primary device that prevents the poetic rhythm from clogging the musical, there are also more subtle techniques, such as the shifts and contrasts of musical accent not only from one section to another but also within sections, and the rhythmic thickening produced by contrapuntal superimposition of successive stanzas simultaneously in the passage commencing 'Recordare Jesu pie'. Towards the movement's end the sections are shorter, in part reflecting the poem's change from three- to two-line stanzas, but the shortened phrases of the abbreviated restatement of 'Dies irae' also promote rhythmic variety. Yet the text is never distorted in accent or quantity. Britten never needs to imitate the variant (and incorrect) stresses that Stravinsky applies to the Latin of *Oedipus Rex*. By its formal, metrical, and rhythmic organization this setting of the *Dies irae* has a totally different effect from Verdi's; it does not evoke a vision of the Last Judgement but rather depicts the fearful sin-laden conscience of guilty mankind.

The refrain and verse-structure the Latin text of the Offertory, one of the very few in the Roman Missal that preserves the medieval responsorial form, are well suited to Britten's scheme of a slow introduction leading to a scherzo and 'trio', the latter consisting of Owen's bitter inversion of the biblical tale of Abraham and Isaac. Britten uses some material from his *Canticle II: Abraham and Isaac*, notably for the scalic motif of the scherzo. The tonal contrast of C sharp and G presents the basic tritone (for the first time in the work) as an opposition of keys. A melody for unison boys' voices, frequently unbarred and recalling the *Missa Brevis* in its punctuating organ arpeggio figures, sets the antiphon's first sentence. The second sentence, for full chorus and orchestra, ushers in the scherzo's fugue on the refrain text 'Quam olim Abrahae promisisti et semini ejus'. The fugal repetitions emphasize Abraham's promised multitudinous progeny, but when the same theme appears at the end of the 'trio' for the final lines of Owen's poem, 'But the old man would not so, but slew his son,— / And half the seed of Europe, one by one', the effect is grotesquely parodistic. As the tenor and baritone continually repeat the last half-line, the boys sing the Offertory versicle in a slower tempo—metrically unaligned with the main body because their music is totally unrelated to the fugal theme, yet to words that underline the murderous horror of the parody: 'We offer to thee, O Lord, a sacrifice of prayer and praise; do thou receive them on behalf of those souls whom we commemorate this day.' When the antiphon refrain returns, the fugue is inverted and sung *pianissimo*.

In any setting of the Requiem Mass, the *Sanctus* should receive completely different treatment from the other texts because in this part of the liturgy any hint of grief is irrelevant. For the *War Requiem* this contrast required stronger emphasis. The blazing theophany of the opening, one of those sublime simplicities that only genius can create, shows Britten's awareness that the *Sanctus* is neither hymn nor canticle but acclamation. Each section underlines this in a different manner. The solo soprano's clarion coloraturas, arching between and around the notes of the basic tritone and giving it entirely new meaning in the work's context, and the cumulative free and unaligned choral repetitions of 'Pleni sunt coeli', which become a tumultuous clamour, culminate in the triumphal D major of the exultant 'Hosanna's, echoed in close dialogue between chorus and orchestra. An interpolated G sharp gives this key a Lydian colouring in the solo soprano line of the *Benedictus*, which thus continues the tritone's new meaning. The effect of the 'Hosanna' is intensified on its return by reworking and abbreviation. The startling effect of the *Sanctus*—the only expression of joy in the entire work—is heightened by its being the first movement without an Owen interpolation. By placing the sonnet questioning the Resurrection *after* the *Sanctus*, Britten hints at the basic theological problem: how can man, saturated with sin, find redemption and thus gain Resurrection? The tritones in both the vocal melody and the accompaniment to the baritone's solo gradually reinstate the initial mood of grief, to which hopelessness is now added, the falling phrases and slackening rhythms finally settling on a low F sharp, four octaves below the pitch on which the *Sanctus* began.

The final F sharp of the *Sanctus* becomes the dominant of B minor, the key of the *Agnus Dei*, in which the liturgical text appears as a refrain to Owen's poem on a wayside Calvary and so emphasizes its final words:

> But they who love the greater love
> Lay down their life; they do not hate.

Thus the movement implies the answer to the query at the end of the *Sanctus*: only by the loving sacrifice of Christ can redemption be achieved. Britten underlines this by adding (unliturgically) 'Dona nobis pacem', the final response to the *Agnus Dei* in Masses for the Living, to the end of the movement. All the music springs from a five-note scale ostinato that fills in, and by inversion resolves, the basic tritone. Both the solo tenor and the choral unison melodies are closely linked to this ostinato, the 5/16 metre preventing the monotony that might arise from constant repetition of so short a motif. Musically and emotionally this movement is the summing up of the work's central message.

Liturgically the remaining Latin texts belong not to the Requiem Mass but to the Burial Service. Though it quotes from and paraphrases portions of the *Dies irae*, the *Libera me* is more ominous than the earlier text because it speaks not only of death and judgement but of eternal death. Britten therefore treats it in a far more terrifying manner which, though in musical terms it arises from the battlefield, evokes a cosmic cataclysm. The overall structure is a long *accelerando*, the main thematic elements being a short choral motif derived from 'Quid sum miser' in the *Dies irae* and the leaping string figure of the *Introit* (especially in the variant for 'What passing bells'), to which are added more figures from the *Dies irae* and other movements. As the orchestra increases its pace the chorus maintains its initial tempo, a metrical conflict generating great momentum. Towards the middle of this process the thematic material begins to disintegrate, especially when at the words 'Tremens factus sum ego' the soprano solo enters with a fragmented version of 'Rex tremendae'. At the height of the acceleration the theme in 7/4 metre of the *Dies irae* is beaten out in the orchestra while the chorus collapses in a flurry of scales. Then the roles reverse, the orchestra returning to the slow tempo and opening theme of the *Introit* while the chorus interject 'Libera me' in rapid repetitions that gradually decrease in frequency as the orchestral restatement of the *Introit* theme grows quieter and fades away into a *pianissimo* G minor triad. Over this a recitative dialogue begins for tenor and baritone on Owen's 'Strange Meeting', which tells of a soldier in a vision escaping down a long tunnel where he meets the ghost of an enemy soldier he has killed. The tenor's line is the more anguished, the baritone's moving more slowly, both being punctuated by thematic fragments from preceding movements in the chamber orchestra. In this, the most compelling and yet the simplest section of the work, forgiveness is offered and accepted as the slow string harmonies move gradually to settle on D. While the male soloists repeat their final 'Let us sleep now', the boys, to a slow scalic theme, commence the 'In paradisum' (which at a funeral accompanies the coffin's transport to its grave) thus making the finale, like the first movement, a processional. Gradually the chorus, solo soprano, and full orchestra take this up, the male soloists and chamber orchestra continuing to expand 'Let us sleep now' until all the performers are combined in quiet rich polyphony whose Lydian G sharps maintain the basic tritone, now seemingly purged of its previous significance. But the boys' 'Requiescant in pace' on the original F sharp–C tritone leads to a repetition of the *Kyrie*'s music, which, as before, closes on a bare fifth based on F—an apparently inconclusive ending which is none the less inevitable. In the light of history, no work could give an adequate assurance of an end to conflict, still less of peace. Concert audiences the world over have recognized the *War Requiem*'s timeless relevance to the human condition.

The Choral Music

After the *War Requiem*, Britten's main choral writing appeared in the church parables and the last operas. The eight smaller works he wrote in the years left to him do not employ the techniques of non-alignment and heterophony that he exploited in the dramas. The *Cantata Misericordium*, composed for the centenary of the Red Cross in 1963 to a Latin text by Patrick Wilkinson on the parable of the Good Samaritan, is scored for chamber forces: string orchestra and quartet, tenor and baritone soloists, harp, piano, and percussion. Its main key-centres, D and F sharp, engender a pattern of relationships of thirds which also influences the thematic material. The many short sections are linked into a continuous whole by the ritornello-like use of a string-quartet motif that expands and develops as the work proceeds. Though there are many felicities of vocal and instrumental colouring, this dramatic narrative has neither the excitement of the *Cantata Academica* nor, despite its theme, the urgency of the *War Requiem*. For this the dull Latin text may be partly to blame.

Voices for Today, commissioned for the celebration of the twentieth anniversary of the United Nations, has an unusual text: an anthology of short quotations, to be sung in the vernacular of the country in which it is performed, is followed by excerpts from Virgil's Fourth Eclogue (in Latin). The rapid treatment of the brief statements does not allow extended musical development. Only with the Eclogue does a more substantial and continuous shape appear, making the listener wish that Britten had chosen to set the entire Eclogue and omit the anthology. A *Welcome Ode* for young people's chorus and orchestra, to celebrate the Queen's Silver Jubilee visit to Suffolk, returns to a more pleasing and more obviously melodious style, charmingly appropriate to the occasion and its performers.

Compared with these occasional works, *Sacred and Profane*, eight medieval lyrics for five unaccompanied solo voices (or small choir) is quintessential Britten. These brief but compelling pieces are filled with pointed detail, economically used but striking material, and above all a response to the rhythms of language that seems to be lacking in the works to Latin or translated texts. They recall many aspects of Britten's choral style from *A Boy was Born* onward and form a fitting conclusion to his achievement in this field.

30

The Beggar's Opera[1]

HANS KELLER

It would seem upon reflection that the most important thing about Britten's version of *The Beggar's Opera* is Britten's version of *The Beggar's Opera*. We therefore propose to dispense with the by now customary Overture-potpourri on Gay, Pepusch, Hammersmith, Brecht–Weill, Dent and the rest, and to plunge instead straight into the Overture of Britten's realization, after reminding ourselves that, like *The Rape of Lucretia* and *Albert Herring*, this work is scored for chamber orchestra, i.e., solo wind—and string—quintets plus harp and percussion.

The Overture, itself a potpourri, introduces the characters through characteristic tunes, with Lucy, who in the opera appears last, coming first, and Peachum, the first to appear on the stage, coming last. Thus Peachum's first song is preceded by its variation in the Overture. The sinister central part (Ex.1b) of this potpourri stands in every way out against the rest. Founded on Mrs Peachum's 'If any wench Venus's girdle wear' (No.3;[2] Ex.1a), it is the only tune which, in the Overture and in the work, appears both in the same key and on the same scale degrees. This because it is the one and only *Leitmotiv*. As such it twice serves to link successive scenes. Its functional significance is further enhanced by the fact that it forms the only section in the Overture which refers to more than one subsequent number, for its threatening timpani figure (Ex.1b) forecasts not just that in Ex.1a, but, more so, the timpani in 'The charge is prepared' (No.52; Ex.1c). With this number the motto tune of Ex.1a–b is in fact linked before the last scene. The common key of these two tunes, E minor, functions, moreover, as '*Leit*-key', for it is exclusively used *re* Rope.

[1] From *Tempo*, No.10 (Winter 1948–9), pp.7–13.
[2] Numbers refer to the Britten realization and not to the Gay original [C.P.].

The Beggar's Opera

ACT I

Another exceptional key is the F minor of Peachum's opening air, 'Through all the employments of life' (which, like his subsequent duets, is marked by canonic imitations). F minor does not recur until Macheath's great scene at the end, which is followed by F major, the key of the Overture's first part. In point of fact F emerges as home tonality, despite the opera's end in G.

Ex.1a

As we now pass on to the song of the motto tune (No.3; Ex.1a), E minor emerges as the only key that has already previously been heard. And the timpani now impress us all the more incisively as this instrument has not been heard since the motto section in the Overture; the body of the opera, in fact, has so far been quite percussionless. Here as in the Overture, E minor is followed by the, throughout the opera, sexual key of D major, i.e. Mrs Peachum's 'If love the virgin's heart invade' (No. 4). This is accompanied by wind and interspaced by the strings, whose very consecutives are out to charm. But with 'A maid is like the golden ore' (No. 5), which concludes Mrs Peachum's trilogy, we return to her aggressive side. The air is set to a harsh C major accompaniment with the tune's initial rhythm persistently in the strings—the chord on the quaver being throughout a bare fifth on C, and the last chord a bare minor seventh on C. (In one performance Mrs Peachum here got herself into D major (*sic*). None of the perspicacious despisers of Britten's harmonies noticed it.)

Polly's (Purcell's) 'Virgins are like the fair flower' (No. 6, A minor), which has been treated in the Overture, is now introduced by a fairly long melodrama in which Polly talks while the instruments rest on a note or an actual rest. Such approach to the problem of melodrama, as cautious texturally as it is structurally captivating, is typical of the opera. Melodrama and air are tenderly scored. So is Polly's 'Can love be controll'd by advice?' (No. 8, G minor). Here the harp flows uninterruptedly through the piece, as in another song of beautifully simple tenderness, Filch's and the females' ''Tis woman that seduces all mankind' (No. 2, B flat).

At the end of Polly's last-mentioned (G minor) air, an unexpected turn to a wrong chord (A flat, yet retaining the G) returns us from her love to the alarming situation into which it has brought her. And in her 'I, like a ship in storms, was tossed' (No. 10, E flat) we recognize the counterpart to Lucy's 'I'm like a skiff on the ocean tossed' (A flat) in Act III; in either case the accompaniment forms a bridge between what the respective young lady describes and what she feels.

With 'A fox may steal your hens, Sir' (No. 11) we return to Mr and Mrs Peachum, to his predilection for canon, and to the initial tonality of F (major) which stays until the end of the scene. Ex.2 gives an idea

Ex.2

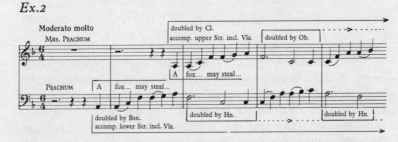

of the canon's texture. Horn and oboe respectively double the end-bars of Mr and Mrs Peachum's phrases, and since the phrases are two bars long and the canon is at the distance of one bar, these doublings alternate continuously. Harp and timpani run through and support the textural design. In the middle and at the end the voices and their orchestral groups rendezvous in a refrain.

Polly's 'The turtle thus with plaintive crying' (No. 13) will be recalled by its trembling flute solo. The tune ends sadly with

The Beggar's Opera

consecutive fifths in the phrases 'Paired in death, as paired in Love'. The instrumentation—flute, harp and strings only—is characteristic of Polly (see Nos. 33, 47 and 51 below).

A melodramatic interlude for Polly (No. 14) follows. It is first based on the motto theme (Ex. 1a), which works up to a climax and leads to a non-thematic section which approximates to the accompaniment of a secco recitative. This, however, is in its turn intensified and thus brings us to Macheath's entry, where the chorus sing the first phrase of his 'Pretty Polly, say' first in A flat, then in F, and then again a sixth further up in D. The dominant of the actual tune (in G minor) having thus been reached, Macheath introduces himself and the tune without a break; Polly and *omnes* join in. His 'Were I laid on Greenland's coast' (No. 16, B flat) is likewise taken up by Polly and the rest. It develops along a continuous quaver movement which persists in the harp, but passes from part to part in the wind, as in the moving texture of ''Tis woman that seduces all mankind' (No. 2, same key). In the present song the composer uses the partial identity of tune and refrain for putting the two on top of each other and letting them meet, go asunder, and meet again, as well as for imitating this vertical combination. In Polly's and Macheath's 'The miser thus a shilling sees' (No. 18, E flat), the mood of departure and separation is suggested in a variety of ways. For instance, the voices part into imitations as the couple turns to leave, and the tune departs rather than ends, in that the phrases are sustained and interrupted, but never concluded.

The Men of the Town's first quintet, 'Fill ev'ry glass' (No. 19), which has been announced in the Overture, returns us to F, but their second quintet, 'Let us take the road' (No. 20), is bitonal and bi-rhythmic: the 2/2 B flat accompaniment of Handel's tune is contrasted with 6/4 muted horn-calls in D flat which suggest the sound of coaches offstage. There is an exact, if germinal, precedent to this number in *Albert Herring*, Act II scene 1, where the *D major* accompaniment of Sid's 'I'd like to see him go for good' is (also bi-rhythmically) contrasted with the muted horn's festival motif in *F major, quasi* offstage—a harmonic, thematic, instrumental, and scenic parallel.

Macheath's 'If the heart of a man is depressed with cares' (No. 21), in which Woman is likened to a fiddle, is in the latter's characteristic key of D, with a coaxing violin solo. Ending itself, like many other numbers, melodramatically, it is followed by the melodrama of

Macheath and the Ladies (No. 22). This consists of interrelated solo cadenzas for various instruments (percussion included), which introduce the various Ladies. Again the violin starts off in D, basing its cadenza on its previous number (No. 21). At Macheath's words 'But hark! I hear music', the harp's C major arpeggio anticipates the accompaniment of the cotillon in the same key, which forms the second part of this number (No. 22): 'Youth's the season made for joys'. Jenny Diver and the Ladies come back to D for their 'Before the barn-door crowing' (No. 23), whose crowing figure in consecutive major seconds derives from the previous melodrama (No. 21). But with 'The gamesters and lawyers are jugglers alike' (No. 24), of which the Overture has given us an unknowingly gay version, the Ladies lead us again to F, and the unknowing Macheath to his imprisonment. The whole spoken dialogue which, in the libretto, succeeds this number and precedes the arrest is here embedded in the music. By the time, however, that Jenny starts to speak, while the Ladies continue their treacherous tune with closed, indeed frozen lips, the listener is so well acquainted with the tune and the nature of the accompaniment that he is able to take in both dialogue and music despite the expanding texture. Tension increases, the Ladies' humming gradually grows into an 'Ah!', and upon a climactic crash chord Macheath is arrested. His own 'At the tree I shall suffer with pleasure' (No. 25) is in the heroic key of C in which we have last heard him, in a happier mood (No. 21).

ACT II

Macheath's 'Man may escape from rope and gun' (No. 26) in the 'rope'-and-motto-key of E minor, introduces for the first time the cor anglais. Combined with strings only, it assumes a solo role in Lucy's first number (No. 27), which is also the first A major number: 'Thus when a good housewife sees a rat'. The instrumentation contrasts her with Polly. Macheath's 'The first time at the looking-glass' (No. 29), where horn and harp 'mirror' the ends of phrases by imitating them, is in the same key, as is Lockit's first number (No. 30), 'When you censure the age', with its tough consecutives.

Lucy's 'Is then his fate decreed, Sir?' and Lockit's 'You'll think ere many days ensue', are combined in a duet (No. 31) in which the affinities between these tunes are made to serve their impeccable integration. First comes Lucy in the, again, unprecedented key of

D minor, her phrases being always anticipated by strings, harp, bassoon and horn, and accompanied by flute, cor anglais and clarinet. After she has sung through her tune and repeated its first phrase, Lockit enters in G minor with his. The first-mentioned orchestral group now accompanies him and alternates, as before, with the other repetitions of her first phrase. Eventually voices and their instrumental groups concur (cf. No. 11), and it now looks for a moment as if Lucy would come round to Lockit's key. The opposite, however, happens: Lockit turns all D minor while Lucy gives up. Far from indicating that he has given way to her, his triumphant acquisition of her key invests his 'Twang dang dillo dee' with sharp yet subtle irony.

After Polly's 'Thus when the Swallow seeking prey' in E flat (No. 32; flute, harp and strings only: cf. Nos. 13, 47, 51) we get another combined number (No. 33, B flat), this time a trio, Macheath's 'How happy could I be with either' and Polly's and Lucy's 'I'm bubbled, Oh how I am troubled'. First Macheath sings his tune in 21/8, then the girls babble theirs in 27/8. Thereupon the combinations indicated in Exx. 3a and 3b ensue. The accompaniment proceeds in the same scheme of accents as do the voices, i.e., 7/4 to 21/8 and 9/4 to 27/8. It is, however, at the same time marked by cross-accents throughout, on the third, fifth and seventh beats in 7/4, and on the second, fourth,

Ex.3a

Ex.3b

seventh and ninth beats in 9/4. (The strong beats of the bar fall on the first, fourth and sixth beats in 7/4, and abnormally on the first, third, fifth and eighth beats in 9/4.)

Polly's and the chorus's 'Cease your funning' in F (No. 34) is movingly constructed as a canon at the half-bar, and at organically varying intervals of imitation. The culmination is reached in the middle as Polly, here doubled by the sopranos, is imitated at the octave by men, harp and bass. The duet (No. 35) of Polly and Lucy also starts in F, but modulates immediately and snappishly to the opera's first E major, Lucy's furious 'Why how now, Madam Flirt!' whence an equally enraged modulation leads to Polly's 'Why how now, saucy Jade!' in the opera's first F sharp major. Mutual rage increases upon a renewed modulation to E, when the two shout at each other in canon at the higher third and at a half-bar's distance, which involves some (rather) cross rhythm, not to speak of the notes. Everyone on and below the stage participates in the last piece of the act, 'No power on earth can e'er divide' (No. 36), which, like the previous duet, increases in excitement as it moves up a tone, i.e. from G major to A major. Thence it again jumps up to B flat major, and the tension which thus and otherwise accumulates leads up to, and is released by, Macheath's release.

ACT III

The final act opens in the relative minor (G) of the last-heard key with Lucy's 'When young at the bar' (No. 37). G minor is also the key in which the act closes. Next follows Lucy's 'My love is all madness and folly' (No. 38) in E flat, which is enclosed by her outcry 'Ungrateful Macheath!' This (originally spoken) sentence is here impressively set in the minor. Of Lockit's F sharp minor 'Thus gamesters united in friendship are found' (No. 39), in triple time, we have heard a relative major version in duple time in the Overture. The tune now appears as a powerfully malicious *maestoso* for the whole orchestra, with an unsociable dotted quaver rhythm in the strings.

Macheath's and the chorus's Lilliburlero 'The modes of the court so common are grown' (No. 40, G major) has also been heard in the Overture, where indeed it has ended at almost the same inconclusive point as it now does. It is preceded by a lengthy melodramatic introduction for the Speaker in which the harp's parallel and open fifths and hidden octaves stress the weird mood that underlies the, on the surface, jolly tune. This introductory music then serves to connect the phrases of the song.

In the D major duet 'What gudgeons are we men!' (No. 41), Lockit imitates Peachum's second strophe freely, as well as, at the end, strictly on the dominant. But there is one striking staccato motif at the beginning of Lockit's part to the words 'that hath been trapped' which characterizes the gaoler all the more sharply since it constitutes his only non-imitational bar.

Though Lucy's 'I'm like a ship on the ocean toss'd' (No. 43, A flat) has already been mentioned, it might be added here that the comparison she makes is not only interpreted by the course of the accompaniment as such, but that even the instruments are 'toss'd': the strings overlap throughout, with the viola on top of the first violin.

With the entry of Polly, three numbers follow which between them make up the episode between the two girls that leads up to Lucy's poisoning attempt. The airs are therefore linked with one another by means of an interesting diatonic suspense. I.e. at the end of the duet 'A curse attends a woman's love' in B flat (No. 44) an ascending chromatic motion leads logically to a D flat which, however, assumes a mysterious significance in that it is left alone by the harmony, sustained, and not resolved: it ends the duet melodramatically. Our expectancy as to the meaning of this D flat is roused and, sure enough, it reappears, again singly and melodramatically, at the beginning of Polly's 'Among the men, coquets we find' (No. 45; flute and strings only). Indeed at first it seems as if we had already arrived at a (re)solution, for the accompaniment of this song starts off A flattishly, with the D flat in apparent dominant seventh function. Anon, however, we find ourselves in E flat, and the D flat, which runs through the air's flute figure, ending up once more as unaccompanied accompaniment to the dialogue, still awaits diatonic elucidation. At last, when we reach Lucy's 'Come, sweet lass' (No. 46, F sharp), we find it as (enharmonically changed) dominant in the clarinet figure which again starts and runs through the number. We have arrived—an impression which is reinforced by this tune's having opened the Overture.

The single C with which this last number ends, after a few bars of melodrama, is the tonic of the women's duet that opens the next episode upon Macheath's return to custody: 'Hither, dear husband, turn your eyes' (No. 47) and which leads to Macheath's enthralling outburst, 'Which way shall I turn me, how cán I decide' (No. 48, G major).

The three airs which now ensue form again a dramatic unity in that they comprise the women's pleading and the father's reaction, and they are linked in a similar way, indeed by the same note, as Nos. 44–6. Polly's D minor 'When my hero in court appears' (No. 49; once more flute and strings only) is distinguished by a beautifully wailing phrase for the flute which appears in straight form at the beginning and inverted at the end, thus starting and finishing the D minor air upon a C sharp. Now follows Lucy's 'When he holds up his hand' in G minor (No. 50), which finishes, enharmonically speaking, with the same single note in the oboe's solo part. And again, as in No. 46, the D flat turns into C sharp in order to become the dominant of an F sharp number, which here is in the minor: 'Ourselves, like the great, to secure a retreat' (No. 51). This is a canon *ad unisonum* between Lockit and Peachum, accompanied by wind only, in a very light texture which lets plenty of air in.

In strong contrast, 'The charge is prepared' (No. 52; Ex.1c) is sung and played by everyone. As Macheath is conducted out by all, this 6/4 march develops into the most threatening version of the motto tune (Ex.1a), the only singer now being Mrs Peachum. True to both its dramatic significance and its structural function, the motto forms the transition to the last scene, or rather scena, 'The Condemned Hold', into which it leads without a pause.

This imposing piece enlarges upon a device that has already previously been applied, i.e. the interruption and sustaining of phrases. The ten tunes of Macheath's scena, that is, develop not so much over as in between a frequently interrupted ostinato (see Ex.4), which derives from the last tune, 'Greensleeves'. Though the tunes begin with a handicap, in that the first of them starts off after the theme has once been stated and its first phrase repeated, they show a firm determination to catch up. And indeed, the tenth and last tune, 'Greensleeves', coincides with the tenth complete statement of the theme (Ex.4).

Ex.4

MACHEATH Since laws were made... for ev'- ry de - gree.... To curb vice in oth-ers, as well as me

(ostinato)

The Beggar's Opera

Lucy's, Polly's and Macheath's F major trio, 'Would I might be hanged' (No. 54) in which gong and cymbal work themselves up to an appropriately deadly noise which an over-reverberate theatre is unable to take, is followed by Macheath's reprieve. This anticlimax cannot, alas, be part of the musical structure (as that in *Herring*),[3] but has of course to occur in the spoken dialogue. The listener consoles himself, however, with the final G minor—major—minor dance, 'Thus I stand like the Turk' (No. 55).

[3] See above, p.132 [C.P.].

31

The Purcell Realizations[1]

ERIC ROSEBERRY

The happy fusion of Britten's exceptional talents as performer and composer attains complete fulfilment, perhaps, in his activity as an interpreter of the music of Henry Purcell—a figure with whom Britten has strong creative affinities, and possibly the greatest single influence on the development of his own vocal and operatic style.

Apart from the many musicological problems which arise in producing a modern practical edition of music belonging to a lost tradition of performance, there is one important aspect of bringing Purcell's music to life which is highly congenial to a vocal composer of Britten's eclectic disposition: the 'realization' of the continuo bass, a tradition of improvisation which, within the limits of the harmonic implications of the 'given' lines to be filled in, is surely no 'humdrum activity' (as Jack Westrup, drily deprecating the term 'realization', once described it) but a stimulating creative challenge. In Britten's view it is the invention of lively figuration and appropriate textures to supply what he calls one's '*personal* reaction to the song' (my italics).

In the preface to their edition of Purcell's works, Britten and Peter Pears refer to those many arrangements which 'do not seem to us to contain much of the Purcellian spirit'. We are indeed all familiar with such editions, in which the 'filling up' consists of a kind of petrified academic cement whose only guiding principle seems to have been the avoidance of consecutive fifths and anything approaching a true keyboard style. Reacting strongly against this, Britten writes: 'Purcell has provided in these given parts a firm and secure musical structure which can safely hold together and make sense of one's wildest

[1] Edited from *Tempo*, No. 57 (Spring 1961), pp. 7–28.

fantasies.'[2] Let it be said immediately, however, that Britten's own 'wildest fantasies' are controlled by a practical musician's intimate knowledge of Purcell's own style: where he has been bold he has done no more than take a hint from Purcell's own extraordinary strangeness, and in no place could it be said that 'the rules of the game' have been broken.

Let us examine the five skilfully chosen songs from *Orpheus Britannicus*, a sequence which could easily form an admirable recital group. They are progressive in key-scheme (A major–A minor–B flat major (Nos 3 and 4)–G major), unified in subject-matter (each dealing with some aspect of love), and contrasting in mood (love-sickness—despair—triumph—carefree cynicism—happy contentment). Practical recital experience has taught Britten and Pears that some introduction is necessary to prepare the audience for the sweet, subtle mood of 'I attempt from Love's sickness to fly', so it is prefaced by a gentle four-bar introduction in simple four-part harmony (Ex.1). The

Ex.1

perfectly acceptable consecutive fifths in the piano's left-hand part of bar 2 announce unmistakably on the first page that the arranger is not too inhibited by text-book rules of traditional harmony when creating an appropriate keyboard texture above Purcell's bass. Britten's accompaniment of Purcell's beautiful melody sustains this texture, with occasional octave doublings in treble and bass of the keyboard part for added emphasis, and more quaver movement to emphasize Love's power 'to make us seek ruin'. Effective here is a most truthful use of the poignant false relation (a device Britten puts to good use in all his Purcell realizations) against the bass in the upper keyboard part.

The second song, 'I take no pleasure', is very much akin to Dowland both in its desolate, restless mood of hopelessness and in the wandering, almost haphazard tonality of the extraordinarily asym-

---

[2] 'On Realizing the Continuo in Purcell's Songs', *Henry Purcell 1659–1695: Essays on his Music*, ed. Imogen Holst (Oxford University Press, 1959), pp. 7–13.

metrical cadential scheme. (It sets out in A minor; the cadences at the end of each six-bar period are on E minor, C major, D major, and G major, before the final A minor full close!) As if to reinforce this affinity, the keyboard texture suggests lute-like figuration. Sharp false relations between Purcell's melody and Britten's figuration in the treble part underline the singer's grief and pain.

In the third song, 'Hark the ech'ing air', Britten concentrates on word-painting to match the happy naïvety of Purcell's setting. Bright staccato fanfares imitate the sound of trumpets and oboes and snappy grace notes the clapping of the 'pleased Cupids' wings'. To introduce 'Take not a woman's anger ill' there is a flippant ostinato-like texture of two bars built over the first four notes of Purcell's bass. This provides a *perpetuum mobile* figure to accompany the whole song. The crisp, clashing major and minor seconds in the right hand of the piano part recall a very personal feature of Britten's own harmonic style, and yet surely Purcell himself would have been delighted with such a happy *trouvaille* on the part of a continuo player. Very Brittenish, too, is the pert and adroit postscript. The seemingly unstoppable momentum of the song is slowed down by means of a rapid *diminuendo* and a couple of rests—an irresistible touch of licence at the end of what is after all a licentious song.

'How blest are Shepherds' brings the group to a close in a mood of happy contentment. The concise eight-bar introduction paraphrases Purcell's melody and harmony. Of special note are the imaginative changes of texture at the repeat of each phrase. Sensitive artistic restraint is displayed in reserving the word-painting for the *repeat*, after the textural realization of the first phrase has emphasized the all-important warmth and serenity of the song. Each repeat is treated as a sprightly echo of the first phrase with the bass rhythmically altered. Here the word-painting is by no means naïve: the 'drums and trumpets' are there, but heard, as it were, through the ears of the lovers, transfigured beyond their real, cruel significance. This is inspired work, matching one of Purcell's most inspired melodies.

Britten's meaningful directions at the head of each arrangement— 'with gentle movement', 'slow and melancholy', 'quick and brilliant', 'gracefully flowing'—all convey something definite and, moreover, something of the true Purcellian spirit. Together with an almost Mahlerian scrupulousness of phrasing and dynamic detail, they reveal the editor's concern to make his intentions clear. Others may feel these songs differently, but there can be no doubt about the immediacy and sharp precision of Britten's sympathetic reaction to the original conception.

The powerful dramatic scena *The Blessed Virgin's Expostulation* provides ample scope for invention in the continuo accompaniment, and Britten has risen to the occasion magnificently, alert to every hint in the highly expressive vocal line. Here too we find a skilful translation of the harpsichord-with-cello-bass idiom into modern piano technique: tremolandi to create a sustained *crescendo* effect, snappy ornaments, dry staccati, abrupt dynamic contrasts, arresting unisons in double octaves, transposition of register (as in 'No Vision from above?'), and so on. In Britten's imaginative treatment of the most dramatic episode (Ex.2) the texture and caesura-cleft vocal line forcibly recall that terrifying moment of recitative over chromatic timpani with staccato string chords in the Wordsworth setting in the *Nocturne* ('The rest was conjured up from tragic fictions . . .'). The

Ex.2

drooping chromatics of the piano texture over the diatonic bass furnish a moving background for the broken farewells to hope in Purcell's own chromatic vocal line—and at the same time establish a surprising harmonic link with Mozart's chromatic textures.

Eloquent, too, is the idea of inventing a touching rhythmical canon in a clear right-hand register of the piano as Mary recalls vanished contentment in a wistful arioso. Purcell's grief-laden melismata in 'Oh! I fear the Child' are yet further intensified by Britten in searing semitonal clashes of piano against voice as the bass plunges downwards towards the fearful full close.

Edward J. Dent's worthy version of *Dido and Aeneas* (1925) enjoyed unrivalled supremacy for many years, but in the absence of a living tradition of performance no edition can be regarded as final, and Britten's fresh, practical ideas on Purcell performance, coupled with new research on the only two manuscripts known to exist (at Tenbury and at Oki, Japan), fully justify the lively, reliable and practicable performing edition he has made in collaboration with Imogen Holst.

Each generation approaches its inheritance of old music from a new angle, and where taste and conjecture play a necessary part in deciding certain questions, what was rejected thirty-five years ago in all good faith as a copyist's error may easily be accepted today as the composer's original intention—especially when new evidence supports it. Music editing has now, we may be sure, progressed beyond the stage of such 'streamlining' and 'smoothing out' as we find in the emasculated Handelian versions of Purcell produced in the eighteenth and nineteenth centuries, but musicians will still disagree violently over an all-important question such as a sharp or natural in an unfigured chord. In such a situation, the harmonic intuition of a composer of Britten's operatic experience is not to be dismissed lightly. I shall comment on the Britten–Holst version from three angles: the purely *harmonic* treatment of the continuo part; Britten's *textural* and *figurative* ideas in realizing the harpsichord part; and the general editing of the instrumental and choral numbers, together with new rhythmical interpretations of certain ambiguous passages (the editors have sensibly provided in the piano part of the vocal score a *playable* and musical adaptation of the string parts).

It is only to be expected that with the raising of 'the norm of dissonance' in the significant music of our time Britten's harmonic interpretation of certain unfigured sections of the continuo part is considerably more venturesome than Dent's. And yet in no such place can the decision be rejected as 'Brittenish' rather than 'Purcellian'. Such personal characteristics as Purcell's own use of false relations and diatonic discords are seized upon to give harmonic vitality to the continuo part. Dent tends to play safe with more 'regular' (in the textbook sense) chord progressions and cadential formulae, smoothing out the accompanying harmony to bring it into line with the voice part itself. Ex.3 demonstrates Britten's preference for the more

Ex.3

pungent root position chord on III to Dent's more insipid first inversion of I. The following examples reveal something of Britten's application of the idiomatic false relation to his harmonic textures. In Dido's 'I am prest with torment' he intensifies the already tormented line with a cruel B flat in the continuo part clashing against Dido's B natural. (The B flat occurs logically as the result of the application of ostinato technique in the accompaniment, but it remains an inspired 'accident'.) In the same aria, at the memorable change to G minor for 'I languish till my grief is known', the F natural/F sharp clash is between the upper parts of the keyboard texture itself, the tied F natural carrying the tension through to the next bar before it is gradually relaxed. In the realization of Belinda's recitative, 'A tale so strong and full of woe / Might melt the rocks as well as you', the bass G at 'woe' is open to a major or minor interpretation. Dent's solution follows the textbook rule of never sounding a note against its harmonic resolution (a 'rule' more honoured in the breach than in the observance in Purcell's own string and chorus parts!); Britten's inspired decision is to make the harpsichord part *major*, which clashes with poignant effect against the *minor* approggiatura inflection of the voice part. A final example of an effective false relation in the keyboard texture is offered in the witches' duet 'But ere we this perform we'll conjure for a storm'. Here a direct hint may have been taken from the 'Dance of the Furies' which finishes the act. In this context, it serves to drive home the preposterous malice of the witches.

An interesting—because personal to Britten—harmonic solution of the unfigured bass occurs in the second chord of the continuo realization of the first bar of 'Fear no danger'. Does the G in the bass imply a 6–4 C major chord, as the voice parts would suggest to a harmonically conditioned reflex? Or is Britten's more rugged dominant chord, clashing against the tonic major third of the voice parts, a more Purcellian solution? True, some of Britten's most fruitful and characteristic harmonic situations are the result of the simultaneous sounding of tonic and dominant, and to realize the bars in this manner must have been gratifying to Britten the composer, whose inner promptings he was no doubt obeying at this juncture. But no one with a knowledge of Purcell's own craggy diatonic discords in his string and chorus parts could condemn his robust enterprise as un-Purcellian. A not dissimilar harmonic situation arises in the realization of the first five bars of the witches' 'But ere we this perform', where a repeated dominant major chord in the right hand clashes against the left hand's sustained tonic minor on the last beat of each bar, momentarily recalling the same kind of harmonic thought that we find in the first song of *Winter Words*.

Elsewhere, Britten's more remarkable deviations from Dent's harmonic treatment occur as a result of his uncompromising habit of realizing Purcell's bass as a plain chord to clash with the ornamental appoggiaturas of Purcell's expressive vocal line. How moving, for instance, is the harmonic effect of the diminished seventh chord sounding against the prolonged, harmonically 'inessential' note A of Purcell's voice part in Dido's poignant recitative after Aeneas' final departure (Ex.4; Dent's smoother solution is to treat the A as an *essential* harmonic note in the continuo part). For a cadential example of the same kind of harmonic treatment of the bass and vocal line we must examine the close of Aeneas' recitative 'Let Dido smile and I'll defy / The feeble stroke of destiny'. Whereas Dent interprets the bass as a conventional 6–4 approach to a V–I cadence, Britten rejects a 6–4 implication on the first beat and boldly sounds the dominant chord against its resolution in the voice part—a very Brittenish harmonic stroke, and yet not un-Purcellian either. A similar clash of dominant chord against tonic 'resolution' in the voice part occurs quite

Ex.4

[Very slow]

But Death, a - las! I can - not shun; Death must come when he is — gone

unambiguously in Aeneas' later meditation 'But ah! what language can I try / My injur'd queen to pacify?' The 6–4 approach to a perfect cadence was by no means a matter of routine in Purcell.

Two other harmonic details must suffice—in this case a matter of textual reading, not realization. This clearly reveals Britten's acceptance of a tougher norm of dissonance than Dent was prepared to concede to Purcell. In 'To the hills and the vales', at the words 'the triumphs of love and of beauty be shown', Dent could not accept the melodic downward leap of an augmented fourth in the soprano part, and the consequent consecutive sevenths between soprano and bass of the chorus parts; nor could Cummings before him. Dent changed the soprano E to C and the alto G to F. Britten, instinctively disposed to these pungent diatonic discords, found that the Oki and Tenbury manuscripts were at one on this point, and accepted this 'tough' passage as Purcell's original intention. Another new textual reading, with interesting harmonic consequences in the continuo part, occurs in Dido's final recitative 'Thy hand, Belinda, darkness shades me'. At the words 'shades me' Dent has A flat in the voice part (bringing it into line with the A flat of the preceding bar), supported by a semibreve F minor chord in the continuo part. Britten's reading is an A *natural* in the voice part (contradicting the preceding bar's A flat), supported by a continuo chord of F *major*. This leads to a sharp passing dissonance (of the kind we may observe in 'If brightness dimmed, and dark prevailed' in 'Before Life and After' from *Winter Words*) between the first two notes of the new minor phrase in the voice part and the sustained F major chord. Its *postponed* submission to the minor follows the voice in the next bar. The semitonal disturbance in the accompaniment is perfectly consistent with the now restored tension of Purcell's vocal line. Moreover, Purcell himself has given a hint of horizontal conflict between instrumental bass and voice part in the final cadence which the forward-looking continuo player can anticipate in the inner lines of his own.

The texture—if one can separate texture from harmonic content—of the highly idiomatic harpsichord part at all times serves to underline the dramatic situation and emotional content of Purcell's word-setting, and contains some memorable inspirations. Perhaps the most beautiful of all Britten's interpretative ideas is in the introduction to Dido's recitative 'Your counsel all is urg'd in vain'. Here the pedal G of the bass line is realized in a most eloquent series of full, spread chords, derived from Purcell's 'weeping' figure in the voice part. This, one feels, could not have been bettered by Purcell himself. It is not pastiche, it is complete identification with the Purcellian spirit.

One of the distinguishing features of Britten's realization, indeed, is that, true opera composer himself, he sees the work as a whole, and looks beyond the bounds of Purcell's short forms in his urge to reinforce the dramatic impact by means of textural consistency and economy of figurative material. A striking instance of this occurs in Act II, where the technical harpsichord device of spreading a single chord in both directions becomes a means of sharpening the characterization of the Sorceress and her spells. The unrelenting, obsessional nature of this arpeggio accompaniment, whenever the Sorceress speaks, invests the texture with something of the power of a supernatural *Leitmotiv*.

A less pervasive example of admirable motivic economy at work in Britten's harpsichord figuration is seen in 'See the flags and streamers curling'. The image cries out for illustration in the continuo part and it suggested to Britten's lively imagination alternating thirds in dotted rhythm. In the duet for the witches, 'Our next motion must be to storm her lover on the ocean', the same linking motif is used (with a splendid disregard for academic inhibitions about consecutive fifths).

Space forbids more than a passing reference to such excellent realizations as Dido's ground, 'Ah Belinda', in which Britten's own increasingly impassioned rhythmic and melodic ostinati intensify the obsessional mood of the piece (Dent is more purely 'decorative', less progressive in emotional intensity here); the throughcomposed realization of the other ground-bass number, 'Oft she visits', with its picturesque 'fountain' motif (Dent seems frankly dull and doodling by comparison); and the small compassionate touch in the harpsichord part at Aeneas' 'Some pity on your lover take'. Wherever one looks there is always the same awareness in the figurative detail which on no occasion degenerates into mere 'humdrum activity'.

The Britten–Holst version reveals a more liberal and varied use of dotted rhythms than the Dent version, which in itself showed a marked advance on the incredible rhythmical flaccidity of Cummings. In the Overture, for instance, the dotted crotchets are double-dotted in the introduction. The middle C of the bass line (which presumably suggested to earlier editors a *piano* opening) is transposed downward in the continuo part to give a firm, tragic *forte* opening, taut and dramatic instead of gentle and romantic. The Sailors' Dance of Act III is made more snappy with a more varied use of and ♫. figures. The last two bars of the dance are notable both for Britten's unharmonized penultimate bar and the substitution of a plagal (bass G instead of F) for Dent's perfect cadence (Ex.5). A more

Ex.5

vital rhythmical departure from the Dent version occurs in the opening number for the Sailors in Act III, where the editors have replaced Cummings's reading with Ex.6a. Unaccountably, Dent chose to alter the energetic cross-rhythmical accentuation of this phrase to the lame Ex.6b.

Ex.6a

The phrasing in this practical edition is lively, detailed and meticulous, with well-chosen metronome markings. A typical example is the sensitive phrasing of the opening ritornello in Act II, which eloquently moulds and characterizes Purcell's tune (Ex.7).

Ex.7

Such things are very much a matter of taste, of course, but this edition is not intended for people who have the time, knowledge, experience and professional skill to make their own arrangement from the original manuscripts. An additional bonus is the music Britten adapted and transposed from *The Indian Queen*, the last of the *Nine Welcome Songs* and an (untransposed) movement from the overture to *Sir Anthony Love* to replace the (presumed lost) chorus and dance music for the end of Act II after the disappearance of Aeneas—all excellent numbers which would otherwise be rarely heard today. As an up-to-date performing edition, prepared with scholarly care and interpreted by a composer whose practical operatic experience and intuitive sympathy with Purcell's music are perhaps unequalled at the present time, it deserves the widest possible use.

INSTRUMENTS

32

The Chamber Music:
An Introduction[1]

DONALD MITCHELL

I am tempted to suggest that there is no distinction to be made—that all Britten's music is, or aspires to the condition of, chamber music. Throughout his work, irrespective of the medium involved, there are qualities which may properly be described as chamber-musical. (In much the same way, the chamber music that Mahler never wrote can be found in his symphonies.) Britten conspicuously prefers relatively small forces (or large forces broken down into select constituencies),[2] very precisely mixed and calculated sound with transparency as the main objective, and spare, often sparse textures; and these preferences naturally embody concentrated, economical and demanding musical thinking. It is in this sense of chamber music that even the operas can and should be approached. Such works as *The Rape of Lucretia* and *The Turn of the Screw* exact a response, make claims on our musicality, which we would expect not in the theatre but, rather confined to the more intimate, intense arena of chamber music. To think of at least certain of the operas in this way can throw fresh light on them and also help us to realize that Britten's development of the idea of chamber opera was by no means stimulated only by practical, economic reasons. The chamber operas—and from a later period one might well include the church parables—are a novel form of chamber music for the theatre and they indicate the extent to which Britten's chamber music was spread throughout his *oeuvre*. Whereas orthodox categorization would suggest that Britten wrote a rather slender

---

[1] Edited from the Programme Book for the 1977 Benson & Hedges Music Festival.
[2] How prophetic, in retrospect, appears his opus 1, the *Sinfonietta* for *chamber* orchestra (1932).

amount of chamber music, he was in fact (according to my methods of calculation) more active in the chamber-music sphere than most of his contemporaries apart from Shostakovich. For an example we need look no further than the series of five Canticles, the first composed in 1947, the last in 1974: a kind of chamber music for the voice (sometimes one voice, sometimes more) displaying the characteristics, and making the demands, which I have outlined above. These highly personal, reflective chamber cantatas were very much Britten's own creation. One of the most ambitious and least frequently performed is *Canticle III: Still falls the Rain* (1954), which introduces the horn as a second 'voice', and illustrates the prominence of variation technique in Britten's chamber works. It is of particular interest in this context that the variation form of *Canticle III* is closely related to the form of the work that immediately preceded it—*The Turn of the Screw*. This is not to say that *Still falls the Rain* is disguised opera (though it is intensely dramatic in conception) but rather that the *Screw* shows all the rigorous organization and close, packed thinking that we find in the chamber-musical canticle.

Britten undoubtedly composed out of a wide and intense experience of the classical and modern chamber-music repertory. Anybody scrutinizing the documents that tell us most about his youthful musical life will be struck by his seemingly ceaseless activity as a performer. (One wonders how he found time as a young man to work so hard at his composing, endlessly revising what he wrote.) His great natural gifts as a pianist meant that he was always busily involved in performances of chamber music, participating with friends in various ensembles and often preparing for a concert, both as a student at the Royal College of Music and, only a little later, as a young professional. He was surrounded by chamber music, and what he did not play himself or read or explore at the keyboard he got to know through assiduous attendance at important concerts and recitals, and above all by listening to the BBC. I doubt if there was a keener listener to radio music than the Britten of College and pre-College days. Very little seemed to escape his ears, and when he came to attempt, say, his own string quartets he had a comprehensive knowledge of the classical and contemporary masterpieces. There was, furthermore, the profound and cosmopolitan influence of Frank Bridge, Britten's revered teacher and friend, himself a distinguished composer of chamber music, a very able viola player and an enthusiast for making chamber music domestically. On many occasions when

The Chamber Music

Britten was visiting the Bridges at their country home in Sussex, as a boy or in later years, the convivial performing of chamber music, as well as exacting composition lessons, would have been on the agenda. So in this context too Britten was continually in touch with, and intimately involved in, the great chamber music tradition and what it meant in terms of art (and sociability). Last but not least, while recognizing that the piano was Britten's principal instrument, we must recall that, like Bridge, he played the viola, which gave him access to chamber music as a string player. He may not have pursued his viola playing very strenuously, especially in later years, but his viola parts reflect his affection for the instrument.

As soon as we start looking through Britten's chamber music we run across characteristic patterns and shapes which lend a remarkable consistency to what he composed in this field. One very persistent and notable feature is the idea of the suite. It was a form that Britten made peculiarly his own: a sequence of movements which could be rather loosely or very rigorously organized, which could be continuous or punctuated, but which almost always gave him scope for introducing one or more of those memorable 'character' movements that marvellously exploit the capacity of the instrument or instruments to make the music appropriate to the title—even to the extent of persuading a solo line to yield the sounds of a miniature band, as in the Marcia from the First Suite for Cello, Op.72 (1964).[3]

At the same time that the instruments are explored to their innermost recesses, so too are the personalities of the players, whose techniques had come to fascinate the composer and eventually to prompt him to write for them. The oboe *Temporal Variations* (1936) for Sylvia Spencer and *Six Metamorphoses after Ovid*, Op.49 (1951), for Joy Boughton; the Suite for Harp, Op.83 (1969), for Osian Ellis; the guitar *Nocturnal after John Dowland*, Op.70 (1963), for Julian Bream; the canticles, for Peter Pears and others; and the three Cello Suites, Op.72 (1964), Op.80 (1967) and Op.87 (1971), and the Cello Sonata, for Mstislav Rostropovich, are all profoundly revealing portraits in sound, not only of the instruments but also of the performers. There can never have been a composer who left so substantial a part of his legacy in the shape of a portrait gallery of his

[3] The Sonata in C for cello and piano, Op.65 (1961), mixes a suite-like form with a genuine sonata gravity and complexity, i.e., the work's subtle and very sophisticated first movement, which strikingly anticipates the first movement of the Symphony for Cello and Orchestra (1963).

virtuoso colleagues and friends. It comes as no surprise then to find a suite among the very early published works—the Suite for violin and piano, Op.6 (1934–5), which was given its first complete performance by the violinist Antonio Brosa, with whom Britten had a close association during his youth and early manhood.[4]

While Opus 6 may have set the pattern for a sequence of character movements, which was to be extended and refined upon in the future—it included a march, a lullaby and a waltz—the first real chamber work of substance, over which Britten laboured hard and long, continuously revising and rewriting, was his Opus 2, the *Phantasy Quartet* for oboe and strings (1932). Not a string quartet, but an oboe quartet; and again a work involved with a particular player, Leon Goossens, to whom it was dedicated and who, with André Mangeot, Helen Perkin and Eric Bray, gave the first performance. A composer as ferociously self-critical as Britten was at this stage[5] would have been unlikely to attempt to add a string quartet proper so early to his rapidly growing list of published works. He would have been too aware of the responsibility, of the standards he would have been judged by and by which he would have judged himself. Nevertheless, the idea of the string quartet did attract and perhaps challenge him; there are numerous complete string quartets among his juvenilia and one from his youth, the String Quartet in D major (1931), which, after only minimal revision and some tightening up in the finale, he was prepared to have published in 1975. Another and important attempt at the form also belongs to his later College days, the unfinished and suite-like string quartet entitled *Alla Quartetto Serioso: 'Go play, boy, play'*, envisaged as a sequence of five character-movements, three of which the somewhat reluctant young composer agreed to have performed in public in London at the end of 1933.[6] This piece is of special significance because, as has been discovered by John Evans, material from one of its discarded movements turns up later to serve one of the songs in *Les Illuminations*—a striking and unexpected translation.

<hr/>

[4] Brosa was a member of the circle of musicians surrounding Bridge and it was he who eventually gave the first performance of Britten's Violin Concerto, Op.15 (1939), in New York, in 1940.

[5] One of the most astonishing things that one learns from studying how he worked in his early days is how hard he found it to satisfy himself; day after day an idea, a passage, would be worked at, scrapped, tried again, scrapped, revised, and so on.

[6] Britten's 1936 revision of three of the 1933 movements is now published as *Three Divertimenti* (Faber Music, 1983) [C.P.].

The Chamber Music

There was then a great deal of practical experience of the medium, and many shots at achieving it, behind the series of three major string quartets which opened with String Quartet No. 1 in D, Op.25, written in California in the summer of 1941, continued with String Quartet No. 2 in C, Op.36, composed in England in 1945, and closed with String Quartet No.3, Op.94, written (after an interval of some thirty years) in Suffolk and Venice and completed in 1975.

The first two quartets represent two peaks of creative energy, innovation and renovation. The first movement of each shows a very fresh and convincing rethinking of the sonata pattern—a formula which Britten declared he never felt wholly comfortable using and avoided altogether in his third and last quartet,[7] which stimulated him to some outstanding formal feats. While the First Quartet followed an orthodox four-movement scheme, the Second introduced an original three-movement form, the slow movement (one of the finest and most majestic of Britten's passacaglias) functioning also as the finale. In the Third Quartet, as if, among many other objectives in this particular work, he was attempting a summing-up of the characteristic overall forms in which he had worked, over the years, in his chamber music, Britten partly reintroduces the suite idea: like the incomplete quartet from 1933 mentioned above, it is in five movements, and the two fast movements which frame the slow movement are vintage examples of 'character' movements.[8] It is again a noble Passacaglia that rounds the work off. There is even a resurgence of the cadenza principle, which is a brilliant feature of the Second Quartet's last movement. Here, in the slow movement of the Third, it is used in quite another way, and, it may be thought, for quite another reason. Finally, in the Third Quartet, with undiminished ingenuity and vitality, Britten continues to invent for the medium—and persuade from it—those fresh sounds and novel textures which he had produced in such abundance in the earlier quartets.

It is natural enough that the composer's final quartet should attract special attention. It would be a mistake, however, to approach it as a last will and testament. Britten was not an artist who thought about himself in those terms, and in any event, as Michael Tippett remarked

---

[7] Hans Keller holds a contrary point of view and expounded it in a BBC Radio 3 talk about the Third Quartet, broadcast on 11 June 1978. See also his article, 'Britten's Last Masterpiece', *Spectator*, 2 June 1979, pp.27–8.

[8] Britten may also have been influenced by the example of Mozart's wonderful six-movement String Trio, K.563, as well as by precedents in his own music, when conceiving the shape of his last quartet.

in his penetrating obituary, he had always been powerfully aware of, and much preoccupied by, death. He was, moreover, even when the last quartet was done, still full of music, which spilled into the robust, throaty *Welcome Ode*, Op.95 (composed in August 1976), and was already filling out the shape of the cantata on a text by Edith Sitwell for chorus and orchestra, which, though unfinished, lacks nothing in energy or commitment. For all that, it would be shallow to pretend that the quartet was not composed out of an awareness that the time remaining to him was at best severely limited; and clearly the use in the finale of materials from *Death in Venice* has a quite specific or symbolic significance. The choice of quotations suggests the composer's recognition of the fact that, like his operatic hero, he too, in the foreseeable future, had to make his crossing; and he meditated calmly on the knowledge with the exemplary courage and serenity which was characteristic of him throughout his illness. And yet the last quartet was *not* the crossing—there were, as we know, more days, more works, to come. Hence, I believe, the deliberate ambiguity, the intended irresolution, of the cadence with which the Passacaglia ends, or rather with which it does not end. The cadence does not so much round the work off as leave the crossing still not quite completed. With this in mind, I think the total shape of the work makes a kind of poetic sense that we respond to instinctively. We feel a logical evolution from the intimate, quiet exchanges of the first movement, through the earthbound energy of the first scherzo to that unique and climactic moment at the centre of the aspiring but serene melody which is the slow movement: the cadenza, when it seems as if the whole work is to expire in a burst of radiant birdsong. But this moment of intense spiritual release passes; calm returns, and so does the world, in the shape of the second scherzo. Then the finale begins, with its undaunted and unsentimental look at what is to come; though *when* it is to come is still unknown, an uncertainty scrupulously documented in the notes.[9] Composers have often reserved some of their finest thoughts for chamber music and especially for the string quartet. Britten's Quartet No. 3 proves no exception to that general rule and also unforgettably consummates the rich contribution to the genre made by a composer who was entirely a chamber musician in whichever field he worked.

[9] The final cadence went through more than one version and was given a great deal of searching thought by the composer.

33

The Solo Chamber Music

ERIC ROSEBERRY

As a chamber music player of distinction himself (viola and piano) Britten the composer was well qualified to address his players as individual artists. The category of 'solo chamber music' may at first seem a contradiction in terms, but the paradoxical truth is that Britten wrote music which challenged the virtuosity of his friends without sacrificing that intimacy and sense of dialogue which is the essence of true chamber music. The dialogue is there, of course, in the music itself—for example in the self-communing fugues of the solo cello suites—but it exists also as a knowing exchange between composer and performer on which we, the listeners, are the privileged eavesdroppers.

This small but not insignificant output, spanning the decades 1951–71, testifies to a matchless ear for sonority and timbre, a ready imagination for apt characterization, and an approach that is both considerately practical yet demanding. It also testifies to that aspect of Britten's creativity which thrived on limitation whether of the medium, the particular circumstances of a performance or even the actual capabilities of the players themselves (as evinced in his resourceful, thoroughly unpatronizing music for children and amateurs).

But more important still, perhaps, and reaching its zenith in the cello suites, we encounter here in its purest state Britten's innate feeling for *line* in music—that supple melodic gift which enabled him to expand, contract, elaborate or transform a musical idea in a seemingly endless number of expressive ways, achieving its total fulfilment across the whole breadth of a composition. The lyrical watershed of *Peter Grimes* is its overwhelming mad scene, when Peter, alone and on the run, expresses the burden of his anguish in an agonized soliloquy of tortured reminiscence; this is the predestined goal of the tragedy—and a single line carries the whole weight of a thematic recapitulation. It is that same sense of the supremacy of line in the expression of human feeling which gives such personal distinction to Britten's solo chamber music.

Looking at this small body of work in its entirety, one is struck at once by the consistency of Britten's predilection for the suite as opposed to the sonata. Here was an appropriately flexible mode of organization that could encompass anything from an unpretentious, loosely connected sequence of character pieces, unified by a particular extra-musical idea, through the thematically interconnected continuity of variations, to a cyclic, progressive scheme akin to that of a five-movement sonata. Britten's early and indeed obsessive interest in suite and variation is amply demonstrated by a glance at the catalogue of instrumental music which he wrote in the mid-1930s. The recent revival and publication of *Temporal Variations* for oboe and piano (December 1936) is a further reminder of this preoccupation, and indicates a youthful partiality for the timbre of an instrument which had already figured prominently in his first published chamber work, the *Phantasy Quartet* for oboe and strings of 1932, and was to attract him later into his first essay in monophony. (In fact *Temporal Variations* was not Britten's first venture into writing for oboe and piano: there are also *Two Insect Pieces*, 'The Grasshopper' and 'The Wasp', of 1935—both deft and idiomatic, and clearly indebted to Bartók and Prokofiev.) Following hard on the heels of *Our Hunting Fathers*, these variations on a sombre processional theme reveal the daring range of the composer's stylistic terms of reference at the age of 23.[1] Echoes of Mahler, Shostakovich, Bartók, Ravel and the twelve-note sonorities of Schoenberg's school—here was an 'escape from Englishry' indeed. But it is no less fascinating to discover in Oration from *Temporal Variations* a pre-echo of the gleaming fanfare imagery of 'Let the florid music praise' in the forthcoming Auden cycle, *On this Island*, a type of imagery more thoroughly to be exploited in the cyclic process of *Les Illuminations*. While the overall span of

---

[1] See Britten's diary entry after attending the first performance of Shostakovich's *Lady Macbeth of the Mtsensk District* in 1936: 'It is the composer's heritage to take what he wants from whom he wants and to write music', Donald Mitchell, 'Britten on *Oedipus Rex* and *Lady Macbeth*', *Tempo*, No. 120 (March 1977), pp.10–12. *Temporal Variations*, interestingly enough, provided Britten with a source for a striking piece of self-borrowing. The Marcia of the Sonata for cello and piano (1961) clearly derives from the March of the earlier work.

gesture and tonal mastery which were so soon to be displayed in the Rimbaud cycle as yet elude the grasp of the young eclectic, the impulse towards them is already struggling to find expression as he hovers between motivic economy (of which the original theme is a splendid example) and expansive rhetoric, between sonority and spareness of texture.

A gap of fifteen years separates the somewhat experimental exuberance of *Temporal Variations* from the assured mastery of the *Six Metamorphoses after Ovid* for solo oboe: a gap in which the composer of *Peter Grimes, The Rape of Lucretia, Albert Herring, The Beggar's Opera* and *The Little Sweep* had found his voice as the leading exponent of opera of his time. This suite of ironic miniatures, written while Britten was at work on *Billy Budd*, is no longer part of a quest for artistic identity; it is the relaxed work of a composer who is able to concentrate much dramatic and expressive experience into a small time-scale, achieving a perfect balance between form and content. As a single example, take the miniature drama of Phaeton. This monothematic sonata movement with the briefest of recapitulations is a perfect tonal analogue to the fateful ride, with its uneasy jerking of the reins, its over-confident ascent followed by plunging catastrophe, the unmanaged horses disappearing into the blue. The work was written for performance by Joy Boughton on the Meare at Thorpeness on 14 June 1951. The fitness of Britten's triadically conceived melodies for extramural chamber performance hardly needs labouring. 'Arpeggiation', as Schenker wrote, 'is an outgrowth of the harmonic series', and whether by instinct or design Britten's melodic inspirations in this suite seem to compensate for the loss of the harmonic dimension (Ex.1).

Ex.1a Phaeton

Ex.1b Niobe

With the *Nocturnal after John Dowland* for guitar, written for Julian Bream in 1963, Britten composed a pendant to his larger vocal

Eric Roseberry

exploration of the theme of night, sleep and dreams in such works as the *Serenade*, the *Nocturne* and *A Midsummer Night's Dream*. In it he draws on a novel adaptation of variation technique, employed some thirteen years earlier in the *Lachrymae* for viola and piano, and to be re-employed with a difference eight years later in the Third Suite for Cello. Both the *Lachrymae* and the *Nocturnal* derive from lute songs by John Dowland, and the technique in each case is to write *partial* variations on aspects of the theme, which is brought to the surface in its original form only at the end of the composition. The two works are to some extent companion-pieces, not only in technique but also in mood, in that both inhabit the same veiled world of fantastic, nocturnal images. But time passes more quickly in the *Nocturnal*. The fleeting, nightmarish episodes generate a motion of tonal unease and ambiguity. Arnold Whittall has pointed out that the tonal principle of this piece is the exploitation of keys a semitone apart.[2] We may also note the avoidance, uncharacteristic for Britten, of the common chord—a point of repose which the *Lachrymae* freely admits and the *Nocturne* sensuously indulges. Still in tonal opposition with itself, the elaborately wrought Passacaglia achieves a terrifying climax of dissonance as it presses on to its E major goal of resolution. The goal reached, the terror is dispersed in a swift scalic dissolution of tension and the mood calms into the acceptance of Dowland's 'Come, heavy Sleep' in its original form, but incomplete. *Distortion* is the essence of the *Nocturnal*, whose grotesque twistings of the thematic material contain naught for our comfort. In style it anticipates the sound-world of the cello suites: the idiomatic *style brisé*, the remarkable harmonic sonorities and the poetic, as distinct from merely technical, exploitation of the instrument's full potential. The difficulties of the piece will confine it to an aristocracy of sensitive virtuosi.

Donald Mitchell has noted[3] Britten's long and memorable attachment to the harp, as pungently idiomatic as it is remote from the florid clichés of nineteenth-century romanticism. The sonority of the harp was unmistakably tethered in Britten's imagination to the idea of innocence, and in the Suite for Harp (1969), written for Osian Ellis, he has not lost sight of its symbolic purity. The prevailing tone is radiantly diatonic, with all but one movement in the major mode, the quality of expression clear and direct, the light, ternary-orientated structures lovingly fashioned as if to dispel the notion of cliché

[2] *BT*, p.210.
[3] Sleeve-note for Decca recording SXL 6788.

The Solo Chamber Music

clinging to the genre. The suite is cast in a characteristically luminous C major, a key that also has connotations of innocence for Britten. The five movements are symmetrically conceived. A central F minor Nocturne is flanked on either side by a D major Toccata and Lydian B flat major Fugue (the latter a dancing arpeggio inspiration, as innocently fresh and unscholastic as Bach's little G major fugue of the 48, Book 2). The whole is framed by a crisply rhythmic C major Overture and sonorous 'white-note' variations on 'St Denio'. This suite, perhaps alone of all the music under discussion, provides its dedicatee with a rich store of detachable encores, but the continuity of conception, which culminates in the pealing sonority of the Hymn, is guaranteed by common tonal and/or motivic pivots from the end of one piece to the beginning of the next.

Britten was always sensitive to the poetry he needed, and his discovery of 'The Death of Saint Narcissus', an early metaphysical poem by T. S. Eliot, must have invaded his creative imagination with the force of an inner light. Eliot's opening lines are charged with a quality of revelation and a beckoning urgency which prepare the mind for a visionary communication far removed from everyday experience:

> Come under the shadow of this gray rock—
> Come in under the shadow of this gray rock,
> And I will show you something different from either
> Your shadow sprawling over the sand at daybreak, or
> Your shadow leaping behind the fire against the red rock:
> I will show you his bloody cloth and limbs
> And the gray shadow on his lips.

There follows, in a fleeting sequence of images, a kind of funeral oration over this shadowy, self-annihilating figure: his self-absorption, his compulsion towards metamorphosis into and recoil from everything in the world, his ultimate and solitary martyrdom as a 'Dancer before God'. This is the terrible ascetic climax of the poem, clashing with the pitiful remains before us.

The emotional reticence, economy, grace and *clarity* of Britten's setting of this poem for tenor and harp (1974) inhibit a discursive response.[4] Three critics have already probed its luminous complexity. Perhaps wisely, Peter Evans[5] concentrated on a precise technical

[4] See Colin Matthews, 'Britten's Indian Summer', *Soundings*, 6 (1977), p.43.
[5] *MBB*, pp.414–18.

analysis of the beauty and aptness of the tonal structure, with its fascinating ambiguities. He also demonstrates the concentrates motivic unity and continuity of its finely spun vocal line—something we can sense at once. Arnold Whittall,[6] briefly confirming Evans's tonal reading of the piece, speculates on the meaning of the poem, its resonances in other works (especially *Death in Venice*) and its personal significance for Britten at this time of crisis. Donald Mitchell[7] sees the pervasive element of the dance and the release of the rhythmic potential of the harp as essential to Britten's setting of the text. Music, Mitchell would seem to imply, has its own self-explanatory role to play in the illumination of metaphysical imagery, and this is a reality we can grasp. But there remains the direct force of Britten's music, which glows with a strange light-heartedness and serenity, for all its terrors. Analysis apart, here is a work to be treasured: a unique distillation of the essence of Britten, compressed into a single brief time-span.

Mstislav Rostropovich was the greatest single influence on Britten as an instrumental composer, inspiring him to produce his greatest symphonic work, the Symphony for Cello and Orchestra (1963), a fine five-movement sonata (his first work so entitled!) for cello and piano (1961) and the three solo cello suites (1964–71). These works seemed to fulfil at last the hopes of his admirers who had waited for a sequel to his earlier instrumental music—the *Variations on a Theme of Frank Bridge*, the concertos for violin and piano, the *Sinfonia da Requiem* and the two string quartets. It would be absurd to imply that 'absolute music' is a higher goal of creative endeavour than vocal music, but we can be grateful to the Russian virtuoso for turning Britten's thoughts once again to these modes of musical discourse and expression.

While Bach is the historical eminence behind the cello suites and the *style brisé* a fertilizing technical principle, one should not make too much here of the model of baroque convention which, even in the case of the two fugues and the Ciaccona, is only intermittently observed. (Closer to the conception of the Third Suite, I suggest, would be the model of Shostakovich's Eleventh String Quartet.) Taken together, the suites present three resourcefully contrasted modes of organization. The first, in G (1964), may be described as a song-cycle without words. The recurring Canto (modified on each of its three returns

6 *BT*, pp.272–3.
7 Sleeve-note for Decca recording SXL 6788.

during the suite, recalling the Promenade in Mussorgsky's *Pictures from an Exhibition*) is the 'motto theme' linking a succession of character pieces which themselves derive subtly from or allude to aspects of it: its pivotal motivic shapes, its characteristic intervals, even its improvisatory phrase-structure. While every lover of Britten's music will have his favourite movement here, I am particularly impressed by the Lamento, which expands only to return each time to a doleful falling E minor arpeggio and climbs via an inversion of the original opening phrase to a top A″ for its final, drawn-out, winding descent to the numb *idée fixe*.[8] The semitonal motivic play of the final Moto perpetuo transforms itself back into the Canto, each phrase of which now reappears in association with the Moto perpetuo until the concluding phrase completely absorbs its figuration in a sonorous climax. The semitonal 'riddle' of the last two bars is a Shostakovich-like grimace, a wry contraction that sums up the motivic concentration of the whole suite, which was implicit from the outset in the austere f sharp'–a–G sonority of the pivotal opening gesture of the Canto.

Certainly the spirit of Shostakovich hovers over the opening gesture of the Declamato of the Second Suite in D (1967), which—consciously or unconsciously—alludes to the opening theme of Shostakovich's Fifth Symphony (Ex.2). Here is an altogether

Ex.2

different proposition from the Canto of the First Suite, providing the rhetorical point of departure for a sonata-like conception whose five-movement scheme suggests the model of Bartók. There are no apparent thematic relationships between the several movements of this suite (discounting the brief quasi-cyclic allusion to the manner of the Declamato in the *tranquillo* at the end of the Ciaccona), but there is a substantial element of thematic development in each of them. There is, moreover, a menacing profundity of expression to be experienced in the fourth movement, Andante lento, with its echoes of serious

[8] This is an example in Britten—one of many in the cello suites—of the influence of Shostakovich. The *reculer-pour-mieux-sauter* extensions of the phrase, the curling expansion of small intervallic cells, the repetitive element of the *idée fixe*, and the contemplative intensity of expression are all features of Shostakovich's style which Britten here makes his own.

passages in earlier Britten—the slow movement of the Cello Symphony, the Wordsworth episode in the *Nocturne*, the preparation for sacrifice in *Canticle II: Abraham and Isaac*. The Ciaccona is an impressive musical edifice (using the theme also in inversion) which is modestly disavowed in a final flippant gesture of dismissal.

The Third Suite in C minor (1971), a genuine multi-movement suite, is a fascinating adaptation of the hidden variation technique of the *Nocturnal* and *Lachrymae*. It is only after experiencing this nine-movement continuity of diverse character pieces that the listener is presented with the thematic source, not just one but four melodies: three Russian folksongs from Tchaikovsky's volumes of arrangements, and the Kontakion (Hymn for the Departed), whose theme Britten took from the English Hymnal. In devising this approach Britten comes close to another characteristic aspect of Shostakovich's style—the melodic collage, such as may be encountered in the fourth movement of the Eighth String Quartet. This allusiveness is but one aspect of a work rich in other readily identifiable attributes of Shostakovich's style—the DSCH motif (encountered in a transposed permutation as early as the third bar of the Introduzione), the brooding parlando soliloquy pivoting on a monotone, the anapaest march rhythms, the extreme contrasts of mood ranging from frenzy to deep introspection. All this suggests that the suite, which the composer actually played to Shostakovich when he visited Russia in 1971, was intended as a double tribute to Rostropovich and Shostakovich, whose own creative relationship had resulted in two great cello concertos. The overall impression of this strange, touchingly personal work is of a sequence of impulsively jotted down moods and reminiscences—as if one were turning over the pages of a private diary.

The solo chamber music has been described by Donald Mitchell as 'a unique portrait gallery of virtuoso colleagues and friends'. It forms a legacy which is a reminder of the vital stimulus Britten derived from individual artistry and personal relationships in his creative life. Mozart and Schubert apart (with whom Britten showed a profound sense of kinship in his own performances), there can be few composers in the history of music who have shared to such an extent this special sense of human *particularity* in their work.

34
The String Quartets and some other Chamber Works

DAVID MATTHEWS

Britten wrote chamber music all his composing life, though more intensively at the beginning and end than in the opera-dominated middle. The majority of these works were written for his friends; at least half are relatively lightweight; a few are masterpieces. The three numbered string quartets are, I believe, the finest of all his chamber works, and the most fruitful to discuss from a technical point of view. Like many of his predecessors, including the two composers closest to him in spirit, Mozart and Schubert, Britten found the string quartet medium a rigorously stimulating challenge to his creative powers.

Apart from the quartets, almost all Britten's chamber music is for one or two instruments. The absence of a major work for solo piano is perhaps puzzling. Although he would not in later life have written anything for himself to play, having diverted his career as a pianist from soloist to accompanist, this would not have prevented him, it might be thought, from writing such a work for one of his friends, as he wrote the Sonata in C and the three Suites for Cello for Mstislav Rostropovich and the guitar piece, *Nocturnal after John Dowland*, for Julian Bream; but significantly the piano piece for Sviatoslav Richter that he began in late 1965 or early 1966 remained unfinished.

So we are left with just two solo piano works: one early, *Holiday Diary*, and one late, *Night Piece* (*Notturno*), plus the set of charming *Walztes* (*sic*) resurrected in 1970 from the vast amount of piano music Britten composed as a child. *Holiday Diary* is dedicated to Arthur Benjamin, his piano teacher at the Royal College of Music. It consists of four genre pieces, of which the last, 'Night', is notable as the first of

Britten's C major tone-poems. (*Night Piece*, composed in 1963 as a test piece for the Leeds International Pianoforte Competition and not as slight as its lack of opus number would seem to imply, is a less static, more Chopinesque nocturne in B flat major, with Bartókian night noises in the middle section.) Peter Evans has suggested[1] the possible influence of the slow movement of Bartók's Second Piano Concerto and of his piano piece 'The Night's Music' on 'Night'; there is also an uncanny resemblance to Ives's *The Unanswered Question* (a piece that Britten almost certainly would not have known) in the way fragments of previous movements drift like dream-images across a background of slowly moving chords (Ex.1). Of the two rarely

Ex.1

performed pieces for piano duo, *Introduction and Rondo alla Burlesca* and *Mazurka Elegiaca* (dating from the American years), the latter in particular is undeservedly neglected. Britten transmutes the rich melancholy of Chopin's mazurka style into a deeply felt memorial for the great Polish pianist and statesman, Paderewski (1860–1941).

The various solo and duet pieces that Britten wrote for his friends are all carefully designed to display each player's individual virtuosity to its best advantage. His concern extended, in several cases, to quoting from, or basing the piece on, appropriate existing music: thus the *Nocturnal* of 1963 for Bream is based on a Dowland lute song (as is the earlier (1950) *Lachrymae* for viola and piano); Rostropovich's Third Cello Suite is based on Russian themes; Osian Ellis's Harp Suite includes the Welsh hymn 'St Denio'; and the *Gemini Variations* written in 1965 for the 13-year-old Hungarian twins Zoltán and Gabriel Jeney are based on an Epigram of Kodály. All the works in

---

[1] *MBB*, p.27.

this category are either suites or sets of variations, with the exception of the Cello Sonata—though this too, with its five character movements, each with a title, might have been called a suite: it is quite closely related in style to the opus 6 Suite for violin and piano.

The three numbered string quartets were preceded by a number of earlier attempts at the medium, including six from Britten's adolescence, as well as a *Phantasy Quintet* for strings dating from 1934 and the 1933/6 'Go play, boy, play' string quartet movements. The only early quartet published during Britten's lifetime (in 1975, in a slightly revised form) was the String Quartet in D major that he wrote in 1931 at the age of 17, a year before the *Sinfonietta*, whose Tarantella finale is anticipated by the Quartet's closing Allegro giocoso. The first movement is unexpectedly Tippett-like in places, the result of a common madrigal influence; while the slow movement has an 'English' quality shared by the slow movement of the *Sinfonietta* and the *Phantasy Quartet* for oboe and strings,[2] but soon outgrown. The pizzicato central episode in the finale obviously derives from Bartók's Fourth Quartet: both Bartók and Stravinsky were seminal influences on Britten in the 1930s, but whereas Stravinsky's influence was soon thoroughly assimilated, bits of undigested Bartók keep appearing in Britten's music even up to the 1960s, for example the aforementioned *Night Piece*, and the Scherzo-pizzicato movement of the Cello Sonata.

By the time Britten came to write his official First Quartet (in the summer of 1941, exactly ten years after the D major Quartet) he had acquired a prodigious compositional technique, and was still young enough to want to show it off. So the First Quartet is intended to impress—which it does, and far from superficially. What is most impressive is the sophisticated way in which Britten handles sonata form and tonality. The majority of Britten's sonata movements are found in his early works, and the First Quartet is the culmination of this early, intensive concern with the sonata. It was the last important piece that he wrote in North America; shortly after he returned to England he became involved with the composition of *Peter Grimes* and, following the success of *Grimes*, opera largely drew his creative energies away from instrumental music for well over a decade.

The first movement's unusual shape (Andante sostenuto alternating three times with Allegro) masks its underlying sonata structure. What appears at first to be a slow introduction returns at the end of the

2 The complex one-movement form of this interesting—if uncharacteristic—early work has been minutely analysed by Paul Hamburger (BS, pp.212–19).

exposition in a key (F major) long prepared for by the nagging
presence of its dominant (C) during the preceding Allegro. (C had
crept in as the lowest note of the cello's pizzicato arpeggios towards
the end of the introduction and hangs on, terrier-like, throughout
three statements of the main Allegro theme.) The introduction
reappears in its original key of D to form a coda; but the master-stroke
in this movement is its return in Allegro disguise to begin the
recapitulation. Comparison of Ex.2 (the opening of the quartet) with
Ex.3 (the beginning of the recapitulation) shows their essential
identity: at the recapitulation the D–E–F sharp chord in bar 1 of Ex.2
and the C sharp–A in bar 3 are sounded simultaneously, while the
cello adds the G sharp at bar 121 and the viola leaps in with the main
Allegro motif **x**: derived from bar 3 of Ex.2) at its initial pitch. Thus
the recapitulation has begun before we are aware of it, Britten
showing himself as cunning a master of such moments as Mahler
(compare the first movement of Mahler's Fourth Symphony).

Ex.2

Ex.3

The tonal structure of the quartet is of crucial importance: of his
contemporaries perhaps only Tippett was as profoundly concerned
with classical tonality as was Britten at this time. The note C continues

to undermine the D major of the recapitulation, so that although the movement ends with an elegant cadence on to the tonic triad, D is hardly felt to have been convincingly established. The rest of the quartet is a gradual journey towards the secure D major of the finale. The device of preparing for a new key by insistence on its dominant, which was a feature of the first movement, is continued. So C, which had persisted throughout the last section of the first movement, becomes the dominant of the second movement's main key, F. This is an Allegretto con slancio whose triadic tiptoeings are thrown restlessly from key to key by explosively interjected triplets. These are finally calmed by the *pianissimo* F major coda, which acts as dominant to the B flat of the Andante calmo slow movement. The introductory passage to this movement, however, treats B flat as the dominant of E flat and seems to be moving towards the establishment of that key; B flat is confirmed only with the entry of the main theme in bar 18—a descending-scale idea which shows how effectively Britten can create memorable tunes out of simple clichés. The finale's first idea (derived from the main Allegro theme of the first movement) is in its dominant, A, a key anticipated in the last few bars of the slow movement; but after twenty-nine bars of boisterous fugato, the second theme, a grandly augmented variant of the first for the three upper instruments in unison, clinches D major. There is a fiery exuberance about this finale; the ghost of Beethoven stalks behind the scenes here as well as in the scherzo. (The well-known fact that the mature Britten found much of Beethoven's music unacceptable is less significant than the schoolboy's total enthusiasm; Beethoven entered his consciousness at a crucial period.)

The Second Quartet was written in 1945, only four years after the First; but with the intervening experience of *Grimes*, Britten had grown to full maturity, and the Second Quartet stands in a similar relation to the First as do Beethoven's Razumovsky Quartets to his opus 18 set. The long opening theme, whose three successive paragraphs, each beginning with the interval of a rising tenth, quietly unfold over a series of pedals, recalls the First Razumovsky Quartet in its calm expansiveness. There is no sense of being in a hurry: C major is unostentatiously asserted. The development begins in an eerie nocturnal atmosphere reminiscent of the Tenebroso of Berg's *Lyric Suite*; it performs its traditional function of disrupting the tonal stability of the exposition so thoroughly that the passionate reassertion of C in the recapitulation does not wholly restore the

David Matthews

equilibrium. The recapitulation is brief: here Britten departs firmly from the Razumovsky model, and with another stroke of great originality restates the three paragraphs of his opening theme simultaneously, a procedure partly anticipated by the exposition's 'second subject', where the second of the two opening paragraphs is superimposed on the first. The calm of the opening is fully restored with the coda, twenty-three bars of the purest C major. Britten rightly sensed that, in composing a sonata movement, the more tonally adventurous he became—and in several places in this movement a sense of key disappears completely—the greater was the need for compensatory passages of maximum tonal stability. Altogether the first movement is a deeply satisfying sonata structure, elegantly summed up by another Beethovenian gesture in the closing bars.

The essentially contemplative nature of the quartet is emphasized by the fact that both subsequent movements are also in C. The scherzo, however, is in C minor and is a dark, rather anxious piece, with a restless energy that drives relentlessly through its three-part structure. The mood and manner of the central trio—a variation of the scherzo—are close to Shostakovich. This movement is notable for being the only one in Britten's quartets where the strings are muted throughout (there is also a brief passage in the Third Quartet's Burlesque for muted first violin).

The finale is a large-scale chaconne, perhaps the outstanding example of a form that fascinated Britten throughout his life (he had recently composed the Passacaglia in *Peter Grimes*) and appropriate for a quartet composed to celebrate the 250th anniversary of the death of Purcell (Britten gives the movement the Purcellian title, Chacony). Its four sections, separated by cadenzas for cello, viola and first violin respectively, form a sonata in miniature with their division into prelude, scherzo, adagio and coda. The theme itself modulates from B flat to C, so that, within an essentially static context, there is a sense of movement throughout each of the twenty-one variations. The adagio is itself a set of variations on a counter-theme, and its close marks the furthest point of development reached; in the coda the theme returns in its original form and advances through a clearing mist of trills and tremolos to a final triumph, celebrated by no less than twenty-three affirmations of the tonic triad, which complements the stable and spacious twenty-three-bar conclusion of the first movement.

It was not until thirty years later that Britten returned to the medium of the string quartet, for what was to be his last major work.

Severely weakened and partially paralysed after his heart operation, he was able to work only for short periods and with difficulty, so that to have produced in his Third Quartet a masterly summing-up of his life's work was an astonishing achievement.

The Third Quartet is explicitly related to *Death in Venice* by the presence of quotations from the opera in the introduction to the Passacaglia finale, which is subtitled 'La Serenissima'. This movement was composed in Venice on Britten's last visit in November 1975 and is a tribute to a city he especially loved, in its own way as evocative a symbol of ideal beauty as Tadzio had been in *Death in Venice*. It seems very likely that Britten intended the quartet as an instrumental counterpart to the opera. The finale is cast in Aschenbach's key of E major, and may be thought of as continuing, on a purely musical level, his quest for transcendence. Since Britten appears to have identified strongly with Aschenbach, the internal programme of the quartet, too, may reasonably be considered autobiographical. Britten comes close to Mahler here; and indeed Mahler's late works make a striking parallel with Britten's, both composers writing under virtual sentence of death, in each case because of serious heart illness, and both accepting the fact of death in their music without despair, but countering it with gestures of tenderness and warmth. Both achieved a serenity that Shostakovich, for example, writing his Fifteenth Quartet in similar circumstances of ill-health, but of course in a very different political climate, was unable to find.

In Britten's later music the sense of tonality, though never wholly abandoned, is often much more blurred than hitherto. The main keys of the first two quartets were defined clearly at the outset; the Third reaches its goal of E major only in the finale, and the first two movements are tonally ambiguous. The first movement, Duets (all the movements bear titles, as in the Cello Sonata and the suites), has a key signature of two flats: B flat major would seem to be implied, though it is never clearly established. B flat is, appropriately, at the furthest tonal remove (an augmented fourth away) from the E that is the quartet's ultimate destination. Ex.4 shows the opening of the movement. Peter Evans has noted[3] the similarity between the main motif (in the second violin) and one of the themes which accompanies Aschenbach's unhappy wanderings through Venice (compare Figure 106 in the opera). So a link with *Death in Venice*, both thematic and

[3] *MBB*, pp.340–1.

Ex.4

With moderato movement ($\downarrow$. = c.56)

psychological, is established from the start; in addition the figure marked **y** in Ex.4 is consciously or unconsciously a retrograde of the opera's 'I—love you' motif as it is presented in the introduction to the Passacaglia (see Ex.5 below). The moment of recapitulation—for this is a sonata movement, if a veiled one—is marked by the first reference to E major (bars 58–9), though its presence is barely sensed before being obscured. There are no literal repeats, but a real sense of return has been created by the radically different textures of the energetic development section.

The second movement, Ostinato, has a key signature of one sharp, implying E minor or G major. The opening takes up the implication of the last chord of the first movement, which was the dominant thirteenth of C, by striding rapidly from a unison E to a chord of C major with added sixths and sevenths. C continues to be stressed in the ostinato bass underlying the E majorish main theme, and later in the B major trio. At the end of the trio (bar 64ff), B major shakes itself free of the accompanying C (we are reminded here of the First Quartet) to emerge, if only very briefly, as the first clearly defined tonality in the piece; it may not be too fanciful to take it as an isolated dominant signpost to the E major of the finale. The movement ends abruptly on a G major triad, which we hear as the dominant of C; and the slow movement, Solo, a rhapsodic cantilena for the first violin, begins with the note C and a passage which sounds as if it is in C minor, though it turns out to be in A flat. But C *major* is the goal of this movement: the rapt twenty-one-bar coda is a last, quiet celebration of the key that Britten had especially made his own.

The fourth movement, Burlesque, is in A minor which, as Hans Keller, the quartet's dedicatee, first pointed out, suggests Mahler's Rondo Burleske in the Ninth Symphony: this, too, is an A minor movement following a C major one; there is also a similarity of thematic material and texture, with use of fugato in both movements. The A majorish closing section, after the trio in E flat (an augmented fourth away), is headed *Maggiore*, recalling Beethoven, whose late

quartet scherzos are also not too far in the background. It is tempting
to extend the Britten–Beethoven parallel to this quartet; certainly I
sense in Britten's Third that indefinable 'late' quality shared also by
Schubert's String Quintet—incidentally a C major work with an
E major slow movement—and there is some general similarity
between Britten's Third and Beethoven's opus 135, both of them very
laconic utterances. But the comparison should not be taken too far.

The introduction to the finale returns to the twilight tonal world of
the first movement, against which solo instruments in turn present
the series of quotations from *Death in Venice* mentioned above. The
last of these is the 'I—love you' motif from the end of Act 1: this is
stated in C in the quartet, a final and appropriate return to that key. A
pedal C remains in the second violin and viola while cello and first
violin introduce the E major of the Passacaglia bass and its
accompanying melody. (The Passacaglia bass (Ex.5), Britten said,

Ex.5

was derived from the sound of some Venetian bells.) The held C does
not fade out until the repeat of the tune; but once the music has
reached E major proper it stays there for a diatonic passage even more
extended than that in the slow movement—the most expansive that
Britten allowed himself in all his late music. We cannot but feel that
the redemption of Aschenbach which had begun in *Death in Venice* is
continued here, with the radiant resurrection of his true key: this and
the obvious derivation of the main melody from 'I—love you' make
Britten's intention clear.

The quartet does not end in E major as we have been led to expect;

instead, Britten chooses ambiguity. Ex.6 shows the last three bars of the work: the question posed by the final chord and its lingering cello D is both enigmatic and profound. Something is glimpsed: 'ist dies etwa der Tod?', we might ask, echoing another great composer's last work. With such an eloquently disturbing gesture Britten takes his leave of the string quartet and of chamber music.

Ex.6

35

The Orchestral Works:
Britten as Instrumentalist

CHRISTOPHER PALMER

By 'instrumentalist' I mean not so much a performer on instruments (though Britten had a disconcerting knack of picking up other player's instruments and showing them that allegedly impossible passages were in fact playable) as a composer whose knowledge and understanding of instruments was thoroughly practical, practised and professional. While it is commonplace to pay tribute to this aspect of Britten's art, it would be misleading to suggest that he was the first fully equipped professional orchestral technician in the history of twentieth-century English music. This does scant justice to the achievement of Elgar and Bridge, to name two fellow Englishmen whose music he recorded. Bridge, of course, was a cardinal influence on the development of his style; but with Elgar he needed some time to come to terms, and much of his attitude to orchestration is revealed by the reasons for his initial antipathy to Elgar. It was above all the quality of the texture he disliked, the specific gravity of the sound. As we know, Britten deals in much of his mature work with the theme of the blighting of innocence; here I want to explore the connection between that theme and its expression in physical sound. The rich heavy proto-Edwardian upholstery of Elgar's orchestra, with its wealth of doubling (prodigious, but not prodigal as in Strauss: Elgar in his way was as concerned as Britten with clarity and firmness of outline), repelled Britten because he regarded it, as it were, as a debaser of innocence, of childlike directness. *His* orchestration is as naked, exposed and vulnerable as any of his child-heroes or sacrificial victims; and this particular relating of technical means to expressive ends is obvious enough to have passed, I think, unremarked before.

. In writing for the orchestra Britten was a democrat, a champion of the individual as opposed to the mass collective, an emancipator; as Donald Mitchell has said, *all* his music is chamber music,[1] however small or large the forces for which it is scored, and this is a large part of the secret of his success as a communicator. Players and audience alike feel that they are being provided for or addressed as individuals rather than as a faceless herd. All Britten's solo vocal and instrumental music is associated with certain performers and reflects both their personal and their artistic qualities; and the extension of this principle beyond the immediate confines of solo voice and instrument gives Britten's purely orchestral work its special poetry and distinction.

In view of this it was entirely appropriate that Britten's 'official' opus I should be a piece for chamber ensemble, the *Sinfonietta*, which exhibits in miniature many Britten fingerprints of the future, not least a highly evolved species of thematic consistency (all three movements are thematically interrelated). It appeared to many critics of Britten's early work that manner occupied a higher place in his scheme of things than matter, that virtuosity of technique served to mask an inner hollowness. Fifty years on it is difficult to see how such a view could have originated, save in feelings of suspicion and envy provoked by one so young seeming to know it all without having to be taught. Even so (comparatively) slight a score as the *Sinfonietta* shows that Britten loved strings above all for their warm, expressive, lyrical quality; he loved the human voice, hence his feeling for its nearest instrumental approximate, the strings, which are vocal and sustaining. Warmth, expressiveness, lyricism, humanity—the very qualities denied in Britten's early music by its commentators, yet all indubitably present from the start. There is nothing arid or cerebral about the *Sinfonietta*'s content; it is revealing to find how often the direction *espressivo* is applied, not simply to long lyrical lines and complete melodic sentences such as the second subject of the first movement, but also to phrases and fragments—none too short or fragmentary, however, that Britten didn't want them articulated in a musical manner. He was one of the most essentially *musical* musicians of the twentieth century; in this he resembled Delius, but unlike the older man Britten took pains, even at this early stage, to furnish his scores, down to their seemingly least significant detail, with precise

[1] P.369 above.

instructions as to how they were to be played. Here his own experience as a practical musician must have been a major contributory factor.

Before leaving the *Sinfonietta*, let me draw attention to the sensuousness of the sound of the widespread pizzicato chords which punctuate the climbing melismatic violin theme in the slow movement. Sensuousness is another 'humanistic' quality for which the young Britten was given little credit. Admittedly the *Quatre Chansons Françaises* of 1928, in which this quality is uppermost, were not performed publicly during his lifetime; yet even had they been, critical antagonism would probably have been much the same, perhaps even worse, in that the precocious professionalism which prompted it would have been seen to be even more precocious. But the strings are not the be-all and end-all of the *Sinfonietta*; they share equal honours with the wind, anticipating in small the incisive and unsentimental sound-world of 'Rats Away!' in *Our Hunting Fathers*. In the scoring for wind too is an early, unselfconscious example of an instrumental trick in which Britten took a lifelong delight—causing one instrument to sound like another. Three bars after Figure 11 a bassoon derivative of the melismatic string motif already mentioned is marked *ppp*; a fourth above it the horn climbs in parallel motion and is marked *pp*. The effect is that of two horns. Two bars later the clarinet (marked *ppp*) instead of the bassoon is below the horn, and the sound is uncannily that of two clarinets! We can probably ascribe this to an instinctive feeling on Britten's part for subtleties of register and dynamic. Another interesting example occurs at the *molto meno mosso* in the final Tarantella, in which the double-bass, playing a syncopated rhythmic pattern on the natural harmonic of his open G string, sounds exactly like a tenor drum without snares (shades of the Funeral March in the *Variations on a Theme of Frank Bridge*. But perhaps the most interesting features of this Tarantella are those which prefigure the work Britten thought of as his *real* opus 1, *Our Hunting Fathers* (for high voice and quite large orchestra), which I take into consideration in this chapter inasmuch as it was Britten's first major orchestral score. Not only do we find in the Tarantella the squealing, scampering woodwind scales which invade and infest the orchestra in 'Rats Away!', but its very rhythm is that of the Ravenscroft 'Dance of Death'. Now that Donald Mitchell has pointed out that *Our Hunting Fathers* is deeply concerned with the rise of Fascism in Europe, and that the real subject of 'Dance of Death' is not partridge-hawking but

Christopher Palmer

Jew-hunting,[2] one wonders if Britten had in mind the old apocryphal association of the tarantella with the bite of the tarantula: perhaps to him the tarantella rhythm denoted pestilence, poison and destruction (the same *moto perpetuo* 6/8 recurs in the 'Dance of Death' in the *Sinfonia da Requiem*).

Our Hunting Fathers was designed by W. H. Auden, according to Britten; but the latter had himself already, in the choral variations *A Boy was Born* (1934), innovatively grouped together poems by different authors relating to a common theme.[3] However, it was Auden's modernization of Anon's 'Rats Away!' which set in motion one of Britten's earliest and most original displays of orchestral (and vocal) virtuosity. Donald Mitchell has drawn attention to Mahler's and Britten's tendency in certain circumstances to make the wind, rather than the strings, the predominant sonority in a tutti,[4] and this is responsible for the bitingly, disconcertingly aggressive sound of 'Rats Away!'—disconcerting in particular to contemporary audiences, since even the symphonies Vaughan Williams and Walton wrote in the 1930s (the F minor and the B flat), belligerently dissonant though they are in places, still employ the conventional (Elgarian) tutti of strings, woodwind and brass. There is no such quarter in Britten: the scoring of 'Rats Away!' is raw-nerved and razor-sharp. Symptomatically the full wind band, not the tutti, delivers the first uncompromising statement of the 'motto'. Simultaneously strings and brass interject a version of the same motif cleft down the middle and in rhythmic diminution—an early, albeit primitive, example of Britten heterophony (Ex.1). The soloist's prayer to sundry saints and holy spirits for deliverance from rats is couched in a naïve, repetitive, incantatory pentatonic formula (accompanied, most originally, by solo muted trumpet and trombone with one solo viola in between), but is constructed with a rodent-like wiliness: gaps are left between each phrase of the prayer, which, though filled in by the orchestra the

[2] *BA*, pp.29–49.
[3] The idea may have been suggested to Britten by Bliss's *Pastoral* (1928) and his *Serenade* (1929). Vaughan Williams's Christmas anthology in *Hodie* (1954) postdates Britten's in *A Boy was Born* and *A Ceremony of Carols*.
[4] E.g. in *Gustav Mahler: The Wunderhorn Years* (Faber and Faber, 1975), pp.325ff. 'Mahler's acute sensitivity to the sounds of Nature was one of the prime reasons for his exploitation of wind instruments, which in general character stand closer to the sound-world of Nature than strings, which are more often associated (at any rate in Mahler's music) with human yearning and human passions . . .' (p.330). This also illuminates much in the orchestral thinking of Delius and Britten (cf. my remarks on the *Nocturne*, above, pp.322–7.

Ex.1

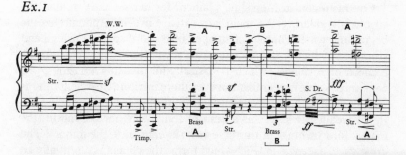

first time round, turn out to be cracks and apertures through which the rats come swarming when the time comes for the *simultaneous* recapitulation of the opening vocal cadenza (on the word 'rats') and the prayer. Mitchell has pointed to the 'pestiferous' sonority of the tuba which is to break out again forty years later to lethal effect in *Death in Venice*; and there is another connection with the same work—with the scene in which the Thomas Cook's Clerk tells Aschenbach about the spread of Asiatic cholera from the Ganges. He does not specifically say that the disease is spread by rats; he does not need to, because we can both hear and see them in the woodwinds employed throughout as accompaniment, nowhere more clearly than at the Clerk's 'Sir, death is at work, the plague is with us!' (Ex.2).

Ex.2

Contrastingly, in Messalina's lament for her monkey we find the strings shouldering the main expressive burden, especially at the beginning, which consists of an open fifth chord spread through and amplified by highly elaborate ten-part string texture (in *Young Apollo* a chord of A major—which is basically all that this amazing piece consists of—receives similar but even more intricate treatment).[5] This hollow open fifth is a recurrent sound in the song and, missing the third, frequently serves as a kind of framework for the motto (the major third turning, in this case *molto espressivo*, to the minor). The great vocal cadenza on 'Fie' which forms the climax is essentially an elaboration of this idea, since Britten alternates major and minor thirds in a sequence of triads which itself descends through thirds (E flat major–B minor–A flat major–E minor). So the musical material is, as often with Britten, of the simplest; and nothing could be simpler than Messalina's hymn-like song of grief with its step-wise melodic motion and rhythmic regularity (Ex.3). Yet the outpouring of woe in

Ex.3

which all culminates must be one of the most impassioned and tumultuous in all Britten; and in this respect the soprano voice is preferable to the tenor, since female hysteria is undeniably more wither-wringing and heartstring-pulling than male, whether inspired by terror, as in 'Rats Away!', or by overwhelming grief, as here. This cadenza expires on a repeated D (surely the only instance in music outside Britten's own *Hymn to St Cecilia* of vocal imitation of a drumbeat), which is then picked up by pizzicato violas (a link here with the double-bass passage in the finale of the *Sinfonietta*) and persists to the end. Above it passes a melancholy procession of instrumental (wind) cadenzas—flute, oboe, clarinet, bassoon, saxophone—each exquisitely disclosed by a soft harp glissando, as it were drawing aside a veil. The drumbeat diminishes to extinction; but now the voice's repeated Ds, having receded into the orchestra, unexpectedly come to the fore again, only not now in mourning for a dead monkey but delivering a roll-call of predators. For without a

---

[5] Such textures can also be described as heterophonic inasmuch as they consist of rhythmically varied or 'staggered' superimposition of the same basic idea.

The Orchestral Works

break the next movement has started, the 'Dance of Death'—and D is very definitely for Death here (as later, in the *Sinfonia da Requiem*). The sound of the voice reeling off these strange names on D is the more chilling for the associations set up in the previous movement, and, in that this movement is at least partly 'about' the hounding and extirpating of the Jews by the Nazis, there is probably significance in the fact that 'Travel' is followed by 'Jew' (i.e. 'Jew—on your way!') Britten makes a point of repeating both names in isolation, and as pointedly juxtaposes 'German' and 'Jew' at the end of the movement. Arresting trombone unisons at regular intervals (they probably had some precise dramatic or representative significance in Britten's mind, perhaps a catch or kill) look forward to the last act of *Billy Budd*, while the abrasive, sardonic, indeed parodistic treatment of folksong and dance bears some relation to Britten's attitude to folksong as demonstrated in the *Suite on English Folk Tunes* (1974). This is in fact an extraordinarily vivid, graphic, 'dramatic and representative' piece in which quasi-visual details abound: the woodwind passage after Figure 38 which suggests a bird coming down in a flurry of feathers, the ingenious use of sparely voiced harp chords to suggest the hawks being released and speeding upwards through the air (before Figure 43). But when we bear in mind that the instrument traditionally associated with the hunt is the horn (just as a traditional hunting rhythm is that of the tarantella), it is not surprising that in the tremendous hurricane which breaks out during the second half of the movement, tearing all the orchestral themes up by the roots and flinging them into the fieriest furnace of symphonic development or distortion, the horns make the strongest impact, whether galloping with the tarantella motif, yelping excitedly and insistently with the dogs' halloo ('Hey dogs hey')[6] or vanishing in the air in a mad flame-like streak of sound (a glissando 'staggered' through the four instruments which only a composer with an intimate knowledge of horn mechanics could have written). As Britten knew, no instrument sounds in its high register quite as hysterical and uncontrolled as the horn; hence the murderously high tessitura in this movement.

Scoring of this virtuoso calibre was unknown in England at the time. For example, Britten requires the chromatic timpani to

[6] To my ears the music is full of suggestions of barking, snapping, scampering and, on the last page, mournful howling or snarling (trombone glissando) and a whimpering final 'whurret' (the pizzicato double-bass slinking off with its tail between its legs).

function in a melodic manner; the part is fearsomely difficult and even today players tend to 'fudge' or 'busk' it at certain points. When played as the composer intended, with hard sticks and in a relatively dry acoustic, the effect is electrifying; and if we look ahead some twenty years we find that in the Wordsworth setting in the *Nocturne* Britten not only associates the timpani with war (the French Revolution) but assigns it a chromatically *melodic* role and on an even more elaborate scale.

It is therefore in this central triptych in D that Britten fires his heaviest orchestral artillery. The scoring of the framing Prologue and Epilogue is more restrained. In the former, where we might well have expected him to illustrate 'the extraordinary compulsion of the deluge and the earthquake' in the orchestra, he does so instead solely by means of vocal inflection—the minor ninth, marvellously realized by Pears on the BBC recording. Donald Mitchell in his sleeve-note for this recording remarks on 'the spacing of the wind and string chords, the transparency of the orchestral colours' in this Prologue, and detects Mahler's influence in the Epilogue and Funeral March, in which 'the xylophone takes over as soloist from the singer and repeats again and again, until its final extinction, a hollow version of the theme which was the basis of the "Dance of Death". . .'. In the Epilogue itself the 'intolerant' lion is characterized by a solo trumpet, the dying quarry by high woodwinds which squeal like an animal caught in a trap—a rat, perhaps? Later, the solo violin's unsentimental, despairing eloquence demonstrates Britten's knack of showing familiar instruments (as well as chords) in a new light.

The relationship of the *Sinfonia da Requiem* to *Our Hunting Fathers* is very close. Both were politically inspired, the one by the gathering storm in Europe, the other by the conflagration at its height. Indeed the *Sinfonia da Requiem* was composed as it were in the heat of the conflict, and at a particularly unsettled time in Britten's personal life; and we may find the third movement, *Requiem aeternam*, somewhat bland or glib until we remind ourselves that its text is a prayer for peace ('Rest eternal grant unto them O Lord'), rather than an expression of peace attained, which was a dim-seeming possibility in 1941. By this time Britten had modified some of the more radical, abrasive stylistic gestures he had made in *Our Hunting Fathers*, to the language of which Shostakovich, as well as Mahler and Berg, had signally contributed. Mahler has now securely established himself as a primary influence. In the powerful, inspiredly simple opening of

Lacrymosa, with its repeated hammerblows on D (D for Death) we can surely hear both an echo of the opening of 'Der Abschied' in *Das Lied von der Erde* (with its massive clods of earth being flung into an open grave) and a foreshadowing of the detonations which bridge the two war-inspired poems in the *Nocturne* (a passage from Words-worth's *Prelude*, and Owen's 'Kind Ghosts'). Donald Mitchell has pointed out to me (in conversation) that the actual model for this opening was almost certainly the funeral cortège (with its obsessive timpani Ds) in the first movement of Mahler's Ninth Symphony. The Mahlerian major–minor third, already incorporated in the motto theme of *Our Hunting Fathers* (see Ex.1), becomes a centrifugal motivic element in the *Sinfonia da Requiem*. All three movements are in D (like the central triptych of *Our Hunting Fathers*). The *Lacrymosa* as it were sets out the twin possibilities: F sharp (=D major), the bringer of peace; or F natural (=D minor), the bringer of war; and is impartial to the extent of presenting, at its climax, major and minor simultaneously. The lamenting alto saxophone of 'Messalina' voices a theme of rising and falling sevenths, as if it were a body being wrenched this way and that by powerfully opposing forces—an impression reinforced when, in the development, horns, trombones and trumpets all vie for ownership in a kind of cosmic tug-o'-war. 'War' is right: the *Dies irae* has chosen F natural in preference to F sharp, war instead of peace, and the resemblances to *Our Hunting Fathers* become even more marked. The flutter-tonguing or trilling of the wind instruments in an all-pervasive simple yet memorable rhythmic motif is chillingly reminiscent of the rolled 'r's of 'whurret' in 'Dance of Death' (Ex.4). The 'pestiferous' tuba of 'Rats Away!' looms and lurches (five bars after Figure 18); a downward-hurtling brass canon over a pedal-point is a specific legacy from 'Dance of Death'; then at Figure 22, *con anima*, the tarantella rhythm of the

Ex.4a Sinfonia da Requiem

Ex.4b Our Hunting Fathers

Sinfonietta and of 'Dance of Death' returns, together with the yapping, baying hunting horns—six of them this time, and more lethal than before: for whereas in 1936 the hunt seemed eventually to peter out in dismal wound-licking disarray, the upshot here is that the music is blown to pieces.[7] Meteoric fragments of sound fly in all directions, yet with the same deadly mechanized precision as in 'Rats Away!'; it is as if all entreaties to the higher powers have failed and the rats have finally accomplished their aim of destroying the civilized world. Yet from these rags and tatters of notes a new hope is born. Matter can be neither created nor destroyed, and from the ashes of the *Lacrymosa* and *Dies irae* arises the *Requiem aeternam*; and it is typical of a master composer that he can satisfy at one and the same time the claims of programmatic versimilitude and of symphonic consistency and logic.

Britten's next orchestra venture after *Our Hunting Fathers* was *Mont Juic*, a suite of four Catalan dances, composed in collaboration with Lennox Berkeley and based on folk tunes they had heard in Barcelona in 1936. *Mont Juic* raises the whole question of Britten's craft as an arranger, and it is a pity that his orchestral versions of certain of his English and French folksong settings are so little known, for in all cases they add a new dimension to the settings themselves. The singer in 'Waly Waly' is drowned heart, soul and senses in love as in the sea; Britten's accompaniment suggests the ebb and flow of the waters in ever-changing sameness, and the strings ebb and flow much more naturally and effortlessly than the piano. In 'Come you not from Newcastle?' Britten depicts the two lovers on horseback, riding after each other and disappearing in the distance (high violin harmonics on the last chord). The old woman in 'Fileuse' sits at her spinning-wheel (harp); as it revolves ever faster it mobilizes a virtuoso orchestra which engulfs her (and us) in a flood of ecstatic, dancing memories, only to leave her, in a poignant *envoi*, still spinning forlornly. 'The Bonny Earl o' Moray' is transformed into a quasi-Mahlerian funeral march complete with bass drum and cymbals and a basic sonority in which wind and brass, rather than strings, take the leading role. Elsewhere the orchestration serves to enhance rather than enlarge upon the piano accompaniments: the solo cello in 'The Salley Gardens' adds an extra note of pathos to the lover's regret; in

---

[7] Much of the impact of the *Sinfonia da Requiem* is diluted on the composer's second Decca recording (SXL 6175) by the mushy Kingsway Hall acoustic. His earlier Danish Radio version, for all its brittleness, gives a truer account of the piece.

the refrain of the exquisite Scots lullaby 'O can ye sew cushions?' the reedy tang of the oboes suggests bagpipes; and the ploughboy's piccolo invests his whistle with delightful pertness. The most extrovert arrangement is 'Quand j'étais chez mon père', whose galumphing *Ländler*-like rhythm Britten drives to a climax of exultant, earthy dissonance with horn-whoops on the downbeats.

In the case of both *Mont Juic* and the two Rossini suites (*Soirées Musicales* and *Matinées Musicales*) Britten is not concerned with any extra-musical connotations (with one possible exception) and is therefore free to go whatever way his purely musical (as opposed to his musico-dramatic) fancy leads him. It is generally assumed that in *Mont Juic* Britten contributed dances 2 and 4 and Berkeley dances 1 and 3, which have conventionally fuller, less soloistic, less Brittenish scoring. Yet I feel that Britten may well have had a hand in the conception of No.3, 'Lament', if not in its execution. Subtitled 'Barcelona 1936', it reflects something of the composers' feelings about a city poised on the brink of civil war. At the outset an elegiac tune firmly establishes itself in C minor and a smooth 3/4; but before long a second tune intrudes, in C major and a gay 6/8, like the sound of distant merry-making. The two continue in surrealistic combination until the merry-makers are engulfed in tragedy. We are reminded of the little boy in the second Hugo setting in the *Quatre Chansons Françaises*, insouciantly fluting his nursery song while his mother lies dying.

Soirées Musicales was written for the GPO Film Unit's *The Tocher*, and was originally scored for a much smaller ensemble (but including voices) than the published version. Rossini exhibits many of the qualities Britten admired in the music of others—fertile, spontaneous, uncomplicated invention, warmth, melodiousness and colour—and in both suites the younger composer was apparently happy to accommodate his own exuberant powers of orchestral invention to Rossini's manner. (He was later to pay a similar kind of tribute to Tchaikovsky in *The Prince of the Pagodas*, although without incorporating any of Tchaikovsky's actual music.)[8] Since Britten does not so much 'arrange' Rossini for orchestra as rethink the music in contemporary orchestral terms, some of it emerges sounding more like Britten than Rossini. A conspicuously brilliant example is the Finale of *Matinées Musicales*, Moto perpetuo (subtitled 'Solfeggi gorgheggi'), in which Britten's relation to Rossini is nearer that

[8] See above, pp.201–2.

Christopher Palmer

of Brahms to Haydn in the *St Anthony Variations*—for instance at Figure 30, where the flutes cut themselves adrift from their harp accompaniment in a manner already familiar from both *Mont Juic* and *Canadian Carnival*. But even when Britten adheres more scrupulously to his text, there are frequent imaginative touches: the solo celesta in the Nocturne, the gurgly, sonorous harp and clarinet triplets in yet another Tarantella, the xylophone solo in the March of *Soirées Musicales* and, in the same piece, the piccolo solo whose oompah bass and harmonies are provided solely by the (unpitched) bass drum and attached cymbal, the ear unconsciously providing the appropriate pitches—surely the *ne plus ultra* of Britten's art as an orchestral illusionist.

Even in so apparently cut-and-dried a case as these Rossini transcriptions it is not easy to mark exactly where arranging ends and composing begins, and it is still less easy in *Canadian Carnival* and the *Suite on English Folk Tunes*, where Britten allows his fantasy free rein. In the folksong arrangements proper, even if he starts out from the premise that the tune is 'his', the text requires that it be preserved intact and retain some of its own emotional resonance (this applies also of course to *Men of Goodwill*, a set of variations on 'God rest ye merry, gentlemen' written for a BBC programme broadcast on Christmas Day 1947 and described as a 'Christmas journey across the world'). But in the case of *Canadian Carnival*, its near contemporary the *Scottish Ballad*, and the *Suite on English Folk Tunes*, these restrictions are lifted. In Peter Evans's words, Britten 'accepts that to "set" a folk tune is artificial, ensures that the nature of the artifice adopted is in some sense prompted by the tune, but then makes no attempt to suppress his own inclinations in developing it.'[9] I suspect the model here was not so much Grainger as Bridge, whose settings for string orchestra of 'Cherry Ripe', 'Sally in our Alley' and, more particularly, 'Sir Roger de Coverley' and 'An Irish Melody', follow the same brief; Bridge was never part of the mainstream folksong movement and was opposed to many of its musical tenets, and in this respect as in so many others he strongly influenced his pupil. We should note too that Britten assumed his emancipated attitude to folksong in a work of totally non-English inspiration. He had left England for North America in search of emotional and physical freedom, and the wide-open Whitmanesque grandeur of prairies, rocks and spacious skies evoked in the Prologue and Epilogue to

[9] *MBB*, p.338.

404

Canadian Carnival (distant trumpet, the cold clear-air *frisson* of the two suspended cymbals, tremolando strings glimmering as the pure blue of mountain peaks in sunshine) is symbolic as well as programmatic. The strings' glacial shimmerings persist around an increasingly animated dialogue of winds and brass (the somewhat slow-speaking sonority of the low register of the horn brightened by the harp), whose B flat tonality is too secure to be dislodged when a lively D major hoe-down irrupts: the two keys form an amiable partnership, as if the merry-making were taking place against a mountain backdrop. This innocuously bitonal episode heralds Britten's inclination, later in the piece, to impose an alternative or even contradictory perspective on the original tune. The central amoroso waltz–lullaby, for example, moves to a slightly out-of-phase accompaniment and consists of a single phrase in endlessly varied expansions, retractions and 'staggered' superimpositions, a far cry from the bland or juicy type of treatment its concertina-like thirds might conventionally have attracted; and as it retreats from its climax with the same studied imperturbability with which it advanced, it features now the harp, now the timpani in a melodic capacity (Britten's 'orchestra of soloists' again). The climactic return of the opening mountain music is preceded by 'Alouette'; but, as Mitchell says,

> . . . it is hardly the cheery arrangement we might have expected. On the contrary, it is spiky in character, ambiguously harmonized and altogether unconventional in sound: the dance is cunningly built up from percussion, woodwind in pairs, brass and lower strings only, gradually increasing in density until the climax, when the whole orchestra joins in the energetic but still waspish revels.[10]

This is preceded by a bleak and increasingly troubled episode in which the mountain-peaks seem to become obscured by mist (close-worked canonic texture for high muted strings) and silently invaded by ominously motionless, unrelated open-spaced triads in the brass. The atmosphere becomes tense, almost anguished, until suddenly dispelled by 'Alouette' with its own brand of edginess.

One reason for Britten's ambivalent response to folksong[11] may

[10] Sleeve-note for EMI ASD 4177.
[11] In an article in the January–February 1941 issue of *Modern Music* (a quarterly review, now defunct, published by the American League of Composers), Britten defines the main attractions of English folksongs as 'the sweetness of their melodies, the close

well have been that he regarded it as a musical incarnation of an 'innocence' destined inevitably to fall prey to the 'experience' of contemporary compositional techniques. The conflict is already expressed in the 'Dance of Death' in *Our Hunting Fathers*, where 'merry folksong and dance' (Britten's words) is specifically associated with killing for personal gratification, and it comes as no surprise to find reminiscences of this movement in the somewhat frenzied virtuoso fiddling of 'Hunt the Squirrel' in the late *Suite on English Folk Tunes*.[12] The same sort of 'confrontation' occurs in the second movement of this suite, 'The Bitter Withy'. (True to his 'soloistic' principles, Britten employs the full orchestra in the first movement and then takes it apart—harp and strings predominate in the second movement, the third, 'Hankin Booby', is a tart quasi-medieval dance for wind and drum, and 'Hunt the Squirrel' is a display-piece for violins—reassembling it in 'Lord Melbourne', an anguished valediction with curlew-cries (muted trumpet and woodwinds) re-echoing over the marshes.) The clear-water diatonic G major of the opening (with its bright chunky harp solo marked, *à la* Grainger, 'ringingly') is soon clouded, first by the E minor of the 'The Mermaid' with its tolling horns and bell, and then, irreparably, by 'The Bitter Withy' itself on its reprise: a canker of wrong notes, distorting the melody, begins in the inner parts, quickly attacks the harp (an F minor arpeggio has no place within a basic G major tonality) and spreads through the whole texture, the sudden downward-swooping, bird-of-prey like harp glissandi reminding us of Aschenbach as he 'rejects the words brought forth by passion'. These are muddy, cloudy waters; that they miraculously clear in a return to G major for the final cadence seems only to emphasize the conflict. I cannot resist quoting a passage from Henry Williamson's *Children of Shallowford* which seems peculiarly apposite to Britten's predicament as here expressed. Williamson is describing a romp with his children in the country around Exmoor:

connection between words and music, and the quiet, uneventful charm of the atmosphere'. However he rejects folksongs as raw material for composition, chiefly because of the severe formal and harmonic restrictions they impose. Interestingly, he remembers 'Scottish fisher-girls who visited my home town of Lowestoft to gut the herrings every fall, singing their lovely, lilting Highland tunes'. Are the latter perhaps recalled in the no less 'lovely, lilting Highland tunes' we find in *A Charm of Lullabies*, *Who are these children?* and *A Birthday Hansel*? Britten's settings of Scottish folksongs (e.g. 'O can ye sew cushions') are among his best.
12 For fuller discussion of this suite, see above, p.74.

Father, thank God, was forgotten; I was one of them, I had got back, for a while, to the land of enchantment, of unselfconsciousness, to the world of otters, deer, salmon, water, moonshine, and Cold Pudding—the only world in which perhaps there was consistency, form, integrity. Back again in the house, with . . . the *ever-pressing need to turn feelings into words*, this world too often faded, and the children were problems of noise, dirt, and even irritation; but never of resentment (my italics).

Britten is less 'irritated' when his thematic *donnée* is not folk-inspired, as in *Russian Funeral* (1936) for brass and percussion (based on a Russian proletarian funeral song, which, though admittedly of 'popular' origin, is treated by Britten in a sombre quasi-liturgical manner which in no way conflicts with its original character), the *Young Person's Guide to the Orchestra* and the overture *The Building of the House*. Peter Evans finds little to admire in the *Young Person's Guide*: he criticizes the clumsiness of the transitions, the conventionality and 'obviousness' of the instrumental writing (e.g. the harp's variation) and much else. Yet the *Young Person's Guide* is exactly what it says it is; it is designed to acquaint young listeners with the basic sounds of the orchestral departments. These departments all make strong, clear, direct statements but in Britten's authentic tone of voice; and what they have to say is never less than relevant and often memorable: the combination of horns and trombones in the brass's initial statement of the theme; the sadly maligned harp variation which, in its string tremolos and resonant gong-strokes, anticipates the music of Pagoda-land in *The Prince of the Pagodas*; the fine unison tune in the trombones' own variation; the use of a timpani 'fanfare' as a ritornello as the percussion are put through their paces, and so on.

The Building of the House employs the old Lutheran chorale 'Vater Unser', a favourite of J. S. Bach but more familiar to the English as the tune of 'O quickly come great Judge of all'. It is one of Britten's most attractive shorter works and his only orchestral score to belong in the stylistic world of the church parables. It makes great play with heterophonic textures among the several sections of the orchestra (e.g. semiquavers against quaver triplets against quavers against crotchet triplets, as at the start); is designed for performance in a resonant acoustic (not a church in this instance but Snape Maltings concert hall); and derives all its essential motivic sustenance from the chorale. The opening complements the cover of the score, a photograph of the Maltings under conversion: the scurrying, racing string figures (excitingly enhanced, of course, by the acoustic) depict the speed of the planning and building and the enthusiasm of those involved. Against this background the chorale begins to assert itself in a proud unison of brass and voices but, remembering that much remains to be done, settles instead for a quiet four-part harmonization in (uncommon-sounding) common chords; a quirky, characteristic touch is provided by the woodwind embellishment of the tune with a series of frolicking, dancing obbligati. After a ruminative central episode in which strings spin a fugal texture in long *dolce espressivo* lines, the chorale finally delivers itself, majestic and now unimpeded, in counterpoint with the work-in-progress figuration. The final chord is a blazing, affirmatory D major; and on the back cover of the score is the completed Maltings.

By way of conclusion, Britten's music for strings calls for special consideration. The would-be orchestrator who plays no orchestral instrument can bluff his way convincingly enough through the successive departments of woodwind, brass, percussion and harp; but the strings are sure to unmask him. Only those who know the strings from the inside, i.e. as players, can write for them as idiomatically and *creatively* as did Britten from his youth. The *Variations on a Theme of Frank Bridge*, the first work to draw attention to him as a composer potentially of international stature, was no bolt from the blue, however it may have appeared at the time; Britten's oft-praised (though more often blamed) facility was, as Donald Mitchell has demonstrated, something of a myth, and he had prepared for the *Bridge Variations* in a series of works for strings, only one of which, the *Simple Symphony*, was published in his lifetime. Here the Boisterous Bourrée, the Sentimental Sarabande and the tarantella rhythms of the Playful Pizzicato look forward to his use of old-style dance-forms in the *Bridge Variations* and elsewhere; but the work's main interest lies in the richly eloquent scoring for strings. It is hard to see why Britten forgot or turned against the *Three Divertimenti* for string quartet (published posthumously in its revised form under this title; originally *Go play, boy, play*, for it is attractive music—the Waltz is one of his most affectingly simple melodic inspirations— besides being prophetic of points of his later style. The movements' titles (March, Waltz, Burlesque) suggest the *Bridge Variations*; whole stretches in the March show Britten's characteristic predilection for euphonious chains of thirds; the Burlesque has the *moto perpetuo* tarantella-like theme that appears time and time again in the music of the following years; and the scoring reveals not only what Imogen Holst called Britten's understanding of the 'feel as well as the sound of strings'[13] but delight in the resonant, natural, 'gutsy' sound of double- or triple-stopped *open* strings which he retained throughout his life (in the *Nocturne*'s 'Kraken', for instance, he directs the players to leave their open A strings twanging and resonating at every opportunity). But more significant than these various technical points is the fine passage shortly before the coda in the Burlesque marked *cantabile ed esultante*, 'singing and exultant'. Robin Holloway charges much of Britten with an 'inability to let go'.[14] I detect no such failure in this music, nor in the best parts of the *Bridge Variations*.

The 'fun' movements of these variations, the March, Aria Italiana and the rest, have attracted comment to the unjust neglect of the others. There has been little appreciation of the Adagio with its keening violins, their expanding melodic flights, *sempre più appassionato*, soaring in flame-like bursts out of the enveloping chordal darkness of violas, cellos and basses; or of the Chant which, with its high pizzicati and harmonics (an unusual combination), inhabits the mysterious, glimmering twilight world Bridge loved; or of the gradual shaping of the Bridge theme against the intense and intricate contrapuntal industry of the Fugue, which gradually retreats and disperses as though to allow the full, radiant emergence of its *raison d'être*; or of the warmth and depth of feeling communicated by this crowning final statement, *lento e solenne*, one of the finest moments in the work. And if Britten's later offering to the Boyd Neel Orchestra, the *Prelude and Fugue* for eighteen-part string orchestra, begins with music of 'thin-ness',[15] i.e. austere, severe, grey, dry (I use the terms in a non-pejorative sense), what 'fat-ness' is unloosed in the Fugue, one of Britten's most exhilarating inspirations. The telescoped diatonic chords which Boyd Neel likens to cathedral chimes[16] originate in the climax of the *Phantasy Quintet* for strings, and reappear in another but very different ecstatic outburst in Britten's last work with strings (alone except for percussion and harpsichord), the cantata *Phaedra*, written for Janet Baker. Here the contrast between 'thin-ness' and

[13] *BR*, p.16.
[14] Above, pp.225–6.
[15] Robin Holloway: see above, pp.225–6.
[16] BS, p.243.

'fat-ness' has dramatic point. Passion has led Phaedra, like Aschenbach, to the abyss; but instead of allowing it to drag her down in a state of acquiescent non-resistance, she throws herself defiantly into it. The 'scrawny' string music[17] with its equally 'scrawny' harpsichord continuo (surely, *pace* Professor Evans, it was precisely *because* the harpsichord does not have the weight or carrying-power of the piano that Britten chose it) and the dry, 'scrawny', sound of the timpani played near the rim with side-drum sticks all represent Phaedra's account of the 'negative' train of events which led to her decision to take a 'positive' stand. Not surprisingly the string agitation in the *presto* episode recalls that of Aschenbach rejecting 'the words brought forth by passion', suspecting the 'easy judgement of the heart'; more startling, though no less logical, is the reminiscence of Mrs Sedley's rather theatrically macabre 'Crime that my hobby is' in *Peter Grimes*, with its rising and falling chromatic shape, at Phaedra's 'The very dust rises to disabuse my husband—to defame me and acuse'. The climactic death scene itself is surely one of the great moments in Britten. The texture of telescoped chords, rich, resolute and commanding, unfurls and expands upwards and outwards like some beautiful gigantic tropical bloom—a wonderful undreamt-of enlarging of perspective. This music consists only of diatonically superimposed triads; but was there ever such a past master in the uncommon handling of 'common' chords as Britten? The basic key is ('Britten's') C major, and the chord to which the music aspires for consummation and transfiguration is that of *Das Lied von der Erde*—C major with the added sixth, A (Britten also adds the second or ninth, D, to form an even more orientally pentatonic-sounding chord than Mahler's). This chord prescribes a limit to our earthly sight; Phaedra goes on, but we cannot see her. The spectral, disjointed recollections of earlier motifs are as chaff in the wind; the only reality is the all-encompassing C major–added sixth chord, which sustains to the end, Mahlerian, Delian and now Brittenian symbol of *die liebe Erde*, the eternally blue horizon.

[17] *MBB*, p.398.

36
The Concertos

JOHN EVANS

Britten's works for solo instrument (or instruments) and orchestra span the entire period of his mature composing career. His earliest published work in this genre is the Piano Concerto, composed in the early summer of 1938, his last the version of *Lachrymae* for viola and strings, Op.48a, which occupied him ten months before his death in December 1976. Though his most substantial essay in this form—the Symphony for Cello and Orchestra—dates from the mid-1960s, the majority of the works considered here belong to the period immediately before and during his sojourn in North America in the early years of the Second World War.

Britten completed the Piano Concerto on 26 July 1938, shortly after moving to the Old Mill at Snape. He was the soloist for the first performance in a Promenade Concert on 18 August 1938 at the Queen's Hall, London, with the BBC Symphony Orchestra conducted by Sir Henry Wood. The concerto was, as much as anything, a vehicle to introduce himself, Mozart-like in the role of composer-performer, to a contemporary audience in London; and he continued to appear as interpreter of his own music—as pianist, accompanist or conductor—throughout his career.

In many respects the Piano Concerto is an uncharacteristic work. In the programme note provided for the Promenade Concert Britten explained that the concerto 'was conceived with the idea of exploiting various important characteristics of the pianoforte, such as its enormous compass, its percussive quality, and its suitability for figuration; so that it is not by any means a Symphony with pianoforte, but rather a bravura Concerto with orchestral accompaniment'. (The 'Symphony', did not appear till 1963, when it turned out to be for *cello* and orchestra.) In the Piano Concerto Britten was content to exercise his unmistakable technical brilliance, composing a truly 'bravura' concerto of an extrovert nature, perhaps surprising from the shy, slight, somewhat introvert figure that Britten cut as a young man.

As in many of his chamber works of the period, Britten sidesteps the 'pure' considerations of form and function established by classical models and constructs his concerto in four character-movements entitled Toccata, Waltz, Impromptu[1] and March. However, he had already proved conclusively in the *Variations on a Theme of Frank Bridge* (and to a degree in the unpublished *Alla Quartetto Serioso: Go play, boy, play* (1933), revised in 1936 as *Three Divertimenti*) that he was able to reconcile classical forms with styles that owe their impact to colour rather than design, and certainly in the Toccata he achieves this reconciliation with remarkable success. It exploits the piano's percussive quality in a sometimes aggressive dialogue with predominantly more sustained orchestral textures. The rising major seventh of the opening figure persists throughout the work, defining the span of the waltz tune in the second movement and penetrating the March via the fanfare-like tailpiece to the soloist's opening gesture. The Toccata remains one of the Britten's largest sonata structures, with a development section juxtaposing the percussive and the sustained over long-ranging pedals and excursions into flat-key regions, notably B flat. The handling of the recapitulation is characteristic of the composer's approach to sonata form: as in the first movements of the *Sinfonietta* and the String Quartet No.2, the reprise of the first subject is underpinned by a simultaneous recapitulation of the second subject in augmentation.

The Waltz, in a simple ternary design, is one of the strangest examples of a form of which Britten was clearly fond; other notable examples from his early period include the last movement of the *Suite*, Op.6 (1935), for violin and piano, and the sixth of the *Bridge Variations*. The waltz tune itself predates the concerto (which makes its motivic relationship with the Toccata and March themes even more extraordinary): in 1933 Britten had begun a part-song setting of 'By the moon we sport and play' from *The Maid's Metamorphosis* (Anon)[2] based on the same waltz tune and in the same key of D major.

---

[1] Composed in 1945 to replace the original Recitative and Aria. See above, n.13, p.34.
[2] In the composition sketch Britten stops just as he is beginning to set the second part of the text from *The Maid's Metamorphosis* with the words 'Round about, round about, in a fine ring a'. His last completed work, the *Welcome Ode*, Op.95, for young people's chorus and orchestra, includes a setting of that very text in the Roundel, its central movement (see above, p.24, Ex.1).

The concerto movement, however, introduces a tonal juxtaposition at the third (B flat against D)—an ambivalence that was later to be exploited in the *Requiem aeternam* of the *Sinfonia da Requiem*.

The Impromptu is a passacaglia with seven variations and was composed at the time of the completion of *Peter Grimes* (1945). Not surprisingly, then, it is a movement of great subtlety and distinction, and shares its form and brooding nature with the most profound of the *Grimes* Interludes. In an attempt to relate the musical language of the Impromptu with the original movements of 1938, Britten took the passacaglia theme[3] (a somewhat curious invention of rising and falling scales in intervals of augmented seconds and semitones) from incidental music he had composed in the same year as the concerto, for a BBC radio drama, *King Arthur*. The theme, although foreshadowed in earlier passages of *King Arthur*, is exposed in unison string tremolandi in Movement IX of the BBC score (Ex.1) and serves

Ex.1

as a leading motif for long stretches of the incidental music. Britten also exploited one distinctive figurative pattern from the original Recitative and Aria, transforming the fourth variation, with the aid of glockenspiel, harp and horn, into the musical box of Dohnányi's *Nursery Variations* (Ex.2). It is interesting to note that this variation is the most closely related to the music of 1938, in that the tremolandi

[3] Walton's *Improvisations on an Impromptu of Benjamin Britten* is based on this theme.

Ex.2

string textures and the horn pedals are precisely those of Ex. 1 from *King Arthur*. The final March is again a sonata scheme with a fanfare-like first subject and, in vivid contrast, a chant-like second subject that achieves its true status in the development. Like the Toccata, the movement betrays the influence of Bartók and Shostakovich, but the thrilling ascent through the cadenza to the recapitulation is pure Britten.

Work began on the Violin Concerto in November 1938, four months after the première of the Piano Concerto. It is a very different work from its predecessor, more symphonic than bravura; not yet the symphony of 1963, but with a solo part so demanding of a virtuoso that even Jascha Heifetz pronounced it unplayable. While working on it Britten left for North America (May 1939), and the score was finally completed in St Jovite, Quebec, on 29 September 1939. The Spanish violinist Antonio Brosa gave the first performance with the New York Philharmonic under John Barbirolli at Carnegie Hall, New York, on 27 March 1940. In Donald Mitchell's BBC radio documentary, *Benjamin Britten: The Early Years*,[4] Brosa recalled that the arresting, recurrent rhythm on percussion at the opening of the concerto (Ex.3) was Spanish in origin; and he suggested that this, and the sombre, intense nature of much of the work, was Britten's musical response to the defeats and horrors of the Spanish Civil War. (Britten and Brosa had visited Spain together in 1936, when they performed the composer's *Suite*, Op.6, at the ISCM Festival at Barcelona.)

Ex.3

In its broadest formal structures the Violin Concerto is the concerto counterpart of the *Sinfonia da Requiem*: a symphonic first movement of moderate pace, a central scherzo in the nature of an Audenesque 'Dance of Death', and a noble, valedictory finale, all played virtually without a break and with the tonal region of D as a central point of departure. However, though described as being 'in D', the work could be said to be in both D major and D minor. The sonata structure

---

[4] First broadcast on 18 April 1980, BBC Radio 3. Antonio Brosa was interviewed by the programme's producer, Anthony Friese-Greene.

of the first movement explores the tonal regions suggested by the D minor triad (D–F *natural*–A) and the hovering trill for the soloist at the end of the work oscillates between F and F sharp over an open fifth on D, sustaining the ambivalence of mode to the very end.

The soloist introduces both the first and the second subjects of the first movement (Moderato con moto), the first being a haunting chromatic melody, as extended in its lyricism as the second subject is muscular in its angular turns of rhythmic animation. The movement achieves its climax at the point of recapitulation—with the roles reversed, the soloist imitating the opening percussion motif under the first subject in the orchestral strings—and there is no reprise of the second subject. The E minor scherzo (Vivace) is a driving, spirited movement, aggressive and at times grotesque in its brilliance. The central A minor trio is somewhat more relaxed, but the 'Dance of Death' is never far beneath the surface and engineers its return via a weird transition scored for two piccolos and tuba[5] (over string tremolandi). After a considerable orchestral tutti, a brilliant cadenza for the soloist forges a link between the scherzo and the Passacaglia. Here the trombones—heard for the first time in the concerto, rather as Brahms had postponed their arrival (also to the beginning of the finale) in the First Symphony—introduce the ground bass in a free fugal exposition. Nine variations arise from the ground, through which the soloist regains a noble supremacy and even dares to invert the ground in the sixth variation (*comodo molto*). This is the first example of Britten's use of the characteristically Purcellian passacaglia form (the passacaglia from the Piano Concerto dates from the wartime revision) that became characteristic of the composer in *nobilmente* mood.

Britten made slight revisions to the Violin Concerto in 1950, slight indeed by comparison with those of the Piano Concerto, and generally undertaken to tighten the forms and occasionally to clarify the textures. In addition, some of the rococo complexities of Brosa's original editorial work on the solo part were brought back into line with the composer's original conception of the relationship between the virtuoso and the symphonic elements of the work.

Young Apollo, a 'Fanfare for Pianoforte solo, String Quartet and String Orchestra', was commissioned by the Canadian Broadcasting Corporation in the summer of 1939, when Britten and Pears were

[5] Cf. the double portrait cadenza in the Prelude to *Owen Wingrave*.

visiting Toronto *en route* for the United States. Writing to Enid Slater (the wife of Montagu Slater, the librettist of *Peter Grimes*) from Woodstock, New York, on 29 July 1939, Britten referred to the new work:

> I've got to go back to Toronto on August 27th to give the first performance of a new bit I've just done—piano and strings—title not yet decided but it is founded on the end of Hyperion 'from all his limbs celestial'. . . . It is very bright and brilliant music—rather inspired by such sunshine as I've never seen before. But I'm pleased with it—may call it 'The Young Apollo', if that doesn't sound too lush! But it *is* lush!

As his letter indicates, Britten once more assumed the role of composer-performer as soloist for the première of *Young Apollo*, which was conducted by the dedicatee, Alexander Chuhaldin. Although it was given an opus number (16) Britten decided to withdraw the work shortly after its première, and it was not heard again until its revival at the 1979 Aldeburgh Festival.

Though one should not overestimate the stature of this score (evidently Britten felt he had good reason to withdraw it, and in comparison with the Violin Concerto or the Cello Symphony it is, indeed, slight), *Young Apollo* is strikingly original in a totally uncompromising way, 'bright and brilliant music' and unquestionably 'inspired'. It is set in Britten's 'Apollonian' key of A major,[6] though at first without the characteristic Lydian inflection that pervades Tadzio's music in *Death in Venice*.

The string writing has all the flair of the composer of the *Bridge Variations* and *Les Illuminations*, the tutti being divisi throughout, contributing much to the 'lush' quality of the score. The solo quartet introduces the principal fanfare theme in the introductory section (*moderato*) between cadenza-like flourishes for solo piano; and this theme strives to widen its span to the leaping major sevenths (Ex.4) which had been the principal unifying motif through the movements of the Piano Concerto. After a brilliant cadenza for the soloist (Apollo

Ex.4

---

[6] See n.11, above, p.315.

shedding his mortal form?) the introductory *moderato* gives way to an *allegro molto*. Thereafter the sun god, as Britten says in his programme note for the première, 'stands before us . . . quivering with radiant vitality'. Within a single-movement structure, not unlike those of the *Phantasy Quartet, Phantasy Quintet* and *Reveille*,[7] Britten manipulates his material with great skill. The *allegro molto* changes the basic pulse from 4/4 to 6/8 but sustains to the very end the emphatic A major tonality. A fantastic dance starts up, demanding a wide variety of string techniques (tremolando, sul ponticello, glissando, 'quasi col legno'—played with an equal amount of wood and hair, with the bow held horizontally) as it becomes more animated. The opening fanfare motif returns in augmentation in the broad *maestoso*, the subject alternating between tutti and solo strings under piano figuration. A new chorale-like development of the fanfare (Figure 16) is entrusted to the string quartet, a rising chromatic bass preparing for the reprise of the *moderato*. After a brief development of the fanfare, the fantastic dance intervenes, providing a heady coda with a final reference to the fanfare in augmentation in the five-bar *lento*.

Britten's *Diversions* for piano (left hand) and orchestra was commissioned by the Viennese pianist, Paul Wittgenstein,[8] who had commissioned similar works from, amongst others, Richard Strauss, Ravel and Prokofiev. As Britten's publication note explains, his objective was not to suggest the illusion of two-handed sonorities and textures, but to exploit the single line in a wide variety of guises; thus in some respects *Diversions* could be compared more closely with the Violin Concerto than with the works for piano and orchestra discussed above. And this would be a fruitful exercise were it not that Britten's structural solution to his declared objective ('to treat the problem in every aspect') was, once more, to avoid the formal problems posed by what could be described as the symphonic concerto, and write an episodic work of 'straight-forward and concise variations on a simple musical scheme'. Thus *Diversions* is yet another set of character-movements: a theme and ten variations with a tarantella finale. (When revising the score in 1951, Britten cut the seventh variation, Ritmico, and modified some of the orchestration in

---

7 Another 'fanfare', a concert study for violin and piano composed in 1937 for Antonio Brosa.
8 Wittgenstein had lost his right arm in the First World War but none the less sustained a brilliant career, and enriched the piano repertoire with a number of distinguished commissions.

the Finale.) This design brings to mind the *Bridge Variations*, but whereas Britten's (brilliantly successful) aim in 1937 was to exploit a wide variety of musical styles and remain poised just short of pastiche, in *Diversions* these adopted styles become pegs on which to hang contrasting pianistic styles and skills. Britten's publication note comments illuminatingly on these styles and skills. The theme on which the variations are based is exposed by the orchestra in the opening Recitative over a persistent pedal C (Ex.5). It bears a very close relation to the twelve-note series on which *The Turn of the Screw* is based, being constructed from open fifths and fourths—an intervallic scheme affording the composer a high degree of flexibility.

Ex.5

Scottish Ballad, one of the last works Britten composed in the United States before returning to the United Kingdom in 1942, was written in Escondido, California, in the summer of 1941 for the husband-and-wife piano duo Rae Robertson and Ethel Bartlett. It may have been composed at their request, and it seems likely that Robertson, who was Scottish by birth, suggested the use of Scottish hymns and folksongs in this ballad for two pianos and orchestra.[9] Britten's intention was 'to evoke a sequence of ideas and emotions that have been characteristic of the life of Scottish people during centuries of stormy history'.

The *Ballad* is constructed rather in the manner of an introduction and allegro: a broad funeral march with a central trio, and a scherzo that begins as a spirited Scottish reel but develops into a more substantial (but no less spirited) argument between soloists and

[9] Britten had previously used original French-Canadian folk tunes ('Là-bas sur les montagnes!', 'Jardin d'amour', 'La Perdriole' and 'Alouette') in the concert overture *Canadian Carnival* (1939). And in 1974 he used original English folk melodies in the orchestral *Suite on English Folk Tunes*.

419

orchestra. The March opens with the noble psalm tune, 'Dundee', scored for the two pianos with punctuating flourishes from the orchestra. This establishes a central juxtaposition of C and A minor (a third apart, as in the Waltz of the Piano Concerto and the *Requiem aeternam* of the *Sinfonia da Requiem*), and the tonal focus becomes yet more blurred as we move into a cadenza for the soloists that gives way to the funeral march rhythm in the timpani, complete with scotch snap, and a move into C minor. 'Turn ye to me' is introduced as counter-subject, at first in the oboes; and the central trio is based on a touching rendering of 'Flowers of the forest', in F major, which reaches a sonorous climax when scored for brass. The March reprise brings back 'Dundee' together with the themes of the March proper, and via a transition (*allegro molto*) we fly headlong into the reel, with the two pianos in competitive dialogue, over an open-fifth drone on A in divisi second violins with a solo violin reinstating a persistent flattened seventh (G natural), introduced in the transition and now reinforced by the two-sharp key signature. Thereafter the eight-bar reel spins in ever more exhilarating variations, sometimes contracting, sometimes extending its phrasing. There are flashes of Prokofiev and Shostakovich (notably in the variation beginning three bars after Figure 270) and a wonderful representation of a misty highland landscape (at Figure 30 with the reel at four-octave unison at the extremes of the keyboard for Piano I and bisbigliando triplets isolated in the middle register for Piano II over pizzicato violins and double-basses), across which distant strains of 'Turn ye to me' are heard from the woodwind. An intoxicating coda (*vivacissimo*) resolves the tonal ambivalence in favour of A *major* and brings the work to a triumphant close.

On his return to the United Kingdom Britten launched into the composition of *Peter Grimes*, and his continuing and deepening fascination with the interrelation of words and music thereafter profoundly affected his entire output. Although between 1938 and 1941 he had composed no fewer than five works that could be described as 'concertos', more than twenty years elapsed before he wrote another work for solo instrument and orchestra.

The Symphony for Cello and Orchestra was written in part as a tribute to the extraordinary virtuosity and consummate musicianship of the Russian cellist Mstislav Rostropovich, whom Britten first met in 1960. It was composed in the spring of 1963 and completed on 3 May, shortly after Britten and Pears returned from participating in a Festival of British Music in Russia organized by the British Council. It was Britten's first substantial composition after the *War Requiem* (1961), and in its musical language it reflects the sound-world of *A Midsummer Night's Dream* (1960) and the *War Requiem* and paves the way for the stylistic advances that Britten was to make later in the 1960s in the three church parables. The make-up of the orchestra is characteristic: two flutes (second doubling piccolo), two oboes, two clarinets (second doubling bass clarinet), bassoon, double-bassoon, two horns, two trumpets, tenor trombone, tuba, timpani, percussion and strings—the combination later used (with additional percussion) for *Owen Wingrave* (1970).

The Cello Symphony is in four movements: an Allegro maestoso, the composer's most substantial sonata allegro in terms of scale and content; a scherzo (Presto inquieto), ghostly and sinewy in its sonorities; an intense, elegiac Adagio with a cadenza for the soloist leading to a passacaglia finale (Andante allegro). In textures that anticipate *Death in Venice* (notably the tuba) the D minor Allegro maestoso opens with a motto motif—a descending scale (tuba and double-bass) and a tailpiece (double bassoon and double-bass, also reminiscent of the sounds of the wood from the *Dream*)—over which the soloist proudly announces the first subject (Ex.6). A more relaxed

Ex.6

transition ebbs into the second subject, where fragmentary motifs for the cello are underpinned by pizzicato figuration for violins and double-basses, the two elements inhabiting the conflicting tonal regions of A (major) and D (minor) respectively. The first subject returns, *agitato*, as the development gets underway. The handling of the recapitulation is again characteristic of Britten's approach to sonata structure; as in the first movement of the Violin Concerto, the roles of soloist and orchestra are reversed, the orchestra having the principal theme and the soloist the accompaniment. The cello remains silent throughout the reprise of the transition (which flirts with the tonic major) and continues as accompanist for the first paragraph of the second subject, but resumes the role of soloist in the second paragraph (at Figure 23) and restores the minor mode to the recapitulation. A finely wrought coda brings back the first subject (cello) and the transition theme (woodwind) over the motto (solo and tutti double-basses with double bassoon), and the soloist finally resolves the movement's tonal argument by cadencing on the tonic major.

The contrapuntal G minor scherzo, with a repeated trio and coda (A–B–A–B–A–coda) exploits a three-note scalic motif contained within a minor third. The final, ghostly, bloodless reprise of the opening of the movement in the coda (sul ponticelli for the orchestral strings and harmonics for the soloist) is a striking example of the original sound-worlds that Britten conjures up in this score.

Thirds again predominate in the Adagio, whose principal theme, introduced and articulated by its own rhythmic version on the timpani, is constructed entirely from a descending sequence of melodic thirds. The second subject (at Figure 52) anticipates the passacaglia: the cello sings the trumpet tune *mezza voce*, while the horn fills in with the cadence figure of the ground. A development and reprise of the first subject prepares for the cadenza (at first accompanied by the timpani's version of the principal subject) which leads straight into the passacaglia, as did the cadenza of the Violin Concerto. Now the solo trumpet has the tune while the cello accompanies and reintroduces the scalic cadence figure adumbrated by the horn in the Adagio (Ex.7). Six variations proceed from this theme, and the work concludes with a majestic coda. It is remarkable that Britten could follow a masterpiece of this order, so consistent in the quality of its invention, with another masterpiece, *Curlew River* (1964), that is equally original but distinctly different in character and form.

Ex.7

Lachrymae, Op.48, for viola and piano, was composed for William Primrose in 1950 while Britten was working on *Billy Budd*. Subtitled 'Reflections on a Song of John Dowland', the work is constructed as a series of variations or 'reflections' on Dowland's 'If my complaints could passion move'. They are unusual in that Britten offers us his reflections, oblique and partial glimpses of the multiple facets of that jewel of Dowland's creation, *before* we hear the viola sing the glorious lament as a conclusion.[10] C minor prevails throughout as a point of departure; Variation VI quotes from Dowland's 'Flow my tears', and the final variation is bound by a pedal C that reaffirms that constant focus before we hear the song itself.

In the spring of 1976 Britten orchestrated the piano accompaniment of *Lachrymae* for strings. Though the work is structurally unchanged, the composer made some slight alterations to the dynamics for the soloist, reassessing the balance in the light of the string textures. The orchestration itself offers a fascinating insight into Britten's approach to the original keyboard accompaniment. The clarity of the textures reflects his sparing use of the sustaining pedal in all his accompanying (particularly of Schubert songs); and an accompanist studying the original version would do well to consult the 1976 orchestration.

When adopting the established forms for presenting a soloist in relation to an orchestra Britten was not always entirely at ease, and it is significant that the Piano Concerto, the Violin Concerto and *Diversions* all underwent revision, and *Young Apollo* was withdrawn altogether. Possibly he remained suspicious of his own facility for

[10] Cf. the *Nocturnal*, also after Dowland, for guitar solo.

writing what could be classed as 'clever, impressive display' (as his critics were often keen to remind him), hence the withdrawal of the show-piece *Young Apollo*. When he conducted *Scottish Ballad* at the 1971 Aldeburgh Festival he was unsettled by the experience and wrily compared his reaction to looking at 'a very old photograph'. But it is difficult to avoid 'impressive display' in works designed to show off the technical and musical excellence of a performing artist.

Real success lay in more symphonically conceived works such as the Violin Concerto, but particularly in the two works that aspire to chamber-music relationships between soloist and orchestra. In *Lachrymae*, the orchestral version benefits from the original conception of 'reflections' for viola and piano—the composer's own instruments and thus a union close to his heart. In the Cello Symphony he avoids the traditional opposition of forces inferred by the term 'concerto' in writing a symphony, literally a 'sounding together' of a solo instrument and orchestra where the symphonic forms aspire to the unity of spirit of the duet sonata. Britten had himself enriched the repertoire for cello and piano in 1960 with the Sonata in C (also composed for Rostropovich); in translating the essence of that work for the orchestra he achieved in one work his finest concerto, his only mature symphony, and one of his greatest masterpieces.

Chronology

This chronology of Britten's works and the major events in his life is based on one originally compiled by Donald Mitchell and John Evans for Benjamin Britten, 1913–1976: Pictures from a Life. *The publishers would particularly like to thank John Evans, to whose further researches this revised chronology is indebted. Original works are set against their composition dates; realizations and editions of music by other composers and folk-song arrangements against their publication dates; incidental music for film, theatre and radio against the year of composition.*

YEAR	COMPOSITIONS	EVENTS
1913		*22 November* Born at 21 Kirkley Cliff Road, Lowestoft, the youngest child of Robert Victor Britten and Edith Rhoda Britten (née Hockey). The elder children were Barbara (1902–1982), Robert (b.1907) and Elizabeth (Beth) (b.1909)
c.1918	Earliest attempts at composition	First piano lessons from his mother, an active amateur singer and secretary of the Lowestoft Choral Society
c.1921		Piano lessons with Ethel Astle, whose pre-preparatory school he attended with his sister Beth.

YEAR	COMPOSITIONS	EVENTS
1922–3	Many songs, including 'Oh, that I'd ne'er been married', and 'Beware!'	
1923		Enters South Lodge Preparatory School, Lowestoft, as a day boy Viola lessons with Audrey Alston of Norwich
1924	Much piano music, including sonatas	*30 October* Hears Frank Bridge's *The Sea*, at Norfolk and Norwich Triennial Musical Festival
1925	More songs and piano music, including ten waltzes, six scherzos, seven fantasies, four bourrées, five suites, etc.	
1926	Sonatas for violin and piano, and viola and piano, duos and trios for strings, and orchestral works	Passes finals (Grade VIII) Associated Board piano examination with honours
1927	Chamber, choral and orchestral works	Head boy at South Lodge *27 October* Hears Bridge's *Enter Spring* at Norwich and meets Bridge for the first time, through Audrey Alston Begins composition lessons with Bridge in London and at Bridge's home at Friston, near Eastbourne, during school holidays
1928	Early settings of de la Mare	*Summer term* Captain of cricket and *Victor*

Chronology

YEAR	COMPOSITIONS	EVENTS
1928	*June–August* Quatre Chansons Françaises	*Ludorum* at South Lodge *September* Enters Gresham's School, Holt. Continues composition lessons with Bridge. Commences piano lessons with Harold Samuel in London
1929	*April* 'A Wealden Trio' *June* 'The Birds'	
1930		Leaves Gresham's; wins open scholarship to Royal College of Music, London
	July A Hymn to the Virgin *August* 'I Saw Three Ships'	
		September Enters RCM: composition lessons with John Ireland; piano lessons with Arthur Benjamin
1931		*5 January* 'I Saw Three Ships' and *A Hymn to the Virgin* performed by Lowestoft Musical Society at St John's Church, Lowestoft
	2 June String Quartet in D major	
		July Wins Ernest Farrar Prize for composition
	Christmas Thy King's Birthday 'Sweet was the Song' Three Two-part Songs	
1932	*11 February* Phantasy in F minor	Certain works published by Oxford University Press

427

Chronology

YEAR	COMPOSITIONS	EVENTS
1932		*May* Awarded Cobbett Prize for *Phantasy* in F minor
	9 July *Sinfonietta*, Op.1	
	October *Phantasy*, Op.2	
		12 December Three Two-part Songs and *Phantasy* in F minor performed at Macnaghten–Lemare Concert at Ballet Club (later Mercury) Theatre
1933		*31 January* First performance of *Sinfonietta* at Macnaghten–Lemare Concert
	February *Alla Marcia* for string quartet	*17 February* First broadcast performance of *Phantasy* in F minor
		16 March *Sinfonietta* performed at the RCM
	May *A Boy was Born*, Op. 3	
	6–8 June Two Part-songs	
		July Again wins Ernest Farrar Prize for composition
		6 August BBC broadcast of *Phantasy*, Op.2
	October *Alla Quartetto Serioso: 'Go play, boy, play'*	
		11 December First performance of three movements from *Alla Quartetto Serioso: 'Go play, boy, play'* at Macnaghten–Lemare Concert
		13 December Passes ARCM examination; leaves the RCM

YEAR	COMPOSITIONS	EVENTS
1934	*10 February Simple Symphony*, Op.4	Certain works now published by Boosey & Hawkes
		23 February First meeting with Peter Pears, during BBC Singers' rehearsal for *A Boy was Born*
		6 March Conducts first performance of *Simple Symphony* at Norwich
		5 April Attends International Society for Contemporary Music (ISCM) Festival in Florence for performance of *Phantasy*, Op.2
	April 'May'	*6 April* His father dies
	17 July Te Deum	
	11 October Holiday Diary, Op.5	
1935	FILM: including *The King's Stamp, Coal Face, The Tocher* and *God's Chillun*	Begins active association with GPO Film Unit, Group Theatre and Left Theatre companies in London
	THEATRE: *Timon of Athens, Easter 1916*	
	16 April Two Insect Pieces	
	Friday Afternoons, Op.7	
	June Suite, Op.6	
		5 July First meeting with W. H. Auden, at Colwall
1936	FILM: including *Night Mail, Peace of Britain, Calendar of the Year, Line to the Tschierva Hut* and *Love from a Stranger*	Signs publishing contract with Boosey & Hawkes

YEAR	COMPOSITIONS	EVENTS
1936	*Russian Funeral*	

February His mother moves from Lowestoft to Frinton
25 February Three Divertimenti (revised from *Alla Quartetto Serioso: 'Go play, boy, play'*) performed at the Wigmore Hall
Joins permanent staff of GPO Film Unit
8 March First performance of *Russian Funeral*
April Attends ISCM Festival in Barcelona for a performance of *Suite*, Op.6

23 July Our Hunting Fathers, Op. 8
Soirées Musicales, Op.9

25 September Conducts *Our Hunting Fathers* at Norfolk and Norwich Festival

12 December Temporal Variations

1937 FILM: *Book Bargain*
THEATRE: *The Ascent of F6, Pageant of Empire, Out of the Picture*
RADIO: *King Arthur, The Company of Heaven, Hadrian's Wall*
Pacifist March
Two Ballads

18 January His mother dies

YEAR	COMPOSITIONS	EVENTS
1937		*March* Friendship with Peter Pears begins
	15 March Reveille	
	May 'Johnny', 'Funeral Blues'	
	12 July Variations on a Theme of Frank Bridge, Op.10	
	October On this Island, Op.11	Acquires the Old Mill, Snape
	November 'Fish in the Unruffled Lakes'; *Mont Juic*, Op. 12 (with Lennox Berkeley Op.9)	
1938	FILM: *Mony a Pickle, Advance Democracy*	Begins regular recital partnership with Peter Pears
	THEATRE: *The Seven Ages of Man* and *Old Spain, On the Frontier*	
	RADIO: *Lines on the Map, The World of the Spirit, Chartism*	
	18 January 'Tell me the truth about love'	
	26 July Piano Concerto, Op.13	
		18 August Piano Concerto is performed at a BBC Promenade Concert with Britten as soloist and the BBC Symphony Orchestra, conducted by Sir Henry Wood
		7 September His first BBC Promenade Concert appearance as a conductor, for the *Bridge Variations*
	29 November Advance Democracy	

YEAR	COMPOSITIONS	EVENTS
1939	THEATRE: *Johnson over Jordan*	
	RADIO: *The Sword in the Stone*	
	29 March *Ballad of Heroes*, Op.14	
		May Britten and Pears leave for North America on the *Ausonia*, first visiting Canada
	29 July *Young Apollo*, Op.16	
	August Settings of poems by Gerard Manley Hopkins (Op.17, withdrawn) 'Calypso'	
		21 August Britten and Pears arrive in New York, meet Dr and Mrs William Mayer and their family, and take up residence with them on Long Island
		3 September Second World War begins
	20 September Violin Concerto, Op.15	
	25 October *Les Illuminations*, Op.18	
	10 December *Canadian Carnival*, Op.19	
1940	RADIO: *The Dark Valley*	Works with Auden on *Paul Bunyan*; continues to give recitals with Pears
	Les Sylphides (Chopin orchestration)	
	Sinfonia da Requiem, Op.20	*30 January* First complete performance of *Les Illuminations* given in London

432

YEAR	COMPOSITIONS	EVENTS
1940		*January–February* Seriously ill with streptococcal infection
	August Diversions, Op.21	Britten and Pears move to
	30 October Seven Sonnets of Michelangelo, Op.22	7 Middagh Street, Brooklyn Heights, where
	November Introduction and Rondo alla Burlesca, Op.23, No.1	Auden is living
1941	RADIO: *The Rocking Horse Winner*	
	Paul Bunyan, Op.17	
		10 January Frank Bridge dies
		5 May First performance of *Paul Bunyan* at Columbia University, New York
	June Matinées Musicales, Op.24	
	July String Quartet No.1, Op.25	Trip to Escondido, California, where Britten
	July–August Mazurka Elegiaca, Op.23 No.2	and Pears stay with Ethel Bartlett and Rae Robertson, for whom Britten writes a number of two-piano works Introduced to the poetry of George Crabbe by E. M. Forster's *Listener* article Britten and Pears decide to return to the UK *September* Awarded Library of Congress Medal for Services to Chamber Music
	27 October Scottish Ballad, Op.26	

433

Chronology

COMPOSITIONS

EVENTS

RADIO: *An American in England, The Man Born to be King*
American Overture (1941/2)

14 March Koussevitzky Music Foundation offers a commission of $1000 for *Peter Grimes*

16 March Britten and Pears sail from New York on the MS *Axel Johnson*, travelling up the coast to Halifax before the Atlantic crossing

2 April Hymn to St Cecilia, Op.27
A Ceremony of Carols, Op.28

17 April Arrival in the UK
Britten and Pears register as conscientious objectors and are exempted from military service. Britten continues composing and gives many wartime recitals with Pears under the auspices of the Council for the Encouragement of Music and the Arts (CEMA)—the condition on which exemption was granted. They also give prison concerts. Britten lives at various London addresses and also spends time at the Old Mill at Snape

YEAR	COMPOSITIONS	EVENTS
1943	RADIO:'Pericles' in *The Four Freedoms, Appointment, Lumberjacks of America, Britain to America, The Rescue* *May Prelude and Fugue*, Op.29 *2 June Folk Songs, Volume 1, British Isles* *17 July Rejoice in the Lamb*, Op.30 *Serenade*, Op.31 *13 December The Ballad of Little Musgrave and Lady Barnard*	
1944	RADIO: *A Poet's Christmas* *8/9 November Festival Te Deum*, Op.32 *Christmas* 'A Shepherd's Carol', 'Chorale' (withdrawn)	
1945	THEATRE: *This Way to the Tomb* *February Peter Grimes*, Op.33	
		7 May Germany surrenders *7 June* First performance of *Peter Grimes*, at Sadler's Wells, London *August* Visits Belsen and other concentration camps as Yehudi Menuhin's accompanist
	19 August The Holy Sonnets of John Donne, Op.35 *14 October* String Quartet No.2, Op.36	

Chronology

YEAR	COMPOSITIONS	EVENTS
1946	FILM: *Instruments of the Orchestra*	
	THEATRE: *The Eagle has Two Heads, The Duchess of Malfi*	
	RADIO: *The Dark Tower*	
	Spring The Rape of Lucretia, Op.37	
	14 June The Queen's Epicedium (Purcell)	
		Glyndebourne reopens with the first performance of *The Rape of Lucretia*
	The Young Person's Guide to the Orchestra, Op.34	
		6 August US première of *Peter Grimes*, at Tanglewood, Mass.
	14 September Occasional Overture (1946)	
	18 September Prelude and Fugue on a Theme of Vittoria	
	The Golden Sonata (Purcell)	
		15 October First concert performance of *Young Person's Guide.*
		29 November First showing of *Instruments of the Orchestra* (FILM), (*Young Person's Guide*)
	31 December Folk Songs, Volume 2, France	
1947	RADIO: *Men of Goodwill*	Forms English Opera Group, with Eric Crozier and John Piper as co-Artistic Directors
	24 January Orpheus Britannicus, 7 Songs (Purcell)	

436

YEAR	COMPOSITIONS	EVENTS
1947	*1 March Albert Herring,* Op.39	
	15 April The Blessed Virgin's Expostulation (Purcell)	
		20 June Conducts the first performance of *Albert Herring* with the English Opera Group at Glyndebourne
		Britten and Pears move to Crag House, 4 Crabbe Street, Aldeburgh
		July EOG European tour of *Herring*, during which Pears proposes the creation of a music festival in Aldeburgh
	12 September Canticle I, Op.40	
		6 November First performance of *Peter Grimes* at Covent Garden
	December A Charm of Lullabies, Op.41	
	Three Divine Hymns (Purcell)	
	24 December Saul and the Witch at Endor (Purcell)	
	31 December Folk Songs, Volume 3, British Isles	
1948	*January The Beggar's Opera,* Op.43 (Gay)	Public meeting at the Jubilee Hall, Aldeburgh, guarantees £200 for the First Aldeburgh Festival

Chronology

YEAR	COMPOSITIONS	EVENTS
1948	*25 March Orpheus Britannicus*, 6 Songs (Purcell)	
		24 May Conducts first performance of *The Beggar's Opera*, at the Arts Theatre, Cambridge
	31 May Saint Nicolas, Op.42	
		5–13 June First Aldeburgh Festival of Music and the Arts
1949	THEATRE: *Stratton April The Little Sweep*, Op.45	
		10–19 June 2nd Aldeburgh Festival *14 June* First performance of *Let's Make an Opera* (*The Little Sweep*), at the Jubilee Hall, Aldeburgh
	June Spring Symphony, Op.44 *September A Wedding Anthem*, Op.46	
1950	*March Five Flower Songs*, Op.47 *3 March Job's Curse* (Purcell) *April Lachrymae*, Op.48	
		17–25 June 3rd Aldeburgh Festival
	29 December What the Wild Flowers Tell Me (Mahler)	
1951	*Six Metamorphoses after Ovid*, Op.49	

YEAR	COMPOSITIONS	EVENTS
1951	Realization of *Dido and Aeneas* (Purcell), with Imogen Holst	
		1 May Conducts first performance of *Dido and Aeneas* realization, with the EOG, at the Lyric Theatre, Hammersmith
		8–17 June 4th Aldeburgh Festival
		28 July Receives Freedom of the Borough of Lowestoft
	September *Billy Budd*, Op.50	
		1 December Conducts first performance of *Billy Budd*, (an Arts Council Festival of Britain commission) at the Royal Opera House, Covent Garden
1952	*January* *Canticle II*, Op.51	Imogen Holst joins him as his music assistant
		14–22 June 5th Aldeburgh Festival
		October First television production of a Britten opera: *Billy Budd*, by NBC TV (USA)
1953	*January* Variation IV of *Variations on an Elizabethan Theme* (*'Sellinger's Round'*)	
	13 March *Gloriana*, Op.53	
		1 June Created Companion of Honour in the Coronation Honours List

YEAR	COMPOSITIONS	EVENTS
1953		*8 June* First performance of *Gloriana* at Covent Garden. Gala performance as part of the Coronation celebrations of HM The Queen
		20–28 June 6th Aldeburgh Festival
	September Winter Words, Op.52	
1954	THEATRE: *Am Stram Gram* (canon) *March The Turn of the Screw,* Op.54	
		12–20 June 7th Aldeburgh Festival
		14 September Conducts first performance of *The Turn of the Screw*, with the EOG, at Teatro la Fenice, Venice
	27 November Canticle III, Op.55	
1955	THEATRE: *Punch Review* 'Old Friends Are Best' *Alpine Suite* and *Scherzo Hymn to St Peter,* Op.56a *Timpani Piece for Jimmy*	*8–26 June* 8th Aldeburgh Festival *November* Britten and Pears leave on a world tour, part of it in company with the Prince and Princess of Hesse and the Rhine, visiting Austria, Yugoslavia, Turkey, Singapore, Indonesia (Java and Bali), Japan, Macau, Hong Kong, Thailand, India and Sri Lanka

YEAR	COMPOSITIONS	EVENTS
1956	*3 February Orpheus Britannicus*, Suite of Songs (Purcell) *30 March Antiphon*, Op.56b	*March* Britten and Pears return to the UK
		Imogen Holst joins Britten and Pears as an Artistic Director of the Aldeburgh Festival *15–24 June* 9th Aldeburgh Festival
	Autumn The Prince of the Pagodas, Op.57	
1957	*January The Holly and the Ivy* (arr.)	*1 January* Conducts first performance of *The Prince of Pagodas*, at Covent Garden *April* Elected honorary member of the American Academy of Arts and Letters and of the National Institute of Arts and Letters, New York *14–23 June* 10th Aldeburgh Festival
	Autumn Songs from the Chinese, Op.58	
		November Moves to the Red House, Aldeburgh
	December Noye's Fludde, Op.59	
1958		*The Story of Music* published (co-author: Imogen Holst) *13–22 June* 11th Aldeburgh Festival *18 June* First performance of *Noye's Fludde*, in Orford Church

YEAR	COMPOSITIONS	EVENTS
1958	*Summer Nocturne*, Op.60 *Sechs Hölderlin-Fragmente*, Op.61	
1959	*March Cantata Academica*, Op.62 *May Fanfare for St Edmundsbury June Missa Brevis in D*, Op.63	
		19–28 June 12th Aldeburgh Festival *Summer* Visits Venice *Autumn–Winter* Enlargement and improvement of the Jubilee Hall, Aldeburgh
1960	*15 April A Midsummer Night's Dream*, Op.64 *10 May Folk Songs, Volume 4, Moore's Irish Melodies*	
		11–26 June 13th Aldeburgh Festival *11 June* Conducts first performance of *A Midsummer Night's Dream*, with the EOG, in the reconstructed Jubilee Hall
	Billy Budd revisions	English Opera Group comes under the management of the Royal Opera House, Covent Garden
	6 September Orpheus Britannicus, 5 Songs (Purcell)	*September* First meeting with Mstislav Rostropovich, in London, introduced by Dmitri Shostakovich

Chronology

YEAR	COMPOSITIONS	EVENTS
1960	*7 September Two Divine Hymns and Alleluia* (Purcell) *4 October Fanfare for SS Oriana*	
1961	*January* Sonata in C, for cello and piano, Op.65 *19 January Corpus Christi Carol* (arr. from *A Boy was Born*) *February Jubilate Deo* *14 February Folk Songs, Volume 5, British Isles* *9 May Fancie* *24 May Orpheus Britannicus,* 6 Duets (Purcell)	
		28 June–9 July 14th Aldeburgh Festival
	7 October National Anthem (arr. for chorus and orchestra) *8 November Folk Songs, Volume 6, England* *20 December War Requiem*, Op.66	
1962	*1 May Psalm 150,* Op.67	*30 May* Conducts, with Meredith Davies, first performance of *War Requiem* for the festival of consecration of St Michael's Cathedral, Coventry *14–24 June* 15th Aldeburgh Festival
	16 June The Twelve Apostles (arr.)	

YEAR	COMPOSITIONS	EVENTS
1962		*22 October* Receives Honorary Freedom of the Borough of Aldeburgh
	29 December A Hymn of St Columba	
1963	The Ship of Rio (arr. from Three Two-part Songs)	*March* Britten and Pears participate in Festival of British Music in USSR, organized by the British Council
	3 May Symphony for Cello and Orchestra, Op.68 *Night Piece (Notturno)* *25 May* Cantata Misericordium, Op.69	
		20–30 June 16th Aldeburgh Festival
	11 November Nocturnal after John Dowland, Op.70	
		22 November Britten's 50th birthday. Concert performance of *Gloriana* at the Royal Festival Hall; BBC TV profile; new production of *Peter Grimes* at Sadler's Wells; collection of 'Tributes' to Britten from friends and colleagues published by Faber and Faber
1964		His music now published by Faber and Faber (later Faber Music) *February* Visits Venice to work on *Curlew River*

YEAR	COMPOSITIONS	EVENTS

1964

12 March Conducts first performance of Cello Symphony in Moscow, with Rostropovich as soloist. During this visit, *Peter Grimes* was performed for the first time in the USSR, at Leningrad Conservatoire

2 April *Curlew River*, Op.71

April Visits Budapest and meets the Jeney twins for whom he is to write *Gemini Variations*

June Cadenzas to Haydn's Cello Concerto in C

10–21 June 17th Aldeburgh Festival
12 June First performance of *Curlew River*, at Orford Church
Imogen Holst retires as Britten's music assistant and is succeeded by Rosamund Strode
31 July Receives First Aspen Award at Colorado, USA
October Travels with the EOG on USSR tour with *Lucretia*, *Herring* and *The Turn of the Screw*
Awarded the Royal Philharmonic Society Gold Medal

December Suite for Cello, Op.72

Chronology

YEAR	COMPOSITIONS	EVENTS
1965		*January* Visits India
	March Gemini Variations, Op.73	*23 March* Awarded the Order of Merit
	6 April Songs and Proverbs of William Blake, Op.74	
		15–27 June 18th Aldeburgh Festival
	July Voices for Today, Op.75	
	August The Poet's Echo, Op.76	Holiday with Pears in Armenia with the Rostropoviches
		28 August Britten Festival at Yerevan
	7 October King Herod and the Cock (arr.)	
		9 October Receives Wihuri-Sibelius Prize in Helsinki
		24 October Triple first performance of United Nations commission, *Voices for Today*, in New York (at the UN), Paris and London
1966	*5 April The Burning Fiery Furnance*, Op.77 'Sweet was the Song' (revision)	
	June Cadenzas to Mozart's Piano Concerto in E flat (K.482)	
		8–21 June 19th Aldeburgh Festival
		9 June First performance of *The Burning Fiery Furnace*, in Orford Church

YEAR	COMPOSITIONS	EVENTS
1966	*26 August The Golden Vanity*, Op.78	
		21 October Successful revival of *Gloriana* at Sadler's Wells
	11 December Hankin Booby	
		Christmas and New Year Britten and Pears, in USSR for recitals, celebrate Christmas and the New Year with the Rostropoviches
1967	Realization of *The Fairy Queen* (Purcell) *16 March The Building of the House*, Op.79	*1 March* Conducts opening concert of the Queen Elizabeth Hall including first performance of *Hankin Booby*
	19 April 'The Oxen'	
		2–25 June 20th Aldeburgh Festival *2 June* HM The Queen opens the Maltings Concert Hall and Opera House *3 June* First performance of *The Golden Vanity*, at the Maltings *25 June* Conducts first performance of *The Fairy Queen* realization at the Maltings
	17 August Second Suite for Cello, Op.80	
		18–25 September EOG participates in Expo '67 at Montreal with performances of *Curlew River* and *The Burning*

YEAR	COMPOSITIONS	EVENTS
1967		*Fiery Furnace*. Britten and Pears accompany the tour, then travel on to New York for recitals
		October They leave New York on a British Council recital tour, visiting Mexico, Peru, Chile, Argentina, Uruguay and Brazil
	November 'The Sycamore Tree' (revision of 'I Saw Three Ships') 'A Wealden Trio' (revision)	
		Receives BBC commission for a television opera (*Owen Wingrave*)
1968		Visits Venice to work on *The Prodigal Son*
	22 April The Prodigal *Son*, Op.81	
		25 May Receives Sonning Prize in Copenhagen
		8–30 June 21st Aldeburgh Festival
		10 June First performance of *The Prodigal Son*, in Orford Church
	Summer Tit for Tat (revisions of 1928–31 de la Mare settings)	
		August–September Edinburgh International Festival programmes built round Schubert and Britten. Britten and Pears participate as performers

Chronology

YEAR	COMPOSITIONS	EVENTS
1968	*10 November Children's Crusade*, Op.82 *Five Spiritual Songs (Geistliche Lieder)* (Bach)	
1969		*February* Conducts BBC TV production of *Peter Grimes* recorded at the Maltings
	18 March Suite for Harp, Op.83 *Spring Five Walztes* (Waltzes) (revision from 1923–5)	
		19 May First performance of *Children's Crusade*, at St Paul's Cathedral, to mark 50th Anniversary of The Save The Children Fund *7–29 June* 22nd Aldeburgh Festival *7 June* Maltings Concert Hall burns down overnight
	Summer Who are these children? Op.84	
		October Britten and Pears give recitals in New York and Boston in aid of rebuilding the Maltings *2 November* BBC TV broadcast of *Peter Grimes*
1970		Chapel House, Horham, purchased *Spring* Britten and Pears accompany EOG on tour of Australia, also visiting New Zealand to give recitals

449

YEAR	COMPOSITIONS	EVENTS
1970	*Spring–Summer Owen Wingrave*, Op.85	*5–28 June* 23rd Aldeburgh Festival *5 June* HM The Queen attends the opening concert at the rebuilt Maltings *14 June* Conducts first performance outside USSR of Shostakovich's 14th Symphony (dedicated to Britten) *November* Conducts BBC TV production of *Owen Wingrave* recorded at the Maltings
1971	*A New Year Carol* (arr. from *Friday Afternoons*) *January Canticle IV*, Op.86 *3 March* Third Suite for Cello, Op.87	*14–21 April* Visits Moscow and Leningrad for a week of British music *16 May* BBC TV broadcast of *Owen Wingrave* *4–27 June* 24th Aldeburgh Festival *October* Visits Venice with John and Myfanwy Piper and Pears. Begins work on *Death in Venice*
1972		*Spring* Visits Schloss Wolfsgarten to work on *Death in Venice* *2–19 June* 25th Aldeburgh Festival

Chronology

YEAR	COMPOSITIONS	EVENTS
1972		*22 September* Last Britten–Pears recital, at the Maltings. This formed part of the first of the masterclass courses from which developed the Britten–Pears School for Advanced Musical Studies Increasing heart trouble curtails his activities
1973	*March Death in Venice,* Op.88	*7 May* Open-heart surgery at National Heart Hospital, London Although the operation was partially successful, he did not fully recover and thereafter never again performed in public *10 May* First stage performance of *Owen Wingrave*, at Covent Garden *16 June* First performance of *Death in Venice*, with the EOG at the Maltings. Britten convalescing at Horham and unable to attend *25 June–2 July* 26th Aldeburgh Festival *12 September* Sees *Death in Venice* for the first time at a special private performance at the Maltings *18 October* Attends London première of *Death in Venice*, at Covent Garden *22 November* Britten's 60th birthday

YEAR	COMPOSITIONS	EVENTS
1973		*25 November (Sunday)* Day of birthday celebrations in the press and on radio and television
1974	*Easter* String Quartet in D major (1931) (revision)	
		7–24 June 27th Aldeburgh Festival *23 June* First European concert performance of excerpts from *Paul Bunyan*, at the Maltings
	July Canticle V, Op.89 *Summer* Paul Bunyan, Op.17 (revision)	
		October Death in Venice performed at the Metropolitan Opera, New York
	16 November Suite on English Folk Tunes (A time there was . . .), Op.90	
		Awarded the Ravel Prize
1975	*January* Sacred and Profane, Op.91 *21 March* A Birthday Hansel, Op.92	
		April BBC Radio 3 recording of revised *Paul Bunyan* *6–23 June* 28th Aldeburgh Festival *7 July* Attends revival of *Death in Venice* at Covent Garden

YEAR	COMPOSITIONS	EVENTS
1975		*9 July* Attends new production of *Peter Grimes* at Covent Garden, his last visit to the Royal Opera House
	12 August Phaedra, Op.93	
	November String Quartet No.3, Op.94	Visits Venice for the last time
1976	*February Lachrymae*, Op.48a (orchestration)	Awarded the Mozart Medal *1 February* First British performance of *Paul Bunyan*, a BBC radio production *4–20 June* 29th Aldeburgh Festival *4 June* First British stage performance of *Paul Bunyan*, by the English Music Theatre, at the Maltings *12 June* Created a life peer, Baron Britten of Aldeburgh in the County of Suffolk, in the Birthday Honours List *July* Begins composition of cantata on Sitwell poem, 'Praise We Great Men'
	August Welcome Ode, Op.95 *Summer Eight Folk Song Arrangements*	
		28–9 September Amadeus Quartet visit Aldeburgh and work on String Quartet No.3 with Britten

Chronology

YEAR	COMPOSITIONS	EVENTS
1976		*October–November* Continues work on Sitwell Cantata, despite increasing physical weakness
		4 December Dies at the Red House, Aldeburgh
		7 December Funeral Service and burial at Aldeburgh Parish Church
		19 December First performance of String Quartet No.3 at the Maltings
1977	*When night her purple veil** (Purcell)	*10 March* Service of Thanksgiving at Westminster Abbey
		11 July First performance of *Welcome Ode* at the Corn Exchange, Ipswich, in the presence of HM The Queen
1978		*21 November* Memorial Stone dedicated at Westminster Abbey

* NB publication date: first performance 1965

Select Bibliography

Blyth, Alan (ed.): *Remembering Britten* (Hutchinson, 1981)

Brett, Philip (ed.): *Benjamin Britten: Peter Grimes*, Cambridge Opera Handbook (Cambridge/New York: Cambridge University Press, 1983) [*PG*]

Britten, Benjamin: *On Receiving the First Aspen Award* (Faber and Faber/Faber and Faber Inc., 1964)

Britten, Benjamin, and Imogen Holst: *The Story of Music* (Rathbone Books, 1958); republished as *The Wonderful World of Music* (Macdonald, 1968)

Crozier, Eric (ed.): *Benjamin Britten: Peter Grimes*, Sadler's Wells Opera Book No. 3 (John Lane, The Bodley Head, 1945) [*SW*]

Crozier, Eric (ed.): *The Rape of Lucretia: A Symposium* (John Lane, The Bodley Head, 1948)

Duncan, Ronald: *Working with Britten* (Bideford: The Rebel Press, 1981) [*WB*]

Evans, Peter: *The Music of Benjamin Britten* (Dent/University of Minnesota Press, 1979) [*MBB*]

Gishford, Anthony (ed.): *Tribute to Benjamin Britten on his Fiftieth Birthday* (Faber and Faber, 1963) [*TBB*]

Headington, Christopher: *Britten* (Eyre Methuen, 1981)

Herbert, David (ed.): *The Operas of Benjamin Britten* (Hamish Hamilton/Norton, 1979) [*OBB*]

Holst, Imogen: *Britten*, Great Composers Series (Faber and Faber/Faber and Faber Inc., 1966, 2/1970; revised 3/1980) [*BR*]

Kennedy, Michael: *Britten*, Master Musicians Series (Dent, 1981) [*BMM*]

Mitchell, Donald: *Britten and Auden in the Thirties: The Year 1936* (Faber and Faber/University of Washington Press, 1981) [*BA*]

Mitchell, Donald, and John Evans: *Benjamin Britten, 1913–1976: Pictures from a Life* (Faber and Faber/Scribners, 1978) [*PL*]

Mitchell, Donald, and Hans Keller (eds.): *Benjamin Britten: A Commentary on his works from a group of specialists* (The Britten Symposium) (Rockliff, 1952, repr. Westport, Conn.: Greenwood Press, 1972) [*BS*]

Slater, Montagu: *Peter Grimes and Other Poems* (John Lane, The Bodley Head, 1946)

Select Bibliography

White, Eric Walter: *Benjamin Britten: His Life and Operas* (Faber and Faber/California University Press, 1970; revised 3/1983)

Whittall, Arnold: *The Music of Britten and Tippett: Studies in Themes and Techniques* (Cambridge/New York: Cambridge University Press, 1982) [*BT*]

Contributors

PHILIP BRETT is Professor of Music at the University of California at Berkeley and editor of the Cambridge Opera Handbook on *Peter Grimes* (1983).

JOHN CULSHAW, who died in 1980, joined Decca after the war where he pioneered the use of stereo for recording opera. In 1967 he became Head of Music Programmes for BBC Television. He worked closely with Britten on the great series of recordings in which the composer, as conductor and pianist, recorded a substantial part of his *oeuvre*.

JOHN EVANS studied at University College, Cardiff, where he specialized in twentieth-century music, percussion, and piano; his postgraduate work has been on *Owen Wingrave* and *Death in Venice*. He assisted Donald Mitchell in the compilation of *Benjamin Britten: Pictures from a Life 1913–1976*, and in 1980 was appointed first Research Scholar at the Britten–Pears Library.

CHRISTOPHER HEADINGTON, from 1965–82 Tutor in Music in the External Studies Department of Oxford University, is a composer, pianist, and broadcaster as well as the author of *Britten* (Eyre Methuen, 1981) and several other books on music.

ROBIN HOLLOWAY is a composer, and lecturer in music at the University of Cambridge.

IMOGEN HOLST was Benjamin Britten's amanuensis and music assistant from 1952 to 1964, and for more than twenty years she was an artistic director of the Aldeburgh Festival. Her 1966 book on Britten in Faber's Great Composers series was revised for a third edition in 1980. She is currently editing her father's music and is responsible, with Colin Matthews, for the Collected Facsimile Edition of Holst's works.

GRAHAM JOHNSON is a concert accompanist, and founder and artistic director of The Songmakers' Almanac. He first met and worked with Britten and Pears as a student in 1969 and has had a long association with music-making and master-classes at Snape. His enthusiasm for performing the song repertoire was initially fired by a Pears–Britten performance of *Winterreise* at the Aldeburgh Festival.

HANS KELLER is a musician, writer, and teacher. After twenty years at the BBC and a visiting professorship in Canada, he is now teaching at the Yehudi Menuhin School and the Guildhall School of Music. He was joint editor (with Donald Mitchell) of *Benjamin Britten: a Commentary on his works from a group of specialists* (1952), and his more recent writings on Britten include 'Operatic music and Britten' in *The Operas of Benjamin Britten*, edited by David Herbert (Hamish Hamilton, 1979).

DAVID MATTHEWS is a composer whose works include five string quartets. He is the author of *Michael Tippett: An Introductory Study* (Faber, 1980) and contributed a chapter to the Cambridge Opera Handbook on *Peter Grimes* (1983).

WILFRID MELLERS was founder and head of the music department at the University of York from 1964 until his retirement in 1981. He has written fourteen books on topics ranging from Couperin, Bach and Beethoven to American music, the Beatles and Bob Dylan. As a composer he has produced music in most media, though with a bias towards the human voice and the theatre. He now teaches part time at the Guildhall School of Music.

ANTHONY MILNER, composer, is Principal Lecturer at the Royal College of Music, London. His compositions include two symphonies; orchestral and chamber works, several chord cantatas and an oratorio.

DONALD MITCHELL is engaged in writing the authorized biography and critical study of Britten's works. He was the composer's close

Contributors

friend and publisher from the 1960s, but has been a student and advocate of his music for far longer. With Britten's encouragement he helped found Faber Music Ltd, of which he is now Chairman. Such time as is left from his work on Britten he devotes to a major study of Mahler, the third volume of which will be appearing shortly.

CHRISTOPHER PALMER is the author of *Impressionism in Music* (1972) and his many contributions to Delius scholarship include *Delius: Portrait of a Cosmopolitan* (1976). He has also published monographs on Miklós Rózsa, Arthur Bliss, Szymanowski (BBC Music Guide), George Dyson, and Herbert Howells, about whom he is currently writing a full biographical and critical study.

PETER PEARS, the great singer. He was Britten's lifelong companion, principal interpreter of his vocal music, and a major influence on the composer's art. Many of Britten's operas were built round him, from *Peter Grimes* in 1945 to *Death in Venice* in 1973. He continues to be at the centre of things in Aldeburgh.

PETER PORTER is a poet of Australian birth, resident in England since 1951. His *Collected Poems* (1983) gathered together his published work of three decades. He has written words for composers and broadcast talks on music for the BBC.

ERIC ROSEBERRY is Senior Lecturer in Music at Bath College of Higher Education. His publications include several articles on Britten's music which appeared in *Tempo*. After completing a doctoral dissertation on Shostakovich in 1982 he is now preparing a book on that composer's musical style.

ERWIN STEIN, born in Vienna, was a distinguished Schoenberg pupil and authoritative advocate of his teacher's music. He came to England in 1938 and worked until his death in 1958 for Britten's publishers, Boosey & Hawkes. He was one of Britten's musical 'fathers', from whom the composer received advice and encouragement over many years.

ROSAMUND STRODE studied at the Royal College of Music, and at Dartington Hall under Imogen Holst. After some years as a freelance musician, she came to work for Britten in 1963, succeeding Imogen

Holst as his music assistant the following year. Since the composer's death she has continued to work for the Britten Estate and, as Archivist and Keeper of Manuscripts, for the Britten–Pears Foundation.

The day this book went to press, Imogen Holst died suddenly in Aldeburgh, where for many years she played such a creative role as music assistant to Benjamin Britten and Artistic Director of the Aldeburgh Festival.

Index of Britten's Works

Compiled by Jill Burrows

The principal entries for the composer's works are shown, exceptionally, in roman type; those in *italic* refer to the titles of plays, films, etc., for which Britten wrote incidental music. Figures in *italic* refer to illustrations, those in **bold** to music examples.

Blessed Virgin's Expostulation, The (Purcell realization), 359–60, **359**, 437; related to *Nocturne*, 359
'Bonny Earl o' Moray, The' (orchestral arrangement), 402
Book Bargain (incidental music), 430
Boy was Born, A, Op.3, 78–9, 81n., 82, 153, 273, 329–31, 345, 396, 428, 429, 443; analysis, 329–30, acoustic, importance of, 78–9, bells in, 81n., boys' voices in, 82
Britain to America (incidental music), 435
Building of the House, The, Op.79, 81, 407, 447; bells in, 81n., 'Vater Unser' in, 81, 407
Burning Fiery Furnace, The, Op.77, 53, 76, 212–14, 215–26, 241, 300, 306, 446, 447–8; analysis, 221, at Expo '67, 447, first performance, 446, instrumentation, 216, percussion-writing, 76; related to *Canticle IV*, 306, *Death in Venice*, 241

Cabaret Songs, 66, 297n., 431, 432; 'Funeral Blues', 431, 'Tell me the truth about love', 431, 'Johnny', 431, 'Calypso', 297n., 432, related to *Winter Words*, 297n.
Cadenzas to Haydn's Cello Concerto in C (Hoboken VII b.1), 445
Cadenzas to Mozart's Piano Concerto in E flat (K.482), 446
Calendar of the Year (incidental music), 429
Canadian Carnival, Op.19, 404–5, 419n., 432; 'Alouette' in 405, 419n., 'Jardin d'amour' in 419n., 'Là-bas sur les montagnes' in, 419n., 'La Perdriole' in, 419n.
Cantata Academica, Carmen Basiliense, Op.62, 26, 81n., 337–8, 345, 442; analysis, 338, bells in, 81n., serial techniques used in, 26
Cantata Misericordium, Op.69, 212, 345, 444, as political statement, 212
Canticle I: My Beloved is Mine, Op.40, 292–3, 297, 370, 437; related to 'Auf dem Wasser zu singen' (Schubert), 293, 297, *Winter Words*, 297
Canticle II: Abraham and Isaac, Op.51, 82, **82n.**, 266, 294–5, 342, 382, 439; related to *Billy Budd*, 295, Second Cello

Suite, 382, *War Requiem*, 295, 342; theme of salvation in, 266
Canticle III: Still Falls the Rain, Op.55, 300, 370, 440; related to *The Turn of the Screw*, 370
Canticle IV: Journey of the Magi, Op.86, 82n., 306, 450; plainsong in, 82n., 306, related to *The Burning Fiery Furnace*, 306
Canticle V: The Death of Saint Narcissus, Op.89, 60, 221, 370, 379–80, 452; related to *Death in Venice*, 380
Ceremony of Carols, A, Op.28, 78, 79–80, 81n., 82, 333, 334, 396n., 434; 'Procession', 80, 333, 'Wolcum Yole!', bells in, 81n., 'There is no rose', bells in, 81n., 'That yongë child', 334, 'As dew in Aprille', 333, 'This little Babe', 80, 333, 'In freezing winter night', 80, 333, 'Spring Carol', 999, 'Deo Gracias', bells in, 81n., 334, 'Recession', 80, 333; boys' voices in, 82, plainsong in, 82; related to church parables, 80
Charm of Lullabies, A, Op.41, 294, 406n., 437
Chartism (incidental music), 431
Children's Crusade, Op.82, 77, 82, 165, 167–9, 212, 225, 317n., 449; analysis, 167–9, as political statement, 212, first performance, 449, percussion-writing, 77, 317n., related to *The Golden Vanity*, 165, 168, text, 169
Coal Face (incidental music), 228, 231n., 429
'Come you not from Newcastle?' (orchestral arrangement), 402
Company of Heaven (incidental music), 430
Corpus Christi Carol, 443
Curlew River, Op.71, 39, 56, 57–8, 153, 201, 204, 206, 212–14, 215–26, 241, 243, 248, 266, 300, 422, 444, 445, 447; analysis, 219–21, at Expo '67, 447, first performance, 445, libretto, 57–8; related to *Death in Venice*, 241, 243, 248, *Peter Grimes*, 213, *The Prince of the Pagodas*, 204; revisions, 57–8, theme of salvation in, 266

Dark Tower, The (incidental music), 436
Dark Valley, The (incidental music), 432
Death in Venice, Op.88, 26, 30, 31n., 36n., 43, **43**, 45, 57, 59–60, 63, 73,

Index of Britten's Works

Index of Britten's Works

26, 49, 65, 82, 92, 154, 177–80, 181–91, 231, 232, 282–3, 320–1, **321**, 340, 378, 421, 442; analysis, 182–91; boys' voices in, 82, first performance, 442, libretto, 177–8, 182, 282–3, *34*, parody in, 65, percussion-writing, 183; related to *Serenade*, 320–1, *The Turn of the Screw*, 186, 191, Symphony for Cello and Orchestra, 421; serial techniques used in, 26

Missa Brevis in D, Op.63, 46, 81n., 337–9, 342, 442; analysis, 338–9, bells in, 81n., related to *War Requiem*, 338–9, 342

Mont Juic, Op.12 (with Lennox Berkeley), 402–3, 404, 431; *Lament*, 403, related to *Quatre Chansons Françaises*, 403

Mony a Pickle (incidental music), 431

National Anthem (arrangements), 315, 443

New Year Carol, A, 450

Night Mail (incidental music), 228, 429

Night Piece (Notturno), 383, 384, 385, 444; Bartók an influence on, 385

Nocturnal after John Dowland, Op.70, 93, 322, 371, 377–8, 382, 383, 384, 423n., 444; BB on, 93; related to *Nocturne*, 322, Third Cello Suite, 382; *Passacaglia*, 378

Nocturne, Op.60, 30–1, 78, 92–3, 181, 182, 249, 278, 279, 283, 308, 314, 322–7, 359, 378, 382, 396n., 400, 401, 409, 441; analysis, 322–7, BB on, 93; instrumentation, 324–6, 327; related to *Blessed Virgin's Expostulation*, 359, *Death in Venice*, 249, *A Midsummer Night's Dream*, 181–2, *Nocturnal*, 322; 'Prometheus Unbound', 278, 322–4, **323**, 359, related to *On this Island*, 322–4, 'The Kraken', 112n., 324, 325, 409, 'The Wanderings of Cain', 324, 325, **325**, 'Blurt, Master Constable', 324, 325–6, 327, 'The Prelude', 93, 326, 382, 400, 401, related to Second Cello Suite, 382, 'The Kind Ghosts', 324, 326–7, 401, related to *Serenade*, 326, *Owen Wingrave*, 326, *War Requiem*, 327, 'Sleep and Poetry', 324, related to *Serenade*, 324, 'Sonnet 43', 30–1, 181, 324, Mahler an influence on, 30–1

Noye's Fludde, Op.59, 48–9, 76, 77, 78, 81, 82, 114, 117, 153–60, 213, 441; analysis, 154–60, audience involvement, 78, bells in, 81n., first performance, 441, hymns in, 81, 114, rehearsal, *33*, related to church parables, 213, *Peter Grimes*, 117, slungs mugs, 48–9, 76, suitability for amateur performance, 77

'O can ye sew cushions?' (orchestral arrangement), 403, 406n.

Occasional Overture (1946), 436

'Oh, that I'd ne'er been married', 426

'Old Friends Are Best' (*Punch Review*), 440

Old Spain (incidental music), 431

On the Frontier (incidental music), 228, 431

On this Island, Op.11, 284, 288–9, 291, 322, 323, 376, 431; 'Let the florid music praise!', 288, 291, related to *Temporal Variations*, 376, 'Now the leaves are falling fast', 288–9, 'Seascape', 289, 'Nocturne', 289, related to *Nocturne*, 322–3, **323**, 'As it is, plenty', 288

Orpheus Britannicus, 6 Duets (Purcell realizations), 443

Orpheus Britannicus, 5 Songs (Purcell realizations), 442

Orpheus Britannicus, 6 Songs (Purcell realizations), 438

Orpheus Britannicus, 7 Songs (Purcell realizations), 436

Orpheus Britannicus, Suite of Songs (Purcell realizations), 441

Our Hunting Fathers, Op.8, 31, 35–6, 75, 284, 288, 310, 318, 331, 376, 395–402, 406, 430; first performance, 310, 430; related to *Lady Macbeth of the Mtsensk District* (Shostakovich), 35, *Das Lied von der Erde* (Mahler), 31, *Sinfonia da Requiem*, 400–2; serial techniques used in, 376, word-setting, 331; 'Prologue', 400, 'Rats Away!', 318, 395, 396, **397**, 398, 402, related to *Death in Venice*, 397, *Sinfonietta*, 395, 398, 'Messalina', 398, 401, 'Dance of Death', 31, 75, 395, 396, 399–400, **401**, 402, 406, Mahler an influence on, 31, related to *Billy Budd*, 399, *Sinfonia da Requiem*, 396, 399, *Sinfonietta*, 395,

465

Index of Britten's Works

Praise We Great Men (incomplete), 23n., 374, 453

Prelude and Fugue, Op.29, 409, 435

Prelude and Fugue on a Theme of Vittoria, 436

Prince of the Pagodas, The, Op.57, 39, 42, 48, 49, 52, 76, 81n., 192–210, **194**, **195**, **196**, **197**, **198**, 203, 208, **209**, 213, 223, 232, 242–3, **242**, 258, 403, 407, 441; Balinese music an influence on, 39, 76, 198, 201, 205–8, 213, bells in, 81n., Cinderella as source for, 205–6n., clusters in, 208–10, first performance, 192, 441, parody used in, 203, Pas de six, 193n., Prelude and Dances from the Prince of the Pagodas (Del Mar), 193–4n., 210n.; related to Curlew River, 204, Death in Venice, 204–5, 242–3, The Turn of the Screw, 204; revisions, 200n., Stravinsky an influence on, 203, Suite (Lankester), 194n., Suite Previn), 194n., synopsis, 194–200, Tchaikovsky an influence on, 201–3, 206n.

Prodigal Son, The, Op.81, 212–14, 215–16, 230, 241, 448; analysis, 221–2, first performance, 448, instrumentation, 216; related to Albert Herring, 213–14, Death in Venice, 241

Psalm 150, Op.67, 334, 443

'Quand j'étais chez mon père' (orchestral arrangement), 403

Quatre Chansons Françaises (1928), 26–7n., 265, 308–10, 395, 403, 427; Berg an influence on, 27n., instrumentation, 309, serial techniques used in, 26n.; 'Nuits de Juin', 26n., **26n.**, 309, 'Sagesse', 309–10, **310**, 'L'Enfance', 309, 403, related to Seven Sonnets of Michelango, 403, 'Chanson d'Automne', 265

Queen's Epicedium, The (Purcell realization), 436

Rape of Lucretia, The, Op.37, 120–6, **122**, **123**, **124**, **125**, 127, 154, 166, 175, 225, 231, 244, 258, 266, 281, 294, 346, 369, 377, 436, 445; analysis, 122–6, Christian element in, 154, first performance, 436, in USSR, 445, libretto, 122–3, 126, 281, quoted in Albert Herring, 121,

166n; related to Death in Venice, 244, Otello (Verdi), 122n.

Rejoice in the Lamb, Op.30, 46, 78, 82, 121, 275–6, 334, 434; boys' voices in, 82, orchestration (Imogen Holst), 46

Rescue, The (incidental music), 435

Reveille (1937), 418, 431

Rocking Horse Winner, The (incidental music), 433

Russian Funeral (1936), 34, 34n., 407, 430; first performance, 430, Mahler an influence on, 34n., Shostakovich an influence on, 34n.

Sacred and Profane, Op.91, 345, 452

Saint Nicolas, Op.42, 52, 77, 78, 79, **79–80**, 81, 82, 212–13, 438; acoustic, importance of, 79, audience involvement, 78, hymns in, 81, Pickled Boys, 212–13, plainsong in, 82n., recording, 30, related to church parables, 213, suitability for amateur performance, 77

'Salley Gardens, The' (orchestral arrangement), 402–3

Saul and the Witch at Endor (Purcell realization), 437

Scherzo, 440

Scottish Ballad, Op.26, 81, 404, 419–20, 424, 433; analysis, 419–20, 'Dundee' in, 81, 420, 'Flowers of the forest' in, 420, Prokofiev an influence on, 420, Shostakovich an influence on, 420, 'Turn ye to me' in, 420

Sechs Hölderlin-Fragmente, Op.61, 264, 277–9, 298–300, 442; 'Menschenbeifall', 299, BB on, 299, 'Die Heimat', 277–8, 299, compared with Eisler's setting, 299, 'Sokrates und Alcibiades', 264, 277, 278, 299–300, related to Death in Venice, 299, 'Die Jugend', 300, 'Hälfte des Lebens', 278, 300, 'Die Linien des Lebens', 278–9, 300

Second Suite for Cello, Op.80, 371, 380, 381–2, 383, 447; Declamato: Largo, 381, related to Symphony No.5 (Shostakovich), 381, Fuga: Andante, 380, Andante lento, 381–2, related to Canticle II, 382, Nocturne, 382, Symphony for Cello and Orchestra, 382, Ciaccona: Allegro, 380, 381, 382

Serenade, Op.31, 66, 92–3, 181, 265, 278, 283, 284, 308, 314, 317–22, 324,

Index of Britten's Works

General Index

Compiled by Jill Burrows

Figures in *italic* type refer to illustrations, those in **bold** to music examples.

General Index

Bachelard, Gaston, 110
Baiser de la fée, La (Stravinsky), 202
Baker, Janet, 62, 230, 409
Balanchine, George, 206n.
Balinese Ceremonial Music (transcribed McPhee), 40–5, 205n., 206n.
  Gambangan, **44n.**, 207n.
  Pemoengkah, **43n.**
  Rébong (unpublished), **44n.**
Ballet Club Theatre (later Mercury Theatre), London, 428
Barbirolli, John, 415
Barrère, Georges, 40
Bartlett, Ethel, 419, 433
Bartók, Béla, 32, 217, 330, 376, 381, 385, 415
  'Night's Music, The', 384
  Piano Concerto No.2, 384
  String Quartet No.4, 385
Basle, University of, 338
Bateau ivre, Le (Rimbaud), 317
Baudelaire, Charles, 254
Bawan, Timir, 40n.
Bayreuth, 65, 66
BBC (British Broadcasting Corporation), 66, 83n., 87, 228, 238, 370, 400, 404, 413, 415, 428, 448, 452, 453
BBC Promenade Concerts (formerly Henry Wood Promenade Concerts), 194n., 411, 431
BBC Scottish Symphony Orchestra, 193n.
BBC Singers, 429
BBC Symphony Orchestra, 411, 431
BBC Television, 62, 66, 67, 87, 231, 444, 449, 450
Bedford, Steuart, 60
Beethoven, Ludwig van, 125, 145, 153, 216, 312n., 335, 387, 390–1
  Coriolan Overture, Op.62, 125
  String Quartet in A minor, Op.132, 189
  String Quartet in F, Op.135, 391
  String Quartets, Op.18, 387
  String Quartets, Op.59 (*Razumovsky*), 387, 388
  Symphony No.3 in E flat (*Eroica*) 335
  Symphony No.5 in C minor, 335
  Symphony No.9 in D minor (*Choral*), 335
'Before Life and After' (Hardy), 278, 279–80
Bellini, Vincenzo, 271, 286

Belloc, Hilaire, 287
Belsen, 435
Benjamin, Arthur, 383, 427
Benjamin, George, 25
Benjamin Britten: The Early Years (Mitchell), 415
Berg, Alban, 27n., 32, 273, 400
  Lyric Suite, 387
  Wozzeck, 36n., 281
Berio, Luciano, 304
Berkeley, Lennox, 402, 403, 431
Berlioz, Hector, 217, 282
Bernini, Gianlorenzo, 274
Bertram, Ernst, 252
Betrachtungen eines Unpolitischen (Mann), 264
Bible, 96
Billy Budd (Melville), 135, 136, 137, 139, 140–1, 142
Blades, James, 76
Blake, William, 69, 245n., 265, 277, 280, 300, 301, 302, 305, 319, *12*
  'Poison Tree, A', 265
  'Sick Rose, The', 265
  Songs of Innocence and of Experience, 69
Blessed Virgin's Expostulation, The (Purcell), 359–60, **359**, 437
Bliss, Arthur
  Pastoral, 396n.
  Rout, 318
  Serenade, 396n.
Blow, John, 335
Blue Angel, The (film), 260
Blythburgh Church, Suffolk, *32*
Boito, Arrigo, 282
Bond, W. H., 275
Book Bargain (film), 430
Boosey & Hawkes (Music Publishers) Ltd, 58, 192n., 194n., 317, 429
Born, Wolfgang, 263n.
Borough, The (Crabbe), 104–5, 134
Boughton, Joy, 371, 377
Boulez, Pierre, 216
  Marteau sans maître, Le, 216
Boyd Neel Orchestra, 409
Brahms, Johannes, 49, 277, 404, 416
  'Academic Festival' Overture, 338
  Liebeslieder waltzes, 59
  'O Tod wie bitter bist du', 292
  Schicksalslied, 277
  Symphony No.1 in C minor, 416
  Variations on a Theme by Haydn, 404
  Vier ernste Gesänge, 292

General Index

General Index

General Index

479

General Index

Massine, Leonide, II, 179
Matthews, Colin, 27n., 60, 61, 309n., 379n.
Matthews, David, 41
Maurice (Forster), 136
Mayer, Elizabeth, 207n., 432
Mayer, William, 432
Mayer family, 39, 40, 432
Mellers, Wilfrid, 117, 255
Melville, Herman, 135, 136, 137, 139, 140–1, 142, 254n., 316, *13*
  Billy Budd, 135, 136, 137, 139, 140–1, 142
  Moby Dick, 254n.
Menuhin, Yehudi, 291, 435
Mer, La (Debussy), 114
Mercury Theatre, London, 428
Messiaen, Olivier, 24–5, 217
Messiah (Handel), 120
Metamorphoses (Ovid), 179n.
Metropolitan Opera, New York, 63, 452, 6
Mewton-Wood, Noel, 298
Michelangelo Buonarroti, 223, 277, 292, 294, 295, 316, 7
Middleton, Thomas, 324
'Midnight on the Great Western' (Hardy), 279
Midsummer Night's Dream, A (Shakespeare), 177–8, 179, 182–3, 185, 282–3, *34*
Mies van der Rohe, Ludwig, 248
Miroirs (Ravel), 27n.
Mitchell, Donald, 71, 121, 125, 228, 235–6, 260, 283, 297n., 309, 315n., 317n., 322, 376n., 378, 380, 382, 394, 395, 396, 397, 400, 401, 405, 408, 415
  Benjamin Britten: The Early Years, 415
  Britten and Auden in the Thirties, 228, 283
'Mitternachtslied' (Nietzsche), 320n.
Moby Dick (Melville), 254n.
Modern Music, 405n.
Moeran, Ernest John, 'Youth is Pleasure', 315n.
'Molly on the Shore' (Grainger), 75
Monk, William Henry, 'Würtemberg', 81
Monteverdi, Claudio, 271
Mony a Pickle (film), 431
Morris, Reginald Owen, 73n.
Moses und Aron (Schoenberg), 240
Mozart, Wolfgang Amadeus, 65, 89, 96,

151, 178, 180, 272, 312n., 360, 373n., 382, 383, 411
  Idomeneo, 54
  String Trio in E flat (K.563), 373
Musical Times, 46
Music in Bali (McPhee), 206–7
Mussorgsky, Modest, 217, 381
  Pictures from an Exhibition, 381
'Mut' (Schubert), 296
Myrthen (Schumann), 290

'Nacht und Träume' (Schubert), 274
National Heart Hospital, 451
National Institute of Arts and Letters, New York, 441
National Theatre (New York), 206n.
NBC Television, 439
Neel, Boyd, 409
New York City Ballet, 207n.
New York Philharmonic Orchestra, 415
Nietzsche, Friedrich Wilhelm, 226, 252–3, 254, 256
  Ecce Homo, 252–3
  'Mitternachtslied', 320n.
Night Mail (film), 228, 429
'Night's Music, The' (Bartók), 384
Nine Welcome Songs (Purcell), 366
Noces, Les (Stravinsky), 217
Nolan, Sidney, 168
Norfolk and Norwich Triennial Festival, 426, 430, *4*
Nutcracker (Tchaikovsky), 202, **202**

Obey, André, 122–3
  Viol de Lucrèce, Le, 122–3
Ode: Intimations of Immortality (Wordsworth), 68
Oedipus Rex (Stravinsky), 33n., 153, 337, 342
Old Hundredth, The, **82n.**
Old Mill, Snape, 110, 411, 434
Old Spain (Slater), 431
'On a poet's lips I slept' (Shelley), 278
On the Frontier (Auden–Isherwood), 228, 431
On Wenlock Edge (Vaughan Williams), 318
Oration (Bridge), 308
Orchestration (Piston), 77
Orff, Carl, 155
Orford Church, 441, 445, 446, 448, *33*
Orpheus Britannicus (Purcell), 357–9, 436, 437, 438, 441, 442, 443

480

General Index

General Index

'Lindenbaum, Der', 296
'Mut', 296
'Nacht und Träume', 274
schöne Müllerin, Die, 279
String Quintet in C (D.956), 49, 391
'stürmische Morgen, Der', 296
'Wetterfahne, Die', 292
Winterreise, 66, 292, 295
Schumann, Robert, 286
Dichterliebe, 279
Myrthen, 290
Scenes from Goethe's 'Faust', 54
Schütz, Heinrich, 248
Scott, Cyril, 'Lullaby', 287
Sea, The (Bridge), 114–15, 308, 426, *4*
Second Viennese School, 338
Serenade (Bliss), 396n.
Seven Ages of Man, The (Slater), 431
Shakespeare, William, 25, 177, 178, 179, 181, 182, 183, 185, 273, 282, 284, 286n.
Midsummer Night's Dream, A, 177–8, 179, 182–3, 185, 282–3, *34*
Tempest, The, 266
Timon of Athens, 429
Shan-kar, Uday, 40n.
Sharp, Cecil, 303
Shelley, Percy Bysshe, 256, 278, 286n., 324
'On a poet's lips I slept', 278
Prometheus Unbound, 322
'Queen Mab', 231
'Shepherd's Hey' (Grainger), 75
Shingle Street, Suffolk, 109
Shirley-Quirk, John, 230, 301
Shostakovich, Dmitri, 32–8, 39n., 302, 370, 376, 381, 382, 388, 389, 400, 415, 420, 442, *2*
Lady Macbeth of the Mtsensk District, 33, 33–4n., 35, 36, 37, 376n.
Piano Concerto No.1 for piano, trumpet and strings, Op.35, 33
String Quartet No.8 in C minor, Op.110, 382
String Quartet No.11 in F minor, Op.122, 380
String Quartet No.15 in E flat minor, Op.144, 389
Symphony No.5 in D minor, 381, **381**
Symphony No.11 in G minor (*The Year 1905*), 34n.
Symphony No.14, Op.135, 335, 450
Sibelius, Jean, 217

'Sick Rose, The' (Blake), 265
Simkie (dancer), 40n.
Sir Anthony Love (Purcell), 366
'Sir Roger de Coverley' (Bridge), 404
Sitwell, Edith, 298, 374, 453, *20*
'Praise We Great Men', 23n., 453
Slater, Enid, 111n., 417
Slater, Montagu, 228, 282, 417, *25, 26*
Easter 1916, 429
Old Spain, 431
Pageant of Empire, 228, 430
Seven Ages of Man, The, 431
Sleeping Beauty, The (Tchaikovsky), 202
slung mugs, 48–9, 76
Smart, Christopher, 273, 275–7, 278, 285, 317, 334, *8*
Jubilate Agno, 275–7, 334
'Song to David, A', 276
Smith, Milton, 28n.
Snape, Suffolk, 307, *26, 41*
'Sokrates und Alcibiades' (Hölderlin), 264, 277, 278
Soldier's Tale, The (Stravinsky), 120, 217
Sonatine (Ravel), 27n.
Song of Solomon (Canticles), 292
Songs of Innocence and of Experience (Blake), 69
'Song to David, A' (Smart), 276
Soutar, William, 273, 280–1, 304, 305, 307, *15*
South Lodge Preparatory School, Lowestoft, 227, 426, 427
'spacious firmament on high, The' (Tallis), 160
Spanish Civil War, 227, 331, 415
Spencer, Sylvia, 371
Spender, Stephen, 227, 228, 283
Stallybrass, Oliver, 136n.
Starkie, Enid, 311
Stead, W. F., 275
Stein, Erwin, 25, 127, 192n., 208n., *27*
Stevens, Wallace, 275
Story of Music, The (Britten–Holst), 48, 441
'Strange Meeting' (Owen), 326, 344
Stratton (Duncan), 438
Strauss, Richard, 393, 418
Stravinsky, Igor, 25, 32, 62, 120, 133, 153, 203, 204, 216, 217, 278, 288, 330, 335, 337, 342, 385
Apollon Musagète, 203
Baiser de la fée, Le, 202, **202**
Noces, Les, 217